LEARNING TO TEACH SCIENCE IN THE SECONDARY SCHOOL

Learning to Teach Science in the Secondary School is an indispensable guide with a fresh approach to the process, practice and reality of teaching and learning science in a busy secondary school. This fourth edition has been fully updated in light of changes to professional knowledge and practice and revisions to the national curriculum.

Written by experienced practitioners, this popular textbook comprehensively covers the opportunities and challenges of teaching science in the secondary school. It provides guidance on:

- the knowledge and skills you need, and understanding the science department at your school
- development of the science curriculum
- the nature of science and how science works, biology, chemistry, physics, astronomy and earth science
- planning for progression, using schemes of work to support planning, and evaluating lessons
- language in science, practical work, using ICT, science for citizenship, sex and health education and learning outside the classroom
- assessment for learning and external assessment and examinations
- educational research and science teachers

Every unit includes a clear chapter introduction, learning objectives, further reading, lists of useful resources and specially designed tasks – including those to support Master's level work – as well as cross-referencing to essential advice in the core text *Learning to Teach in the Secondary School*.

Learning to Teach Science in the Secondary School is designed to support student teachers through the transition from graduate scientist to practising science teacher, while achieving the highest level of personal and professional development.

Rob Toplis is Senior Lecturer in Secondary Science Education at Brunel University, UK.

LEARNING TO TEACH SUBJECTS IN THE SECONDARY SCHOOL SERIES

Series Editors: Susan Capel and Marilyn Leask

Designed for all students learning to teach in secondary schools, and particularly those on school-based initial teacher training courses, the books in this series complement *Learning to Teach in the Secondary School* and its companion, *Starting to Teach in the Secondary School*. Each book in the series applies underpinning theory and addresses practical issues to support student teachers in school and in the training institution in learning how to teach a particular subject.

Learning to Teach in the Secondary School, 6th edition
Edited by Susan Capel, Marilyn Leask and Tony Turner

Learning to Teach Art and Design in the Secondary School, 3rd edition
Edited by Nicholas Addison and Lesley Burgess

Learning to Teach Citizenship in the Secondary School, 3rd edition
Edited by Liam Gearon

Learning to Teach Design and Technology in the Secondary School, 2nd edition
Edited by Gwyneth Owen-Jackson

Learning to Teach English in the Secondary School, 3rd edition
Edited by Jon Davison and Jane Dowson

Learning to Teach Geography in the Secondary School, 2nd edition
David Lambert and David Balderstone

Learning to Teach History in the Secondary School, 4th edition
Edited by Terry Haydn, James Arthur, Martin Hunt and Alison Stephen

Learning to Teach ICT in the Secondary School
Edited by Steve Kennewell, John Parkinson and Howard Tanner

Learning to Teach Mathematics in the Secondary School, 3rd edition
Edited by Sue Johnston-Wilder, Peter Johnston-Wilder, David Pimm and Clare Lee

Learning to Teach Modern Foreign Languages in the Secondary School, 3rd edition
Norbert Pachler, Ann Barnes and Kit Field

Learning to Teach Music in the Secondary School, 2nd edition
Edited by Chris Philpott and Gary Spruce

Learning to Teach Physical Education in the Secondary School, 3rd edition
Edited by Susan Capel

Learning to Teach Religious Education in the Secondary School, 2nd edition
Edited by L. Philip Barnes, Andrew Wright and Ann-Marie Brandom

Learning to Teach Science in the Secondary School, 4th edition
Edited by Rob Toplis

Learning to Teach Using ICT in the Secondary School, 3rd edition
Edited by Marilyn Leask and Norbert Pachler

Starting to Teach in the Secondary School, 2nd edition
Edited by Susan Capel, Ruth Heilbronn, Marilyn Leask and Tony Turner

LEARNING TO TEACH SCIENCE IN THE SECONDARY SCHOOL

A companion to school experience

4th edition

Edited by
Rob Toplis

Routledge
Taylor & Francis Group

LONDON AND NEW YORK

Fourth edition published 2015
by Routledge
2 Park Square, Milton Park, Abingdon, Oxon OX14 4RN

and by Routledge
711 Third Avenue, New York, NY 10017

Routledge is an imprint of the Taylor & Francis Group, an informa business

First edition published by Routledge 1998
Third edition published by Routledge 2010

British Library Cataloguing in Publication Data
A catalogue record for this book is available from the British Library

Library of Congress Cataloging in Publication Data
Learning to teach science in the secondary school: a companion to
    school experience / edited by Rob Toplis. – Fourth edition.
        pages cm
    1. Science–Study and teaching (Secondary) I. Toplis, Rob.
    Q181.L497 2015
    507.1'241–dc23

                                                    2014030147

ISBN: 978-0-415-82642-6 (hbk)
ISBN: 978-0-415-82643-3 (pbk)
ISBN: 978-1-315-73128-5 (ebk)

Typeset in Times New Roman
by RefineCatch Limited, Bungay, Suffolk

CONTENTS

CONTENTS ▦ ▦ ▦ ■

CONTENTS ■ ■ ■ ■

FIGURES

FIGURES ▪ ▪ ▪ ▪

TABLES

TASKS

CONTRIBUTORS

Ruth Amos is Lecturer in Science Education at the Institute of Education, University of London. Her interests include learning science in field visit settings, using ICT to support learning science, chemistry education, environmental education and global dimensions and curriculum enrichment projects.

Sandra Campbell is Lecturer in Education at the Institute of Education, University of London, where she teaches on the Science PGCE and MA programmes. Previous posts include working as a Science Educator for the Science Learning Centre London at London's Science Museum and Head of Biology in a London comprehensive school. Her research interests include teacher development and biology education.

Steven Chapman is Head of Physics at Croydon High School. Before that he was Lecturer in Science Education at the Institute of Education, University of London, where he worked on the Physics elements of the secondary and primary PGCE. His research included teachers' subject knowledge and teaching Physics outside the classroom.

Ann Childs is Associate Professor in Science Education at the Oxford University Department of Education and a Fellow of Lady Margaret Hall, and she leads the science strand of the Post Graduate Certificate in Education (PGCE) at Oxford. She taught science in secondary schools in the UK and West Africa for 11 years, seven of these as a Head of Chemistry and Head of Science. Her research has focused on the professional learning of science teachers both nationally and internationally and the implications of government education policies for teacher education. Her current research is focused on working with teachers and pupils on explanations in science classrooms at both primary and secondary level.

Paul Davies is Lecturer in Science Education at the Institute of Education, University of London, where he teaches on the Science PGCE and MA programmes. He previously worked in schools in London, most recently as Head of Biology.

Caro Garrett taught sciences, mainly physics and chemistry, in secondary schools and a sixth form college for 25 years before joining the Education School at the University of Southampton in 2008. She introduced the pre-ITE 24-week physics Subject Knowledge Enhancement course and is currently the lead tutor for the Science PGCE. She is chair of the Association of Tutors in Science Education (ATSE). Her research interests are in physics education, particularly related to girls in physics.

Marcus Grace is Head of Science Education Research in the University of Southampton's Education School. Previously, he taught science at state schools in London. His main interests centre on learning and teaching about socio-scientific issues, particularly health, biodiversity and environmental issues, and outdoor science education. His current work focuses on developing realistic teaching approaches to improving health-related attitudes and behaviour among young people.

Christine Harrison works at King's College London where she trains secondary science teachers, teaches on several Master's courses and carries out research in assessment and science education. Chris taught in London schools for 13 years prior to her university career and is known for the seamless way she bridges the gap between research and the classroom.

Ralph Levinson is Reader in Education at the Institute of Education, University of London. He taught science in London comprehensive schools for 12 years before working in higher education, mainly as a teacher educator and researcher.

Katherine Little currently teaches Biology at a girls' grammar school in Plymouth. Prior to training to be a teacher at the Institute of Education, University of London, she was awarded her doctorate in anthropology, researching the genetics and behaviour of Indian monkeys.

John Oversby has experience as a teacher of the sciences, mathematics and ICT, as well as research in chemistry and education in the sciences. Currently, he is working on diagrams in mathematics and sciences education, climate change education, and teacher subject knowledge.

Michael J. Reiss is Pro-Director: Research and Development and Professor of Science Education at the Institute of Education, University of London, and an Academician of the Academy of Social Sciences. The former Director of Education at the Royal Society, he has written extensively about curricula, pedagogy and assessment in science education.

Kevin Smith has worked in education for 25 years as a teacher, middle manager and a science consultant/adviser. He is now a freelance consultant, specialising in teacher training and curriculum and resource development.

Pete Sorensen is Lecturer in Science Education in the School of Education at the University of Nottingham. He teaches on ITE courses, the PGCE (International) and Master's programmes, supervises higher-degree students, and researches in the field of teacher education. He has previously taught and held leadership and management positions in schools and teacher education institutions in the UK and Ghana.

Rob Toplis is Senior Lecturer in Science Education at Brunel University, London, where he teaches and supervises on pre-service, PhD, EdD and MA programmes. His research examines teaching and learning science in secondary schools with a particular emphasis on science for engagement and science for all.

PREFACE TO THE FOURTH EDITION

As with the previous editions of *Learning to Teach Science in the Secondary School*, this fourth edition is written in conjunction with the generic text, *Learning to Teach in the Secondary School*, 6th edition (Capel, Leask and Turner, 2013), which we assume readers can access. Therefore, we have attempted to avoid repetition of material in the generic text though there may be some inevitable overlap to aid clarity. The suggested tasks, set in boxes, are an integral part of each unit and the intention is that they should be read in conjunction with the text. As with the generic book, these tasks can be done on your own or in collaboration with your mentors in school, your tutor or your fellow student teachers. The tasks frequently provide opportunities to link theory with practice: it is often very difficult to separate theory and practice and very often theory is essential in order to understand and interpret much of the practice and procedures you will encounter as a student teacher. It may be worth highlighting that in a number of texts and journals, the term 'student' is used instead of 'pupil'; that 'trainee teacher', 'trainee', 'beginning teacher' or 'pre-service teacher' may all be used to mean 'student teacher' and that 'school-based tutor' may be used instead of 'mentor'. Although the term 'student' instead of 'pupil' is now becoming commonplace to mean a learner in 11–19 secondary education, there is a risk of confusing 'student' with 'student teacher' and we have therefore kept to the terms 'pupil' and 'student teacher'.

Since the publication of the third edition, there have been a number of important changes in teacher education and in science education. These changes include:

- a new set of Teachers' Standards;
- the introduction of School Direct for school-based teacher education and training;
- changes in the names and status of schools that now include terms such as colleges, academies, 'all-through' schools (from 5–19 years) and free schools;
- changes in assessment and examinations;
- new Ofsted (Office for Standards in Education) inspection frameworks for both schools and teacher education and training;
- changes in the National Curriculum.

Many teacher education and training courses include Master's level work and readers are directed to the relevant sections of the units that address these requirements. Many of the suggested 'Further Reading' lists include references to books and book chapters that will provide appropriate background for Master's level work.

ACKNOWLEDGEMENTS

When Jenny Frost, the editor of the previous editions of this book, approached me to take on the role of editor for this fourth edition, I was both flattered and rather daunted. How can anyone follow on from the direction that Jenny had set out for the book? I once commented to one of the contributors that this is really Jenny's book, I am just looking after it.

I am grateful to all the previous authors who remained on the team and were able to bring their Units up-to-date with the sometimes radical changes in both the school science curriculum and in science teacher education. I am also grateful to those new authors whom I approached and who enthusiastically agreed to contribute. I would like to thank those contributors with whom I had a very professional dialogue about terminology and meanings. These discussions have, I hope, added to the clarity of ideas in the Units and to our own thinking as science teacher educators.

Together with the contributors, I would like to express my thanks for permission to reproduce or use materials from the following individuals and organisations. These include, from the third edition, Cengage Learning Services Ltd for the reproduction of Figure 1.2.1; Caroline Allen for her drawing of a scientist in Unit 3.1; Nick O'Brien, Satomi Saki and Jamie Styles for ideas and drawings which appear in Unit 5.3; and the pupils and student teacher who appear in the photographs in Unit 5.6. In addition, I would like to thank Herschel Grammar School for permission to reproduce the pro-forma example in Figure 4.3.4 and Brunel University for the pro-forma example, Figure 4.3.5 and the lesson evaluation pro-forma in Figure 4.4.6.

Marcus Grace (Unit 5.4) would like to acknowledge the advice and helpful discussions with Jackie Smith, Personal Development Learning Coordinator and Careers Coordinator at The Mountbatten School, and with Maxine Farmer, Citizenship Coordinator at Hounsdown School.

I would like to express particular thanks to Helen Pritt, Sarah Tuckwell and Natasha Ellis-Knight of Routledge for their advice and support, to Kat Troth for editing some of my sections and asking awkward but important questions, and to Jenny Frost herself for her advice and for easing the transition to my editorship.

ABBREVIATIONS

AAIA	Association for Achievement and Improvement through Assessments
ACCAC	Qualification Curriculum and Assessment Authority for Wales
ACT	Professional Association for Citizenship Teaching
AfL	Assessment for Learning
AIDS	Auto Immune Deficiency Syndrome
A-level	Advanced level (GCE)
APP	Assessing Pupil Progress
AQA	Assessment and Qualifications Alliance
ARG	Assessment Reform Group
AS level	Advanced Subsidiary level (GCE)
ASE	Association for Science Education
AST	Advanced Skills Teacher
BEI	British Education Index
BTEC	Business and Technical Education Council
CASE	Cognitive Acceleration in Science Education
CAU	Centre Assessed Unit
CCTV	close circuit television
CLEAPSS	Consortium of Local Education Authorities for the Provision of Science Services
CLISP	Children's Learning in Science Project
CPD	Continuing Professional Development
DARTS	Directed Activities Related to Texts
DCSF	Department for Children, Schools and Families
DfE	Department for Education
DfEE	Department for Education and Employment
DfES	Department for Education and Skills
DNA	deoxyribonucleic acid
DoH	Department of Health
EAL	English as an Additional Language
ECM	Every Child Matters
EBD	Emotional and Behavioural Difficulties
EPPI	Evidence for Policy and Practice Information and Coordinating Centre
ESTA	Earth Science Teachers Association

ABBREVIATIONS ▨ ▨ ■ ■

EVC	Educational Visits Coordinator
EVS	Electronic Voting System
GCE	General Certificate of Education
GCSE	General Certificate of Secondary Education
GP	General Practitioner
G & T	Gifted and Talented
GTC	General Teaching Council
GTP	Graduate Teacher Programme
GUM	Genito-urinary Medicine
HEI	Higher Education Institution
HIV	Human Immunodeficiency Virus
HoD	Head of Department
HoS	Head of Science
IB	International Baccalaureate
IDEAS	Ideas, Evidence and Argument in Science project
IEP	Individual Educational Plan
IoB	Institute of Biology
IoP	Institute of Physics
ISA	Investigative Skills Assignment
IT	Information Technology
ITE	Initial Teacher Education
ITT	Initial Teacher Training
IWB	interactive white board
KS	Key Stage
LA	Local Authority
LRS	Learner Response System
LSA	Learning Support Assistant
LSD	lysergic acid diethylamide
MA	Master of Arts
MA	Management Allowances
MedFASH	Medical Foundation for Aids and Sexual Health
MI	Multiple Intelligences
NHSS	National Healthy School Status
NQT	Newly Qualified Teacher
Ofqual	Office of Qualifications and Examinations Regulation
PACKS	Procedural and Conceptual Knowledge in Science project
PCK	pedagogical content knowledge
PDP	Professional Development Portfolio
PHSE	Personal Health and Social Education
PLTS	Personal Learning and Thinking Skills
PSA	Practical Skills Assessment
PSHE	Personal, Social and Health Education
PSMSC	Personal, Social, Moral, Spiritual and Cultural
QCA	Qualifications and Curriculum Authority
QCDA	Qualifications and Curriculum Development Agency
QTS	Qualified Teacher Status
RSC	Royal Society of Chemistry
SASP	Science Additional Specialism Programme

SATs	Standard Assessment Tasks
SCITT	School Centred Initial Teacher Training
SEN	Special Educational Needs
SEP	Science Enhancement Programme
SLT	Senior Leadership Team
SMT	Senior Management Team
SoW	Scheme of Work
SRE	Sex and Relationship Education
STEM	Science, Technology, Engineering and Mathematics
STI	sexually transmitted infection
TDA	Training and Development Agency for Schools
TGAT	Task Group on Assessment and Testing
TIMSS	Third International Mathematics and Science Survey
TLR1	First Teaching and Learning Responsibility
TLR2	Second Teaching and Learning Responsibility
TLRP	Teaching and Learning Responsibility Payment
TTA	Teacher Training Agency
VAK	Visual, Auditory, Kinaesthetic

BECOMING A SCIENCE TEACHER

INTRODUCTION

Becoming a science teacher involves a diverse range of different tasks covering a wide range of skills, knowledge and understanding. No day is the same and very often no hour is the same. This is by its very nature a function of dealing with human beings. The humans you are dealing with on a daily basis are not just ordinary humans; they are teenagers and have all the features that go with an age group who are going through some of the most important changes of their lives. As a secondary science teacher you are in a privileged position to witness and even to some small extent, to be part of those changes. Therefore, the skills of a beginning or student science teacher are not those that just involve science knowledge and skills but are those of an individual who may, at various times, be a counsellor, careers officer, adviser, psychologist, carer and actor, to name but a few. After all, that is probably why you decided to be a teacher. At this point it might be useful to read the first unit, Unit 1.1, 'What do teachers do?' by Andrew Green and Marilyn Leask from the companion volume, *Learning to Teach in the Secondary School* (Capel *et al.*, 2013).

The units in this section provide an early introduction to starting out as a student science teacher. It provides some background about starting points and some of the skills and knowledge you may bring with you that can enhance pupils' experiences. It provides the backdrop to developing as an individual who is deeply involved with science *learning* – in Keith Taber's words, a 'learning doctor' (Taber, 2001, p. 53) – and with a proactive approach to managing your own learning and professional development as a science teacher. It also gives an overview about the ways in which schools and science departments are structured and some of the different jobs that science teachers undertake. In essence, this first section is about an induction into a community of practice that relies not only on science knowledge, but also on a variety of skills required when dealing with people. And the people in secondary schools are a diverse but extremely interesting lot!

REFERENCES

Capel, S., Leask, M. and Turner, T. (2013) *Learning to Teach in the Secondary School: An Introduction to School Experience*, 6th edn. London: Routledge.

Taber, K. S. (2001) *Chemical Misconceptions: Prevention, Diagnosis and Cure*, vol. 1: *Theoretical Background*, London: Royal Society of Chemistry.

UNIT 1.1

LEARNING TO BE A SCIENCE TEACHER

Rob Toplis

INTRODUCTION

Science education can be a rather tricky business. Not only do you need to know the science itself, to 'know your stuff', you also need to know a lot about education, that is teaching and learning, and know quite a lot about people. There is a myth – and one that is unfortunately still prevalent in the minds of some people with little experience inside schools – that science is something that can somehow be imparted to pupils, that science knowledge can be transmitted directly from the teacher to the pupil by some unseen conduit, a kind of learning cable from one stock of knowledge to an empty vessel at the pupil end. The mere act of telling someone can somehow convey all the information needed. Nothing could be further from the truth.

OBJECTIVES

By the end of this unit, you should:

- be aware that science teaching and learning is a complex process;
- know that your own enquiry skills are needed to develop knowledge about science education;
- understand some of the requirements for Master's level work.

WHAT DO SCIENCE TEACHERS NEED TO KNOW?

Starting points: what do you know already?

Beginning or student teachers come from a wide variety of starting points in terms of their academic experience, social and cultural experiences and work experiences. Added to this are their values, attitudes and beliefs about science, what it is and how it should be taught.

Academic experiences may be varied. They may include a first degree from a fairly narrow area or one with a mixture of different modules; they may include a higher degree in an even narrower area with research based on one specialist topic. Examples may be a biology student teacher with a first degree in genetics but with little or no ecology; a physics student teacher with a degree in electrical engineering but with little content in astrophysics, or a chemistry student with a degree in medicinal chemistry but little inorganic chemistry. In these examples, further subject knowledge enhancement would be required before being able to confidently teach all aspects of the specialist science.

An individual's social and cultural experiences can often be a valuable addition to the daily interactions with teenage pupils. Personal experiences and interests, memberships of groups, travel experiences and hobbies can contribute to the positive professional relationships that occur between teachers and pupils. At one level, involvement in the clubs and societies in schools not only helps forge these positive interactions but helps the informal education of pupils: the hidden curriculum. At another level, the richness of a diversity of backgrounds and cultures can add to the overall pupil experience in school.

A student teacher's prior work experience can provide opportunities that will enrich their science teaching, whether it be through new ideas to teaching science, approaches to organising the classroom, dealing with individuals – the so-called 'life skills' – or simply some of the anecdotes from work that can be used to illustrate ideas in the science laboratory. However, it is important to point out that schools and classrooms are very complex social situations and often work very differently to the workplace; it may not always be possible to simply transfer practices from the context of work to the context of school.

You will, inevitably, arrive with a number of very different views, values, beliefs and attitudes. Some of these may be based on your own education; some will be based on your views of the world, your experiences and even the ways you view learning. When you begin teacher education and training, a number of these will alter, and may even be in conflict with new experiences and change as a result. It is important to be open-minded. As you observe, reflect on and evaluate your previous ideas and current experiences, you may start to develop a personal philosophy about science teaching and learning, and your role in this.

Task 1.1.1 **Starting out**

Make a list of some of your skills and beliefs about science teaching and learning. These might include: subject knowledge; 'transferable' skills such as organisation, time management and creativity; 'people skills' such as empathy, diplomacy, enthusiasm, and beliefs, attitudes and values that might address the question, 'why do I want to teach science?'

Then look at this list and consider how you can enhance these skills, and how you hope to address some of these areas during your teacher training and education.

An outline of some of the different roles of teachers can be found in Unit 1.1 of the companion volume to this book, *Learning to Teach in the Secondary School* (Capel *et al.*, 2013).

Subject knowledge, content knowledge and pedagogy

There has been a certain amount of debate about the nature of subject knowledge. Teachers need to know *what* to teach, the content knowledge necessary. They also need to know *how* to teach this knowledge, the pedagogy involved. Shulman (1986) has contributed to our understanding about subject knowledge and has proposed the term *pedagogical content knowledge*, or PCK, to refer to the practical knowledge used by teachers in classrooms. This practical knowledge is, understandably, complex as it involves the knowledge that specialist teachers possess that includes pupil misconceptions, examples, analogies and models. Added to this are the illustrations, conceptual difficulties and connections with other aspects of learning such as assessment and the curriculum (Berry, 2012). If we take the example of teaching a very simple topic such as the forces on a cyclist pedalling at a constant speed along a flat road, the teacher will need to know a number of important facts. They will need to know the content knowledge about the forces acting on the cyclist such as friction, forward motion, gravity and Newton's Laws. They will also need to know pupils' misconceptions or alternative frameworks about forces and motion, how force arrows can be drawn, balanced forces, some possible simple demonstrations or observations about Newton's Laws, other possible examples that can add to pupils' understanding, 'what if' questions and even the kinds of questions that may arise in assessment tests or examinations. The PCK involved in this apparently straightforward example on forces and motion is rather more complex than it immediately appears and the teacher needs to draw on a wide range of knowledge to deal with this.

Task 1.1.2 **Simple photosynthesis**

List the items of PCK needed to teach a simple outline of photosynthesis, involving the production of carbohydrate and oxygen from carbon dioxide and water, using light energy.

Curriculum knowledge

Subject knowledge is not the only form of knowledge a teacher needs. They also need to know *what* needs to be taught, i.e. curriculum knowledge. This is further complicated by the frequency of curriculum change but change is inevitable as the curriculum is revised in response to changes in policy and evolving ideas about what kind of science needs to be taught to all pupils in the secondary age range. Curriculum change is not just something to hit the news in England; it occurs throughout the world as governments and international educators react to the need for both a scientific and technological workforce while at the same time enhancing the scientific literacy of twenty-first-century populations who need to be better informed about some of the major scientific, ethical and environmental issues facing them.

One of the biggest curriculum changes in more recent years has been the arrival of and changes to the General Certificate of Secondary Education (GCSE) with a shift towards what pupils can do, rather than what they can remember for a final examination – and recent shifts back again. The second major curriculum change is the National Curriculum and its revisions.

The National Curriculum arrived in 1989, resulting from a mixture of historical events, initiatives and a not inconsiderable degree of political influence. Although the biological, chemical and physical science content was familiar, AT1, later to be called Sc1, covered experimental and investigative work and was the first time investigations in school science were now part of a statutory curriculum. With Sc1, pupils were required to predict, carry out, analyse and evaluate investigative work in science. This type of practical work in science was a noticeable departure from the 'recipe-following' form of practical work that was being carried out across the country, designed to illustrate scientific phenomena and explanations.

Since 1989 there have been five versions of the National Curriculum in 1991, 1995, 2000, 2004 with another in 2013. What does this indicate? Changing criteria for the science curriculum? Different political agendas? Or the realisation that previous versions of the curriculum were in need of change? Two earlier areas of the National Curriculum were open to general criticism as far as teachers were concerned: its manageability in practice and its assessment. A third criticism relates to scientific literacy and the question: 'Who is the science curriculum for?' A rapid level of curriculum reform in the early days led to 'mass reading activities' (Wellington, 1994, pp. 3–4) where teachers attempted to interpret the new requirements, a difficulty for a group of professionals more used to *controlling* aspects of the curriculum (certainly below the examination years) than *delivering* a centralised and prescribed format over which they had no influence. Teachers then had to write complex schemes of work to accommodate all of these factors – and have been doing so ever since. The later versions of the National Curriculum attempted to address some of the problems and simplify them by relying more on the professional judgement of teachers in their interpretation and implementation.

In response to criticisms that the curriculum was prescriptive and assessment-driven in nature; that there was an overload of factual content, little contemporary science, and coursework that was restricted to a few tried and tested investigations that were divorced from day-to-day science teaching, the 2004 version of the National Curriculum introduced 'How Science Works' with its emphasis on evidence, investigative science, communication, and applications and implications. These now form the 'working scientifically' part of the latest version of the National Curriculum.

More recently, there have been continuing international concerns about school science education, including a reduction in the numbers of pupils studying the physical sciences beyond the age of 16, gender differences, and pupils' attitudes and motivation for studying science. The Relevance of Science Education (ROSE) study of pupils' attitudes to science shows that in over 20 countries, pupils' response to the statement: 'I like school science better than other subjects' is increasingly negative the more developed the country (Osborne and Dillon, 2008, p. 13), that science is 'important but not for me' (Jenkins and Nelson, 2005, p. 41). Against this backdrop has been the most recent version of the National Curriculum with greater emphasis on content knowledge. It remains to be seen if this initiative is able to reverse some of the trends in attitudes to school science and can engage *all* pupils in further study and for greater scientific literacy.

LEARNING SCIENCE

The science teacher needs to have some understanding about theories of learning. A biologist would not expect to understand many aspects of the subject without Darwin's theory of evolution by natural selection; a chemistry teacher would be expected to know about atomic theory; a physics teacher would need to be conversant with both Newton's Laws as well as quantum theory. Similarly a science educator needs to be aware of theories of learning: it is, quite simply, their business to know.

One comment that is sometimes heard from science teachers is, 'Oh, I don't need to know all that educational theory stuff.' The same teacher may also come out with the comment: 'I taught them that topic three months ago and they still get it wrong' or 'Why can't they grasp this idea about energy conservation?' We only have to look at the educational theories of, for example, Piaget and the Russian educator Vygotsky to suggest some possible answers to these questions. Piaget's suggestion that children actively construct knowledge in order to make sense of the world around them, and can assimilate new learning that may or may not fit with the previously constructed knowledge, helps us to understand why they may 'get it wrong' at a later stage. The *active* construction of knowledge, as opposed to the passive reception of knowledge provides a clue here. Work by Rosalind Driver (Driver, 1983) also shows us that children's science, the knowledge they construct themselves, may not be accepted scientific knowledge but is still coherent to the child. Furthermore, these constructs are alternative frameworks of understanding that are difficult to change. The pupils in the first teacher's comment above appear to have reverted to their previous, unscientific, ideas three months later. Going back to the Introduction, the invisible conduit between teacher and pupil does not exist; the act of telling is not pupil learning. Pupils need to actively construct meaning and Vygotsky's theories show this is done socially by using language, internalising ideas and with the help of informed others; this is where the teacher comes in by providing that other construction metaphor, scaffolding learning.

Piaget's theories do not stop at constructing knowledge. His suggestion that children move from the concrete level of understanding to the more abstract, formal operational, stage at about age 11 helps us to understand the second of the teacher's comments above about grasping the idea of energy conservation. Energy is an abstract concept. Furthermore, the transition from the concrete to the formal (more abstract) may not necessarily occur at age 11 but may come later. The intervention strategies of the Cognitive Acceleration in Science Education (CASE) programme (Adey *et al.*, 1989) are firmly grounded in the learning theories of Piaget and Vygotsky. This is covered in more detail in Unit 4.1 and other theories, such as those of Bruner, Ausubel, and Lave and Wenger, all have relevance to science learning. Jon Scaife's chapter in the 'Further Reading' list provides a more comprehensive review of the area and is recommended reading (Scaife, 2009).

ASSESSMENT

Assessment is an essential part of teaching and learning science. It is necessary for both the teacher and the pupil. For the teacher, it evaluates their teaching and informs planning for the future. For the pupil, it can inform their current progress and what they need to do to progress further. Assessment is often broken down into formative assessment, often called assessment *for* learning (AfL), and summative assessment, assessment *of* learning. Summative assessment has probably been the dominant form for a long time with its familiar terminal examinations, end-of-topic tests and coursework assignments. Formative assessment is part of the day-to-day assessment that teachers carry out during lessons and inform both pupils and teachers about their knowledge, understanding and skills. These two assessment approaches are covered in detail in Units 6.1 and 6.2.

When planning lessons and setting objectives and outcomes, student teachers are asked to evaluate their lesson following their teaching. Apart from a regular focus on the negative rather than the positive features of a lesson, they will frequently state that all pupils met the planned objectives or outcomes. When questioned, they will often come up with answers such as: 'I questioned them', 'They nodded', 'They put their hands up.' This begs the question, 'How do you know?', more specifically, 'How do you know all of them met the outcomes?' This is where assessment strategies as part of normal class planning, routines and feedback *for all pupils* become important. One further question could be 'How do *they* know?'

Task 1.1.3 **Outcomes and assessment**

Consider the simple outline of photosynthesis in Task 1.1.2:

1   What outcomes would you expect Year 8 pupils to have achieved at the end of an introductory lesson on this topic?
2   Suggest three ways you could assess pupils in the class during this lesson.

PROFESSIONAL LEARNING AND ENQUIRY

What is it to be a professional science teacher? Hoyle and John (1995) have suggested two kinds of professional: the restricted professional and the extended professional. Some of the features of the restricted professional include: a high level of classroom skill, using skills derived from practical experience; does not reflect on or analyse their practice; avoids change. In contrast, the extended professional exhibits features such as: using a broader range of knowledge and skills; linking theory *and* practice; reflection and analysis of problems; adoption of intellectual approaches; experiments with and welcomes new ideas. This is not to say that practical approaches to teaching science are without value and these are, of course, extreme ends of a spectrum. Some individuals will at various times occupy different positions along this spectrum. However, a spirit of enquiry, of being open to and trying out new ideas, of reflecting on those ideas and of inspiring others, are all features that can contribute to the development of science education and provide a high level of job satisfaction and effectiveness.

WORKING AT MASTER'S LEVEL

Leading on from the idea of the extended professional, one who adopts an enquiry approach to teaching and learning, is working at an academic level that meets Master's level criteria. Many initial teacher education courses, whether they are university or school-based, have assignments credited at Master's level (M level). This requirement carries with it a set of characteristics or criteria about the level of thought and writing needed for work at this level which encompasses theory, reflection and enquiry.

As part of this Master's level work you will very likely be asked to focus on an aspect of science teaching from your own school experience and may be asked to prepare and carry out a small-scale project in school that collects and analyses qualitative or quantitative data and is informed by some theoretical perspective. The key features of this work will be:

■   A suitable project based on your direct classroom experience. Although it may appear daunting at first, there will be no shortage of problems or experiences to investigate. Do boys answer more frequently than girls? What are the learning characteristics and support approaches for a pupil with individual needs? How are exercise books used in science lessons? What do pupils think about homework?

■   A clear and tightly focused research question.

■   Work that will require reading and a critical review of the literature in your chosen topic, or literature that is closely linked to it. A heavy reliance on web resources is not advisable; the literature should include academic books and journals. Increasingly, journals are available as e-journals on library intranets and you should be able to search using suitable keywords.

■   Ethical implications. You will be asked to gain permission from all concerned, including setting out rights of voluntary participation, the right to withdraw, anonymity and storage of data.

■   A clear set of reasons to justify your methods of enquiry.

■   Clear presentation of data and analysis.

■   A clear discussion that uses the literature.

■   Conclusions and possible implications for future practice.

The key points are that there must be clear and critical argument, using the literature; the research question has a clear and concise focus; the enquiry methods are justified, and the findings are clearly discussed in the light of the literature. A well-written and presented topic will very often have implications for your own practice and the science department where you work may well ask you to present this at a department meeting.

SUMMARY AND KEY POINTS

This unit has introduced some of the considerations that need to be taken into account when learning to be a science teacher. It has provided an overview of the complexities of science teaching and learning and of the professional role of science teachers. Some of the areas covered are:

■   the learning and skills you bring to science education as starting points;

■   subject knowledge, pedagogy and pedagogical content knowledge (PCK);

■   the nature of curriculum knowledge, pupil learning and assessment;

■   the nature of being a professional and carrying out work at Master's level.

REFERENCES

Adey, P. S., Shayer, M. and Yates, C. (1989) *Thinking Science: Student and Teachers' Materials for the CASE Intervention*, London: Macmillan.

Berry, A. (2012) 'Pedagogical content knowledge (PCK): a summary review of PCK in the context of science education research', in J. Oversby (ed.) *ASE Guide to Research in Science Education*, Hatfield: ASE.

Driver, R. (1983) *The Pupil as Scientist?* Milton Keynes: Open University Press.

Hoyle, E. and John, P. D. (1995) *Professional Knowledge and Professional Practice*, London: Cassell.

Jenkins, E. W. and Nelson, N. W. (2005) 'Important but not for me: students' attitudes towards secondary school science in England', *Research in Science and Technological Education*, 23(1): 41–57.

Osborne, J. and Dillon, J. (2008) *Science Education in Europe: Critical Reflections*, London: Nuffield Foundation.

Shulman, L. S. (1986) 'Those who understand: knowledge growth in teaching', *Educational Researcher*, 15(2): 4–14.

Wellington, J. (1994) *Secondary Science: Contemporary Issues and Practical Approaches*, London: Routledge.

FURTHER READING

Driver, R., Rushworth, P., Squires, A. and Wood-Robinson, V. (2004) *Making Sense of Secondary Science*, London: Routledge.

This important book provides a research digest of many of the learning difficulties in science education. It is an important part of background reading, as well as preparation and reference for lesson planning.

Green, A. and Leask, M. (2013) 'What do teachers do?' in S. Capel., M. Leask and T. Turner (eds) *Learning to Teach in the Secondary School: A Companion to School Experience*, 6th edn, London: Routledge.

This chapter provides a broad introduction to many of the roles and tasks of the professional teacher.

Scaife, J. (2009) 'Learning in science', in J. Wellington and G. Ireson (eds) *Science Learning, Science Teaching*, 3rd edn, London: Routledge, pp. 61–118.

Jon Scaife's extended chapter in this book provides an excellent introduction to learning theories with practical examples.

UNIT 1.2 MANAGING YOUR PROFESSIONAL LEARNING

Caro Garrett

INTRODUCTION

Your professional journey as a teacher will have begun when you prepared to apply for a teacher training place, observing real classrooms and deciding which route to take to Qualified Teacher Status (QTS). At that point you may not have been able to interpret much of what you saw happening in the classroom, but you will have observed a variety of practices and begun to appreciate the wide range of strategies that teachers use to carry out their professional role on a day-to-day basis. At interview, you will have been asked a question such as: 'What qualities do you think you have that will make you a good teacher?', and your interviewer would hope for an answer that implied that you understood what some of those qualities are, and that you could relate them to observations and conversations you had already had in the classroom and with teachers. The expectation throughout your life as a teacher involves you taking responsibility for your own development as a professional, and this unit is aimed at helping you to manage your own professional development from the varied experiences you will have on the course.

OBJECTIVES

By the end of this unit, you should:

- understand a model of professional development that helps you to learn from experience;
- recognise how to use the Professional Standards for Qualified Teacher Status as an aid to learning;
- know how to work effectively with mentors;
- be able to identify your starting points;
- appreciate the progressive complexity of learning experiences that will be an intrinsic part of your course.

SETTING THE SCENE

There is an ongoing debate about whether we should refer to the courses followed by beginning teachers as Initial Teacher *Education* (ITE) or Initial Teacher *Training* (ITT). Put simplistically, the argument centres round the need for beginning teachers to understand something of the theories underpinning ideas about children's learning, and the pedagogical strategies that are considered effective (the 'education' bit), and to develop their application of these theories and strategies through teaching practice supported by experienced teachers (the 'training' bit). These two aspects are neatly summed up by a quote from Sir Stuart Sutherland in the Dearing Report (NCIHE, 1997): 'the purpose of teacher education and training should be to produce professional teachers who have the theoretical knowledge and understanding, combined with practical skills, competences and commitment to teach to high national standards' (Report 10, point 9). They are, of course, mutually inclusive, and both aspects make important contributions to the development of the teacher as a professional.

This chapter will use the expression ITE to refer to the whole programme, though the government for England and Wales has for some time used the term ITT. Beginning teachers, undergoing some form of education/training, for the purposes of this chapter, will be referred to as student teachers. Student teachers will all be working towards gaining Qualified Teacher Status (QTS), and most will also be working towards a university-awarded Master's level qualification, the Post Graduate Certificate in Education (PGCE). Some Higher Education Institutions (HEIs) may call their post-graduate qualification something slightly different, but we will refer to PGCEs here.

Significant changes to ITE in England occurred following the White Paper, *The Importance of Teaching* (DfE, 2010), but the statutory requirement that all training programmes are designed to provide student teachers with at least 60 days of training activity per year remained in place. Those student teachers following the 'Core' PGCE route will receive these 60 days of training activity in their HEIs. School Direct, Teach First and School Centred Initial Teacher Training (SCITT) student teachers will receive these 60 days through a varying mix between their provider (usually a HEI) and their placement school. Reference to your 'school' could also mean a school in your school alliance.

So during your ITE course you will have two types of professional base: the school and the HEI provider. In school, you work as an individual student teacher (or possibly as one of a pair of science student teachers) alongside teachers and technicians. Early experiences in school involve observation of teachers and pupils, working with small groups of pupils, and team teaching. You gradually take over whole classes. One science teacher acts as your mentor and meets with you on a regular basis, with others also giving you advice. A professional studies programme in school allows you to learn about whole school issues that are not unique to science and in this you are likely to work with student teachers of other subjects also in the school. In your other professional home, the HEI, you are part of a bigger group of science student teachers attending a highly structured programme of lectures, seminars, workshops and tutorials. Here you have access to a strong research and literature base in education and, of course, your science tutors. This second base provides you also with a community of peers who share the ups and downs of learning to become a science teacher, with whom you can gain a perspective on all your own particular experiences.

To make best use of the resources at these two professional homes, you need to understand the nature of professional learning, and not only your own role but also the role of the science teachers and tutors with whom you work.

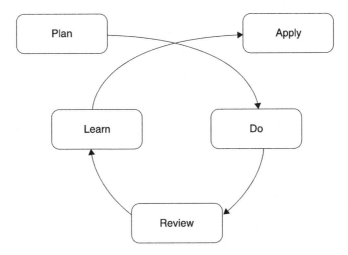

■ **Figure 1.2.1** A model of active learning

Source: Watkins *et al.* (2007, p. 27).

A MODEL FOR PROFESSIONAL LEARNING

Some of the most important attributes that a teacher as a professional needs to develop are those of reflecting on practice, being able to be critical of that practice and using knowledge to move that practice along. A useful model which can be applied to this cycle is that of an active learning cycle, as represented in Figure 1.2.1.

This cycle involves:

■   *Planning*: deciding what to do (possibly as a result of an iteration of the cycle).
■   *Doing*: the carrying out of the plan, which, as well as delivering a lesson, could also be observing other teachers' lessons, including in subjects other than science, working with a tutor group, marking pupils' work, organising a science club or a visit or a meeting with parents.
■   *Reviewing*: standing back, describing the event, analysing it and evaluating its effect. The ability to reflect constructively and self-critically is essential. Research shows that reviewing is most effective if done with another person, often a teacher in school or your tutor, or a fellow student teacher. In the review, other ideas are brought in to make sense of what has happened and to help in identifying general points that can be applied elsewhere. It is in this phase that links are made to the more theoretical parts of the course, because these provide 'frameworks' for reviewing the event;
■   *Learning*: consideration following review, of what you might do differently next time will lead to new goals and actions, some of which may be to definitely not try that again, or alternatively to acknowledge that the latest strategy has worked rather well and will be used again;
■   *Applying*: applying your new learning and going through the cycle again.

This cycle can be illustrated by the following example:

A student teacher had prepared a lesson on microprotein for a bright Y10 class. Her resources were well constructed and consisted of:

- a worksheet with clear diagrams and information followed by questions which required pupils to interpret the information and apply scientific principles;
- clear diagrams of the fermenter on a data projector;
- cooked microprotein for pupils to taste for 'acceptability'.

In the review afterwards, her perception was that she had talked for about a quarter of the lesson. Her observer's notes, however, identified that she had, in fact, talked for about three-quarters of the lesson. She recognised that she felt under pressure to make sure that she told the pupils all the facts even though she knew this was not how pupils learned. Discussion focused on how she could provide pupils with more time when they were engaged in problems, which would, in turn, provide her with more information about their understanding. The discussion also focused on the personal courage she would need to 'let learners off the leash'. With her mentor, she set her goals for the next lesson, to talk for no more than 50 per cent of the time and to use the extra time to monitor pupils' achievements more thoroughly.

Effective mentors will be able to support you in all the phases of the active learning cycle (Figure 1.2.2).

Mentors support active learners in the different phases of their learning in the following ways:

The 'plan' phase
They help students plan what to do by:

- encouraging students to come up with ideas
- acting as a sounding board for ideas
- helping students to work out their ideas in greater detail.

The 'do' phase
They help students get the activity done by:

- supporting motivation
- checking out practical details
- smoothing communication with others.

The 'review' phase
They help students review an experience by:

- encouraging students to make an account
- providing frameworks of questions to consider
- making suggestions for comparisons and evaluations.

The 'learn' phase
They help students to learn from experience by:

- bringing in useful ideas from a range of sources: reading, theories, others' views.

The 'apply' phase
They provide students with tools to promote application by:

- giving support to the question of 'what would you do differently next time?'
- leading to action planning and goal setting.

■ **Figure 1.2.2** Ways in which mentors can support an active learner

Some people will be better at some parts than others and there may be other professionals you work with (teachers, technicians, student teachers, tutors, etc.) who are exceptionally good at helping you find resources and ideas for getting something done, while others may be much better at helping you to analyse what has happened. Your responsibility is to use the varying expertise of the people around you to best effect. All teachers at all stages of their professional journey will use a cycle with similarities to this one, and the most effective teachers are constantly learning by adjusting their practice according to the results of their reflections.

WORKING WITH THE TEACHERS' STANDARDS

The current Teachers' Standards came into effect on 1 September 2012 (DfE, 2012). They replaced the standards for Qualified Teacher Status (QTS) and the Core professional standards previously published by the Training and Development Agency for Schools (TDA), which had been in place since 2007, as well as the General Teaching Council for England's *Code of Conduct and Practice for Registered Teachers*. The standards define the minimum level of practice expected of student teachers and teachers from the point of being awarded QTS: in other words, they are the standards you must reach by the end of your training in order to achieve QTS. They form an important framework for your development, so early familiarity with them is essential (see Task 1.2.1). The standards are divided into three main sections:

■ The *Preamble* which summarises the *values and behaviour* that all teachers must demonstrate throughout their careers.
■ *Part 1* which comprises the *Standards for Teaching*;
■ *Part 2* which comprises the *Standards for Professional and Personal Conduct*.

The Standards in Part 1 are numbered from 1–8, each of which is accompanied by a number of bulleted subheadings. The bullets, which are an integral part of the standards, are designed to amplify the scope of each heading, and are not separate standards in their own right.

> [They] should be used by those assessing student teachers and teachers to track progress against the standard, to determine areas where additional development might need to be observed, or to identify areas where a student teacher or teacher is already demonstrating excellent practice relevant to that standard.
>
> (DfE, 2012)

Task 1.2.1 **Familiarising yourself with the Teachers' Standards for QTS**

Read through the standards in detail and discuss with your tutor what they mean and what has to be done by the end of the course to show that you have achieved them. They will form the basis on which you are assessed to have gained QTS, so finding out the specific requirements of your course is extremely important. There are likely to be several ways in which they are used: as an advance organiser; for personal profiling; and as a vehicle for discussion with others, for instance.

Be aware that most providers (if not all) will also use the Higher Education Academy (2012) *Working with the Teachers' Standards in Initial Teacher Education: Guidance to Support Assessment for Qualified Teacher Status (QTS)* document, which was developed in 2012 following the publication of the Teachers' Standards, to support a consistent approach to making professional judgements as to whether each student or student teacher has demonstrated the range of skills, knowledge and understanding required to be recommended for QTS at the end of their programme. This is a document you should also familiarise yourself with, or your provider's equivalent.

Using the Teachers' Standards as an advance organiser

The Standards indicate the various areas that need to be developed by you as a student teacher, and you need to identify your individual starting point in relation to each one. You will find this easier to do once you have started your first practice, and can take stock of where you are. You will then be able to start setting targets including short-term goals, and project forward to later targets; this will usually be done in discussion with mentors and/or tutors. This will be an on-going activity throughout your course; consistent reflection on how you are progressing against each Standard will guide your future planning and target setting, and anticipate the answer to 'What next?' in your progress towards gaining QTS.

Using the Teachers' Standards for personal profiling

Using the Standards to map the learning ahead goes hand-in-hand with reviewing your progress. You will be required to produce *evidence* of your progress against the Standards, and to develop some sort of a portfolio of this evidence, often called a Professional Development Portfolio (PDP). The PDP, or its equivalent, will serve a number of key purposes:

■ It will support you in identifying what you need to focus on to meet the Teachers' Standards required for QTS.
■ It will provide a record of your progress.
■ It will indicate what evidence you have accumulated to meet the Standards and where this can be located.

Your institution's PDP will make it clear what evidence should be recorded, how and where, with the following likely to contribute: lesson plans and resources (PowerPoints, worksheets, etc.), lesson evaluations, lesson observations, feedback from teachers on your lessons, mark books, reports, notes on meetings and activities outside the classroom (science clubs, visits, departmental meetings, parents evenings, etc.), attendance at university and school-based subject sessions and professional studies sessions.

Effective progress with your PDP necessitates you organising your documentation and filing efficiently and in a timely manner. Multiple files will be needed (whether on paper or electronically) and you will quickly learn that good administration and organisation skills are a necessary part of a teacher's repertoire. As your portfolio of evidence develops, you will begin to appreciate which parts contribute to which Standards, and annotating your lesson plans/evaluations/observations/feedback/etc. *at the time* indicating which Standards they evidence will be very useful. Your mentors and tutors will be looking for consistency and reliability, and several pieces of evidence over a range of contexts for each Standard; course documentation may indicate how much constitutes enough.

Using the Teachers' Standards as a vehicle for discussion

The Standards contribute to a shared language with which to discuss educational issues, including the type and quantity of evidence you collect. They help to shape the programme you follow, they affect the way in which feedback to you is structured and the way you review and evaluate your teaching. They are, however, not sufficient on their own as there are practical and theoretical ideas underpinning each standard. Take, for instance, Standard 4 that requires you must 'impart knowledge and develop understanding through effective use of lesson time' (DfE, 2012, p. 6). This opens a large agenda: what methods does a teacher use to impart knowledge? How do you cope when different children in the class develop understanding at different rates? What are the appropriate strategies to use, and for how much time in a lesson, such that lesson time is used effectively? What constitutes imparting new knowledge as opposed to just having new knowledge?

As another example, Standard 3 states: 'Have a secure knowledge of the relevant subject(s) and curriculum areas, foster and maintain pupils' interest in the subject, and address misunderstandings' (DfE, 2012, p. 5). As a science student teacher, you will undoubtedly find yourself teaching outside your specialist area during your course, and finding ways not only to improve your own subject knowledge, but also familiarise yourself with common misconceptions and ways of overcoming these, will form part of your professional development.

WORKING WITH YOUR OWN EXPERIENCES AND REFLECTIONS

You will already have given thought to your own experiences as a pupil in your decision to train to become a teacher. Your perception of what teaching is and the kind of teacher you wish to become are powerful factors in teacher formation. You will probably also have thought about how you will start to develop a professional relationship with your pupils, and how you wish to be perceived by them. Consideration of these experiences and images can be a starting point for your professional development. Task 1.2.2 requires you to make explicit the characteristics you associate with a good teacher by reflecting on your experience as a learner.

Task 1.2.2 **Reflections on your experiences of learning science**

Think back to your own schooling and recall an educational experience, preferably in science, which you remember and value. Why was this a successful learning experience for you? List all the points that you remember as being distinctive about this experience. You may find it helpful to think first of the qualities of the particular teacher, followed by the nature of the learning activities. With other science student teachers, discuss and compare your responses to this task. Collate the positive features identified into a list of the qualities a good teacher of science has.

The second part of this task is to repeat the above exercise, but this time focusing on an educational experience that failed to engage or motivate you.

Once again, compare and collate your responses with those of fellow student teachers.

Keep your notes in your Professional Development Portfolio and at the end of the course, consider how much your ideas have developed and how much you have achieved.

The features you have listed in your answers to the first part of Task 1.2.2 are those that you consider resulted in a successful learning experience from your perspective. When science student teachers are asked questions similar to those in Task 1.2.2, they generate a list that usually includes the attributes listed in Figure 1.2.3.

One of the challenges of the student teacher year is to incorporate the qualities that learners value into your work as a teacher. Task 1.2.3 helps you identify your starting point.

Task 1.2.3 **Auditing your own starting points**

The range of qualities possessed by good science teachers may seem daunting at the start. You may already have many of these skills through the life experience you bring to teaching, but they may need adjusting to the classroom context. The generic qualities of good teachers can be categorised in three ways:

▨ the nature, temperament and personality of the person;
▨ the commitment to young people and the profession of teaching;
▨ the professional skills acquired through need and practice.

Use the lists generated above (Task 1.2.2) to audit your personal qualities using these three categories in turn. What qualities do you need to acquire during school experience? In what ways do you expect your school experience to help you to develop these qualities, and how?

The teacher:

▨ was knowledgeable and enthusiastic about science
▨ was approachable
▨ knew and treated pupils as individuals
▨ had the ability to make science relevant to everyday life
▨ was able to explain scientific concepts and ideas clearly and logically
▨ was able to manage practical work safely and to support learning
▨ adopted a firm, but fair and consistent, approach
▨ was patient
▨ was willing to give up their time to go over material
▨ was well prepared.

▨ **Figure 1.2.3** Students teachers' list of good teacher attributes

WORKING WITH MENTORS AND TUTORS

There will be a variety of patterns of working with a range of different people, depending on the HEI where you are registered, and the route you are following to QTS. It is likely that there will be one HE science tutor who has oversight of your progress during the year, and acts as a personal tutor, and that one science teacher in the school will act as your school mentor. In addition, there may be another teacher in the school (often a senior teacher) who has oversight of all the student teachers in their school or alliance and who organises a professional studies programme. You will also work closely with science teachers whose classes you teach and these teachers give you guidance on your lessons and feedback on your teaching. Some student teachers may be teaching their own classes without supervision, and in this case there will be teachers who observe you teaching and give you feedback on a regular basis. These teachers will be involved in working with you on the Plan–Do–Review–Learn–Apply cycle, as much as your main science mentor. You will also form working relationships with the technical teams in both the school and the HE institution, and a good working relationship with your technician in school is essential.

School-based mentors organise the induction period in school, plan your timetable, and support you as you move from observing classes to working with small groups and then taking over whole classes. They ensure that you have class lists with appropriate inform-ation about particular pupils. They meet with you on a regular basis to discuss your learning. They teach you more skills, such as how to mark books, how to give constructive feedback and how to monitor practical skills. They discuss feedback you are receiving from other teachers and your own evaluations, to help you identify targets in your next phase of development and ways of reaching those targets. They may well take an active interest in your coursework and reading. You must take a proactive part in these meet-ings, going to them with the necessary documents and items you want to discuss.

Your HEI tutor has responsibility for overseeing the collation of your experiences, monitoring your progress as a whole and ensuring that the course components add up to a coherent experience. Your tutor contributes to the lecture, seminar and workshop programme and is the main supervisor of your written work. Tutors are also involved in periodic profiling with student teachers. When they visit schools, they spend time talking with the mentors about the school programme as well as discussing your progress. They are likely to observe your teaching and to give feedback. The list of 'good practice' in Figure 1.2.4 gives the tenor of conversations you should anticipate with both your tutor and school mentor.

Good practice occurs when:

- trainees take an active role in the feedback sessions
- trainees are able, and given the opportunity, to evaluate their own teaching
- the lesson's aims or means of assessing pupil progress and achievement are used to structure feedback
- feedback is thorough, comprehensive and, where appropriate, diagnostic
- there is a balance of praise, criticism and suggestions for alternative strategies
- points made in feedback are given an order of priority of importance, targeting three for immediate action
- trainees receive written comments on the lesson observed.

■ **Figure 1.2.4** Good practice in giving and using feedback on teaching

WORKING WITH AND THROUGH LESSON OBSERVATIONS

Throughout your training, but particularly at the beginning, you will observe other teachers teaching. Classrooms are complex and busy places and observation of exactly what is going on and why can be difficult. Focused observations, however, when you are directed to observe specific, targeted aspects can be very useful. Task 1.2.4 suggests an activity you might try and Figure 1.2.5 has a schedule that focuses on the flow of activities in a lesson and on classroom management. You could use all, or more probably, some of these foci during your observations.

Make notes about how the teacher accomplishes all or some of the tasks at the different phases of a lesson and about what the pupils are doing.

1   Throughout the lesson

- ■ timing
- ■ use of praise and/or sanctions
- ■ use of body language and tone/volume of voice
- ■ movement around the class.

2   Starting the lesson

- ■ bringing in the class
- ■ settling and registration
- ■ opening up the topic

  - ☐ gaining interest
  - ☐ eliciting prior knowledge
  - ☐ explaining the purpose of work
  - ☐ telling pupils what to do.

2   Equipment/resources

- ■ location and evidence of pre-ordering with technician
- ■ working order
- ■ management of distribution
- ■ collecting in.

3   Main activity of lesson

- ■ What is the class doing?
- ■ What is the teacher doing?
- ■ How does the teacher gain the attention of the class?
- ■ How does the teacher ensure pupils are on-task?
- ■ How does the teacher manage transitions from one activity to the next?
- ■ How does the teacher manage group and/or independent work?
- ■ What problems arise? How are they managed?

4   End

- ■ signal to stop/clear up
- ■ clear up/collect equipment
- ■ identifying/drawing out/summarising learning
- ■ setting homework
- ■ dismissing class.

■ **Figure 1.2.5** Example of a guide for observing a lesson to focus on particular aspects of the lesson and to record strategies and management skills being used (see Task 1.2.3)

Task 1.2.4 **Watching science teachers: teaching skills**

With the prior agreement of the teacher, arrange to observe a science lesson. Share the purposes of your observation and any particular focus you have. If possible, find a time for a short debriefing with the teacher after the lesson. Use an observation schedule to help in focusing your observation (the list in Figure 1.2.4 suggests examples of what you might focus on). Make a list of questions to discuss with the teacher after the lesson. Write a summary for yourself identifying the implications of your observation for your lesson planning and those practices that you might adopt.

As you progress through your training and take on whole lessons and an increasing timetable, you will be observed yourself, initially for the majority of your lessons. These observations may be formal (as part of your evidence against the Standards) or informal, but in all instances you should expect some sort of feedback. As part of your development, it is useful for observers if you explain the focus of your practice for that lesson, e.g. that you are trying out some strategy in order to improve your practice and/or evidence for a particular Standard. Highlighting your personal targets for that particular week can also be helpful. This will focus the observation points for your observer, and give them a context in which to give you feedback.

WORKING IN YOUR SCHOOL CONTEXT

As you start your time on school placement, there will be many questions to ask of school colleagues, and you may feel that the contribution you can make in return is insignificant. However, schools welcome the knowledge, skills and enthusiasm that student teachers can bring to the school community, often accompanied by 'real-world' experience. Science is a rapidly changing world and recent graduates will have up-to-date knowledge of their subject area, and those recently employed in the STEM community will bring knowledge of careers and the world outside education. Student teachers will be working on development of resources and will bring new teaching materials, teaching and learning strategies and innovative ideas, many of which will become part of the resources bank for the school.

SUMMARY AND KEY POINTS

Any cohort of student teachers will include a wide range of previous experience, and consequently a variety of starting points from which to embark on their professional journey. Whatever the starting point, understanding and using the Plan–Do–Learn–Review–Apply cycle encourages student teachers to reflect on their professional practice, and makes it easier to seek appropriate help and to make best use of support and input from your tutors, mentors, other science teachers, the technicians and fellow student teachers. Using the Standards as an advance organiser, for professional profiling and as a vehicle for discussion contributes to professional development.

Progress will be marked by an increasing sophistication of the analyses in which you engage and the move towards a time when your focus is entirely on the pupils' learning. This professional learning involves a complex mix of classroom experience and theoretical understanding; one without the other will not maximise productivity. Above all, remember that you are in charge of your professional development. Your commitment to taking an active part in it is crucial to your success. Learning to teach will take a toll on your personal reserves; it takes stamina and persistence, it requires good administrative skills as well as skills and knowledge needed for the classroom. It will draw on your personal attributes of being able to deal with complex situations, of establishing authority and showing leadership. By the end of the training year you will be aware that you have learned 'a new way of being yourself' (Black, 1987) and will derive a great deal of professional satisfaction from this 'new you'.

REFERENCES

Black, P. (1987) 'Deciding to teach', *Steam, ICI Science Teachers' Magazine* No. 8.
DfE (Department for Education) (2010) *The Importance of Teaching*. London: HMSO.
DfE (Department for Education) (2012) *Teachers' Standards*, available at: www.gov.uk/government/publications/teachers-standards (accessed 1 November 2013).
General Teaching Council for England (2009) *Code of Conduct and Practice for Registered Teachers*. Available at: http://webarchive.nationalarchives.gov.uk/20111213132132/http://www.gtce.org.uk/teachers/thecode/ (accessed 11 September 2014).
Higher Education Academy (2012) *Working with the Teachers' Standards in Initial Teacher Education: Guidance to Support Assessment for Qualified Teacher Status (QTS)*. Available at: http://www.heacademy.ac.uk/assets/documents/events/SS_assets/Working_with_the_Teachers%E2%80%99_Standards_in_ITE.pdf (accessed 20 October 2013).
NCIHE (1997) *Higher Education in the Learning Society*, Report of the National Committee of Inquiry into Higher Education: The Dearing Report, London: HMSO.
Watkins, C., Carnell, E. and Lodge, C. (2007) *Effective Learning in Classrooms*, London: Sage.

FURTHER READING

Capel, S., Leask, M. and Turner, T. (eds) (2013) *Learning to Teach in the Secondary School: A Companion to School Experience*, 6th edn, London: Routledge.

Chapters in Capel *et al.* are:

▮ Allen, M. and Toplis, R., Unit 1.2, 'Student teachers' roles and responsibilities', pp. 25–41.
▮ Capel, S., Unit 1.3, 'Managing your time, workload and stress', pp. 42–54.
▮ Redondo, A., Unit 2.1, 'Reading classrooms. How to maximise learning from classroom observation', pp. 83–98.

Parkinson, J. (2002) *Reflective Teaching of Science 11–18*, London: Continuum.

The chapter 'Learning to become an effective teacher' discusses the attributes of good teachers. It outlines issues of professional attitudes and responsibility including the need to review your practice regularly, and suggests ways of doing this.

UNIT 1.3

WORKING IN A SCIENCE DEPARTMENT

Rob Toplis

INTRODUCTION

The majority of your experience will be spent in schools and working in a science depart-ment. This will involve daily interactions with science teachers, science technicians, form tutors, teaching assistants and cover supervisors as well as occasional interactions with other school staff such as caretakers, maintenance staff, visitors and the school's senior management. In addition, you will also be working within pastoral or year group teams that will include teachers from a range subjects and pastoral team leaders, and possibly the Special Needs Co-ordinator (SENCO) and the Gifted and Talented Co-ordinator: teaching in schools is not just about teaching your own subject. This unit will give you an overview of school organisation and will help you explore the ways in which a science team works in your placement school.

OBJECTIVES

By the end of this unit, you should:

- appreciate the main differences between how primary and secondary schools are organised;
- recount how teachers are organised in a number of different teams in a school and know the meetings you are expected to attend;
- explain the structure of the science team and know the key responsibilities which individuals, both teachers and technicians, hold;
- form appropriate and constructive professional relationships as a student teacher with other members of the science team;
- appreciate the place of the science team within the workings of the whole school.

MOVING FROM THE PRIMARY SCHOOL TO THE SECONDARY SCHOOL

In many cases you will have spent some time in a primary school and will therefore be in a position to appreciate the very different ways in which the schools operate in these two phases of education, both on a structural and on a daily basis. When pupils move from primary to secondary schools they frequently experience enormous changes, so much so that the first day or two can end in tears!

Task 1.3.1 **Differences between primary and secondary schools**

Keep a diary or notes from your experience of observing in a primary and a secondary school. At this stage, a focus on the following will be relevant to your understanding of how primary schools work and will provide a comparison with secondary schools:

1 the different ways in which teachers teach;
2 the contributions made by Teaching Assistants during the lesson;
3 the variety of learning activities taking place;
4 the different ways in which pupils appear to learn;
5 how pupils are motivated to work;
6 what structures exist to organise the school as a community;
7 what different responsibilities do teachers and pupils have;
8 how the environment affects the learning and the activities of the school.

ORGANISATION IN SCHOOLS

Despite calls for greater collegiality in schools (Hargreaves, 1994) or the views of some Senior Leaders about a 'flatter' pyramid of management with a more distributed leadership style, schools are still very hierarchical places. The structure of schools and departments reflects the need to respond to external pressures, to get a multitude of tasks associated with teaching and school organisation completed, a need to provide incentives to do so, and at the same time allowing teachers to see a route to personal and career advancement.

The overall school structure often consists of a single Headteacher or 'Head' at the top of the pyramid, followed by Deputy Headteachers and then Assistant Heads. These constitute the Senior Leadership Team or Senior Management Team (SLT or SMT) in the school. Below this senior level are teaching teams based around subjects or groups of subjects and year group or Key Stage teams with pastoral responsibilities for pupils. In charge of these teams are middle managers who may have a variety of different titles such as Heads of Department or Heads of Year/Heads of Key Stages, Curriculum Leaders, Curriculum or Pastoral Managers, Directors of Departments or Key Stages (Figure 1.3.1).

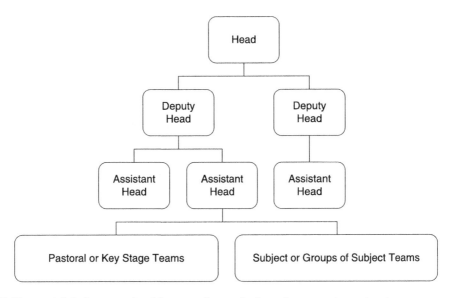

■ **Figure 1.3.1** An example of the overall organisation of a secondary school

The science department may be organised in a number of different ways. The first model – and probably a more traditional one – is of separate sciences. In some schools these are very distinct departments and the level of communication between them may or may not be limited. The separate departments may have their own Heads of Biology, Chemistry and Physics, their own laboratories, their own budgets, their own technicians and even their own places to drink coffee at morning break (Figure 1.3.2). In other schools, these separate science departments may still exist but may be more fluid with greater movement of science teachers between the separate science areas, especially so at Key Stage 3. Typically schools with this model of organisation are independent schools, grammar schools and comprehensive schools still following grammar school models of organisation.

An increasing number of science departments in schools have become organised around Key Stages. This is largely a response to the National Curriculum and its assessment, as

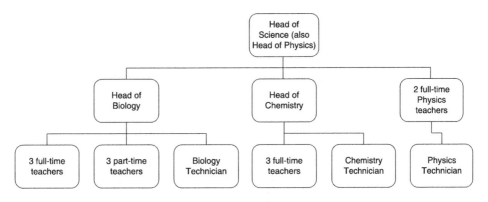

■ **Figure 1.3.2** An example of separate science departments

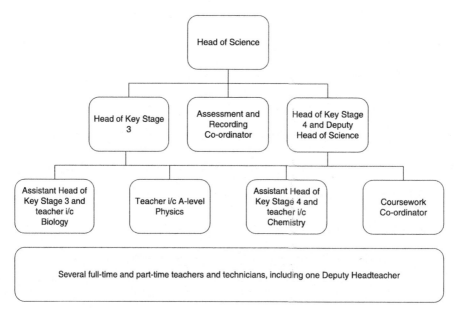

▨ **Figure 1.3.3** An example of a Key Stage departmental structure

well as the provision of laboratory space for lower school, Key Stage 3, classes and the way in which different specialist teachers are deployed. Although the subject specialist departments from the model above have been removed, there is still a need to have specialist teachers of biology, chemistry and physics at post-16 and the need to provide incentives to manage various aspects of the science curriculum as well as retain existing staff and recruit new science teachers. Within this structure there may be graded posts of responsibility, Teaching and Learning Responsibility points, with associated payments. These points could be for responsibilities for the Key Stage 3 curriculum, the Key Stage 4 curriculum, assessment and recording within the department, being in charge (i/c) of a separate science at Key Stage 4 and A level, coursework co-ordination, and so on. One example from a large science department is shown in Figure 1.3.3.

A third model of science department organisation does not include a science department as such but has a faculty structure (Figure 1.3.4). In this example, the faculty is called the 'STEM Faculty' where STEM is an increasingly common term for Science, Technology, Engineering and Mathematics. It should be noted that this is a much less common type of organisation but variations of it do occur in some schools. In this case the separate sciences are retained as part of the structure but the faculty also includes the areas of Mathematics, Design and Technology and a vocational strand that includes Health and Social Care, and Information Technology and Computing.

These models are examples of some of the structures that exist within different schools. However, they do not indicate the other roles of teaching staff in these departments. Some science staff may have responsibilities for Year groups, some may have whole school responsibilities for such areas as work experience, careers, examinations, co-ordinator for continuing professional development (CPD) and, relevant to student teachers, Professional Tutor with overall responsibility for initial teacher education in the school.

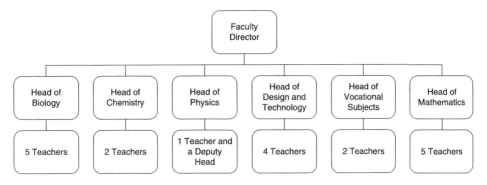

■ **Figure 1.3.4** An example of a faculty structure

Task 1.3.2 **Who's who in the school**

You are now joining the school staff and one of the early tasks you will need to do is to find out how staff teams are organised. This information may be in a staff handbook so it is worth finding this out.

1 Who is the Headteacher? Who are the Deputy Heads and Assistant Heads and what are their main responsibilities?
2 Who is the Professional Tutor?
3 How are subject or curriculum teams organised?
4 How is the pastoral system organised?
5 Which pastoral team or year group will you be part of? Does this include members of the science team?
6 What school meetings and committees are there?
7 Who is the Special Educational Needs Co-ordinator? The Gifted and Talented Co-ordinator?

THE SCIENCE DEPARTMENT

Everything will appear a little daunting at first but it will help you a great deal if you know about the roles of different members of the science department. You will, after all, be approaching them for help and advice in addition to your mentor.

Ancillary staff in the department

First, a few words about the role of technicians. Technicians are often (sadly) overlooked outside the science department. Unfortunately some student teachers also overlook them, possibly assuming that as they are classed as 'ancillary staff' they are of less importance. Nothing could be further from the truth. The myth that technicians hide in the prep room (preparation room) and do the washing up is simply not the case. Technicians are rarely noticed as they move through and between laboratories but they see everything. During your first day or two, it is very worthwhile to talk to the technicians and find out how the apparatus, the provision of books and worksheets, stationery and photocopying are organised. Are there class sets of books? Is there a number for the photocopier? Are the worksheets on a CD-Rom? How do you get class sets of copies reproduced?

Task 1.3.3 **The roles of the technician**

One way of finding out exactly what sorts of jobs a technician does is to observe them and talk to them. This can be recorded in a notebook or diary and referred to a later date. Your records may form part of your portfolio for fulfilling your wider professional responsibilities. Some questions may be:

1 Are there subject specialist technicians?
2 How much of a technician's time is spent repairing, preparing and moving apparatus?
3 How much time is spent cleaning apparatus?
4 Do they keep records? Do they order equipment?
5 Do they advise on health and safety issues with practical work?
6 Do they have responsibility for setting up data logging and/or computer resources?
7 What is the teacher:technician ratio? What is the technician:laboratory ratio?
8 Do they help with distribution and collection of apparatus during practical lessons?
9 What are the procedures for ordering apparatus and chemicals? How much notice is needed?

One of the important things you will need to find out early is the procedure for ordering apparatus and chemicals. You will need to talk to the technicians about this with some very specific questions that relate to:

■ *Technician order forms.* Does the science department use a standard order form? If so, it may be a good idea to keep copies for your evidence records.
■ *How does the risk assessment work?* It may be that the scheme of work used by the department includes specific risk assessments for particular practical work activities. However, you will also need to make sure that you can demonstrate that you can assess risk, are aware of the possible hazards with different age groups and classes, and can show this in your evidence.
■ *How much notice do the technicians require?* Frequently this is a week but different technicians in different schools may have other arrangements. It will be up to you to find out about this and keep to the notice periods. You cannot rely on coming into a prep room on a Monday morning with a list of apparatus needed for later that day or, worse still, the first teaching period.
■ *You will need to specify exactly what you want* for apparatus and materials; you cannot assume they will be there in the laboratories. It is also inappropriate to just order 'beakers' for a practical – you will need to specify size. Similarly just stating 'hydrochloric acid' is not enough. How much? In how many bottles? At what concentration? Ordering materials also applies to non-laboratory items as well. It is

very easy to forget basic things such as a class set of pencils, writing paper, glue sticks or scissors.

The technician can be one of the most important allies of a student teacher so it is important to treat them as you would any other member of staff.

The second group of people you will need to consider in your planning, teaching and learning is the Teaching Assistants (TAs), also called Learning Support Assistants (LSAs) or Classroom Assistants (CAs). Different schools may have different numbers of TAs and they will have different roles. In a number of cases they will be employed to support specific pupils, in other cases they may have more of a whole class role. TAs are colleagues with whom you work and it is important that they are included in your planning and teaching. Your work with TAs can be regarded as part of the Teachers' Standards (DfE, 2012) where you are required to develop effective professional relationships with colleagues, knowing how and when to draw on advice and specialist support, and how to deploy support staff effectively. It is therefore important that you are not only able to evidence this but also to take a proactive approach to involving TAs in your work on a daily basis.

Task 1.3.4 **The roles of Teaching Assistants**

A way of finding out exactly what a teaching assistant (TA) does is either to talk to one or to note their activities during your classroom observations. Some questions about their role might be:

1 How many pupils are they assigned to in the class? Or are they assigned to a whole class?
2 What are the reasons for TAs being assigned to pupils?
3 Do they spend all their time with the assigned pupils? If not, who else do they help?
4 What exactly do they do with the pupils they help?
5 What resources do they prepare for pupils?
6 Do they help organise the pupils?

One important part of your planning and teaching is how you can involve the TA. It is really inappropriate to expect to get the most from a TA if they are unprepared or have to second-guess what you are doing in your lesson as the lesson unfolds. One way to avoid this is to make sure they know what you are doing in advance of your lesson. At the very least they should have a copy of your lesson plan and have this in advance, ideally several days before the lesson itself so that they have an opportunity to review it and plan for their individual pupils. This might sound obvious but is something that is all too frequently overlooked by student teachers, especially in the early stages of your teaching when the focus is very much on what *you* will be doing. However, successful lessons are those that have a focus on learning and on the learning of all pupils; catering for all requires managing for the work of TAs. Part of the planning for TAs may involve talking to them about the needs of pupils in the class, how other teachers cater for these pupils, a copy of the lesson plan, some ideas about the resources that might help the pupil and any preparatory work the TA might need to do beforehand.

Task 1.3.5 **Involving the TA**

You are planning to teach a Year 8 lesson that includes testing a range of different foods for starch using iodine solution and a white tile. Imagine you have a pupil with a visual impairment. Consider how you might plan a lesson and the work of the TA who supports that pupil so that:

1 You know the exact nature of the visual impairment and what the pupil *can* see.
2 How the TA can appreciate the subject knowledge intended for the class.
3 How the TA helps the pupi carry out and record the results without being over-dependent on the TA's input.
4 How the TA can help with recording the results.
5 Any resources you can prepare that may help this pupil, e.g. size of script, contrast, positioning of words, number of words, use of diagrams, etc.

A third dimension of working with support staff may be your awareness of the role of outside agencies. Clearly at this stage you will not be expected to liaise with these but you should be aware of their roles. It may be worth discussing some of these with the school's SENCO, pastoral leader or Deputy Head. Pertinent questions might include the roles of the Psychological Service, the Educational Welfare Officer, the Careers Service, work experience placements or the Pupil Referral Unit. Within the science department there may also be additional 'outreach' work with museum staff, the CREST award scheme, a science club or with a partnership scheme involving undergraduate science students or professional scientists or engineers such as those run by the Royal Society.

The role of the Head of Department

The traditional role of the Head of Department (HoD) has changed a great deal in the last few years. No longer do they just administer the budget and advise staff about in-service courses but they have become an important part of the school's Middle Leadership team. As part of their leadership role they have responsibility for the overall performance and development of the science department and this includes monitoring pupils' attainment as well as the performance and professional development of teachers. This forms an important part of their role in school improvement. Such tasks may include:

- managing the science department's overall strategy, including an improvement plan;
- raising attainment in science by monitoring pupil progress;
- making sure all schemes of work are in place and are reviewed as necessary;
- team building within the science department;
- managing resources;
- timetabling and room allocation in the department;
- promoting professional development for staff.

These tasks are in addition to those of a departmental manager that include the smooth running of the department, keeping up-to-date with science education and national initiatives, preparation for Ofsted inspections or reporting, performance management, supporting classroom management and to report at meetings with the Senior Leadership Team and Governors.

The Second in Department

The Second in Department will very likely be a teacher who aspires to a Head of Department post at some point in the future. As Second in Department they will be expected to deputise for the Head of Department in their absence and to carry out tasks as delegated or negotiated. One of these tasks may be as a mentor for science student teachers.

Science teachers

The numbers of science teachers in the department will vary according to the number of pupils in the school, the number of full-time and part-time staff and the number of pupils in the sixth form studying science at post-16 level, often A-levels. It is also worth remembering that a number of these science teachers may have delegated roles both within the department and outside it, as outlined above. It is not unusual to have a Deputy Head teaching science.

A number of teachers in the department may receive a salary addition to carry out these responsibilities as part of the Teaching and Learning Responsibility Payments (TLRPs) that form a structured system aimed at recognising additional responsibilities related to teaching and learning and as a way of providing incentives to retain teachers in schools. Different schools use the TLRPs in different ways and there is no one model that can be applied to all schools as these are largely at the discretion of the individual school's governing body. These payments were introduced from 2006. First Teaching and Learning Responsibility (TLR1) post-holders also have line management responsibility for a significant number of people compared with TLR2 teachers whose payment will be of a lower value (National Union of Teachers, 2012). The situation in Academies varies as these are able to set their own pay, conditions and working time arrangements for newly appointed teachers joining the Academy. In some Academies, pay and conditions arrangements for new teachers are similar or identical to those for teachers in local authority maintained state schools; in others, teachers' pay and conditions can be different. This situation is different for teachers who transfer when an Academy replaces an existing school or schools where teachers who transfer to the Academy from the predecessor school(s) are protected in respect of pay and conditions.

Meetings

As a student teacher you may be expected to attend meetings. However, it is worth checking first as there may be some meetings – usually very rare – where confidential or contentious issues are discussed and where it would be more comfortable for those involved if you were not there. The vast majority of meetings will involve the policies, practice and day-to-day workings of the department and will help you to be part of the professional life of the school.

Most departments produce improvement or development plans that are linked to the whole school improvement plan as part of the drive to raise standards. The way in which these policies are planned and developed further, and how they contribute to the effectiveness of the department in improving the quality of learning for pupils, depend on a consensus that is part of the decision-making process in the department. Agreed decisions are understood and implemented via discussion at department meetings where the quality of discussion is crucial to the effectiveness of the department. The issues discussed are often varied, e.g. teaching and learning strategies, issues with curriculum continuity or problems associated with particular pupils. A department meeting usually has an agenda and the Head of Department will often invite members of the department to suggest items for the agenda in advance of the meeting. Agenda items may include: requests for information from the SLT; a review of progress with the department's improvement plan; a request to provide data on pupil attainment; announcements of professional development opportunities; feedback from department members about professional development activities they have attended; changes to the department's handbook; individual pupil concerns; pupil grouping, and the choice of published schemes of work or examination specifications.

Task 1.3.6 **Departmental policies**

You will need to consult the department's handbook or related documents to familiarise yourself with various policies. You will need to concentrate at first on those directly related to you as a student teacher in the department. Some starting points are:

■ health and safety policy
■ equal opportunities
■ inclusion policy
■ behaviour policies, including rewards and sanctions
■ assessment
■ homework.

BEYOND THE SCIENCE DEPARTMENT

Although most of your observation, planning and teaching will be within the science department, it is worth valuing observations of teachers and classes in other departments as a contribution to your overall experience in schools. It is always illuminating to see how classes respond to teachers in other subjects, to the different styles of other teachers in other departments and the ways in which personalities and contexts vary. How does an English teacher manage pupil discussions? How do Geography teachers organise group work? How does the context of the Art department alter the way pupils work? How do Mathematics teachers display pupils' work? In observing these subject teachers and departments and gaining other experiences, you can learn about different strategies and think about widening the range of approaches you can use develop your own teaching in science.

SUMMARY AND KEY POINTS

In this unit we have explored the range of different ways that schools are organised, the roles, responsibilities and diversity of different individuals in the science department and ways in which the student teacher can appreciate and work effectively in this environment.

We have reviewed the changes that pupils experience as they move from primary to secondary school, the professional relationships that science teachers forge and how you as a student teacher can develop these and play a part in the life of the school. You will need to use these departmental experiences and tasks to widen your own understanding and relate these to the Teachers' Standards.

REFERENCES

DfE (Department for Education) (2012) *Teachers' Standards*, available at: www.education.gov.uk/schools/leadership/deployingstaff/a00205581/teachers-standards1-sep–2012 (accessed 30 December 2013).
Hargreaves, A. (1994) *Changing Teachers, Changing Times*, New York: Teachers College Press.
National Union of Teachers (2012) *School Teachers' Pay*, available at: www.teachers.org.uk/payandconditions/pay (accessed 30 December 2013).

FURTHER READING

Dillon, J. (2000) 'Managing the science department', in M. Monk and J. Osborne (eds) *Good Practice in Science Teaching: What Research Has to Say*, Buckingham: Open University Press.

This chapter looks at what research tells us about effective management, particularly at departmental level.

Greenway, T. and Kirk, T. (2004) 'The changing role of the head of department', *School Science Review*, 85(313): 41–7.

This article explores the impact of changes on the diversity and complexity of the role of the head of department within the context of school improvement and leadership.

Peters, A. (2004) 'Our first year as a specialist science college' *School Science Review*, 85(313): 60–1.

This snapshot outlines the changes that one school made to the management structure and the outreach activities as a result of becoming a specialist science college.

The Wellcome Trust (2009) *Perspectives on Education 2 (Primary–Secondary Transfer in Science)*.

Leading experts in primary–secondary transfer issues look at the dips in attitudes and attainment often associated with the move from primary to secondary school, their particular relevance to science education, and what improvements are being made to better support students through this transition.

Available at: www.wellcome.ac.uk/stellent/groups/corporatesite/#camsh_peda/documents/web_document/WTX054697.pdf (accessed 15 October 2012).

USEFUL WEBSITES

Cambridge Primary Review: www.primaryreview.org.uk (accessed 15October 2012).
National Union of Teachers: www.teachers.org.uk (accessed 15 October 2012).

THE SCIENCE CURRICULUM

INTRODUCTION

Two terms you will come across regularly are: 'the curriculum' – what is taught, and 'pedagogy' – how it is taught. This section provides a focus on the curriculum. Until the introduction of the National Curriculum in 1989, the curriculum was determined by schools themselves where they had a choice of different examination boards and sometimes their own examination schemes for Mode 3 examinations in the upper school (now Years 10 and 11). Schools often devised their own schemes for the lower school for the 11–14 age range. The National Curriculum changed that and is still changing. Indeed, one of the problems we encountered when writing this section is that we were experiencing one of these changes with the National Curriculum, its drafts and its consultation process. As a result, there is now a Key Stage 3 (KS3) National Curriculum for Years 7 to 9 but a draft Key Stage 4 (KS4) curriculum. At the time of writing, examination boards are planning their specifications for 2015 with new GCSEs ready for teaching from 2016. Nevertheless, science departments and individual teachers have flexibility about their pedagogy, how they teach the curriculum. When teachers meet outside of their classes, conversation frequently turns to the topic of how they teach certain areas of the curriculum and what resources they use.

The focus of this chapter is the formal science curriculum. Designing any curriculum involves making choices about what should, and should not be included. In the countries of the United Kingdom those choices are made at different levels. National bodies provide guidelines through their own curriculum bodies or through the criteria for science courses leading to qualifications. Science departments in schools interpret these guidelines when producing their schemes of work and individual teachers use their own interpretation when developing lessons from the schemes of work. Pupils, themselves, after the age of 14, may make choices about which science courses they follow.

As a science teacher you need to be aware of the national guidelines, to know how these might be translated into more specific course outlines and to recognise the flexibility that schools and individual teachers still have when creating learning activities for their pupils. This last point is particularly important because teachers can sometimes feel they have no 'voice' and are subject to doing what the curriculum tells them. In school, you may need to be aware of this and help to maintain a degree of teacher autonomy and creativity.

Unit 2.1, Science in the National Curriculum, gives the background to the National Curriculum in Science, the changes that have occurred in the 25 years since its introduction and the reasons for the changes. We have focused on the situation in England; however, there are sufficient similarities to make the chapter relevant to the contexts in Wales and Northern Ireland, because the early history and principles on which the National Curriculum is based apply to them all. Scotland has an advisory, not a statutory, curriculum. Again, many of the principles apply. Relevant websites for the National Curriculum documents for the four countries are given at the end of Unit 2.2, Science 11–14.

Unit 2.2, Science 11–14 helps you to understand the detail of the English science curriculum for the 11–14 age range. The tasks are easily adapted for people working with the Welsh, Northern Irish or Scottish curricula.

Unit 2.3 examines the diversity of the 14–19 science curriculum. This diversity arises because only one part of the curriculum in England is specified by the National Curriculum; the rest is determined by the choices that pupils make between different courses. Those choices are always shifting, but recently, there has been the development of more vocationally based courses alongside academic courses, meaning studying science post-16 is becoming ever more flexible. The unit has been written in the context of GCSE (General Certificate of Secondary Education) and GCE (General Certificate of Education) courses, used in England, Wales and Northern Ireland, but the tasks are easily adaptable to the courses leading to Scottish qualifications.

It may be worth noting that at the time of writing, the curriculum in England for pupils after the age of 14 is in a process of change – sometimes at short notice – and you should therefore check current curriculum documents, examination board news and examination boards' specifications for these changes.

SCIENCE IN THE NATIONAL CURRICULUM

Paul Davies

INTRODUCTION

The National Curriculum is a series of government-produced documents which describes the subject knowledge content that children from the ages of 5–16 years, studying in maintained schools in England and Wales should be taught. Academies, Free Schools and Independent schools are under no statutory obligation to follow the National Curriculum, but most choose to. Covering most school subjects, the National Curriculum was introduced in 1989 to provide a framework for teachers to guide their planning of learning experiences. However, the National Curriculum is an evolving document and has undergone many iterations since its inception. All teachers need a sound understanding of the curriculum for the specific subject and age range that they teach, but they also need an awareness of how ideas are built up throughout a child's experience of school, and the requirements within other subjects. This unit explores some of the developments and evolution of the National Curriculum and then, in Units 2.2 and 2.3, looks in greater detail at the National Curriculum in Science for the 11–14 and 14–19 age ranges, respectively.

OBJECTIVES

By the end of this unit, you should:

- be familiar, in broad terms, with the aims and purpose of the National Curriculum in science;
- be aware of associated assessment;
- understand something of the history of the development of the National Curriculum.

NATIONAL CURRICULUM ASSESSMENT

The National Curriculum (NC) was first introduced in 1989. Until that time, teachers had much greater freedom to decide what to teach, and in many respects, how they would teach their subject. This was something that was often decided upon by individual school departments and helped promote a particular 'subject ethos' within schools, an echo of which can still be felt in many schools. While both liberating for teachers, and potentially exciting for pupils, this approach ran the risk of children learning very different things and so caused problems in terms of standardising assessment outcomes between schools and the equity of knowledge base that a child could be expected to have when leaving school.

In response to this, the government at the time decided to implement major changes to what was taught in schools. To do this, educational experts, in both school and tertiary education, as well as representatives from subject-specific professional bodies worked to produce a document that would provide clear guidelines as to what specific content should be taught throughout primary (5–11 years) and secondary (11–16 years) in maintained schools. Development was a long process and involved trialling within certain schools and lengthy consultation with interested parties. Education, being an important focus for governments, meant much was at stake in the development of the NC and, in many ways, it became a politician's tool.

Together with mandatory subject content, the NC brought with it an entirely new language associated with the names of different school years and assessment opportunities. Prior to the NC, schools were free to call their year groups whatever they wanted. However, the NC divided learning in Key Stages and, to help provide clarity, linked these to specific year groups which started at the beginning of compulsory education at aged 5 years in Year 1 (Y1) and ended at the end of compulsory education at aged 16 in Year 11(Y11). The Key Stages span certain year groups as follows: Key Stage 1 (KS1) (Y1 and Y2), Key Stage 2 (KS2) (Y3–6), Key Stage 3 (KS3) (Y7–9) and Key Stage 4 (KS4) (Y10–11). At its inception, the NC did not provide a name for post-16 year groups and, for a long time, many schools retained the familiar Lower 6th and Upper 6th to identify pupils aged 16–18 years. However, as the NC has evolved, and schools have become inculcated into the language of the NC these groups are now often referred to Year 12 and 13, respectively, and Key Stage 5. For fuller details about the background to these changes, refer to Unit 7.3 in the generic text, *Learning to Teach in the Secondary School*, 6th edition (Capel *et al.*, 2013).

The final iteration of the NC identified Science as a 'core subject', meaning that, along with English and Mathematics, it formed part of compulsory education for all pupils in primary and secondary schools. Interestingly, this meant that 'Science' was seen to consist of the three separate sciences of biology, chemistry and physics. This categorisation was seen as an important step towards the formation of a scientifically literate society who would be educated in the language and technical issues surrounding science which might be useful in terms of pursuing a scientific career, but also for living as a scientifically literate citizen in the modern, Western world. Being a core subject means that Science occupies a privileged position within the curriculum with around 30 per cent of curriculum time being allocated to science teaching. There are several pathways that pupils can take when studying science, the most able pupils taking Triple Science leading to three separate GCSEs in Biology, Chemistry and Physics. Less able pupils are able to follow a pathway which leads to Additional Science with two GCSEs being awarded. There are also a number of other pathways that a pupil may follow in science, including BTEC and IGCSE.

Since its inception, NC Science has undergone several changes, the most important one affecting secondary schools occurring in the last few years. The culmination of this is its sixth implementation, with first teaching in September 2014.

Along with Key Stages and new Year Group names, the arrival of the NC brought with it a new assessment model which allowed pupils' progress to be monitored throughout their school career. The Task Group on Assessment and Testing (TGAT) developed a scheme for Key Stages 1–3 where pupils are awarded 'Levels'. The criterion for achieving levels was set out as a series of 'level descriptors' which provided guidance on a number of different aspects of learning which led to the awarding of nine different levels, termed Levels 1–8 and 'Exceptional Performance'. Originally, these attainment targets were linked to Key Stages 1–4, however, more recently, these have been reduced to encompass only Key Stages 1–3. Together with these levels was an expectation that a certain proportion of pupils in each Year Group cohort would reach a certain attainment level. These targets were used to assess the 'value added' achievement of schools and allow comparison in pupil achievement between schools; but this is something which has been perceived by many teachers and educationists as potentially divisive. In 2014, changes to the NC led to an abandonment of levels and their replacement with in-house assessment grading (see Unit 2.2 for further details).

Before the arrival of the NC, no national assessment was carried out in primary schools or the first three years of secondary school, with teachers charged with internal assessment duties until national testing at age 16. However, as well as developing assessment level descriptors, the TGAT were tasked with producing standardised tests that could be used at the end of certain Key Stages. These were designed to be used to assess the progress of individual pupils and to allow for comparison between schools, something which led to the development of School Performance Tables. The tests are called Standard Assessment Tests (SATs) and were originally developed to be used at the end of KS2 and KS3 in English, Mathematics and Science. In addition, teachers developed their tests for use at the end of KS1. Driven by the pressure of performance tables and teachers feeling they had to 'teach to the test' there has been a slow abandonment of SATs with none now taking place at the end of KS3 and only English and Mathematics testing at the end of KS2. However, this has not marked the end of national testing, with, for example, KS1 assessment being put in place for literacy and newly developed tests appearing for KS2.

THE PRINCIPLES IN THE DEVELOPMENT OF THE NATIONAL SCIENCE CURRICULUM

Developing a new curriculum is not straightforward and involves the input of many 'stakeholders'; for example, educationalists, government policy advisors, and sometimes teachers. It is noteworthy that pupils are rarely asked directly about what they would enjoy learning in a particular subject area, however, much research has been carried out and some of this is used to guide curriculum content (see Further Reading). The five most important considerations in the development of the NC Science were: breadth and balance, inclusion, continuity, progression and opportunities for cross-curricular teaching and learning.

Breadth and balance

Breadth refers to the scope of the subject content with the curriculum; deciding upon what this means for each Key Stage is not easy but experts are brought together to consider what pupils should be learning concerning the major ideas within the sciences (biology, chemistry and physics) as well as technological application of science, the social consequences of science and the skills of being a scientist. *Balance* is concerned with providing equal weighting of the three main sciences as well as the nature of science, that is, something about understanding the way that science is carried out and the implications of the development of scientific knowledge.

Consideration of breadth and balance in the curriculum is important because, before the establishment of the NC, pupils had much more freedom regarding which subjects they studied, with no requirement to study any science after the age of 14. The consequence of this was that certain subjects might be identified by pupils as not suitable for them, with the best understood example of this being physics, in which girls at the post-16 level are still underrepresented. Being a compulsory subject to 16 years means that now all pupils are given the opportunity to study various important areas of the sciences; however, this may be to the detriment of other, non-core subjects which are squeezed out of the curriculum to become 'optional' at post-14 age.

Inclusion

Central to the development of the NC was that it should be for everyone. For science, this means it should be accessible for all learners, irrespective of how interested they are in science and how good they are at science. While a laudable aim at its inception, the reality of how the NC Science has evolved is that pupils are very often streamed to study only certain strands of the science curriculum in preparation for national examinations at 16 years (see Unit 2.3). The reasons that underpin this are twofold. First, schools are, quite understandably, keen to support pupils in developing their knowledge in subjects where they are strongest, and are thus likely to study post-16. But, second, schools are mindful of the proportions of high level examination grades their pupils collectively amass, meaning that pupil interest in a particular subject may be considered less important than their potential examination success. The implications of this are that, for a large number of pupils, the opportunities they are afforded for studying science may be curtailed and somewhat limited.

Continuity

An important feature of the curriculum is that it supports continuity. Continuity refers to the content of each Key Stage being designed to support what has been learnt before. This means more than only thinking about the sensible ordering of the curriculum but also considering how each Key Stage supports development into the next, as well as reflecting back on what has been learnt before. This is harder than it sounds because it relies on teachers having in-depth knowledge of a potentially rapidly changing curriculum beyond the Key Stages that they teach, as well as a good understanding of the pedagogical approaches that are adopted at different Key Stages. Aspects of the NC have been criticised for being too repetitive in this respect as well as some of the content being too challenging for pupils at particular Key Stages (see Further Reading).

Progression

Progression in learning is not guaranteed but relies on a combination of appropriate content that makes links with prior learning, as well as carefully designed teaching and learning opportunities which support conceptual development in pupils. True progression happens when the learner is able to make sense and use more complex information; this may mean making links between apparently disparate ideas, as well as advanced thinking skills.

The theoretical considerations underpinning progression within the curriculum are complex (see Unit 4.1 for a fuller discussion on progression) and teachers need to fully understand the criteria that are developed to assess progress, and plan for progression.

Cross-curricular learning opportunities

A welcome addition that was a consequence of the inception of the NC was that it made explicit reference to cross-learning opportunities. For science, this means teachers having to be mindful not only of the content of the science curriculum but also mindful of opportunities to develop pupils' ICT, numeracy and literacy skills. Science also plays a key role in supporting pupils' awareness of the 'Global dimensions' strand of the curriculum as well as contributing to sex education (see Unit 5.5) and issues surrounding citizenship (see Unit 5.4). These opportunities need planning for and so teachers of science have to be flexible in their thinking, and broad in their subject knowledge, to be able to identify and build on these ideas within their teaching of the science content.

THE CHANGING CURRICULUM

No curriculum is static and there are many good reasons why curriculum changes are made. The current NC has undergone six major revisions since 1989 with the latest being a major rewriting across all Key Stages in 2013 to produce a curriculum for first teaching in September 2014. Changes are sometimes made in response to teachers finding aspects of the curriculum unsuitable, for example, it being too content heavy, but more often it is because it is not seen to be serving its purpose of providing pupils with the education that they need. An important example of this was that the NC Science did not present pupils with an accurate perception of how real science is carried out and what the implications of science for society might be and that, being driven by assessment, it was extremely prescriptive, even in the way that investigative work was supported.

A major review of the NC curriculum in 1998 produced an important and influential report called *Beyond 2000: Science Education for the Future: A Report with Ten Recommendations* (Millar and Osborne, 1998). This report arose for a five-year project where mainly science educators met to discuss and debate the nature of the NC Science and consider how it could be modified to meet the needs of the learners in the twenty-first century. The influence of the report was far-reaching and it should be essential reading for all science teachers. A key recommendation was that the NC Science was severely lacking in its ability to develop 'scientific literacy' in citizens of the future. Essentially, this meant that pupils were learning much about scientific content, but very little about the nature of science and the relevance of science in their everyday lives, either as children or adults. In light of the report, the curriculum has come to include much more about the working of science, so that pupils are now encouraged to be creative in their thinking, to draw on different types of evidence and to consider the implications of scientific developments in much greater detail. These ideas have become embedded in newer versions of the NC Science as the 'How Science Works' strand, and from 2014 as 'Working Scientifically'. These aspects of the curriculum are further explored in the Units 2.2 and 2.3.

Another important recommendation from the report was to make science more accessible and to provide pupils with greater opportunities to consider science in contexts that are meaningful for them; this was especially true of KS4 science. The result of this was that new courses were developed for KS4 science which took a 'context-led' approach. This was not something completely new, with aspects of some KS4 courses of the early 1990s and various post-16 courses taking this approach, but it was the first time that a complete KS4 course was specifically designed in this way; this is a good example of the concrete way that research can influence classroom practice. It is worth considering how a 'context-led' approach course addresses the same ideas as a 'concept-led' approach and the benefits, as well as problems that teachers and pupils may face (see Unit 2.3).

SUMMARY AND KEY POINTS

The National Curriculum in science is designed to support teachers in understanding the breadth of scientific content they need to teach to provide pupils with a balanced understanding of science. It covers all branches of science, as well as the nature of science. Ideas of continuity and progression are central in its design as well as in preparing pupils to live in a technologically advanced society.

Since 2000, a key feature of the NC Science has been the idea of scientific literacy. The inclusion of this strand of the curriculum has led to major changes and developments, aspects of which are becoming increasingly important in the science classroom.

REFERENCES

Capel, S., Leask, M. and Turner, T. (eds) *Learning to Teach in the Secondary School: A Companion to School Experience*, 6th edn. London: Routledge.

Millar, R. and Osborne, J. (1998) *Beyond 2000: Science Education for the Future: A Report with Ten Recommendations.* London: King's College. Available at: www.nuffieldfoundation.org/sites/default/files/Beyond%202000.pdf (accessed 25 March 2014).

FURTHER READING

Cerini, B., Murray, I. and Reiss, M. (2003) *Student Review of the Science Curriculum: Major Findings.* London: Planet Science.

A review which asked pupils what they think about the science curriculum. On reading this you will gain insight into what the pupils you teach might be thinking.

Corrigan, D., Dillon, J. and Gunstone, R. F. (eds) (2007) *The Re-emergence of Values in Science Education.* London: Sense Publishers.

A book that reviews important ideas about the aims of a science curriculum.

Millar, R. and Osborne, J. (1998) *Beyond 2000: Science Education for the Future: A Report with Ten Recommendations.* London: King's College. Available at: www.nuffieldfoundation.org/sites/default/files/Beyond%202000.pdf (accessed 25 March 2014).

Although now more than 15 years old, this report has had a major influence on the current shape of the science curriculum. Its influence can still be felt in both curriculum design and schools.

Osborne, J. (2008) 'Engaging young people with science: does science education need a new vision?' *School Science Review*, 89(328): 67–74.

This is a well-argued article that challenges the widely held belief that more scientists are needed. Its extensive literature on research into pupils' attitudes to science and reports on the need for scientists, with international comparisons, is valuable.

Osborne, J., Simon, S. and Collins, S. (2003) 'Attitudes towards science: a review of the literature and its implications', *International Journal of Science Education*, 25(9): 1049–1079.

This provides a synthesis of what research has to say about pupils' attitudes towards school science.

USEFUL WEBSITES

Websites for the National Curriculum documents from England, Wales, Northern Ireland and Scotland are given at the end of Unit 2.2.

SCIENCE 11–14

Paul Davies

INTRODUCTION

Most pupils enter secondary school at age 11 years and most find the transition from primary to secondary school a difficult time. Secondary schools are very different to primary schools; they are large, have a great age range of pupils who are normally free to mix together outside of lessons, and pupils are expected to move between classrooms and be taught by a large number of teachers (see Unit 1.3). Fortunately, most pupils enter secondary schools very excited at the prospect of learning science, and will arrive with varied experiences from their primary education. One important role for the science teacher at the 11–14 age range is to develop this enthusiasm and prepare pupils for when they are 14–16 years old and studying for national examinations. The NC Science at KS3 is designed to provide teachers with a framework to ensure continuity and progression from KS2, while, at the same time, being general enough to give teachers the chance to explore the programme of study with innovative and imaginative approaches which help to further engage and motivate learners. The tasks in this unit are designed to enable you to understand the NC framework and identify topic areas where you feel most confident, and those that you need to develop. They also provide you with opportunities to examine the way that schools implement the NC Science in their schemes of work and consider why these approaches are adopted. The final task requires thinking at M-level and encourages you to reflect on learning a specific scientific concept.

OBJECTIVES

By the end of this unit, you should:

- understand the guidelines for NC Science at KS3;
- be aware of the areas of expertise that you need to develop in order to teach the whole of science at KS3;
- be able to analyse achievements in your own teaching.

FRAMEWORK FOR THE PROGRAMMES OF STUDY (POS) AT KEY STAGE 3

The KS3 curriculum that was introduced in September 2014 is more streamlined than its predecessor and, for non-core subjects, is designed with a much greater emphasis on the development of skills rather than extensive subject knowledge. Being a core subject, the same is not true for science which has a more traditional structure and is designed to provide pupils with the breadth and depth of subject content, as well as the key skills associated with science.

For each NC subject the POS identifies the following sections:

▦ Purpose of Study
▦ Aims
▦ Attainment Targets
▦ Subject Content.

As you enter the teaching profession as a teacher of science, it is worth considering something about the design of the curriculum. The job of a science teacher is about much more than 'imparting knowledge' but is also about designing opportunities for learners to develop understanding and to also make links between what they are learning. Task 2.2.1 encourages you to take some time to examine the NC Science; doing this will help you look for these links yourself, as well as consider ideas surrounding the aims of science education and how the curriculum has evolved since you were are school.

Task 2.2.1 **The design of the NC Science at KS3**

See the Useful Websites section and download the NC Science and POS Science for KS3.

1 Imagine a friend asked you: 'What is the point of studying science at school?' Write down a short response to this question.
2 Read the Purpose of Study and Aims sections and compare this to what you have written. How are they similar and different? Can you explain any differences? What does what you have written tell you about your perspectives about learning science and the aims of learning science?
3 Look through the POS and make a list of any topics and concepts that you did not study, or cannot remembering studying when you were aged 11–14 years.
4 Share your responses to these three questions with other student teachers.

THE NATIONAL CURRICULUM SCIENCE AT KEY STAGE 3

The NC Science at KS3 is divided into two areas: the first, Working Scientifically, outlines the procedural knowledge that pupils should learn about how scientific data are collected, analysed and reported; the second, Subject Content, identifies key concepts (see Table 2.2.1) and provides details of 'What pupils should be taught about' in Biology,

■ **Table 2.2.1** The key concepts of each of the NC Science at KS3 subject content areas

Science	Key concepts
Biology	Structure and function of living organisms Materials cycles and energy Interactions and interdependencies Genetics and evolution
Chemistry	The particulate nature of matter Atoms, elements and compounds Pure and impure substances Chemical reactions Energetics The Periodic Table Materials Earth and atmosphere
Physics	Energy Motion and forces Waves Electricity and magnetism Matter Space physics

Chemistry and Physics. Before you start to think about how you plan to support pupils' understanding of these two areas, it is important that you consider your own knowledge and understanding. Task 2.2.2 encourages you to start this process; for most teachers, this is an on-going process but, in the first instance, it requires you to be open and honest.

Task 2.2.2 **Audit of prior knowledge: Subject Content and Working Scientifically in science**

1 Download a copy of the NC Science.
2 Look at Table 2.2.1 for your specific subject specialism and make a list of the concepts that you think pupils should be taught under each of the key concept headings. Compare your list to the content in the NC Science. Repeat this activity for the two other science areas.
3 The Working Scientifically section contains the following headings:

■ Experimental skills and investigations
■ Analysis and evaluation
■ Scientific attitudes
■ Measurement.

4 For each heading, make a list of what you think pupils should learn.
5 Compare your list to those in the NC Science. Does the NC science list accurately reflect your experiences of science?

See the Further Reading section for more information on the aims of science education and the nature of science.

THE SCIENCE CURRICULUM ▨ ▨ ▨ ■

Subject Content section

The subject content for the three sciences outlines the specific scientific knowledge that should be taught. An essential feature of your teaching will be being familiar with this content but also being able to teach the content is much more than simply knowing the statements in the NC Science. Task 2.2.3 is designed to support your thinking about the subject content across the sciences by focusing on three important themes: (1) the scientific story or explanation; (2) the evidence on which on which it is based; and (3) the arguments that are used to link the evidence to the story. For example, the story of the cellular organisation of life says that all living things are made up of cells. Some organisms are unicellular (composed of just one cell), others are multicellular (composed of many cells). Cells have certain features in common, such as a cellular membrane and cytoplasm but there are many different types of cell which are identified as having specific structures, which are related to their specific functions. The evidence on which this story is based is that cells can be seen under microscopes, cells can be removed from organs and many different types of cell have been observed. Their functions can be observed directly, for example, sperm cells swimming, or indirectly through experimentation, for example, the behaviour of root hair cells in the presence of solution of different water potential. The arguments that relate the story and observations show how the story of the cellular basis of life explains these observations and how other theoretical perspectives are needed (e.g., how cell organelles evolved from bacteria, the Endosymbiotic Theory).

Task 2.2.3 **Audit of personal confidence on range and content of science**

Thinking about the Science Story, Evidence and Arguments, audit how confident you are in relation to the Subject Content in the NC Science; to do this, use Table 2.2.2 as an example as a starting point. It shows the statements from NC Science for Biology: *Cells and organisation*; for each statement identify how confident you feel using the key:

Confident ✓
Unfamiliar ✗

When thinking about each statement, you should consider what you think you would be able to do in the classroom. For example:

1 *Scientific story*: I could give a detailed account of the scientific story of the cellular basis of life and support this with a range of examples.
2 *Evidence*: I know the different types of evidence on which this is based and the strength of this evidence.
3 *Arguments*: I can explain the link between the evidence and the story.

Repeat this for all the statements in the NC Science. You should do this at the start of your course, but as the course progresses, go back and revisit this task to reflect on how your confidence is changing. By the end of the course, you should feel confident in all areas.

The statements in Table 2.2.2 are shortened versions of those that appear in the NC so you should also refer to this as you complete the task.

■ **Table 2.2.2** Statements from NC Science Biology, KS3: cells and organisation for an audit of confidence

Subject content of Science at KS3		Science story	Evidence	Arguments
Cells and organisation	Cells as the fundamental unit of living organisms			
	Functions of the parts of cells			
	Similarities between different types of cell			
	Movement into and out of cells			
	The structural adaptations of some unicellular organisms			
	Hierarchy of cells to organisms			

Working Scientifically section

Having an understanding of the nature of science is becoming increasingly important in the NC Science at KS3. The Working Scientifically section of the NC Science is discussed under the following headings:

■   Experimental skills and investigations
■   Handling information and problem solving
■   Scientific attitudes
■   Measurement.

The ideas taught in this section are meant to support pupils to feel confident about their interactions with science in everyday life and to see science as part of their cultural heritage. Working Scientifically is also designed to allow pupils to engage with public debate in science, for example, making sense of how a scientific story might be reported in the media. A major criticism of how these ideas were introduced into the curriculum (until 2014 as a strand called How Science Works) was that, rather than being integrated, they were 'bolted on' to the teaching of Subject Content (see Further Reading section for more details). This is unsurprising because very few science teachers study the philosophy in their undergraduate training, and so most feel unprepared to talk about these ideas in the classroom, and the rapidity with which the new strand was introduced into the curriculum meant that providers of teacher training and schools were ill-prepared to support both student and in-service teachers. This situation has now changed, with science departments becoming much more familiar with what is expected to be taught and aware of the appropriate strategies to support learning in this area. Task 2.2.4 requires you to consider the nature of these strands.

Task 2.2.4 **Examining the Working Scientifically strand in the NC Science**

1 Read each section carefully (Experimental skills and investigations, Handling information and problem solving, Scientific attitudes and Measurement).
2 Underline the terms and key ideas that you think are important.
3 Choose two areas where you feel less confident and prepare a short presentation to explain them. Think up examples to illustrate your explanations.
4 Look back at the Subject Content strand and identify a topic from Biology, Chemistry and Physics that is a useful way to illustrate with each section of the Working Scientifically strand. Share these ideas with other student teachers.

Breadth and balance

In Unit 2.1, the ideas of breadth and balance in the NC Science were explained. Use Task 2.2.5 to check on the extent to which these have been achieved in the current NC Science at KS3.

Task 2.2.5 **Identifying breadth and balance in the NC Science**

From your examination of the NC Science in Tasks 2.2.1–2.2.4, consider the following questions:

1 Do you think the balance between Working Scientifically and Subject Content is right? If not, what changes would you make and why?
2 Is there balance in the Subject Content between Biology, Chemistry and Physics? Is there any overlap between the three sciences? Are other areas of science well represented?
3 Is the history of science represented, and are there opportunities to learn about the significance of the relationship between culture and scientific discovery, and the implication of scientific advancement?
4 Is there anything to help pupils think about the breadth of scientific knowledge and about careers in science?
5 List other aspects of breadth and balance that you identify in the NC Science or think are missing or problematic.

ASSESSMENT OF PROGRESS

Before 2014, each curriculum subject had a specific list of criteria that were designed to allow teachers to judge the progress of pupils. There were four attainment targets related to the How Science Works strand and three science Subject Content strands. The criteria contained a description of expected performance at six levels at KS3 (levels 4–8 and 'Exceptional standard'). The levels were designed to make it easy for teachers to monitor individual, and cohort progress but this proved to be difficult for teachers and their pupils, and understandably led to a focus on levels rather than the learning that was taking place. They were also hard for parents to interpret and often too general in nature to be useful.

These problems led to an abandonment of attainment levels in the 2014 curriculum, leaving methods of pupil assessment at the discretion of individual schools, though governmental guidance is provided and constantly updated in light of good practice. Schools are expected to develop a robust assessment system which allows teachers and pupils to assess progress throughout each Key Stage and report to parents. Importantly, schools have to show evidence of the effectiveness of the system in supporting their pupils and how equity between different teachers and across the school is maintained. Assessing pupils' progress, and understanding how assessment approaches work can be challenging. Task 2.2.6 requires you to test your skills in this area. Also see Units 6.1 and 6.2 for further details.

Task 2.2.6 **Assessing pupils' progress**

1   Talk with teachers in your training school and ask about how the school has developed its own assessment approaches since the introduction of the new curriculum. Focus on how teachers apply the approaches and how assessment is moderated within the department.
2   Share the outcome of these conversations with other student teachers.
3   For a piece of pupil work, devise your own assessment criteria and apply them in your marking. Reflect on how easy, or difficult it is to mark work in this way. What does this tell you about the role of assessment in teaching and learning?

WIDER ASPECTS OF THE CURRICULUM

The National Curriculum as a whole has wider objectives than those attributed to specific subject areas and it is the responsibility of whole-school policies to ensure that these are embedded in teaching and learning. The two most important, and explicit, are:

■   Inclusion
■   Language, literacy and numeracy.

Inclusion

Inclusion is about providing learning opportunities for all. The guidance in NC about inclusion is separated into *Setting suitable challenges* and *Responding to pupils' needs and overcoming potential barriers for individuals and groups of pupils.* The former is concerned with teachers designing learning activities with strength and to challenge the most able, and support those pupils who have lower levels of attainment, or come from disadvantaged backgrounds. The second is concerned with providing equal opportunities for all learners to succeed, despite having special educational needs (SEN), disabilities or where English is not their first language.

Look at these sections of the curriculum and find out what strategies have been developed in your school to promote inclusion of all learners.

Language, literacy and numeracy

This section of the curriculum has especial relevance to science and because of this importance, language and literacy are dealt with elsewhere in Unit 5.1. All teachers are required to develop pupils' mathematical fluency and confidence in using mathematics in their learning, and everyday life. Science uses mathematics as a tool but there are several difficulties associated with this:

▨ Pupils find it hard to transfer skills learnt in one subject to other subjects.
▨ Mathematics education is often approached with little context, meaning that pupils do not see the relevance of the skills they are learning. This makes transferability more of a challenge.
▨ The language used in a mathematics lesson may not be the same as that used in a science lesson.
▨ Science teachers may not be aware of the conceptual challenges that pupils face when learning about, and using mathematical skills.

There are several things that a science teacher can do to overcome these challenges. The first is to read the National Curriculum for mathematics, especially the Subject Content areas, which are:

▨ Number: calculation and accuracy
▨ Number theory
▨ Algebra: expressing relations
▨ Algebra: using equations and functions
▨ Ratio, proportion and rate of change
▨ Geometry and measures
▨ Probability
▨ Statistics.

As you read these sections, identify any areas where you feel less confident and update your own knowledge and skills. It is also a good idea to speak to teachers in the mathematics department, and maybe observe them. Find out the teaching order of mathematics at KS3 and ask them about the approaches and language that they use in their teaching. It would be also useful to read about the conceptual difficulties that pupils commonly have (see Further Reading). Finally, you should work through the NC for science and identify opportunities when mathematical skills can be used and developed.

REVIEWING YOUR WORK WITHIN THE NATIONAL CURRICULUM

Despite all the documentation that is available in the National Curriculum and the schemes of work that may be found in schools, these do not tell you how to teach, they contain nothing about what to say to the pupils and provide little guidance about how you develop and assess conceptual understanding. Planning for these is much of what teaching involves and Task 2.2.7 (an M-level task) is designed to encourage you to analyse what you have achieved in terms of NC aims.

Task 2.2.7 **Evaluating your teaching of a key concept**

1 Consult the NC Science and identify one of the key concepts in the Subject Content section, for example, Cells and organisation.
2 Explain in writing why you chose this particular area.
3 Do some reading on this area and research common challenges that pupils face in their understanding of this concept.
4 Design a short sequence of lessons that could be used to support pupil progress in this area; pay particular attention to how you would provide learning opportunities for all pupils and the different ways that both you and the pupils will assess progress.
5 Evaluate the extent to which pupils engaged with your planned teaching and learning strategies and learnt what you intended.
6 Discuss your evaluations with your tutor.

MODIFICATION OF THE AGE RANGE FOR KEY STAGE 3

While 11–14 years is intended as the age range for KS3, many schools have decided to teach their KS3 programmes in less than three years so that they can start KS4 during, or even at the beginning of, Year 9. If you are working in a school that adopts this approach, talk with the teachers about the rationale behind this decision and find out how the department has compressed the NC Science three-year programme into a shorter space of time. Consider the advantages and disadvantages of this approach.

SUMMARY AND KEY POINTS

The National Curriculum in science is about much more than pupils only learning established scientific facts. It is designed to allow them to explore some important scientific ideas for themselves, as well as learn about the processes of science and develop their skills in doing science. It is also designed to support pupils' understanding of science in their lives, and the wider community. As your training progresses, you should become more confident in meeting these demands as you develop imaginative and creative ways to engage and support pupils in their learning of science.

FURTHER READING

Hollins, M. (ed.) (2011) *The ASE Guide to Secondary Science Education*. Hatfield: ASE.

A handbook with short and readable chapters which covers aspects about the aims of science education, teaching and learning in science and assessment.

See also the themed issues of *School Science Review* given at the end of Unit 2.3. These have articles relevant for KS3 as well as KS4.

A selection of Key Stage 3 text books and resources:

The 'Activate' series from Oxford University Press. More details from: https://global.oup.com/education/content/secondary/series/activate/?region=uk (accessed 2 January 2014).

'Exploring Science'. More details from: www.pearsonschools.co.uk/exploringchapter (accessed 12 January 2014).

'Science Progress'. More details from: www.hoddereducation.co.uk/Product?Product=9781471801426 (accessed 12 January 2014).

'Smart Science'. More details from: www.smartscienceonline.co.uk/ (accessed 2 January 2014).

USEFUL WEBSITES

ASE, Association for Science Education: www.ase.org.uk. ASE has a lot of resources for teachers and *It Makes You Think*, an online set of downloadable resources for teaching the global dimensions of science.

Department for Education (schools section): www.education.gov.uk/schools/teachingandlearning/curriculum/nationalcurriculum2014/ (accessed 24 December 2013). This page has links to curriculum documents, information about assessment and suggestions about teaching and learning approaches.

The Draft National Curriculum in Science at KS4: http://media.education.gov.uk/assets/files/pdf/s/science%20-%20key%20stage%204%2004-02-13.pdf (accessed 24 December 2013).

The National Curriculum in Science (for the KS1 and KS2 Science Curriculum): www.gov.uk/government/uploads/system/uploads/attachment_data/file/239132/PRIMARY_national_curriculum_-_Science.pdf (accessed 24 December 2013).

The National Curriculum in Science at KS3: www.gov.uk/government/uploads/system/uploads/attachment_data/file/239134/SECONDARY_national_curriculum_-_Science.pdf (accessed 24 December 2013).

The Northern Ireland Curriculum (all Key Stages): www.nicurriculum.org.uk/ (accessed 24 December 2013).

Scotland: www.scotland.gov.uk/Topics/Education/Schools/curriculum (accessed 24 December 2013). Scotland has an advisory, not a statutory, curriculum for the 5–14 age range.

Welsh Assembly Government Education and Skills: National Curriculum at Key Stages, 2, 3 and 4: www.wales.gov.uk/topics/educationandskills/schoolshome/curriculuminwales/arevisedcurriculumforwales/nationalcurriculum/?lang=en (accessed 24 December 2013).

UNIT
2.3

SCIENCE 14–19

Paul Davies

INTRODUCTION

The science curriculum in the 14–19 age range covers Key Stages 4 and 5 and is designed to provide learners with a broad and balanced education in biology, chemistry and physics. There is choice in terms of the routes that individuals can follow, which lead to a variety of qualifications that prepare citizens of the technological age, as well as those wanting to go on to study science beyond the age of 19 years. The awarding bodies (previously referred to as Examination Boards) are the main source of information on what is taught in these Key Stages in the specifications that they design. There are three main awarding bodies in England (AQA, Edexcel, and OCR), one in Wales (WJEC) and one in Northern Ireland (CCEA). Scotland has the Scottish Qualifications Authority (SQA). Each awarding body has its own designated website (see Useful Websites) which contains information about how they organise the curriculum and their assessment materials. The awarding bodies are overseen by the Office of Qualifications and Examination Regulation (Ofqual), a body that sets out and monitors the quality of the materials developed by the awarding bodies, and reports directly to Parliament.

At the time of writing, 16 years is the age that compulsory education ends, and it is the time when most pupils receive their first nationally recognised qualification. For this reason, it is most useful to consider science education in the 14–19 age range in two parts: 14–16 years and 16–19 years.

OBJECTIVES

By the end of this unit, you should:

- understand the guidelines of the National Curriculum in science at KS4;
- be aware of the range and nature of science courses which are available to the 14–19 age range;
- be able to distinguish features of the different types of courses available.

A. Compulsory
  GCSE *Additional Science*; or
  GCSE *Additional Applied Science*

B. An alternative: Triple Science
  Triple Science: GCSE *Biology*, GCSE *Chemistry*, GCSE *Physics*

Currently, pupils study either A or B. Triple Science contains all the course elements of A, plus some extra material.

▪ **Figure 2.3.1** The most common pattern of GCSE Science courses in 14–16 age range

14–16 SCIENCE

The main qualification that over 90 per cent of pupils in England, Wales and Northern Ireland will study in science is the General Certificate of Education (GCSE); see Figure 2.3.1 for the most common model of how GCSE Science is provided in schools in this age range.

NC SCIENCE AT KEY STAGE 4

The current GCSE Science, the compulsory course, is designed around the statutory programme of study for NC Science at KS4. The course is expected to support pupils in understanding the important concepts in biology, chemistry and physics, as well as provide them with an appreciation of the skills and knowledge needed to carry out science and the implications that science has on society.

As with KS3, the NC Science at KS4 is divided into two main sections:(1) the Working Scientifically section deals with the knowledge, understanding and skills associated with carrying out science; and (2) the Subject Content in the three separate science areas.

As at KS3, the Working Scientifically section is divided into four themes:

▪ Experimental skills and investigations
▪ Handling information and problem solving
▪ Scientific attitudes
▪ Measurement.

Task 2.2.4 in Unit 2.2 (Science 11–14) required you to review this section of the KS3 curriculum. Task 2.3.1 encourages you to compare Working Scientifically between KS3 and KS4.

Task 2.3.1 **Making a comparison between Working Scientifically at Key Stage 3 and Key Stage 4**

1 Look back at the notes you made for Task 2.2.4 (in Unit 2.2, Science 11–14).
2 Download and study the draft programme of study for NC Science at KS4.

3 Make a list of any differences between the Working Scientifically content in both key stages.
4 Why do you think these differences exist?
5 Does Working Scientifically for KS4 present a better representation of how science is carried out and the implication of science on society?
6 Do you think that anything is missing? If so, what, and why do you think this is important?

SUBJECT CONTENT

The NC Science Subject Content statements describe the science content that pupils should be taught but these statements are then interpreted by the awarding bodies in their specifications and examinations. It is the responsibility of Ofqual (the Office of Qualifications and Examinations Regulation) to ensure equity among the awarding bodies.

As with KS3, having a secure subject knowledge in the areas of science that you are going to be teaching is essential. Sometimes, science teachers are responsible for teaching all aspects of biology, chemistry and physics. Even if this is not the case, it is important that you are aware of what is being taught in the other science areas; this will help you make links between different parts of the specification and so help pupils make connections in their learning. Task 2.3.2 requires you to examine the GCSE Science specification from your training school and to audit your subject knowledge, as well as to identify overlap between the sciences.

Task 2.3.2 **Audit of personal confidence on range and content of science**

As with Task 2.2.3 in Unit 2.2, think about the scientific story, the evidence that supports the story and the arguments that support the evidence for the Subject Content of your science specialism. Audit how confident you are in relation to the Subject Content in the NC Science for the subject(s) you will be teaching. To do this, use Table 2.3.1 as an example. It shows the statements from NC Science for Biology, Cell biology; for each statement identify how confident you feel, using the key:

Confident ✓
Unfamiliar ✗

When thinking about each statement, you should consider what you think you would be able to do in the classroom. For example:

1 *Scientific story*: I could give a detailed account of the scientific story of the cellular basis of life and support this with a range of examples.
2 *Evidence*: I know the different types of evidence on which this is based and the strength of this evidence.
3 *Arguments*: I can explain the link between the evidence and the story.

Repeat this for all the statements in your subject(s). You should do this at the start of your course, but as the course progresses, go back and revisit this task to reflect on how your confidence is changing. By the end of the course, you should feel confident in all areas.

The statements in Table 2.3.1 are shortened versions of those that appear in the draft NC for science, so you should also refer to this as you complete the task.

▨ **Table 2.3.1** Statements from NC Science Biology, KS4: cells and organisation for an audit of confidence

Subject content of Science at KS4		Science story	Evidence	Arguments
Cell biology	The role of the electron micro-scope in understanding cells			
	Function of important cell organelles			
	Similarities between proka-ryotic and eukaryotic cells			
	Cell cycles			
	Stem cells and their use			
	Cell differentiation and specialisation			
	Transport across the cell membrane			
	Cellular respiration			
	Enzyme structure and function			

CONSTRUCTION OF GCSE SCIENCE

A consideration of the different ways that awarding bodies design their GCSE Science courses is useful for any teacher of science. Some courses take a more traditional approach in both the organisation of the material and the way the material is approached. For example, in Chemistry, this could mean starting the course with atoms as the building blocks of elements, before moving on to molecules and bonding, and so on. Courses taking this approach are often described as 'concept-led' course.

In contrast, 'context-led' courses take a different approach. Here, the content is organised into themes and often approached through story telling. For example, the structure and function of the heart may be approached through the story of a person suffering with heart disease and the way that different treatments are designed to help them. Although context-led courses are not a new idea, the publication of *Beyond 2000: Science Education for the Future* (Millar and Osborne, 1998) highlighted the importance of courses of this type and led to the development of the twenty-first-century Science course (see Useful Websites). Research has shown that both types of course are effective in supporting pupil progress in science, but that context-led courses are often perceived by pupils as being more engaging.

All awarding bodies provide clear aims and objectives for their interpretation of NC Science and support teachers in providing information about contexts which may help in the design of schemes of work. Additional support is also provided through extensive materials, such as textbooks, worksheets, guidance about practical work and digital resources. They also provide additional information through links to their websites and teacher training sessions. Becoming familiar with the organisation of the specification for the awarding body that is used in your school is something to do as soon as possible. Task 2.3.3 asks you to examine the course that is running in your school and to compare it with one other specification.

Task 2.3.3 **Comparing the organisation of two different GCSE Science courses**

Use the specification of the GCSE Science course running in your training school and the specification for GCSE Science from another awarding body.

1 For the two courses, compare (noting differences and similarities):

   ▧ the aims;
   ▧ the module/topic headings;
   ▧ the details given in two or three modules/topics.

2 Analyse how confident you are with the content of the topics. What are the areas you need to develop? Plan how you will develop you knowledge. A good place to start is reading about what ideas pupils have about these topics and comparing these to your own.

3 Find out about the organisation of teaching of the course in your training school. How is the specification divided up? What is taught when and why? Do subject specialists teach the biology, chemistry and physics content? Why/why not?

4 Look for broader themes within the specifications: how does the Working Scientifically section complement the Subject Content section? Do they suggest out-of-school learning experiences? How is mathematical thinking integrated into the Subject Content section? Is ICT promoted and, if so, how?

5 Reflect on which of the two specifications you prefer and consider why. What are your reasons? Compare your findings with a fellow student teacher.

Keep the notes you have made. They may well be useful when you come to apply for your first teaching post.

GCSE Additional Science courses and GCSE Triple Science

All pupils must study at least one course in Additional Science, where two different routes are currently available. One route, studying GCSE Additional Science, is focused on scientific concepts while the other route, Additional Applied Science, has a greater emphasis on application of science. Schools are under no obligation to offer pupils a choice in Additional Science. Having studied to the level of Additional Science, pupils are able to proceed to post-16 study of science and should not be disadvantaged in their progress compared to those who study Triple Science.

Task 2.3.4 requires you to compare the Additional and Additional Applied Science courses.

Task 2.3.4 **Comparing GCSE Additional Applied and Additional Science courses**

For any awarding body, compare the content of the specifications of GCSE Additional Applied Science and GCSE Additional Science. This is similar to Task 2.3.3.

1 Study and compare:

   - the aims;
   - module headings;
   - resources;
   - suggested contexts;
   - suggested visits for the two courses.

2 Which course would you like to have studied?
3 Which would you like to teach?
4 Find out whether your school offers both Additional Science and Additional Applied Science.
5 Who makes the choice about which course pupils take – teachers, pupils, parents?
6 How is the teaching of these additional courses divided between teachers?

Keep the notes you have made. They may well be useful when you come to apply for your first teaching post.

Triple Science must be made available to pupils but exactly which pupils are allowed to continue with this course is partially at the discretion of the school. The material in Triple Science is no more complex than that covered in Additional Science but it does address content that has not previously been covered. There is some evidence that pupils who study Triple Science are more likely to go on to study it post-16 but no evidence shows that they perform any better in their final post-16 examinations. Task 2.3.5 requires you to make a comparison between the extra material that is found in Triple Science compared to Additional Science and consider the way your school supports the teaching of Triple Science.

Task 2.3.5 **Content and provision of Triple Science (Biology, Chemistry and Physics)**

1   Find out what additional material is found in the Triple Science course compared to the Additional Science course. The best place to find this information is in the specifications of the various awarding bodies.
2   If your training school offers both routes, find out how the decision to study which route of the GCSE is made: is it down to the teacher, the pupils or the parents?
3   How does the school timetable Triple Science? Is it accommodated in the normal timetable?
4   Investigate the extra material that is covered in Triple Science. Are the concepts more difficult than those found in Additional Science? Does the material build on what has already been learnt?

While these courses are the mainstream GCSE courses in sciences found in schools in the 14–16 age range, they are not the only ones available. For example, GCSE qualifications are also available in Engineering, Astronomy, Computer Science, Environmental Science and Human Health and Physiology.

Assessment and tiers of entry for GCSE courses

The GCSE examination system awards students grades in the form of numbers (8–1, with 8 being the highest grade). In the case of the Triple Science course, students are able to achieve different grades in Biology, Chemistry and Physics. In the Additional Science course, two GCSE grades are awarded but they must be the same.

All GCSE examinations are assessed in a linear way. This means that pupils do not study for modules, which are individually assessed but, instead, take all their examinations at one sitting in the summer at the end of the GCSE course. The principle behind this approach is twofold: (1) it gives teachers more freedom to organise the curriculum as they wish; and (2) there is an expectation that it makes the examination system more rigorous. This second point is especially important because it is linked with pupils not being able to re-sit modules where they have performed less well. You should discuss with the teachers in your training school how they organise the curriculum, what decisions they have made and why.

In addition to written examinations, GCSE Science has an internally assessed practical component. This is organised in different ways by the various awarding bodies but is designed to encourage teachers to incorporate practical work into their teaching, using activities which are important in understanding both scientific content and processes.

There are currently two tiers of entry for GCSE Science courses: foundation and higher. Foundation leads to grades in a lower range and the higher tier leads to grades in an upper range. It is useful to examine the content of the material covered for each tier and discuss this with teachers in your training school. You will want to find out how decisions are made about which pupils study which tier.

OTHER KEY STAGE 4 SCIENCE COURSES

Although the vast majority of pupils in KS4 study GCSEs, there are other qualifications available to schools. You may find that your school offers a variety of different courses to cater for its pupils. Task 2.3.6 requires you to compare these courses to a GCSE Science course, and consider the rationale that explains the reason why pupils study science at KS4 through different routes.

Task 2.3.6 **Comparing the different KS4 Science qualifications**

1 Find out which science qualifications your school offers.
2 Compare the content, organisation of these courses and find out how each is assessed.
3 Talk to teachers in your school and find out how pupils are selected to study the different routes.
4 Are pupils able to transfer between courses? If so, how is this organised?
5 Make some notes about which of the courses you would like to teach the most and say why.
6 Compare your thoughts with other student teachers.

Entry level

Science courses leading to an entry-level qualification are designed for pupils for whom GCSEs seem inappropriate. The content of them draws heavily on NC Science at KS4, meaning that pupils who make sufficient progress can then transfer onto the GCSE pathway. Unlike GCSE courses, entry-level science courses are composed of short topics which take one or two weeks to teach.

BTEC

Business and Technology Education Council (BTEC) certificate qualifications are designed to be more vocational in nature. While drawing on much of the content in GCSE Science courses, BTEC courses tend to be organised around projects which pupils complete independently, normally using a website interface. This approach to teaching offers both benefits and challenges for teachers.

IGCSE

Some independent schools teach the International GCSE science course which gives pupils IGCSE qualifications in Biology, Chemistry and Physics. Despite its name, the structure and content of this course are different to GCSEs. Especially designed for the international market, this qualification is closely linked to other international post-16 qualifications.

16–19 SCIENCE

Science courses in the 16–19 range can lead to a range of qualifications. They include GCSE; GCE Advanced Subsidiary level and Advanced level; Diplomas and the International Baccalaureate. There is no National Curriculum for this age range, but this does not mean that awarding bodies are free to include whatever content they wish. Instead, national criteria (see Useful Websites) set out the 'core' subject content, which accounts for around 60 per cent of what must be included. This provision means that each awarding body provides a broad and balanced post-16 curriculum.

General Certificate of Education (GCE), Advanced Subsidiary level and Advanced level, sciences

The majority of pupils who wish to continue to study science after KS4 follow courses that lead to either Advanced Subsidiary level (AS-level) or Advanced level (A-level) qualifications in KS5. These are offered by all the major awarding bodies, in a variety of science, and science-related subjects. Figure 2.3.2 shows the science available for the AS-level and A-level awards from the various awarding bodies, at the time of writing. Most pupils begin their studies for AS-level and A-level qualifications in Year 12, age 16. AS qualifications are designed to take one year to complete, and A-level qualifications are designed to take two years to complete. The two qualifications are quite separate, with AS levels not forming the first year of the two-year A-level course. Many students complete Year 13 with three A-level qualifications and one or two AS qualifications. Typically, a pupil who is interested in studying post-16 science would take a combination of AS-level and A-level subjects in biology, chemistry, physics, mathematics and further mathematics. However, the flexibility afforded by being able to choose a broader range of subjects at AS-level in Year 12 means pupils often study for a mixture of subjects from the sciences, technology, the arts and the humanities. Increasingly, universities and other post-18 education institutes are encouraging this broad approach to education in their applicants.

As with GCSE Science, AS level and A-level Science courses are divided between subject content knowledge and procedural knowledge. This latter section builds on the Working Scientifically section of GCSE Science and encourages pupils to consider how scientific knowledge is accumulated and communicated, as well as the limitation of science in society. This aspect of the qualification is becoming ever more important.

AS-levels and A-levels are assessed in a linear way with examinations at the end of the course. As with GCSE Science, this approach is taken to increase the rigour of the qualification. This is also encouraged with the individual examination papers having

---

AQA: Biology, Human Biology, Chemistry, Physics A, Physics B: Physics in Context, Applied Science, Environmental Science, Science in Society, Electronics

Edexcel: Biology, Chemistry, Physics, Psychology

OCR: Biology, Chemistry A, Chemistry B (Salters), Geology, Human Biology, Physics A, Physics B (Advancing Physics), Psychology, Science (Applied), Science (AS only)

WJEC: Biology, Human Biology, Applied Science, Chemistry, Physics, Psychology, Geology

---

■ **Figure 2.3.2** Science courses available at AS-level and A-level

synoptic aspects to them where pupils are expected to draw on their knowledge and understanding from different parts of the course.

Task 2.3.7 helps you identify characteristics of the three post-16 courses.

Task 2.3.7 **Comparison between the three GCE specifications: Biology, Chemistry or Physics between two different awarding bodies**

1 Study the specification of any awarding body for the GCE in your science specialism (biology, chemistry or physics). Look at aims, range of content and the way that the ideas of Working Scientifically are addressed. How familiar are you with the content? What knowledge and understanding will you need to develop if you are asked to teach it?
2 Compare your responses to question 1 with the specification for the same science from a different awarding body.
3 How are they the same? How do they differ? Which specification would you like to teach and why?
4 If you have time, look at the specifications of the other sciences. Is there any overlap between them? Would it be useful to highlight any overlap for pupils?
5 Compare your thoughts with your mentor and other student teachers.

Other science courses

In addition to AS-level and A-level science qualifications, the awarding bodies offer science, and science-related courses that lead to other qualifications, with the three most common being BTEC, Extended Project Qualification (EPQ), and Diplomas. The BTEC and Diploma qualifications at KS5 are more vocational in nature than the GCE courses and sometimes involve pupils combining their academic studies with work experience. In both cases, the qualifications are more closely tailored to skills that are directly linked to careers than GCE, for example, the BTEC in Forensic Science. These qualifications are highly valued by many employers and are a useful route for many pupils who have a clear focus on what career they wish to pursue upon leaving school.

The Extended Project Qualification (EPQ) is fairly new and is equivalent to an AS level qualification. An EPQ involves pupils completing an R&D-based project. The qualification involves two parts: the first is a taught module on philosophical and practical aspects of doing research and developing a project, and the second is the project itself. An EPQ in science typically involves pupils carrying out an extensive literature review on a science subject of their choice but it could also be a piece of investigative or design work. Universities are encouraging candidates to study for an EPQ alongside their other qualifications as it demonstrates the ability to carry out research and work independently.

In Scotland, KS5 pupils study for Scottish Highers, which are qualifications that are equivalent to AS levels. 'Highers' are available in all main subject areas with the most able pupils taking five over a two-year course. Universities in England and Wales recognise Highers in their selection procedures and treat them much as they do AS levels.

International Baccalaureate and other baccalaureates

Baccalaureates are not single-subject qualifications but incorporate a suite of subjects to provide a holistic education. The International Baccalaureate (IB) Diploma for 16–19-year-olds is composed of a core and subject groups. The core is compulsory and involves pupils learning about extended writing, theories of knowledge, and working collaboratively. Pupils study six subjects from the subject groups which must include languages, social sciences, experimental science and mathematics. In addition, arts subjects may be chosen. In terms of studying science, only two 'pure' science subjects may be selected.

The provision of this qualification is restricted to schools which are registered for the IB and it is most commonly found in international and independent schools. If you are in a school running the IB qualification, find out the reasons why the school is following it and what the pupils think about this provision. The IB is not covered by statutory legislation, so you will not find information about it on government websites.

Wales and Northern Ireland offer Welsh and Irish Baccalaureates, respectively.

SUMMARY AND KEY POINTS

The learning of science to age 16 is compulsory in the UK, with most pupils following a course that leads to GCSE science qualifications. The NC KS4 outlines the content of what should be taught and this is interpreted by awarding bodies into specifications that schools then use in their teaching. There is no NC for post-16 study but national criteria stipulate the majority of what should be taught in each subject area. Typically, pupils study for AS-level and A-level qualifications but other routes are available to them, with vocational and more holistic approaches becoming more popular. The curriculum is politically important and, because of this, it can change rapidly. It is important that science teachers keep abreast of these developments in order to best meet the needs of their pupils.

FURTHER READING

Hanley, P., Osborne, J. and Ratcliffe, M. (2008) 'Twenty-first century science', *School Science Review*, 90(330): 105–12.

The authors give an account of research into how teachers and pupils adapted to the demands of a course based on scientific literacy.

Hollins, M. (ed.) (2007) special issue, *School Science Review 2007*, 89(326): 25–91.

The theme 'Beyond core science' provides a collection of articles that illuminate the debates about the nature of the science curriculum. It contains arguments for the inclusion of earth sciences, electronics, engineering and psychology.

Murray, C. (2007) 'Reflections on the UK National Curriculum', *School Science Review*, 88(325): 119–123.

An interesting account of how it was only through teaching in another country (Zambia) that the author realised how much ideas about teaching and learning in science had progressed in the UK.

Wardle, J. (ed.) (2009) special issue, *School Science Review*, 90(332): 29–94.

The theme of this edition was 'Creativity in science'. It was produced in response to the new science curriculum requiring teachers to help pupils understand creativity in science, and to learn to be creative themselves.

Themed issues of the ASE publication, *School Science Review*, Hatfield: ASE, with articles aimed at KS3, KS4 and KS5:

Applied science (2006) 88(321).
Argument, discourse and interactivity (2007) 88(324).
Beyond core science (2007) 89(326).
Science now and then: discovering how science works (2008) 90(330).
Creativity in science (2009) 90(332).
Education for sustainable development (2010) 92(338).
Contemporary topics in school science (2011) 3(343).

USEFUL WEBSITES

Awarding bodies in England, Wales, Northern Ireland and Scotland AQA (Assessment and Qualifications Alliance): www.aqa.org.uk (accessed 31 December 2013).
CCEA (Council for the Curriculum, Examinations and Assessment): www.rewardinglearning.org.uk/ (accessed 31 December 2013).
Department for Education (2012), *The Importance of Teaching*, White Paper: www.education.gov.uk/ schools/toolsandinitiatives/schoolswhitepaper/b0068570/the-importance-of-teaching (accessed 26 March 2013). This provides details of the government's vision for education.
Edexcel: www.edexcel.com/Pages/Home.aspx (accessed 31 December 2013).
International Baccalaureate: www.ibo.org (accessed 31 December 2013).
OCR (Oxford, Cambridge and Royal Society of Arts): www.ocr.org.uk (accessed 31 December 2013).
National Curriculum websites, see Unit 2.2.
Ofqual (Office of Qualifications and Examinations Regulation) for criteria. National Criteria for GCE Sciences can be downloaded: www2.ofqual.gov.uk/downloads/category/191-gce-as-and-a-level-subject-criteria (accessed 31 December 2013).
Ofqual (2011) Criteria for the Diploma Qualifications at Foundation and Higher Levels: http://ofqual.gov. uk/documents/criteria-for-the-diploma-qualifications-in-science-at-foundation-and-higher-levels/all-versions/ (accessed 12 January 2014).
Twenty-First Century Science: www.twentyfirstcenturyscience.org/ (accessed 31 December 2013).
Scottish Qualifications Authority: www.sqa.org.uk/sqa/1.html (accessed 31 December 2013).
WJEC (Welsh Joint Examining Council); www.wjec.co.uk (accessed 31 December 2013).

GETTING TO GRIPS WITH SCIENCE

INTRODUCTION

The units in this section provide an overview of the main areas associated with the knowledge of science needed to teach the subject in schools. These units do not try to provide an alternative to the detailed subject knowledge that can be obtained from good textbooks or subject knowledge enhancement courses at differing levels but rather give something of an orientation towards the main areas in science, to encourage you to think about some of the ideas and issues with teaching these subject areas and to provide further reading. Therefore, this section includes units on: the Nature of Science (3.1); Biology (3.2); Chemistry (3.3); Physics and Astronomy (3.4); and Earth and Atmospheric Science (3.5).

Many science teachers are required to teach outside their subject area at times, whether this is at Key Stage 3 or even Key Stage 4. This section provides a starting point that will allow you to develop your broader knowledge of the sciences, bring to mind some of the areas that may need to be revised and possibly lead you to think about science subjects in a new way, with a particular focus on pupils' learning in science and some of the difficulties they encounter.

UNIT 3.1

THE NATURE OF SCIENCE

Michael J. Reiss

INTRODUCTION

In the UK, most university students who study science are taught little explicitly about the nature of science. And yet the science National Curriculum in England requires pupils to be taught about 'working scientifically'. Perhaps unsurprisingly, research evidence suggests that most pupils leave school with a somewhat partial knowledge of this area of science.

This unit explains what is meant by the terms 'working scientifically' and 'the nature of science'. It looks at whether science always proceeds by the objective and rigorous testing of hypotheses, or whether there are other factors at play in deciding whether one scientific view comes to hold sway within the scientific community over alternatives.

In schools, there are different views about the nature of science among both pupils and science teachers. These different views are important in terms of how people see scientific knowledge. Ways of discovering people's views of the nature of science are given below. It is hoped that these will be of interest and lead to richer teaching and learning in this area. This is important as it can be argued that long after pupils have forgotten much of the content of science that they are taught at schools, they will still hold a view as to how science is done and as to whether scientific knowledge is trustworthy or not.

OBJECTIVES

By the end of this unit, you should be able to:

- distinguish between alternative understandings of how science is carried out;
- contrast science as undertaken by scientists and science as undertaken in school science lessons;
- help your pupils develop a deeper understanding of the nature of science.

WHAT DO WE MEAN BY HOW SCIENCE WORKS AND THE NATURE OF SCIENCE?

In the science National Curriculum, the section 'Working Scientifically' is described under four headings:

■ Experimental skills and investigations
■ Analysis and evaluation
■ Scientific attitudes
■ Measurement.

Interchangeable?

This covers a lot of ground but encapsulates quite well what is meant by 'the nature of science'.

WHAT DO SCIENTISTS STUDY?

It is difficult to come up with a definitive answer to the question 'What do scientists study?'. Certain things clearly fall under the domain of science – the nature of electricity, the arrangement of atoms into molecules and human physiology, to give three examples. However, what about the origin of the universe, the behaviour of people in society, decisions about whether we should build nuclear power plants or go for wind power, the appreciation of music and the nature of love, for example? Do these fall under the domain of science? A small number of scientists would argue 'yes' to all of these and the term *scientism* is used, pejoratively, to refer to the view that science can provide sufficient explanations for everything.

However, most people hold that science is but one form of knowledge and that other forms of knowledge complement science. This way of thinking means that the origin of the universe is also a philosophical or even a religious question – or simply unknowable; the behaviour of people in society requires knowledge of the social sciences (e.g. psychology and sociology) rather than only of the natural sciences; whether we should use nuclear or wind power is partly a scientific issue but also requires an understanding of economics, risk and politics; the appreciation of music and the nature of love, while clearly having something to do with our perceptual apparatuses and our evolutionary history, cannot entirely be reduced to science.

While historians tell us that what scientists study changes over time, there are some reasonable consistencies:

■ Science is concerned with the natural world and with certain elements of the manufactured world, so that, for example, the laws of gravity apply as much to artificial satellites as they do to planets and stars.
■ Science is concerned with how things are rather than with how they should be. So there is a science of gunpowder and *in vitro* fertilisation without science telling us whether warfare and test-tube births are good or bad.

HOW IS SCIENCE DONE?

If it is difficult to come up with a definitive answer to the question 'What do scientists study?', it is even more difficult to come up with a clear-cut answer to the question 'How is science done?'. Indeed, there is, and has been for many decades, active disagreement on this matter among academic historians, philosophers and sociologists of science. A useful place to start is with the views of Robert Merton and Karl Popper. In my experience, most working scientists have almost no interest in and know little about the philosophy and sociology of science. However, they do like the views of Merton and Popper once these are explained to them – though they generally think their arguments so obvious as not to need stating. The same working scientists are a great deal less keen on the views of Thomas Kuhn and others, to which we shall come in due course.

Robert Merton characterised science as open-minded, universalist, disinterested and communal (Merton, 1973). For Merton, science is a group activity: even though certain scientists work on their own, all scientists contribute to a single body of knowledge accepted by the community of scientists. There are certain parallels here with art, literature and music. After all, Cézanne, Gauguin and van Gogh all contributed to post-Impressionism. But while it makes no sense to try to combine their paintings, science is largely about combining the contributions of many different scientists to produce an overall coherent model of one aspect of reality. In this sense, science is disinterested; in *this* sense it is (or should be) impersonal.

Of course, individual scientists are passionate about their work and often slow to accept that their cherished ideas are wrong. But science itself is not persuaded by such partiality. While there may be controversy about whether the works of J. S. Bach or Mozart are better (and the question is pretty meaningless anyway), time (almost) invariably shows which of two alternative scientific theories is nearer the truth. For this reason, while scientists need to retain 'open-mindedness', always being prepared to change their views in the light of new evidence or better explanatory theories, scientific knowledge grows (though not uniformly) over time. As a result, while some scientific knowledge ('frontier science') is contentious, much scientific knowledge ('core science') can confidently be relied on: it is relatively certain.

Karl Popper emphasised the falsifiability of scientific theories (Popper, [1934] 1972). Unless you can imagine collecting data that would allow you to refute a theory, the theory is not scientific. The same applies to scientific hypotheses. So the hypothesis 'All swans are white' is scientific because we can imagine finding a bird that is manifestly a swan (in terms of its appearance and behaviour) but is not white. Indeed this is precisely what happened when early explorers returned from Australia with tales of black swans (Figure 3.1.1).

Popper's ideas can give rise to a view of science in which knowledge steadily accumulates over time as new theories are proposed and new data collected to discriminate between conflicting theories. Much school experimentation in science is Popperian: we see a rainbow and hypothesise that white light is split up into light of different colours as it is refracted through a transparent medium (water droplets); we test this by attempting to refract white light through a glass prism; we find the same colours of the rainbow are produced and our hypothesis is confirmed. Until some new evidence causes it to be falsified (refuted), we accept it.

There is much of value in the work of Robert Merton and Karl Popper but most academics in the field would argue that there is more to the nature of science. We now turn to the work of Thomas Kuhn (Kuhn, 1970). Thomas Kuhn made a number of seminal contributions but he is most remembered nowadays by his argument that while the Popperian account of science holds well during periods of *normal science* when a single paradigm holds sway, such as the Ptolemaic model of the structure of the solar system (in which the Earth is at the centre) or the Newtonian understanding of motion and gravity, it

■ **Figure 3.1.1** Black swans (*Cygnus atratus*) are native to Australia. Until they became known to people in the West, the statement 'All swans are white' was thought to be true. Now we say that it is both falsifiable (i.e. capable of being falsified) and false. Karl Popper argued that scientific statements, hypotheses and theories all need to be falsifiable

breaks down when a scientific *crisis* occurs. At the time of such a crisis, a scientific revolution happens during which a new paradigm, such as the Copernican model of the structure of the solar system or Einstein's theory of relativity, begins to replace the previously accepted paradigm. The central point is that the change of allegiance from scientists believing in one paradigm to their believing in another cannot, Kuhn argues, be fully explained by the Popperian account of falsifiability.

Kuhn likens the switch from one paradigm to another to a gestalt switch (when we suddenly see something in a new way) or even a religious conversion. As Alan Chalmers puts it:

> There will be no purely logical argument that demonstrates the superiority of one paradigm over another and that thereby compels a rational scientist to make the change. One reason why no such demonstration is possible is the fact that a variety of factors are involved in a scientist's judgment of the merits of a scientific theory. An individual scientist's decision will depend on the priority he or she gives to the various factors. The factors will include such things as simplicity, the connection with some pressing social need, the ability to solve some specified kind of problem, and so on. Thus one scientist might be attracted to the Copernican theory because of the simplicity of certain mathematical features of it. Another might be attracted to it because in it there is the possibility of calendar reform. A third might have been deterred from adopting the Copernican theory because of an involvement with terrestrial mechanics and an awareness of the problems that the Copernican theory posed for it.
>
> (Chalmers, 1999, pp. 115–16)

Kuhn also argued that scientific knowledge is validated by its acceptance in a community of scientists. Often scientists change their views as new evidence persuades them that a previously held theory is wrong. But sometimes they cling obstinately to their cherished theories. In such cases, if these scientists are powerful (e.g. by controlling which papers are published in the most prestigious journals), scientific progress may be impeded – until the scientists in question retire or die!

In a unit of this length there clearly is not space to provide an account of many other views of how science is done but there is one philosopher of science whom you will either love or hate – Paul Feyerabend. In many ways Feyerabend anticipated the post-modernists with their suspicion of a single authoritative account of reality. His views are succinctly summed up in the title of his most famous book, *Against Method* (Feyerabend, 1993). Feyerabend is something of an intellectual anarchist (another of his books is called *Farewell to Reason*) and the best way to understand him is for you to read him rather than for me to provide too tidy a summary of his thinking. Here are a few quotations – to either whet your appetite or put you off for life:

> No theory ever agrees with all the facts in its domain, yet it is not always the theory that is to blame. Facts are constituted by older ideologies, and a clash between facts and theories may be proof of progress.
>
> (Feyerabend, 1993, p. 39)

> The events, procedures and results that constitute the sciences have no common structure.
>
> (Feyerabend, 1993, p. 1)

> The success of 'science' cannot be used as an argument for treating as yet unsolved problems in a standardized way.
>
> (Feyerabend, 1993, p. 2)

> There can be many different kinds of science. People starting from different social backgrounds will approach the world in different ways and learn different things about it.
>
> (Feyerabend, 1993, pp. 2–3)

Task 3.1.1 **Getting pupils to consider the scope of science**

It is all too easy for pupils to take for granted that they get taught different 'things' in their different subjects in school. The aim of this task is to help pupils to become more aware of why there are certain things they study in science lessons as opposed to in other lessons.

You can start by having a discussion with pupils about whether there are some things in science that they also learn about in other subjects (e.g. rocks in geography, muscles and breathing in PE, sound in music). Then get them, perhaps in pairs or small groups, to talk about the similarities and differences between what they are taught in, for instance, geography and what they are taught in science. Pupils should end up appreciating that there are overlaps but that science is more interested in experiments, is more universal (so that most science is much the same in any country whereas geography is very interested in differences between countries) and has less to say about human action unless such action can be studied objectively.

Task 3.1.2 **What is your view of the nature of science? (M-level)**

There have been a number of research instruments devised to enable a person's views on the nature of science to be determined. Probably the easiest for you to get hold of and use is that provided by two leading UK science educators – Mick Nott and Jerry Wellington (Nott and Wellington, 1993). If you quite enjoy reading questionnaires along the lines of 'Does your partner find you boring?' in the backs of magazines while at the dentist, this task is for you. Once you have completed this questionnaire, reflect on *why* the scoring system came up with the result it did. Do you feel content with your view of the nature of science? How would your answers have needed to differ for you to have been classified differently? Discuss whether there is a single ideal view of the nature of science that science teachers should hold.

'REAL SCIENCE' COMPARED TO SCHOOL SCIENCE

There is much in the 5–16 science National Curriculum in England with which to be pleased. However, one of the less successful areas has been what in the 2014 version is called 'Experimental skills and investigations'. For one thing, we do not do a very good job of getting pupils in school science lessons to ask the sorts of questions that scientists actually ask or to ask the sorts of questions that the rest of us ask and to which science can make a contribution. Instead, pupils are too often restricted to uninteresting questions about the bouncing of balls or the dissolving of sugar in what are misleadingly termed 'scientific investigations'.

The history of this part of the science curriculum since the first National Curriculum Science Working Group, which published its report in 1987, up to the year 2000 has been analysed by Jim Donnelly (2001) and remains relevant to this day. Donnelly argues convincingly that two conflicting understandings of the nature of science can be detected in the battles of those years (and they felt much like battles to those participating in them). One is what Donnelly terms 'essentially empiricist'; in other words, straightforwardly concerned with how factual data are collected with which to test hypotheses. The other stresses social and cultural influences on science. In the language of the first part of this unit, this is a contest between Popper and Kuhn (Feyerabend doesn't get a look in).

The reasons for this battle need not greatly concern us except in so far as the very existence of the battle indicates the lack of consensus in this area among those responsible for the Science National Curriculum. This contrasts with many other parts of the Science National Curriculum. There is, for example, little controversy over the inclusion of food webs, evaporation and series circuits.

Much school science operates on the assumption that 'real science' only consists in doing replicated laboratory experiments to test hypotheses. When I started teaching social biology to 16–19-year-olds in England, the Examinations Board (it was in the mid-1980s, before awarding bodies) that set the syllabus included a project. One of my students was a very fit athlete who lived in Bahrain out of term time. He undertook measurements on himself of such physiological variables as body temperatures and body mass just before and just after completing a number of runs both in the UK and in Bahrain under very different environmental conditions. Another student was interested to see whether a person's astrological sign (determined by their birth date) correlated with their choice of school subjects at advanced level (e.g. sciences versus arts) or with their personalities. Accordingly she carried out a large survey of fellow students.

Both students had their projects scored at 0 per cent. Nor were these marks changed on appeal. I'm not claiming that either of these projects was the finest I have ever seen. But I am convinced that the marks they were given reflected too narrow an assumption in the examiners' minds about what constituted a valid piece of scientific enquiry (Reiss, 1993).

Those who write science curricula and mark students' work are powerful determinants of what passes in school for 'real science'. A more valid approach to finding out what science actually consists of is to study what real scientists do. Careful ethnographic work on this only began in the 1970s – one classic book is Latour and Woolgar (1979). Much of this writing is rather difficult to read and it is much easier to read any really good biographical account of a scientist – though such biographies, in concentrating on individuals, do rather give rise to the 'Great scientists' view of scientific progress.

The take home message from the ethnographic work on science is that while scientific practice is partly characterised by the Mertonian and Popperian norms discussed above, there is plenty of support for Kuhn's views and even for Feyerabend's. For example, school accounts of science often underplay the political realities of scientific research (not to mention the monotony of much of it). Nowadays governments and companies are far more interested in funding botanical research on genetic modification than on moss reproduction. Actually, it's the exception that proves the rule. If your moss only lives in Antarctica, chances are you may indeed find funding as many countries are keen to undertake research there so as to stake a territorial claim should the wilderness ever be exploited for natural reserves.

Task 3.1.3 **Get pupils to research how science is done**

Get your pupils to research using books in the school library or internet sources one example of the history and practice of science. For example, you might get pupils to research one of these topics:

- the theory of evolution;
- Rosalind Franklin's contribution to determining the structure of DNA;
- *in vitro* fertilisation;
- the Periodic Table;
- the history of glass;
- plate tectonics;
- the competition between DC and AC among domestic suppliers of electricity;
- the life and work of Galileo;
- the use of X-rays.

This exercise works best if pupils have a choice and have some opportunities to work collaboratively.

Pupils' views of the nature of science

In the UK, a classic piece of research was carried out on pupils' views on the nature of science from 1991 to 1993, i.e. in the early years of the National Curriculum. The work was undertaken with pupils aged 9, 12 and 16 years in England and came up with the following findings (Driver *et al.*, 1996):

- Pupils tend to see the purpose of science as providing solutions to technical problems rather than providing more powerful explanations.
- Pupils rarely appreciate that scientific explanations can involve postulating models. Even when they do, models are presumed to map onto events in the world in an unproblematic manner.
- Pupils rarely see science as a social enterprise. Scientists are seen as individuals working in isolation.
- Pupils have little awareness of the ways that society influences decisions about research agendas. The most common view is that scientists, through their personal altruism, choose to work on particular problems of concern to society.

One technique that has been used to examine how pupils see science is to ask them to draw a scientist (Figure 3.1.2). The drawings are then examined to see whether pupils tend to draw scientists as male or female, white or black, in laboratories or in other settings, etc. It has been suggested that the images produced are becoming less stereotypical, show less gender bias and are more realistic (Matthews, 1996).

Task 3.1.4 **Get pupils to do the 'draw a scientist' test**

Get your pupils to do the 'draw a scientist test'. (This probably works better at KS3 than at KS4.) Explain to them before they start their drawings that this isn't a test in the sense of some people gaining more marks than others and that you aren't interested in the artistic quality of their drawings. Ensure they write their names on the back of the drawing (in case you want to analyse the results by gender, ethnicity, performance in science or something else that requires knowledge at the individual level).

Usually researchers get pupils to do this individually but you might decide that it would be interesting to get pupils to discuss in pairs what they are going to put in their drawings before they do them.

If you want to go beyond what most researchers do, you might:

- require pupils to write a few paragraphs explaining why they drew what they drew;
- interview pupils about their drawings;
- try to untangle whether pupils are really drawing what they think scientists are like or whether they are drawing stereotypes or caricatures.

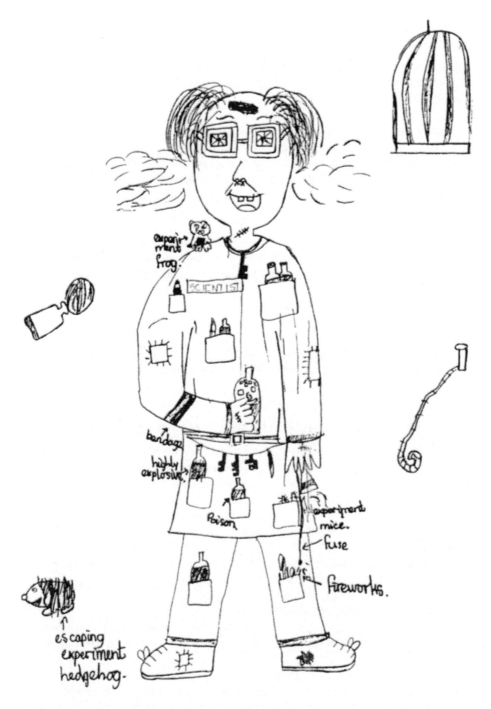

▪ **Figure 3.1.2** Caroline Allen's drawing of a scientist

SUMMARY AND KEY POINTS

Science is concerned with the natural world, with certain elements of the manufactured world and with how things are rather than with how they should be.

The nature of science is a controversial area and there are several competing understandings of how scientific knowledge is produced. Robert Merton saw science as open-minded, universalist, disinterested and communal. For Karl Popper, the distinctive thing about science is that all its ideas are testable and thus are falsifiable. Thomas Kuhn went beyond these views in seeing certain crucial episodes in the history of science as inexplicable within Mertonian and Popperian thinking. Kuhn emphasised that when scientists switch from one way of seeing the world to another, i.e. as the paradigm changes, they do so for a variety of reasons, not all of which are scientific in the narrow sense of the term.

Pupils generally have rather a limited understanding of the nature of science. The tasks presented here are intended to help deepen their understanding.

REFERENCES

Donnelly, J. (2001) 'Contested terrain or unified project? "The nature of science" in the National Curriculum for England and Wales', *International Journal of Science Education*, 23: 181–95.

Driver, R., Leach, J., Millar, R. and Scott, P. (1996) *Young People's Images of Science*, Buckingham: Open University Press.

Feyerabend, P. (1993) *Against Method*, 3rd edn, London: Verso.

Latour, B. and Woolgar, S. (1979) *Laboratory Life: The Social Construction of Scientific Facts*, London: Sage.

Matthews, B. (1996) 'Drawing scientists', *Gender and Education*, 8: 231–43.

Merton, R. K. (1973) *The Sociology of Science: Theoretical and Empirical Investigations*, Chicago: University of Chicago Press.

Nott, M. and Wellington, J. (1993) 'Your nature of science profile: an activity for science teachers', *School Science Review*, 75(270): 109–12.

Popper, K. R. ([1934] 1972) *The Logic of Scientific Discovery*, London: Hutchinson.

Reiss, M. J. (1993) *Science Education for a Pluralist Society*, Buckingham: Open University Press.

FURTHER READING

Chalmers, A. F. (1999) *What Is This Thing Called Science?*, 3rd edn, Buckingham: Open University Press.

An extremely clear and very widely read introductory textbook on the philosophy of science. If you want a readable account about any of the major questions on the nature of science, here is an excellent place to look.

Kind, V. and Kind, P. M. (2008) *Teaching Secondary: How Science Works*, London: Hodder Education.

A really well-written and intelligent overview of how science works at both Key Stages 3 and 4. It comes with a very useful CD-ROM that contains pupil worksheets.

Kuhn, T. S. (1970) *The Structure of Scientific Revolutions*, 2nd edn, Chicago: University of Chicago Press.

A classic in the history and philosophy of science. This is the book which undermined the straightforward Popperian view of science and convincingly argued for the importance of culture in the growth of scientific knowledge. Kuhn introduced the notion of paradigms in science.

USEFUL WEBSITES

Australian websites: Australia introduced 'Working Scientifically' into schools before we did in England. Try entering '"working scientifically" Australia' into a search engine. For example, see www.angelfire.com/sc/staws/Working_Scientifically.pdf (accessed 1 March 2014).

Getting practical: www.gettingpractical.org.uk/ (accessed 26 March 2013). A website about a project on practical work, undertaken across England.

BIOLOGY

Katherine Little

INTRODUCTION

The study of biology in schools is mainly concerned with green plants and animals, meaning that there are only slightly more than a million organisms to come to terms with. Occasionally, there may be a brief consideration of fungi or bacteria, if threatening or useful to us. However, because life on Earth has a single origin, all living things share common characteristics – they respire, reproduce, respond to their surroundings, move, excrete waste, take in nutrients, and grow (known as MRS GREN, to school children). Therefore by understanding some basic concepts, it is possible to extend and apply ideas to a wide range of organisms.

OBJECTIVES

By the end of this unit, you should:

- know the key concepts in biology;
- be aware of the distinctive features of living things;
- be aware of the role evolution plays in explaining how our living environment came to be as it is.

CELLS AND DNA

One of the most fundamental and important ideas in biology is that all living things are made of cells. Named by Robert Hooke, who observed that the tissue of cork resembled the regular, bare cells of monks under the microscope, it has since been found that far from empty, cells contain many components. Though contents of cells differ – from mammalian nerve cells to photosynthetic plant cells, muscle cells to gametes – they all share essential constituents, including a nucleus, cell membrane, and cytoplasm.

The nucleus contains a cell's chromosomes, along which a complete set of instructions for its life are arranged as beads on a string in the genes, written in the four-letter code of DNA. Genes are translated into proteins, which are responsible for the functioning of a cell. The genetic code is the same in all organisms, allowing the technology of genetic engineering, for example, a bacterial cell can be induced to produce human insulin by the insertion of the human insulin gene into its DNA strand. Within an organism, different types of cells function differently because different genes are 'switched on'; between organisms there are differences in the forms, or alleles, of genes, for example, that which controls blood group. When genes, chromosomes and gametes become so different that they are incompatible, two different species are considered to exist. However, because of the common ancestry of living things, all living organisms share a wide range of cellular reactions governed by the same genes. For example, we share 98 per cent of our DNA with chimpanzees, our closest relative, but also share 60 per cent with mice. DNA technology is increasingly used in taxonomy, as it is possible to calculate how recently different species have diverged from one another.

DNA is copied faithfully during cell replication by enzymes. The double helix structure, proposed by Watson and Crick in 1953, lends itself to information carrying as one strand complements the other, allowing proofreading of the new strands to occur. Depending upon the type of cell division, the daughter cells may be identical (mitosis), or genetically different (meiosis). In sexual reproduction, the number of chromosomes is reduced by half in the gametes (the name given to male and female sex cells, either the sperm and egg, or contents of pollen and ovules). At fertilisation, the full number of chromosomes is restored, giving rise to an organism that has inherited half of its mother's and half of its father's genes. In this way, the genetic essence of an individual can be passed down through generations.

If the sole purpose of an organism's existence is to pass its genes to future generations, then the complexity of life shows the variety of ways in which this can be achieved. There are around one million named living species of animals, with most recent estimates of 7.8 million in existence. Add to that the other kingdoms – plants, fungi, protists and monera – and numbers of up to a billion species have been proposed (it is the bacteria that account for such wild uncertainty at the upper end). Plants and animals, the kingdoms concentrated on in school biology, represent two main groups of organisms; the first is able to produce its own source of food, while the second is dependent upon the first for its supply of nutrients.

PLANTS AS THE POWERHOUSES OF THE LIVING WORLD: PHOTOSYNTHESIS

In 1648, Jan Baptista van Helmont, a Flemish scientist, planted a willow tree in a pot in the first recorded quantitative experiment. After five years, he observed that its mass had increased by 74kg, but the soil had only lost 60g. He concluded that water was the source of the extra mass, and also the plant's source of life. Subsequent experimentation by Joseph Priestley and Jan Ingenhausz demonstrated that plants produce oxygen and need sunlight to do so. It became apparent that green plants, often overlooked as inanimate and rather dull, are the powerhouses of the living world. Without the ability of these plants to harness the energy in sunlight, the carbon-based life would not have developed as it has today. This most crucial of chemical reactions, photosynthesis (literally, building up by light), occurs in every green leaf. Simple molecules of carbon dioxide, from the air, and water, absorbed through the plant's roots, are combined in the leaf's chloroplasts using the sun's energy captured by the green pigment chlorophyll to form glucose, a sugar built around six carbon atoms. The chemical energy in the glucose–oxygen system then becomes available for the plant – a producer – and any animal – a consumer – that might use that plant as a food source. Additionally, glucose can be polymerised into starch or glycogen for food storage, or cellulose for structural use in plant cell walls. Alternatively, they may combine with other molecules to form either amino acids, the building blocks of proteins, or fats and lipids. Proteins are structurally important – for example, skin and hair contain the protein keratin – and have a vital role as biological catalysts in their action as enzymes. Fats and lipids are the main constituent of cell membranes, and are also used for long-term food storage – both walnuts and polar bears depend on their high energy content. Without photosynthesis to capture the sun's energy, there would be no glucose production, or its subsequent conversion into more complex biological molecules, and no atmospheric oxygen; hence it is true to say that the natural world is driven by sunlight.

SUPPLYING ENERGY: RESPIRATION

The majority of organisms respire aerobically – that is, they combine glucose with oxygen to release a supply of energy that can be used to drive cellular reactions. The reactions of aerobic respiration occur in the mitochondria, organelles dedicated to the oxidation of glucose and the simultaneous formation of adenosine triphosphate, or ATP, the biological currency of cellular energy. Carbon dioxide and water are produced as waste products. This process occurs in every living cell, and the number of mitochondria is indicative of how active a cell is; muscle fibres and intestinal epithelial cells are packed full. Anaerobic respiration can take place under extreme conditions when oxygen is less plentiful, but the amount of energy released is far less. In very small organisms, oxygen and glucose needs can be met by simple diffusion of molecules from the external to the internal environment. However, as the size of an organism increases, the surface area to volume ratio is reduced, so not every cell can meet its requirements by diffusion. Large organisms have therefore evolved complex systems for the exchange of vital molecules with the environment and for their transport within the organisms to the cells, and to remove potentially toxic waste products from them.

TRANSPORTATION OF MATERIAL

Both plants and animals use the process of mass transport to move large amounts of substances. Animals' transport systems are often illustrated by the example of the mammalian heart (demonstrating the often human-centred view of biology). In this system, the heart – a mechanical pump – moves the transport medium – blood – around the body in a system of arteries, capillaries and veins. These specialised vessels bring the blood's contents into close contact with every single cell, from where it is only a short distance for substances to diffuse into and out of cells. It is in this way that oxygen and nutrients are delivered to cells, brought from the lungs and intestines respectively, and carbon dioxide, water and other waste products are removed, mainly via the lungs and kidneys.

Plants, being generally less active than animals, do not have such high energy requirements; their rate of respiration can therefore be lower, and delivery and removal of molecules are not as urgent. Nevertheless, plants do need to distribute glucose produced in their leaves to the rest of the plant, and must raise water from their roots to their photosynthesising leaves. Plants have two transport systems: xylem and phloem vessels.

Xylem vessels can be thought of as long thin tubes that can stretch the height of the tallest trees, through which water and minerals move from the roots to the leaves as a result of the polar nature of water molecules. Cohesive forces between individual molecules create an unbroken column of water that is pulled up the plant by evaporation from the leaves – no active energy-consuming transport process is needed and so xylem vessels are made of dead cells, containing no organelles. Calculations of the maximum height to which water could be lifted by this mechanism match closely with the recorded heights of the tallest Californian redwoods – around 125 metres.

The second plant transport system is the phloem system. Phloem tissue also comprises tubes, but these tubes are living, and need to respire. The liquid moving in these tubes is far more concentrated than that in the xylem, being a solution of sugars being transported from the leaves to other parts of the plant, particularly the roots. The direction of flow in the phloem is from a source to a sink and will vary depending on conditions, for example, in summer, roots may act as a sink, storing products of photosynthesis, whereas in the spring they will act as a source to feed growing shoots.

CHANGING LARGE MOLECULES TO SMALL ONES: DIGESTION

Whereas plants can build more complex organic molecules from their synthesised glucose and minerals absorbed from the soil, animals are dependent upon their diet to obtain many essential nutrients. However, food that is ingested is rarely in an appropriate form to be used by cells. It must first of all be digested – broken down mechanically and chemically into its constituent molecules. For example, the energy-rich starch polymer is too large to pass through a cell membrane, so must be digested into glucose monomers before absorption. This breakdown is catalysed by specific enzymes in the human gut, amylase and maltase. Even as the enzymes get to work, mechanical processes of chewing and churning will have begun the physical breakdown, giving the enzymes a greater surface area to act upon.

Surface area is a factor that affects many processes in the living world; so many are dependent on the diffusion of substances across membranes, hence their rate is dependent on the surface area of membrane available. Thus, the rate of absorption of nutrients in the small intestine is maximised by the convolutions of the surface into villi and further into finger-like microvilli; plants' absorption of water and minerals from the soil is aided by the fine projections of root hair cells from the finest of roots; gas exchange in organisms occurs in the spongy, air-filled mesophyll of leaves, across the surface of many-branched air sacs of the mammalian lungs, across the richly blood-supplied feathery gill lamellae of a fish. Equally, the shape of animals and even their behaviour are influenced by heat loss, which increases with increasing surface area: volume ratio. Hence we see the large ears of the desert-dwelling fennec fox to aid cooling, and the huddling of emperor penguins to maintain warmth in the Antarctic chill.

CONTROLLING CONDITIONS: HOMEOSTASIS

To carry out the functions of life, organisms strive to maintain constant internal environments, a process known as homeostasis. To consider a single factor, the water content of cells: if the water content of a cell becomes reduced, the cell will collapse; if the water content is too great, the cell will over-expand which can result in the membrane of the cell rupturing. The movement of water into and out of cells is governed by the concentration of solutes on either side of the membrane. In humans, two important osmotically active solutes are salt and glucose. If salt or the glucose concentration is high in the bloodstream, water will be drawn out of the cells causing them to dehydrate; this could occur through the ingestion of salty foods, or in the case of glucose, with the condition diabetes, where glucose is not effectively removed from the bloodstream. To moderate the extremes of solute content, and to eliminate metabolic waste, humans have kidneys that filter the blood to remove excess water and solutes. These organs use mechanisms of high pressure filtration to remove all particles below a certain size from the blood, then employ active transport and diffusion to return a correct balance of substances to the body. The final concentration of reabsorbed substances is governed by a hormone – a chemical messenger carried in the bloodstream – released from a gland in the brain, which affects the uptake of water in the kidney.

COMMUNICATION AND CONTROL: HORMONES AND THE NERVOUS SYSTEM

Many biological processes are governed by hormones, and their effects may be both long-lasting and wide-ranging. One dramatic hormone is adrenaline, released from the adrenal glands on top of the kidneys, that elicits the increased heartbeat, raised breathing rate, dilated pupils and sweating palms of fear, preparing the body for 'flight or fight'. Longer-acting hormones include the sex hormones, testosterone, oestrogen and progesterone, released from the sex organs and responsible for growth and development of sexual characteristics and the development of gametes over months and years. The growth of plants is also governed by hormones, the effects of which can be demonstrated by exploring tropisms of plants, or in the practices of pruning and training to achieve desirable growth and flowering.

The action of hormones is in contrast to the nervous system of animals. Nerve cells carry electrical impulses at great speed to and from the central nervous system. They are typified by their long length, their numerous connections to other nerve cells, and in mammals by their associated Schwann cells, which act as insulation to speed signal transmission. Nerves can elicit lightning reactions – fractions of a second – between sensing and responding to a stimulus. For example, whereas a plant will respond to light and grow towards it as a result of a hormone over a course of days, a star-nosed mole will detect prey with its tentacle-like nose and capture it within 120 msec.

EVOLUTION AND GENETICS

The perfectly engineered solutions to problems of maintaining life presented here are the result of billions of years of successive minute changes in design, the designer being the pressures of the environment they inhabit. The theory of evolution by natural selection was famously developed by Charles Darwin, over 150 years ago. His work was the result of many years of careful observation of evidence from such diverse sources as fossils from South America; pedigrees of fancy pigeons from London's enthusiasts, and observations of weed competition in his own garden. Natural selection explains how changes in organisms occur with clarity and simplicity; subsequent research and evidence continue to support and strengthen the theory, without the need for more complicated explanations for evolution. At the time of publication of Darwin's (1859) *Origin of Species*, the mechanism for the inheritance of characteristics was unknown. It was not until the early twentieth century, with the appreciation of Gregor Mendel's formative work on genetics that the mode of information transmission by 'factors' (now genes) was elucidated; further advances in the field of genetics sees us 100 years later with the understanding and technology to influence our own genes and inheritance.

In a world where resources are finite, it is not other species with whom individuals compete most intensely, but their peers, as they have the most similar needs. In a population of similar organisms, some will be better suited to the conditions and be able to produce more surviving offspring than those individuals struggling to survive. For example, in a field that is home to white rabbits and brown rabbits, white rabbits are more likely to be seen and eaten by foxes than their brown counterparts. Of the brown rabbits, those with long legs for fast running will escape the foxes. Only those individuals that are not eaten will go on to breed, and pass on their characteristics; eventually, the field will be home to only brown, long-legged rabbits. Slight changes in species generation after generation have led to the living world we see today, and continue to shape it. Evolution is dependent upon there being a diversity of genes within a species to begin with, and the continuing introduction of new genes by mutation – random mistakes in the replication of DNA. In the present day, when human activity is adversely affecting many habitats, organisms do not have the genes present in their populations that might enable future offspring to adapt to rapid environmental changes. As they cannot evolve to exploit their changing habitats in one or few generations, they are becoming extinct.

ECOLOGY: THE INTERDEPENDENCE OF ORGANISMS AND THEIR ENVIRONMENT

In any study of biology, it is disingenuous to study an organism in isolation from its environment. No plant or animal can exist free from the effect of other members of its community, be it through direct competition for resources within or between species, feeding relationships between successive trophic levels, or the alteration of abiotic factors by successive seral stages as an ecosystem progresses to a climax community. An ecosystem is driven by energy from the Sun that is harnessed by photosynthesising plants; this energy, and nutrients, are transferred up the food chain from producer to primary consumer to secondary consumer. Crucially, energy is lost at each level, left locked up in uningested food, as heat energy radiated to the environment as animals move and maintain body temperature, and in waste (dried cow dung is a rich energy source). Some of this energy can be considered to move 'sideways' out of a food chain and be used by detritivores – bacteria, fungi and other decomposers – but ultimately all energy will be lost to the environment in the form of heat. Transfer from one trophic level to the next is at best 10 per cent efficient. This has significant effects on how we raise animals for meat; reducing energy losses through restricting movement in heated environments means more feed is converted to muscle mass. Equally, losses through energy transfer provide a strong argument for reducing meat consumption. It is possible to grow sufficient crops to feed the world's seven billion humans, but not if we persist in growing food crops to feed livestock to satisfy our desire for meat; each kilogramme of meat requires six kilogrammes of grain.

Nutrients, on the other hand, follow a cyclical path. Any molecule in an organism is there for a relatively short time – a lifetime at most – before being recycled through the abiotic environment. It is possible to imagine the path of an atom of carbon as it passes from carbon dioxide in the air, into the leaf of a photosynthesising plant where it is incorporated into an organic molecule, through the tissues of the animal that eats that plant, until it is respired and returned to the atmosphere. A deviation from this short cycle may take millions of years; it is the carbon that was trapped by plants when the dinosaurs roamed the Earth that is now being released as fossil fuels are burnt, and is causing world-altering climate change.

BIOLOGY: THE HUMAN ANIMAL

Biology is the study of living organisms, among which *Homo sapiens* is included. We are part of the continuing evolution of life, a species at present enjoying a successful period thanks to a few spontaneous mutations, including those leading to speech and larger brains. There is no way that we can separate our existence from the influences of the natural world. Plant life provides us with food and oxygen; different habitats influence our available and desirable resources; our drive to propagate our genes drives many individual and cultural practices.

Our application of biological knowledge is amply demonstrated in the field of medicine. For millennia plant products have been used as drugs to help treat ailments, some passing into folklore and others into the research lab. The spread of infectious diseases has been controlled through our understanding of germ theory. An early proponent of this idea was Ignaz Semmelweis, a Hungarian obstetrician. He observed that many women died of puerperal fever after having given birth attended by doctors, whereas the death rate of those under midwife care was much lower. Doctors came straight to deliveries from autopsies. By insisting that doctors washed their hands before attending labour wards, Semmelweis cut mortality rates to 2 per cent. In other areas, the study of anatomy has led to microsurgery as opposed to butchery; prophylactic immunisations stimulate our immune system into producing antibodies to pathogens that might otherwise overcome us; endocrinologists have allowed diabetics who would have died in childhood 80 years ago to lead relatively normal lives with the discovery of insulin. As our understanding of biology at a cellular level advances, so technologies such as therapeutic stem cell cloning and treatments for degenerative diseases will become widespread. These future possibilities are necessarily also laden with ethical implications; part of our role as biology teachers is to give pupils the tools to make informed decisions on lifestyle choices – whether to use drugs (legal and illegal), what impact different diets may have on their health and environment, how funding for research should be allocated. At the time of writing, the US Supreme Court has ruled that natural human genes cannot be patented, and the cost of having one's genome sequenced has fallen from $2.7 billion to $5000. A wealth of information is about to become available to everyone, and its use will move from science fiction to science fact. Biology has the potential to give rise to some of the most heated debates in science, because as part of biology we find it difficult to maintain an objective viewpoint.

SUMMARY AND KEY POINTS

From the elephant to the ant to the bacteria that live upon and within the ant, from the giant redwoods of California to the algae in a garden pond, all organisms are performing the processes of living things. They have arrived at a multitude of different ways in which to carry out these processes – remaining in the same place and producing their own food or moving around in search of nutrition; transporting substances throughout their systems actively or passively; sensing and responding to their environments in a multitude of ways. The diversity of life that is so remarkable is the result of billions of years of evolution. From LUCA (the last universal common ancestor) has evolved the wealth of living things upon which David Attenborough has built his illustrious career. Biology provides answers for such questions as: 'Why are trees green? How do fish breathe underwater? Why do elephants have big ears? Why do animals become extinct?' To study biology so enhances our appreciation of our own selves and of the world of which we are both an integral part and self-appointed guardians, that to disregard the discipline would be to go through life blind to the truly awe-inspiring nature of our unique planet.

The tasks below provide ideas for stimulating thinking and interest in the living world.

Task 3.2.1 **Plants**

- ▨ Take a walk in a wood, or a flight over the countryside in Google Earth. All those trees and plants are made of carbon dioxide and water. That's quite a feat.
- ▨ Grow cress seeds on the windowsill, and marvel at the tiny plants' ability to respond to sunlight. Try turning them on their side after a few days – they can sense gravity too!
- ▨ Always effective: stand a white carnation in a small depth of strong food dye, and leave it overnight. The dye will be transported in the xylem to the petals, where the intricate network of veins will be revealed in glorious technicolour. For added fun, split the stem and use different colours.
- ▨ Tie a clear polythene bag over a pot plant. After a few hours, droplets of water will start to collect on the inside. This is water that has been transported from the soil through the root hairs, into the xylem vessels and out through the leaves into the air. The process at work here is multiplied a thousand fold in taking water to the tops of the tallest trees.

Task 3.2.2 **Our bodies**

1 A favourite: stand on your head and drink a glass of water through a straw. Why doesn't it run back out of your mouth? Peristalsis – waves of muscular contraction moving towards your stomach, regardless of gravity.

---

2   Hold your breath. What caused you to breathe again? Not a need for oxygen, but an urge to rid the body of carbon dioxide. While you do this, think of the abilities of some sea mammals to dive to depths of over 2 km for half an hour or more.

3   In front of a mirror, cover one open eye with your hand. The other pupil will expand in response to the darkness experienced by the other pupil. Tiny muscles in the iris are constantly adjusting the size of the pupil in response to the light level. This represents a fraction of the stimuli from our environment to which our bodies are constantly reacting.

4   Look at a flower. Look at a tree. Look at a snail. Look at birds in the sky. Aren't these the most amazing pictures you have ever seen? Created by a collection of light-sensitive cells on your retina sending electrical signals to the back of the brain, these images enable us to appreciate the natural world.

REFERENCE

Darwin, C. (1859) *On the Origin of Species*, London: John Murray.

FURTHER READING

Attenborough, D. (1979) *Life on Earth: A Natural History*, Boston, MA: Little, Brown, and Company.

Attenborough, D. (1995) *The Private Life of Plants: A Natural History of Plant Behaviour*, London: BBC Books.

Carey, N. (2011) *The Epigenetics Revolution*, London: Icon Books Ltd.

Dawkins, R. (1989) *The Selfish Gene*, Oxford: Oxford Paperbacks.

Diamond, J. (2006) *The Third Chimpanzee: The Evolution and Future of the Human Animal (P.S.)*, New York: Harper Perennial.

Fong, K. (2013) *Extremes: Life, Death and the Limits of the Human Body*, London: Hodder and Stoughton.

Goldacre, B. (2008) *Bad Science*, London: Fourth Estate.

Goulson, D. (2013) *A Sting in the Tale*, London: Jonathan Cape.

Jones, S. (1999) *Almost Like a Whale: The Origin of Species Updated*, New York: Doubleday Publishing.

Reiss, M. (ed.) (2002) *Teaching Secondary Biology*, London: John Murray for ASE.

Rutherford, A. (2013) *Creation: The Origin of Life; The Future of Life*, London: Penguin.

Shubin, N. (2009) *Your Inner Fish*, London: Penguin.

Wilson, E.O. (1992) *The Diversity of Life*, New York: W.W. Norton and Co.

USEFUL WEBSITES

Bank of biology resources and experiments from D. G. Mackean: www.biology-resources.com/ (accessed 2 February 2014).

Guardian **Education**: www. education.guardian.co.uk/higher/links (accessed 2 February 2014).

Lots of animations of cell processes: http://highered.mcgraw-hill.com/sites/dl/free/0072437316/120060/ravenanimation.html (accessed 2 February 2014).

New Scientist **magazine**: www.newscientist.com/ (accessed 2 February 2014).

Nuffield Foundation teaching resources: www.nuffieldfoundation.org/practical-biology (accessed 2 February 2014).

SciShow: www.youtube.com/user/scishow; www.youtube.com/user/crashcourse (accessed 2 February 2014).

TED: Ideas worth spreading: www.ted.com/ (accessed 2 February 2014).

Wellcome Trust's *Big Picture* magazine: www.wellcome.ac.uk/Education-resources/Teaching-and-education/Big-Picture/index.htm (accessed 2 February 2014).

CHEMISTRY

Ann Childs

INTRODUCTION

> It was quite the most incredible event that has ever happened to me in my life. It was almost as incredible as if you fired a 15-inch shell at a piece of tissue paper and it came back and hit you. On consideration, I realized that this scattering backward must be the result of a single collision, and when I made calculations I saw that it was impossible to get anything of that order of magnitude unless you took a system in which the greater part of the mass of the atom was concentrated in a minute nucleus. It was then that I had the idea of an atom with a minute massive center, carrying a charge.
>
> (Ernest Rutherford, cited in Pais, 1986, p. 186)

> I write because I am a chemist. My trade has provided my raw material, the nucleus to which things join . . . Chemistry is a struggle with matter, a masterpiece of rationality, an existential parable . . . Chemistry teaches vigilance combined with reason.
>
> (Primo Levi)

This unit looks at chemistry as a school subject and focuses on two key themes. The first theme is the interplay between the macroscopic world of materials, their properties and their uses with the atomic/sub-atomic level (which encompasses atoms, molecules, ions, protons, neutrons and electrons) because, as Taber (2002, p. 162) says, 'Many explanations in chemistry require transitions between the macroscopic and molecular levels' and throughout the unit it will be shown how these transitions, between the macroscopic and the molecular, help explain some key ideas in chemistry. The quotes above capture some of the key ideas within this theme. The first from Ernest Rutherford represents one of the major steps forward in our understanding of the structure of the atom. In 1899, J. J. Thomson had proposed the 'plum pudding' model of the atom where the pudding was positive charge in which the plums, electrons, were embedded. In 1909, Hans Geiger and Ernest Marsden, under the direction of Ernest Rutherford, performed the gold foil experiment where they fired alpha particles at a thin sheet of gold atoms. If J. J. Thomson's model was correct, then the alpha particles should have passed straight through the gold foil but they did not and Rutherford's quote above vividly illustrates the research team's surprise. This led to Rutherford, in 1911, proposing that the atom had an incredibly small, positively charged nucleus. Later it will be shown how an understanding of the structure of the atom helped to explain why, for example, elements in the same group of the Periodic Table have similar physical and chemical properties. The second quote by the Italian chemist, Primo Levi, simply illustrates the importance of the sub-atomic world and that, fundamentally, chemistry deals with matter. Which leads to the second theme: how the study of chemistry can help us make sense of the incredible variety of matter or materials in the world we live in that occur naturally or have been made by humans. For example, think about how many chemicals/materials you have used or inter-acted with from the time you wake every day to the time you go to sleep. The number would be vast! It might include various lotions and potions used in the bathroom for washing to the chemicals you are wearing, that you ate for breakfast, that made up the transport to go to school/work and all the materials you use in your workplace. How can chemistry make sense of this bewildering yet useful array of different kinds of materials? This unit will therefore also demonstrate how chemistry helps us group, classify and understand some of the properties of these materials and of their chemical reactions.

Miodownik sums up many of the issues addressed in these two themes in his new book, *Stuff Matters*:

I have delved into our material world in an attempt to show that although the mater-ials around us might seem like blobs of differently coloured matter, they are in fact much more than that: they are complex expressions of human needs and desires. And in order to satisfy our need for things like shelter and clothes, our desire for chocolate and the cinema – we have had to master the complexity of their inner structure.

(2013, pp. 236–7)

OBJECTIVES

By the end of this unit, you should:

▨ appreciate the scope of chemistry;
▨ be able to identify how the microscopic story of particles contributes to explaining the macroscopic properties and behaviour of materials;
▨ appreciate some of the future directions of chemistry and its connection to other areas of science.

PRIMARY AND LOWER SECONDARY CHEMISTRY: MACROSCOPIC TO THE MOLECULAR LEVEL

The study of chemistry in school begins firmly rooted in the macroscopic world of mater-ials. In the early stages of studying chemistry students learn that materials can be grouped according to properties such as whether they are strong or weak, brittle, or conduct elec-tricity, are magnetic, shiny, malleable or ductile and many more. Classifying materials in this way is also used to begin to get students to think about how the properties of materials make them useful in our everyday lives. For example, a brittle transparent material like glass is obviously used for windows (see Miodownick, 2013, Chapter 7, for a full discussion of the history of glass as a material); and metals like copper are used in electrical wiring because they are good conductors of electricity. In the final years of primary education students are taught that materials can be classified as solids, liquids or gases and there is strong focus on physical changes such as melting, freezing, evaporating, dissolving and condensing. Chemical changes such as burning are also introduced. Therefore, changes can be classified into physical changes or chemical changes and a key difference between the two, for example, is that chemical changes are irreversible changes and physical changes are reversible. At primary level this classification could be considered as a helpful way of understanding change in chemistry but at higher levels in secondary school it will be seen to be an over-simplification because, for example, chemical changes are reversible (e.g. equilibrium reactions). Furthermore, Taber outlines in some detail other challenges and complexities of classifying changes as physical or chemical (2002, pp. 97–100). Kind also reports challenges in this area and, in particular, that students find 'difficulty in recognising when a chemical reaction occurs' and they find it hard to 'discriminate between a chemical change and a change of state, which chemists call a "physical change"' (2004, p. 24). Therefore, a seemingly simple classification at this level needs some careful thought.

By the end of primary school, pupils are still firmly in the macroscopic world and they know that materials have different properties but they do not know why. At early secondary level, the kinetic theory of matter is introduced. Pupils learn how particles are arranged in solids, liquids and gases. However, it is worth noting that the use of the term particle also has its challenges, as Taber says: 'The word "particle" is not very helpful, as it is used for small (yet still visible and macroscopic) particles such as salt grains or dust specks, as well as a collective term for molecules, ions, etc.' (2002, p. 90). This causes some confusion for pupils and it is important at this stage to establish the relative size of the particles in solids, liquids and gases in relation to these 'macroscopic' particles (see Website 1 for help). However, the introduction of the particle theory of matter allows pupils to begin to explain physical changes such as melting and boiling rather than just describing them. Therefore, we are beginning to make sense of the material world now at molecular level where explanations can emerge!

THE POWER OF THE PERIODIC TABLE

The introduction of the Periodic Table at lower secondary level helps to group and make sense of the 92 naturally occurring chemical elements. A simple classification of these elements could be as solids, liquids and gases. Using this method, the majority of elements are solids, some are gases and two only, bromine and mercury, are liquids at room temperature. The solids are very different and range from sulfur, a non-metal, which is a bright yellow and brittle solid, to a metal such as gold, which is shiny and malleable, to a number of metals that are very reactive in water such as lithium, sodium and potassium. Therefore classifying the elements as solids, liquids or gases at room temperature is not massively helpful in explaining this diversity.

The Periodic Table was developed by a number of significant scientists in the late 1800s. By 1850, 59 of the 92 naturally occurring elements had been discovered and chemists at the time, Döbereiner and Myer in Germany, Newlands in England and

Mendeleev in Russia were trying to look for patterns in their properties to group these elements. The work of Dmitri Mendeleev, in particular, is significant because it shows how the power of the emerging Periodic Table allowed Mendeleev to predict the properties of undiscovered elements. Website 2 shows Mendeleev's table (Table 3.3.1), and note that there is a question mark in the fourth row where there is a missing element. Mendeleev predicted the properties for this element which he called eka-aluminium. The element was eventually discovered by Paul de Boisbaudran in Paris in 1875. He named the element gallium which is the Latin name for France. Table 3.3.1 shows just how remarkably close Mendeleev's prediction was to gallium's actual properties, which illustrates how powerful these early attempts at producing a Periodic Table were in being able to predict the properties of, as yet, undiscovered elements. More information on these scientists working on the Periodic Table can be found in Website 3.

Website 4 gives a good visual representation of the chemical elements in the current Periodic Table and Website 5 is a lively song by Tom Lehrer which includes all 92 naturally occurring elements and others that have been made.

Although these early chemists could describe many of the physical and chemical properties of elements and then group them, they could not explain why elements in the same group, for example, Group 1, the Alkali Metals, or Group 7, the Halogens, had similar physical and chemical properties. This could only come once the structure of the atom had been understood. The idea of matter being made of atoms began with Democritus in 400 BC. He called the particles atoms from the Greek *atomos* which means indivisible. But it was not until 1803 with John Dalton, again proposing an indivisible atom, that the idea of atoms emerged again and the structure of the atom was finally worked out (for the stories of all the scientists involved, see Warren, 2001). As we saw above, in 1899, J. J. Thomson proposed the plum pudding model of the atom which was later challenged by Rutherford's gold foil experiment and, in 1911, Rutherford proposed an atom that had an incredibly small positive core, where the majority of the mass of the atom was concentrated, with electrons orbiting around this positive nucleus. In 1914, Bohr modified Rutherford's model by introducing the idea that the electrons were arranged in energy levels or shells. Finally, in 1932, Chadwick discovered the neutron and we now think of the atoms as having a nucleus containing protons (positively charged) and neutrons (no charge). Surrounding the nucleus are negatively charged electrons orbiting the nucleus in shells or energy levels. Returning then to the Periodic Table, the structure of the atom can now help explain why, for example, the elements in Groups 1–8 have similar physical and chemical properties. This is because elements in the same group of the Periodic Table have the same number of electrons in their outer shell. So all the elements in Group 1, the Alkali Metals, have one electron in their outer shell and, similarly, all the elements in Group 7, the Halogens, have seven electrons

▪ **Table 3.3.1** Mendeleev's predicted properties of 'eka-aluminium'

Property	Eka-aluminium (Mendeleev's prediction)	Gallium
Atomic mass	68	69.72
Density (g/cm^3)	6.0	5.9
Melting point (°C)	Low	29.78
Formula of oxide	Ea_2O_3	Ga_2O_3
Formula of chloride	Ea_2Cl_6	Ga_2Cl_6

in their outer shell. It is the electrons in the outer shell of the atoms of the elements that are involved in chemical reactions and in chemical bonding and so this begins to explain why elements in the same group have similar properties. In addition, another group or block, the transition elements or D-block elements, are grouped together because in their major oxidation states they have similar electron configurations too. Therefore, the macroscopic world interacts with the atomic/sub-atomic world, providing explanations why elements in the same group of the Periodic Table have similar physical and chemical properties.

STRUCTURE AND BONDING IN THE PERIODIC TABLE: ANOTHER WAY OF GROUPING ELEMENTS

So far, elements have been grouped as solids, liquids and gases and then grouped in the Periodic Table. Another way to group elements is to look again at the molecular level and consider their structures. Elements can be grouped into four main structures:

1   *Giant metallic structures*, e.g. all the metal elements. The outer electrons of the metal atoms are delocalised to form a 'sea of electrons' and positive metals ions. The positive metals ions are organised into a giant structure of ions (see Website 6 for more information). Metallic bonds are the forces of attraction between the delocalised electrons in the 'electron sea' and the metal ions. Metallic bonds are strong so metals usually have high melting and boiling points. Taber (2002, pp. 133–5) discusses in detail the problems students can have with understanding metallic structures, for example, the use of the analogy 'sea of electrons' can imply that the metal ion is seen as 'being like an island surrounded by electrons' and 'floating in a sea of delocalised electrons' (Taber, 2002, p. 134), which makes it difficult for students to understand that metallic bonds are, relatively speaking, strong.

2   *Simple molecular structures*, e.g. nitrogen, oxygen and hydrogen. The atoms of these elements form simple molecules, N_2, H_2, O_2, where the atoms in the molecules are held together by covalent bonds (see Website 6 for more information). Although the covalent bonds (the intramolecular bonds) holding the atoms together in the molecule are strong, it is the relatively weaker van der Waals forces of attraction (intermolecular bonds) between the molecules that are broken when these elements melt or boil. Therefore, elements with this structure have low melting and boiling points (see Website 6 for more information). For example, the boiling point of nitrogen is $-195.8°C$ and it is a gas at room temperature.

3   *Giant molecular structures*, e.g. the two allotropes of carbon, diamond and graphite. Here atoms of carbon are covalently bonded in a massive three-dimensional giant structure. Atoms of carbon in both allotropes are joined together by covalent bonds (see Website 6 for more information). The structures of diamond and graphite do have important differences (see Website 6 for a full description of the structures of these two allotropes). However, they do show an important similarity in that it is the relatively strong covalent bonds that need to be broken in both structures to melt or boil diamond and graphite so they have very high melting and boiling points.

4   *Simple atomic structures*, e.g. the Noble gases. These consist of single atoms which have weak van der Waals forces of attraction between the atoms so, like the simple molecular structures of nitrogen, oxygen and hydrogen, the Noble gases have low melting points and boiling points. The boiling point of Argon, for example, is $-185.8°C$ and it is a gas at room temperature.

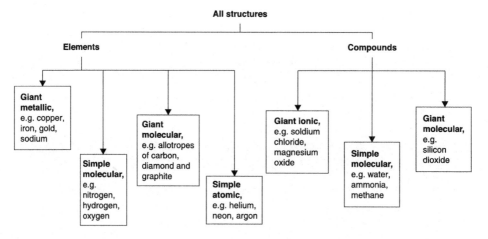

Figure 3.3.1 gives a summary of all these structures, and for more details on some of these structures, see Website 6.

Note in the descriptions of the structures above that the terms 'bond' and 'forces of attraction' have been used and these terms will be found in many school chemistry text-books used in very similar ways. However, they can cause confusion for students and pose a series of questions, for example: what is a chemical bond? What is a force of attraction? What is the difference, if at all, between a chemical bond and a force of attrac-tion? A detailed discussion of this issue is beyond the scope of this chapter but Taber's Chapter 1 (2002, pp. 6–8) and Chapter 8 (2002, pp. 125–6) look at these questions and consider in detail how, for example, the commonly used 'octet rule' or 'full shells explan-atory principle' can, if taken too far, lead to confusion and misconceptions when it comes to what constitutes a bond and can create a less than helpful distinction between a force of attraction and a bond.

CHEMICAL CHANGES

Types of chemical change

In the last section we looked at elements but have yet to say how they react to form compounds but also how compounds can react together to form new substances. Kind (2004, p. 23) talks about chemical changes occurring 'when atoms (or ions) in reactants are rearranged to form new substances'. Taber (2002, p. 141) says:

> The main defining characteristic of a chemical reaction is that it is a process where one or more new substances are formed, i.e.:

$$\text{Reactants} \longrightarrow \text{Products}$$

In a chemical change, bonds break in the reactants to form new substances called products where new bonds are formed. Reactions can be classified in different ways, so, for example, when the reactants such as an acid and alkali react to form the products salt and water, we can classify this as a neutralisation reaction. Other types of chemical reaction are precipitation reactions, redox reactions and thermal decomposition reactions and their names describe the key processes that are occurring in the reaction.

Chemical reactions can also be classified as exothermic or endothermic reactions. Exothermic reactions transfer energy to the surroundings which can be measured by a temperature increase in the surroundings. For example, in the chemical reaction between magnesium and oxygen, there is a transfer of energy to the surroundings and so this is said to be an exothermic reaction. Endothermic reactions have energy transferred to them from the surroundings so the temperature of the surroundings decreases. Examples of endothermic reactions are much less common but the reaction between ethanoic acid with sodium carbonate and photosynthesis in plants are both endothermic reactions.

Sodium carbonate + ethanoic acid ⟶ sodium ethanoate + carbon dioxide + water

Water + carbon dioxide ⟶ glucose + oxygen (photosynthesis)

Why do we get exothermic and endothermic reactions? Here we need to go from the macroscopic level of temperature changes in the surroundings to the molecular level and look at chemical bond breaking and formation. In any chemical reaction, energy is required to break the bonds between the atoms, ions or molecules in the reactants (an endothermic process). At the same time, energy is released when new bonds are formed in the reactants (an exothermic process). Therefore, in all chemical reactions both processes occur at the same time but it is the balance between the energy required to break the bonds and the energy released when new bonds are formed that determines *overall* if a chemical reaction is exothermic or endothermic. In exothermic reactions more energy is released in bond formation than is required to break bonds in reactants. Therefore overall energy is transferred to the surroundings and the temperature of the surrounding increases. In endothermic reactions, more energy is required to break bonds in the reactants than is released when new bonds are formed in the products. Therefore, overall energy is transferred from the surroundings to the reaction and the temperature of the surroundings decreases.

In chemistry, we can measure these energy changes and we call them enthalpy changes because they denote an energy change for a set number of particles. Working with a set number of particles is important in chemistry but it also presents challenges for students. For example, in everyday life when baking a cake, 250g of butter, 250g of sugar and 250g of flour, with a few eggs thrown in would be measured out. In this example the same mass of sugar, butter and flour are considered to be equivalent. However, imagine instead we wanted to buy a dozen (12) cherries and a dozen (12) oranges. Buying the same mass of cherries and oranges would not give the same number of cherries or oranges because, obviously, an orange has a much greater mass than a cherry. See Figure 3.3.2 to illustrate this point.

In chemistry, we have much the same issue. If, for example, we want the same number of aluminium atoms and gold atoms then we cannot weigh out the same masses of aluminium and gold because the mass number of an aluminium atom is 27 (13 protons and 14 neutrons) and the mass number of a gold atom 197 (79 protons and 118 neutrons). Therefore, gold atoms have much greater mass than aluminium atoms, much like an orange has a much greater mass than a cherry.

This issue is solved in chemistry by using a quantity called the mole as the basic unit of measurement to define the amounts of a chemical substance rather than using mass.

1 dozen cherries (number = 12)

Mass of one cherry = 7g
Mass of a dozen cherries = 84g

1 dozen oranges (number = 12)

Mass of one orange = 150g
Mass of a dozen oranges = 1800g

1 mole of aluminium (number = 6.023 × 10²³ atoms of aluminium)

Relative atomic mass of aluminium = 27
Mass of one mole of aluminium = 27g

1 mole of gold (number = 6.023 × 10²³ molecules of oxygen)

Relative atomic mass of gold = 197
Mass of one mole of gold = 197g

▪ **Figure 3.3.2** Relative atomic mass

The mole is defined as the amount of any substance that contains as many elementary entities (e.g. atoms, molecules, ions, electrons) as there are atoms in 12g of the carbon–12 isotope which has a relative atomic mass of 12. In a dozen, there are 12 'particles' but in a mole, because we are working at molecular level, there are approximately 6.023×10^{23} atoms in 12g of the carbon–12 isotope and this is called the Avogadro number. Thus, 1 mole of aluminium would have a mass of 27g and would contain 6.023×10^{23} atoms of aluminium, 1 mole of gold would have a mass of 197g and would contain 6.023×10^{23} atoms of gold. So although the masses of aluminium and gold are different, 27g and 197g respectively, the number of atoms, the Avogadro number, is the same and Figure 3.3.2 helps illustrate this point further. For a fuller discussion of the relationship between mass number and relative atomic mass, including a discussion of isotopes, see Websites 7(a), (b) and (c).

Then going back to our enthalpy example, having a set number of particles, i.e. the mole, then when 1 mole of methane (16g), containing 6.023×10^{23} molecules of methane, combusts completely in oxygen, it transfers 890KJ of energy to the surroundings and so it is an exothermic reaction and the temperature of the surroundings increases. The equation for this reaction is shown below and the enthalpy change which has the symbol ΔH is negative, −890, to show that this is an exothermic reaction and overall energy has been transferred, from the chemical system to the surroundings and so while the surroundings may have had energy transferred to them, the chemical system has 890KJ less energy for every mole of methane that combusts.

$$CH_4(g) + 2O_2(g) \longrightarrow CO_2(g) + 2H_2O(l) \; \Delta H \text{ is } -890\text{Kjmol}^{-1}$$

Rates of chemical change

Chemical changes go on all around us and vary considerably in how fast they occur. The reaction of magnesium and oxygen occurs very rapidly, superglue sets in seconds, a banana goes brown in minutes, jelly sets in a matter of hours, and geological processes such as the formation of metamorphic rock from sedimentary rock can take millions of years.

As chemists, we can speed up the rate of a chemical reaction in four ways:

1   *By increasing the concentration of particles in a reaction.* This can be done by making reactants in solution more concentrated or by increasing the pressure of gaseous reactants.
2   *By increasing the temperature of a reaction.*
3   *By increasing the surface area of solid reactants* so, for example, powdered calcium carbonate, which has a large surface area, will react much faster with hydrochloric acid than a solid lump of calcium carbonate of the same mass, which has a much smaller surface area.
4   *By adding a catalyst.* A catalyst is a chemical substance which speeds up chemical reactions but does not itself get used up. In biological systems biochemical reactions are also speeded up using catalysts called enzymes. For example, the decomposition of starch in the mouth is catalysed by the enzyme amylase.

To explain why, for example, increasing the concentration of reactants increases the reaction rate, it is again necessary to go to the molecular level and consider collision theory (see Website 8 for details). The collision theory states that for a reaction to occur, reactant particles have to collide. When, for example, gaseous reactants are under higher pressure, there is a greater density of gas particles per unit area and so the probability that the gas particles involved in the reaction will collide increases which increases the reaction rate (see Website 8, for a detailed discussion of collision theory and for the discussion of why increasing temperature, increasing the surface area of a solid and using a catalyst also speed up chemical reactions).

There are some interesting examples where the criteria indicated above become somewhat strange and different. For example, one would expect that chemical reactions in interstellar space, where it is very cold and the reacting particles are very far apart, might be very slow or nonexistent. But this is not necessarily the case and there is some fascinating chemistry in interstellar space which students will find interesting (see Website 9 and the cold chemistry resources under resources for schools).

Will it, won't it?

A final question chemists ask themselves in chemical change processes is whether a chemical change is feasible or not. In order to determine this, we need to know two things about a particular chemical change:

■   its standard enthalpy change;
■   its standard entropy change.

Entropy is an interesting concept – it measures the order/disorder of a system, and a system that is more disordered, where energy is more spread out, is a more stable system and so physical and chemical changes that tend to occur in a more disordered system, in the universe, are favoured ones. For example, there would be an increase in the entropy/ disorder of a system if a solid was heated to produce a gas. This is because in a solid, the particles are in a regular and ordered state and in a gas they are randomly distributed. Other examples where entropy increases would be where a solid dissolves in a solute, for example, sodium chloride in water.

An example of a decrease in the entropy of a system would be a reaction where two gases (for example, ammonia and hydrogen chloride) react to form a solid (ammonium chloride) as shown below:

$$NH_3 \text{ (g) and HCl (g)} \longrightarrow NH_4Cl(s)$$

Entropy is given the symbol S, standard entropy S° (linked to the number of moles) and a change in entropy is denoted by the symbol ΔS. Both the change in enthalpy (ΔH) and the change in entropy (ΔS) are important in deciding whether a physical or chemical change will take place when they are combined in an equation suggested in the nineteenth century by Josiah Willard Gibbs (1839–1903), which is shown below, whether the feasibility of a chemical reaction can be predicted:

$$G \text{ (free energy)} = H \text{ (enthalpy)} - (T \text{ (temperature/K)} \times S \text{ (entropy)})$$

$$G = H - TS$$

At constant temperature:

$$\Delta G = \Delta H - T\Delta S$$

For a spontaneous physical or chemical change to take place, there needs to be a decrease in free energy, i.e. ΔG must be negative. Looking at the equation then, an exothermic reaction (ΔH is negative) coupled with an increase in entropy (ΔS is positive) will give a highly negative ΔG and make the reaction feasible.

However, reactions can be feasible even for endothermic reactions where ΔH is positive if ΔS, the change in entropy is positive, i.e. the system becomes more disordered. An example of this is the dissolving of potassium chloride, which is endothermic, but this is counteracted by a large increase in entropy as the ordered solid becomes very disordered as it dissolves in water. Equally, a reaction could involve a large decrease in entropy but this could be counteracted by the reaction being exothermic. An example of this is the reaction between ammonia and hydrogen chloride which has a large decrease in entropy as discussed above but this is counteracted by it being an exothermic reaction.

STRUCTURE AND BONDING IN COMPOUNDS: MATERIALS, MATERIALS, MATERIALS

So far, we have considered elements and their grouping in the Periodic Table and also ways of grouping them according to their structures. We have also looked at elements and compounds reacting in chemical reactions and considered different types of chemical reactions, how fast they go, and if a chemical reaction will occur or not. We will now consider compounds in their own right.

Compounds are usually defined as materials where two or more elements are chemically combined. The macroscopic world of compounds, both those that occur naturally and those which have been made by humans, is complex and vast. How do we even begin to group compounds and make sense of them? Indeed, we now may be feeling that the grouping of the 92 naturally occurring elements was a simple job by comparison! Again, as with the elements, compounds can be grouped according to their structures, and we again move to the molecular level to both group and explain the properties of compounds.

Giant ionic structures

Ionic compounds (e.g. sodium chloride, NaCl) are giant structures of positive metal ions (e.g. sodium ions, Na^+) and negatively charged non-metal ions (e.g. chloride ions, Cl^-) held together by ionic bonds. Ionic bonds are the strong electrostatic forces of attraction between the oppositely charged positive and negative ions. Because the bonds between the ions are strong ionic compounds, they have high melting points and boiling points. The melting point of sodium chloride, for example, is 801°C (see Website 6 for more information).

Simple molecular structures

Examples of simple molecular structures which are compounds are water (H_2O), ammonia (NH_3) and methane (CH_4). The intramolecular bonds between the atoms in the molecules are covalent bonds, as we saw with the same structures in the elements, and the forces of attraction (or bonds) between molecules (intermolecular bonds) are again weak van der Waals forces of attraction. In melting and boiling, it is these weak intermolecular bonds that are broken and so these compounds have low melting points and boiling points. Water, for example, has a melting point of 0°C (see Website 6 for more information).

Giant molecular structures

The most common example of a compound with a giant covalent structure is silicon dioxide (SiO_2), a major component of sand. This giant structure of atoms of silicon and oxygen is held together by covalent bonds. It is the covalent bonds, which are strong that have to be broken to melt or boil silicon dioxide and so the silicon dioxide has a high melting point and a high boiling point. The melting point of silicon dioxide is 1600°C (see Website 6 for more information).

Figure 3.3.1 shows all the structures described for elements and compounds in this chapter. These have some similarities but also some important differences. For example, there are elements and compounds which have simple and giant molecular structures. However, *elements only* have metallic structures and *compounds only* have giant ionic structures. Both of these structures contain giant structures of ions, as we have seen, but metallic structures contain only one kind of ion, the metal ion, whereas ionic compounds contain positive metal ions and negative non-metal ions. The distinctions between metallic and ionic structures must be made because students can easily confuse them and think they are the same structure. A final difference between structures found in elements and compounds is the presence of simple atomic structures, e.g. the Noble gases. Why do you think compounds do not have simple atomic structures? Again, for all the structures, the questions raised earlier about what constitutes a chemical bond and the use of terminology like forces of attraction still applies and is an important issue which can be pursued further, as suggested above, in Taber (2002).

A final word on an incredibly important group of materials in the modern world which merit a special mention here, polymers and plastics such as polyethylene, polystyrene PVC (polyvinylchloride).These are part of the group of compounds that might well be grouped as having simple molecular structures – they are mostly compounds of carbon and hydrogen but with other atoms added in such as oxygen, nitrogen, chlorine and fluorine. However, there is a vast array of different polymers that have become a crucial part of our day-to-day lives and their structures take us beyond just describing them as simple molecular. Websites 10 and 11 begin to capture some of the different structural features of polymers and why they are so useful.

MATERIALS AND THE FUTURE

> Chemistry lies at the heart of much current and future technology. It is essential to the understanding of molecular biology, materials science, the environment, health-care developments, energy . . . Indeed, to all of the foundation stones upon which a modern industrial nation stands.
>
> (David Phillips, President of Royal Society of Chemistry, 2012, p. 3)

In summary, we have seen how chemistry has helped us group the vast macroscopic world of materials for example, in the Periodic Table or in terms of their structures. Chemistry can also classify chemical reactions into different types such as endothermic and exothermic reactions or as neutralisation or redox reactions. We have also seen how the molecular level can help provide explanations of why, for example, elements in the same group of the Periodic Table have similar physical and chemical properties, why some reactions are exothermic and some are endothermic, how increasing the pressure of gaseous reactants speeds up chemical reactions and why elements and compounds have different physical properties. But chemistry is an ever expanding world and new materials are constantly being made. In the media every day there are stories about how chemists are at the forefront of developing new materials and how they have very close links to other scientific disciplines as illustrated in the quote above by David Phillips.

We will now consider just a few examples of advances in materials science and links with other sciences. There are a whole group of *Smart materials* that have been designed to have one or more properties that change when there is a change in the external environment. For example, photochromic pigments have been synthesised which go darker when they are exposed to sunlight and so are used in sunglasses. Website 12 gives many more examples. Nanochemistry works at the atomic level and there are now a large number of nanomaterials, for example, fullerenes. Some fullerenes have tube-like structures and have been used as semi-conductors in electric circuits or, because they are exceptionally strong and light, they have been used to make tennis racquets. To find out more about nanochemistry and nanomaterials, see Websites 13 and 14. More recently, chemists have synthesised a group of compounds called nullomers which are biological molecules that can theoretically exist naturally but don't [and] have been shown to kill breast and cancer cells as well as those causing leukaemia, while sparing healthy cells and this development clearly has the potential to make a key contribution to healthcare. (Coughlan, 2012, p. 9)

Chemists have also synthesised materials known as phase change materials (PCM) which 'are attractive energy-savers because of their ability to absorb or release massive amounts of energy while maintaining a near-constant temperature' (McKenna, 2012, p. 17). These materials are hoped to be able to completely revolutionise energy storage and have a wide number of uses from warming bed rolls in the day, using cooking stoves to keep people warm at night or in keeping vaccines cool in developing countries, thus making key contributions to developments in energy conservation and to the environment. Finally, Miodownik (2013) describes how scientists have made material scaffolds out of synthetic materials which have been used to grow a new windpipe for a cancer patient. Chemists synthesise the scaffold and then implant it with the patient's mesenchymal stem cells taken from his/her bone marrow. The stem cells create a new windpipe and, as this is happening, the synthesised scaffold begins to dissolve and disappear. The really key issue then is that the new windpipe is made from the patient's own cells so they are not rejected by the patient and this development has the potential to make a significant contribution to transplant surgery.

Miodownik also gives an exciting vision of materials for the future and strays into the realms of science fiction when he says:

> There are living things which we call life and there are non-living things which we call rocks, buildings and so on. As a result of our greater understanding of matter, though, this distinction is likely to become blurred as we usher in a new era of materials. Bionic people with synthetic organs, bones and brains will be the norm.
>
> (2013, p. 246)

Chemistry and chemists are here to stay but their work is becoming even more varied and interconnected with important issues in the real world and with scientists from a wide range of disciplines!

REFERENCES

Coughlan, A. (2012) 'Unnatural molecules are cancer assassins', *New Scientist*, 2889.
Kind, V. (2004) *Beyond Appearances: Students' Misconceptions about Basic Chemical Ideas*, Royal Society of Chemistry. Available at: www.rsc.org/images/Misconceptions_update_tcm18–188603.pdf
McKenna, P. (2012) 'Melt buildings to save fuel', *New Scientist*, 2846.
Miodownik, M. (2013) *Stuff Matters: The Strange Stories of the Marvellous Materials That Shape Our Man-Made World*, London: Penguin.
Pais, A. (1986) *Inward Bound: Of Matter and Forces in the Physical World*, New York: Oxford University Press.
Phillips, D. (2012) 'Chemistry goes boom', *New Scientist*, 2848.
Taber, K. S. (2002) *Chemical Misconceptions: Prevention, Diagnosis and Cure*, vol. 1: *Theoretical Background*, London: Royal Society of Chemistry.
Warren, D. (2001) *Chemists in a Social and Historical Context*, London: Royal Society of Chemistry.

USEFUL WEBSITES

Website 1: www.powersof10.com/
Website 2: www.bbc.co.uk/schools/gcsebitesize/science/edexcel_pre_2011/patterns/periodictablerev4.shtml
Website 3: www.rsc.org/education/teachers/resources/periodictable/pre16/develop/mendeleev.htm

Website 4: Visual elements Periodic Table, Royal Society of Chemistry. www.rsc.org/periodic-table

Website 5: A flash animation by Mike Stanfill of Tom Lehrer's 'The Elements' song: www.privatehand.com/flash/elements.html

Website 6: www.bbc.co.uk/schools/gcsebitesize/science/add_aqa_pre_2011/atomic/differentsubrev1.shtml

Website 7:

    (a)   www.bbc.co.uk/schools/gcsebitesize/science/add_aqa_pre_2011/chemcalc/chemcalc_bothrev1.shtml

    (b)   www.bbc.co.uk/schools/gcsebitesize/science/add_aqa_pre_2011/chemcalc/chemcalc_bothrev2.shtml

    (c)   www.bbc.co.uk/schools/gcsebitesize/science/add_aqa_pre_2011/chemcalc/chemcalc_bothrev3.shtml

Website 8: www.bbc.co.uk/schools/gcsebitesize/science/add_ocr_pre_2011/chemical_synthesis/ratereactionrev3.shtml

Website 9: Oxford Sparks is Oxford University's online science portal to access exciting scientific developments at Oxford University. It has a section on teaching resources for schools with supporting animations: www.oxfordsparks.com

Website 10: www.bbc.co.uk/schools/gcsebitesize/science/aqa_pre_2011/oils/polymersrev1.shtml

Website 11: www.bbc.co.uk/schools/gcsebitesize/science/21c_pre_2011/materials/molecstructpropertiesrev3.shtml

Website 12: www.bbc.co.uk/schools/gcsebitesize/design/resistantmaterials/materialsmaterialsrev5.shtml

Website 13: www.bbc.co.uk/schools/gcsebitesize/science/add_gateway_pre_2011/chemical/nanochemistryrev2.shtml

Website 14: www.bbc.co.uk/schools/gcsebitesize/design/textiles/productiontechniquesrev6.shtml

Another useful website: www.rsc.org/learn-chemistry.

The Royal Society of Chemistry website that allows teachers to search for a wide variety of resources to teach chemistry in schools. (All websites accessed 2 February 2014).

PHYSICS AND ASTRONOMY

Steven Chapman

INTRODUCTION

When I mention the word 'Physics' to any group of people, they respond with a number of words, not all of them nice. Mainly, though, certain words (or their synonyms) like 'hard', or 'boring', or even 'boring' and 'hard' together top the list.

Yet as you read this chapter your hand provides just enough force to exactly support your book's (or e-reader's) weight. It does not bounce off your hand or pass through it to the floor. How is this possible?

Physics helps us understand not only why we don't fall through the floor, but also how the rest of the universe works. It helps explain everything from the very smallest sub-atomic particles to large clusters of galaxies. However, most children have little experience of particle theory and galactic evolution, but they do have experience of everyday phenomena and these are our gateway to improve their understanding of physics. Nevertheless, it is an arduous job. Physics is difficult to understand. It is also counter-intuitive and astounding at the same time, in the words of Carl Angell: 'Physics is frightful but fun' (Angell *et al.*, 2004, p. 684). Young people are both afraid of and fascinated by the Big Ideas of Physics.

What physics allows us to do is to join the everyday world to the strange world of particles, forces and energy using models and mathematics. In defining what physics is we need to think about both the Big Ideas that underpin all of physics and the topics that are taught at school. This is a key point, as a science teacher one needs to think about the difference between Science and *School* Science.

As a teacher of physics, whether you have a background in physics or not, it is important to realise that physics is not the same as other sciences; it has a different epistemology, a different rationale and a different way of thinking to biology and chemistry for example. Having said that, it is still a science, it is underpinned by a framework of ideas verified by experimental evidence. So before we go further, it is worth trying to answer an important question: What is physics?

OBJECTIVES

By the end of this unit, you should:

- ▪ be aware of the scope of Physics and Astronomy;
- ▪ have some insight into the unique ways of thinking in this area of science;
- ▪ have some idea where to get help on teaching Physics and Astronomy;
- ▪ be more confident to explore the area further.

WHAT IS PHYSICS?

In theory, we could say physics is the Science of Everything, however, trying to define very complex systems, like fluid transport in trees, or China's economy using exclusively physics is beyond our imagination and the computational power of even Douglas Adams' (2013) fictional super-computer *Deep Thought*. The *Oxford English Dictionary* defines physics as:

> The branch of science concerned with the nature and properties of non-living matter and energy, in so far as they are not dealt with by chemistry or biology; the science whose subject matter includes mechanics, heat, light and other radiation, sound, electricity, magnetism, gravity, the structure of atoms, the nature of subatomic particles, and the fundamental laws of the material universe. Also: the physical properties and phenomena of a thing.

This gargantuan definition (much longer than the equivalent ones for biology and chemistry) helps frame the problem in trying to answer what seems a straightforward question. Can we think about what elements make up physics? In the UK, the Institute of Physics (Main and Tracy, 2013) have tried to think about how to define physics and came up with a series of Big Ideas, based not on topics but on underpinning ideas. I think it is helpful to list these here:

- ▪ *Reductionism* – we can reduce physics to a few universal laws. In fact, the longer one studies physics, the fewer the ideas needed. Compare this with biology which gets more complicated as one studies it further.
- ▪ *Causality* – an event caused by a previous event never precedes that event.
- ▪ *Universality* – the laws of physics apply across the Whole Universe.
- ▪ *Mathematical modelling* – we can use calculations to predict what real objects and systems will do.
- ▪ *Conservation* – there are some things that do not get used up, like charge or energy.
- ▪ *Equilibrium* – how do things balance out?
- ▪ *Differences cause change* – how do things start moving, or heat up or cool down?
- ▪ *Dissipation and irreversibility* – the Second Law of Thermodynamics
- ▪ *Symmetry and broken symmetry* – crucial to all kinds of physics, like crystallography.

Now no examination specification or curriculum uses these terms very often, if at all, instead they break down physics into a series of topics. However, it is worth mentioning that the physics of familiar topics (forces and movement, for example) contains the ideas above.

Although physics has some common themes across its whole run, it is worth breaking them down into smaller subsets or topics. These groupings are my own and are used for convenience and relevance to schools. Physics, if nothing else, is a triumph of reductionism and many of the above topics could be grouped together into even fewer categories. However, I have made an attempt to do so below, by stating the kinds of questions that can be addressed by each topic.

Forces and fields

How do objects interact with each other? What effects do these forces have on each other? How can we characterise the effect mass and charge have on space? What is the relationship between work, energy and force?

The nature of matter

What is matter made of? How are the building blocks organised and catalogued? What interactions take place between them? How do the building blocks behave both individually and collectively? How is the microscopic world linked to the world we see around us?

Materials

What are the bulk properties of matter? How can we explain ideas about a material's physical properties in terms of its atomic structure and arrangement?

Electricity and magnetism

What happens when materials have charges? How do charges affect each other when they are stationary? What happens when they start moving? What happens when charges are moved? How can we get magnetic effects in materials and from moving charges? What happens when we interact a current with a magnetic field? What happens when we drive charges around wire loops? How can electricity shift energy from one place to another?

Electromagnetic radiation

How can a combination of electric and magnetic fields produce waves that transfer energy? How are the properties of these waves related to the size, frequency and energy of the waves? What do we use these waves for in everyday life, medicine and other areas of science?

Radioactivity

Why do some atoms break down by emitting particles or electromagnetic radiation? Why is it only certain particles are emitted? Why do large nuclei emit helium nuclei (alpha particles) and smaller ones high-speed electrons? Why do very large nuclei sometimes split in two and give out energy? Why can small nuclei sometimes combine to form larger atoms and also give out energy?

Energy transfer

What is energy? Where can it be stored? How can it be shifted from one place to another by particles, radiation, electric or mechanical work? Why is it that when we try and work out how much energy is in a system we always get the same number? How efficient are our energy transfers? How does heat transfer from a hot object to a cold? Why does heat go from hot to cold but not the other way around?

The Earth in space

How do everyday ideas like day, month, year or seasons relate to astronomical phenomena? What evidence is there that we live in a heliocentric solar system? What observations can we make in the classroom?

The universe

What are stars? How do they form? How do they die? What is their life cycle? What happens when you have groups of stars? How did the universe form? What evidence do we have for that? What tools do we have for observing the universe? Is there life elsewhere in the universe?

EXPLANATIONS AND MISCONCEPTIONS

As a teacher of physics, you will have to think not only about the correct science but about how to explain it to young people. This pedagogical content knowledge is crucial. Which explanations are helpful? What misconceptions do young people have about particular parts of physics? Which teaching approaches help deal with these misconceptions? What simplifications are used? Which models help link the unseen world to the world of observables? Some of the references at the end of the chapter help with this and work done by the Institute of Physics is available at www.talkphysics.org.

MODELLING

There are a number of models that help us begin to understand physics and it is sometimes helpful to think about how we use these to help us. Two important images in physics to help us imagine what the world is 'really' like and help us understand a range of phenomena are:

▓   *particles* (dust, molecules, atoms, electrons, protons, neutrons, quarks, photons . . .);
▓   *waves* (water, sound, earthquakes, radio, microwaves, infrared, light, ultraviolet, X-rays, γ-rays).

We can also use predictions with pencil and paper; for example $E = mc^2$ or Maxwell's equations.

In electricity, we need models to help us understand what is going on inside the wire and to make predictions about what circuits might do. While these may be useful, it is important to realise that these models have limitations and thinking about where they break down is as important to learning as when they are useful.

PHYSICS IS COUNTER-INTUITIVE

Often when teaching about forces, I throw a ball in the air and ask trainee teachers or pupils what forces are acting on it. This seemingly simple question exposes quite a lot about people's ideas about forces. Almost everyone (including many of those with a physics degree!) includes gravity and air resistance but also adds an upward pushing force from the hand, even though the hand is no longer touching the ball. Why do they do this? Well because the ball is moving upwards, they feel there must be a force pushing it upwards.

Of course, once the ball leaves my hand, that's the end of my involvement with the ball, I have no magic powers so I can't control it without touching it. This is difficult to understand and great minds like Aristotle struggled with this. Isaac Newton spent 12 years formulating his laws of motion, so why should a class of 15-year-olds completely get it after 45 minutes of your teaching? It's important to look at work done on misconceptions (see Driver *et al.*, 1994, for example) to anticipate and think about the right approach to take with teaching these tricky topics.

CONTEXTS

Are there real-life examples that help you explain the concepts? Are those contexts relevant to the young people you are working with? Contexts can help young people cement the concepts they have been working on. Picking a good context is a crucial skill. This involves the teacher trying to get inside the mind of a student.

Take forces, for example, if you are trying to think about the forces acting on a moving object, what would a good context be? Is a bicycle a better example than a jet aeroplane? After all, most young people have seen and ridden a bike but few have piloted a plane.

Are your contexts and examples alienating members of the class? Have you thought about how you might teach girls differently from boys? A great deal of work has been done on this, but it is still not effectively used in classrooms (see the guide in the references for some suggestions).

However, you can find contexts in even the most seemingly non-physics scenarios. When a pupil says that it's their birthday, for example, that means they have just completed another orbit of the Sun.

SUMMARY AND KEY POINTS

There are a couple of Big Things to bear in mind when teaching physics. The first is to be very honest about your own physics subject knowledge. Having to teach physics requires a very deep and secure understanding of a subject. As one graduate said to me recently: 'It wasn't until I started teaching that I realised that all the stuff I had done at university had just happened to me and now I really had to learn it.'

It is sometimes helpful to use a traffic light system:

RED: I have no idea what the answer is.
AMBER: I know the right answer, but I have no idea why it's the right answer.
GREEN: I get it

As an experienced teacher I never think I completely understand anything, rather I prefer to think that each year I have a slightly *lower* level of misunderstanding of physics.

NEXT STEPS

The suggested reading will help you, as will trying problems on the BBC Bitesize website. However, you might like to try the explanations in the following task. If you are feeling confident you might like to try explaining some at both the macroscopic and microscopic level.

Task 3.4.1 **Questions**

1 Why does a satellite stay in orbit and not fall to Earth if gravity is the only force acting on it?
2 Where do stars go during the day?
3 What is the difference between being radioactive and being irradiated?
4 How do we know how far away the Sun is?

REFERENCES

Angell, C., Guttersrud, O., Henriksen, E.K. and Isnes, A. (2004) 'Physics: frightful, but fun', *Science and Education*, 88(5): 684–706.

Driver, R., Squires, A., Rushworth, P. and Wood-Robinson, V. (1994) *Making Sense of Secondary Science: Research into Children's Ideas*, London: Routledge.

Institute of Physics, *Girls in the Physics Classroom: A Teachers' Guide for Action*, Bristol: IOPP. Available at: www.iop.org/education/teacher/support/girls_physics/action/file_41603.pdf (accessed 1 March 2014).

Main, P. and Tracy, C. (2013) 'Defining physics', *Physics World*, April, pp. 17–18.

FURTHER READING

Adams, S. and Allday, J. (2013) *Advanced Physics*, Oxford: Oxford University Press.

Sang, D. (ed.) (2011) *ASE Science Practice Teaching Secondary Physics*, London: Hodder Education.

USEFUL WEBSITES

www.bbc.co.uk/bitesize/
www.practicalphysics.org
www.stellarium.org
www.talkphysics.org
http://tap.iop.org
(All websites accessed 1 March 2014.)

EARTH AND ATMOSPHERIC SCIENCE

Paul Davies

INTRODUCTION

Within the curriculum, Earth science deals with a broad range of ideas concerning the structure and composition of the Earth. These include its origins, physical features and the changes that take place through time. It is also concerned with the origin and evolution of the atmosphere and, in particular, changes that are currently taking place.

Earth science was once the domain of Geography, or more specifically Geology, but as much of this curriculum area has become more human-focused and, as in the case of Geology, disappeared, it has moved into the realm of science. However, Earth science does not slot 'neatly' into the curriculum areas of Biology, Chemistry and Physics; this should not be seen as a threat but an exciting teaching and learning opportunity because, unlike many other curriculum areas, Earth science lends itself easily to cross-science, and cross-curricular ways of thinking. For example, consider what knowledge you would need to draw on to explain the presence of marine fossils in the rocks five miles above sea level that form the peak of Mount Everest. This question requires some knowledge of palaeontology (the study of fossils), the physics of the movement of land masses and an appreciation of the chemistry of the rocks that contain the fossil remains; it also draws on the history of science as it seeks to explain the significance of this understanding in terms of human culture.

Although for many people, rocks are thought to be solid materials which do not change, we know that they are recycled and modified through processes that occur only a few miles below our feet. An examination of a rock tells you something of its history, and who has not been amazed by the site of a volcano spewing liquid rock hundreds of metres into the air?

OBJECTIVES

By the end of this unit, you should:

- be aware of the scope of Earth science across different science subjects;
- understand how human activity affects the atmosphere and water sources;

■ be able to give some examples of how humans can prevent and reduce environmental damage;

■ be confident to explore these areas further.

THE STRUCTURE OF THE EARTH

Finding out about the structure of the Earth is not easy. Geologists gather data to answer this question from two important sources: seismic surveys and the examination of volcanoes. When earthquakes happen, two different types of waves called p-waves and s-waves pass through the Earth over long distances and their analysis allows geologists to determine the nature of the material deep below the Earth's surface. Sometimes, instead of waiting for an unpredictable earthquake, geologists carry out controlled explosions in specially dug shafts which also help them understand the nature of the rocks nearer to the surface.

Examination of the molten (liquid) rock, called lava that explodes out of volcanoes during volcanic eruptions also helps geologists to make sense of the ways that rocks are recycled and modified through time. The data from these analyses has allowed geologists to build, with some confidence, a model of the interior of the Earth (Figure 3.5.1).

The Earth's structure is divided into four layers and the surface that we stand on is the crust. The upper mantle is, on average, 100 km thick and is thinner beneath the ocean compared to dry land. It can be divided into two distinct layers: the lithosphere (*litho*

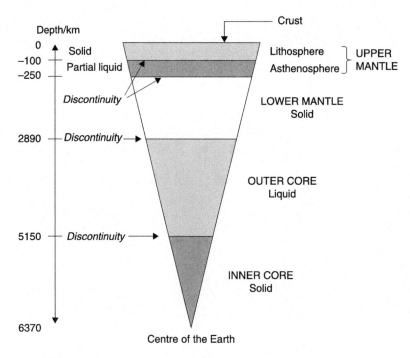

■ **Figure 3.5.1** Segment through the Earth showing rock layers

meaning 'stone'), which is solid rock and the asthenosphere (astheno, from *asthenia*, meaning 'weak'), which is mainly composed of solid rock but some molten rock as well. Below this layer, the solid lower mantle is about 2500 km thick and surrounds the equally thick liquid outer core. The molten rock contains liquid iron, the movement of which many scientists believe to be the source of the Earth's magnetic field, though this is disputed by some. Below the outer core is the solid inner core.

TYPES OF ROCK

Rocks are composed of minerals. Some rocks are made of only one type of mineral, for example, marble (calcite), while others are composed of a mixture of different minerals. It is the minerals and the conditions in which the rocks were formed that give them their particular characteristics, for example, colour, crystal structure and patterning. Studying the chemical and physical properties of rocks reveals much about the minerals that they contain and how they were formed. For example, the sizes of the crystals found in granite, a rock formed from cooling magma, give clues to how quickly it was formed. Geologists use a range of tests when they are investigating rocks from very simple visual inspection using a hand lens, to careful chemical analysis in a laboratory.

Sorting rocks into groups uses principles of classification, an important tool in many aspects of science. In the simplest system, rocks can be divided into three main groups called igneous, sedimentary and metamorphic; the groups are determined by the way that the rock was formed, see Table 3.5.1.

Igneous rock is formed from molten rock that has cooled and solidified; the rate of cooling determines the crystal size. For example, granite is formed when magma cools down very slowly, often over thousands of years, maybe in underground chambers; this produces large crystals in granite, as they have time to grow. In contrast, gabbro is formed when lava quickly cools down and, consequently, has very small crystals. Although normally very hard, some igneous rocks are unusual, for example, pumice, formed when lava cools down very rapidly as it flies through the air from erupting volcanoes, is full of air pockets and powdery in nature. Often being hard, igneous rock is typically used where hard-wearing surfaces are needed, e.g., kitchen table tops and paving.

Sedimentary rocks are the most common on the Earth's surface and show considerable variation in appearance. They sometimes contain the impressions of dead organism (fossils) and are formed from the eroded fragments of other rock types. Sometimes living things give rise to sedimentary rocks, for example, chalk (calcium carbonate) is very often formed from parts of microscopic sea organisms including forminifera, ostracods and molluscs, while coal is formed from dead plants. Other sedimentary rocks have

■ **Table 3.5.1** Details of rock types, formation and physical characteristics

Rock type	How formed	Physical characteristics
Igneous	Cooling and solidification of molten rock	Interlocking crystals
Sedimentary	Cementing of sediment that has been deposited in bodies of water	Grains and small particles cemented together
Metamorphic	Modification of igneous or sedimentary rock, through heat and/or pressure	Often smooth and hard with swirling patterns in layers (called foliation)

inorganic origins, for example, mudstone and sandstone. Sedimentary rocks have many important uses, for example, their softness often means they are easy to carve, so they are often used for buildings and especially when intricate designs are called for, such as the gargoyles found on cathedrals. Calcium carbonate is an extremely important raw material in the cement industry, glass production and iron extraction.

Metamorphic rocks are always formed through the recycling of other rocks. High temperatures and pressures deep in the Earth provide the conditions to modify rock by baking and squeezing. These conditions often change the chemistry of the rock and so new rock is formed. For example, when heated and squeezed, limestone becomes marble; while under great pressure mudstone becomes slate. Metamorphic rocks are normally very hard and often aesthetically appealing. For these reasons they are typically used for decorative purposes, such as statues or the interiors of important buildings.

The following task requires you to investigate how different types of rock are used in, and around your school. You may find it helpful to read Unit 5.6 before completing the task.

Task 3.5.1 **Investigating how different types of rock are used in, and around your school**

1 Walk around the inside and outside of your school and make a list of the different rock types you find and their uses. Think about why the rock has been chosen for its particular function. You may like to take photographs to record what you have observed.

2 Use the information you have gathered to plan and design a short 'learning trail' for pupils. This should be designed to encourage pupils to examine the different rock types in their school and make links between the type of rock and its use. To do this, design some questions that you could ask at each 'stop' on the trail, e.g., What does the rock look like? What is the rock being used for? You could design it like a treasure hunt or game.

3 If possible, try your trail out with pupils; this could be something you do as part of a Science Club. If you are not able to do this, share your plan with other student teachers and ask for their feedback.

Rocks are constantly being modified and changed; this process is described in the rock cycle (Figure 3.5.2). Over hundreds of thousands of years rocks become weathered by changes in temperature, the wind and chemical and biological attack which results in small fragments breaking off. These are then carried by wind and rivers where they are further broken down and eroded. The fragments may eventually settle in water and slowly form into layers. Eventually the layers become so thick that their weight squashes the particles together and they become cemented to form sedimentary rock. Great movements in the upper mantle then move these rocks around, perhaps pushing up into high mountains or forcing them deep into the Earth's interior where they are heated and squeezed, and so may form metamorphic rock. If they remain molten, they may eventually reach the Earth's surface through a volcano or cracks in the crust and cool to form igneous rock. It is important to notice that the rock cycle is actually made up of a number

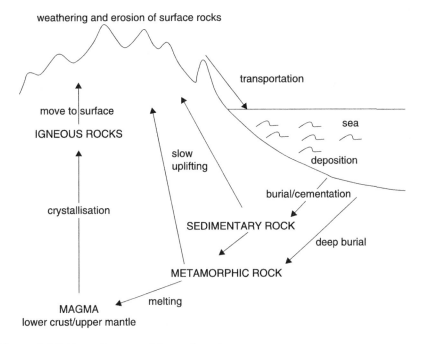

■ **Figure 3.5.2** Some features of the rock cycle

of smaller cycles, rather than a simple cycle which moves through a series of stages to return to the start. Geologists know about the stages of the rock cycle through careful chemical and physical analysis of rocks, as well as direct evidence, for example, observing lava from a volcano cooling down, and from indirect evidence such as finding fossils of marine organisms in rocks now forming dry land.

PRODUCTS FROM ROCKS: THE EXAMPLE OF CALCIUM CARBONATE

Calcium carbonate ($CaCO_3$) is an important raw material for many useful products and is obtained from limestone. As well as being a useful building material in its own right, for example, much of St Paul's Cathedral in London is made of limestone blocks, it is also used in the production of cement which, when mixed with water, sand and crushed rock, forms concrete – arguably the most important building material of the past 100 years.

To become useful, calcium carbonate must first be heated to form calcium oxide (CaO), also known as quicklime. When reacted with water, calcium oxide forms a new product called calcium hydroxide ($Ca(OH)_2$) or slaked lime. Slaked lime can be used to produce mortar; when it reacts with carbon dioxide in the air, it forms calcium carbonate again, which is hard and can be used to stick blocks of rock and bricks together. This technology is ancient, and was understood by the Egyptians around 6000 years ago and used in the construction of the pyramids. In the eighteenth century a discovery was made that if limestone is heated with clay, it forms a very hard and waterproof material we now call cement.

Limestone is quarried out of the ground, an environmentally damaging activity. Not only does the quarrying industry involve large, noisy machinery and vehicles; the largest reserves of limestone in the UK are found in some of the most unspoilt and beautiful land-scapes. One of the largest limestone quarries is near Buxton in the Peak District National Park, an area of outstanding natural beauty and popular with tourists. The decision to build a quarry here was not an easy one and there are still frequent demonstrations surrounding the continuation of quarrying in the park. This is an example of a socio-scientific issues (see Unit 5.4).

FOSSILS

Fossils are the remains of living things that are found in rocks. Sometimes these remains become impregnated with minerals from the surrounding rocks and in doing so, become rock themselves; dinosaur bones are typical of these types of fossils. Other fossils are much less modified and have a composition much more similar to that found when the organism was alive, for example, 'ice mummy' fossils and those preserved in tar pits. Sometimes organisms leave behind a record of their activity, for example, footprints, which then become fossilised; these are called trace fossils. The most famous trace fossils are the Laetoli footprints in Tanzania, which were formed by the oldest known hominid around 3.6 million years ago.

Fossils are very important to provide both correlation among different rock layers and evidence about past environments. For example, excavations at Trafalgar Square revealed that 150,000 years ago, central London was covered in a mixed mosaic of forest and grassland, populated with animals we now find in central Africa, for example, hippopot-amus, lion and an extinct type of elephant.

TECTONIC PLATE THEORY

It seems almost unbelievable now but, until the mid-1960s, there was no consensus among geologists to explain some of the massive changes that are observed in the rocks on the Earth's surface; for example: How it is that mountains are formed from sedi-mentary rocks that were deposited in the sea? What causes the massive earth movements that lead to earthquakes? In the mid-1960s, J. T. Wilson, along with others, developed a theory to explain these observations. Like many theories that appear very straightforward, an important aspect of his 'Tectonic Plate Theory' was that it had far-reaching explan-atory powers. The theory, which is now fully accepted in both the geology and wider scientific communities, states that the Earth's crust is made up of large plates which carry the continents and the ocean floor. As Figure 3.5.3 shows, there are six major continental plates, though there are lots of small ones too. These plates sit on the solid lithosphere and move around because of forces below the lithosphere. These movements cause the plates to collide with one another or, sometimes force one deeper in the Earth while the other rides above. Where these plates collide, we often observe geological activity, for example, earthquakes and volcanoes (see Further Reading and Useful Websites for more informa-tion and further resources related to Tectonic Plate Theory).

Understanding how the plates actually move around is not straightforward but it is best explained through convection currents in the hot asthenosphere. Here the molten rock slowly rises, and then cools which pulls the lithosphere, on which the plates rest, along with it. The movements of the plates are very small (about 2–3 cm per annum) but, over long periods of time, these small changes have given rise to mountains, such as the Himalayas, and account for the devastating power of huge earthquakes, for example, the

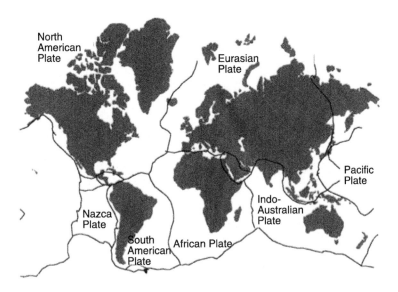

■ **Figure 3.5.3** Map of the Earth showing plate boundaries

2004 earthquake in the Indian Ocean near Sumatra which caused the huge tsunami wave, resulting in the deaths of over 200,000 people.

Understanding the Tectonic Plate Theory requires skills associated with the Working Scientifically strand of the Science section of the National Curriculum and is a good example of how evidence is used to develop scientific theories.

There are five compelling pieces of evidence that support the Tectonic Plate Theory:

1   examination of a map of the continents shows them to fit together like a jigsaw and that at one time they formed a large land mass called Pangea (see Figure 3.5.4);
2   the same rock strata and patterns are observed in rock formation in different continents, this is called stratigraphic data;
3   similar fossils are found on different continents, in the same stratigraphic areas, this is called biostratigraphic data;
4   the alignment of magnetic particles on either side of mid-ocean ridges, formed as the continents drift apart;
5   the patterns of volcanoes, especially where they form islands on the plate boundaries.

GEOLOGICAL TIME

The Earth is thought to be around 4.6 billion years old. Understanding geological time periods, often called 'deep time', is an essential element of Earth science but is very difficult for humans to think in this way. A useful way of considering geological time is to divide the time since the Earth was formed into a calendar year; doing this we see that modern humans appeared just a few minutes before midnight on 31 December (see Useful Websites for further resources related to understanding geological time).

▨ **Figure 3.5.4** Arrangement of continental plates around 300 million years ago showing the supercontinent Pangea

To make it easier to understand, and so that geologists have a 'common language' geological time is divided in eons, which themselves can be separated into era, which are, in turn, formed from periods (Table 3.5.2). The different episodes are identified through a combination of the layers of rock (or strata) that are characteristic of the episodes; for example, the rocks of the Carboniferous period are dominated by coal while the Cretaceous period is characterised by rocks rich in calcium carbonate. Fossils are also used to date rocks and assign them to specific geological episodes. Doing this on one fossil type can be problematic and a matter of controversy for palaeontologists. However, groups of fossils, called assemblages, provide much more convincing evidence. Some good examples are the end of the Triassic Period being marked by the disappearance of non-avian dinosaurs, as well as lots of other taxa. The names of the geological episodes often arise from places in the world where rocks characteristic of a particular episode are common, for example, the rocks common to the Cambrian Period are very abundant in Wales, the ancient name for which is *Cambria*.

Assigning time periods to geological episodes is not straightforward but two methods are commonly used: those which give absolute dates and those providing relative dates. Radiometric dating, which relies on the constant rate of half-life decay of certain radio-active elements such as uranium, provides accurate absolute dates of even the oldest rocks. More modern rocks can be dated through radio-carbon dating; this relies on the

■ **Table 3.5.2** Geological eons, eras and periods

Eon	Era	Date (mya)	Periods	Origin of name: feature or place
Pre-Cambrian (now divided into several eons)	See websites for details	Beginning of universe 4500–545		
Phanerozoic	Palaeozoic (Ancient life)	542–251	Cambrian	Wales (old name Cambria)
			Ordovician	Ordovicas – ancient Welsh tribe
			Silurian	Silures – ancient British tribe
			Devonian	Devon
			Carboniferous	Coal-bearing
			Permian	Perm – Russian area
	Mesozoic (Middle life)	251–65	Triassic	'Three layers' outcrop in Germany
			Jurassic	Jura Mountains
			Cretaceous	Chalk
	Cenozoic (Recent life)	65–present	Paleogene (Tertiary)	Birth of distant past
			Neogene (Tertiary)	'New born'
			Quaternary	Fourth age after Tertiary period

same methods as other radiometric dating, through comparison between different isotopes of the element. Radio-carbon dating is particularly useful for dating organic material, for example, fossil remains, and yields data which are much more repeatable than the methods used to date older rocks (see Useful Websites for details of simulations that support understanding radiometric dating).

THE CHANGING ATMOSPHERE

Understanding how the Earth's atmosphere has changed is not easy, but by examination of gases trapped in some of the oldest rocks on the planet, and by investigating the atmosphere of other planets in our solar systems, scientists have started to reconstruct a history of how the atmosphere has evolved. At the start of its 4.6 billion-year history, the Earth was a molten ball of rock and minerals and for around a billion years was covered in volcanoes. As well as releasing lava, the volcanoes released carbon dioxide, water vapour and nitrogen which formed the early atmosphere. As the Earth cooled down, the water vapour condensed and fell as rain, forming the first oceans. The early atmosphere also contained large amounts of methane and no oxygen, very like the atmosphere on the planet Mars today.

Life first appeared around 3.4 billion years ago in the form of bacteria which were able to harness the methane in the atmosphere to provide a source of energy. Some of these bacteria evolved to be able to carry out photosynthesis and, together with early types of algae, began removing large amounts of carbon dioxide and releasing large quantities of oxygen into the atmosphere. Since then the atmosphere has gradually changed so that by about 200 million years ago, it formed the composition with which we are now familiar (78 per cent nitrogen, 21 per cent oxygen, 0.9 per cent argon, 0.04 per cent carbon dioxide and trace amounts of other gases).

Coupled with the changes in the atmosphere were changes in the Earth's mean temperature. This was sometimes brought about through the composition of gases in the atmosphere trapping more heat. For example, during the Carboniferous period, around 300 million years ago, it was slightly hotter, and much more humid than it is today, conditions which promoted the growth of huge forests over much of the planet. Some changes in temperature are not related to the composition of the atmosphere but caused by slight variations in the tilt of the Earth on its axis and orbit around the Sun. These variations drive ice ages – periods characterised by a cycle of cold periods (glacials) and warm periods (interglacials). The last glacial period ended around 20,000 years ago and we are now in the middle of an interglacial.

These variations in temperature have been happening throughout Earth's history, and occur over huge periods of geological time. However, the current changes in climate we are experiencing – often called global warming (but, more correctly climate change) – is happening much more rapidly and is related to human behaviour (often termed anthropogenic climate change). Although the proportion of carbon dioxide in the atmosphere is small (0.04 per cent), this is increasing very quickly; additional carbon dioxide is coming mainly from when humans burn fossil fuels, an important feature of all industrialised countries. In addition, humans release large amounts of other atmospheric pollutants, including carbon monoxide, sulfur dioxide, methane, oxides of nitrogen and chloro

▨ **Table 3.5.3** Details of common atmospheric pollutants showing their anthropogenic source and environmental effects

Pollutant	Sources	Environmental effect
Carbon dioxide	▨ Combustion of fossil fuels used in industrial processes and vehicles ▨ Deforestation	Increase in global temperature
Carbon monoxide	▨ Incomplete combustion of fossil fuels	Increase in global temperature through chemical reactions that increase methane concentration
Chlorofluorocarbon	▨ Refrigeration systems	Damage to ozone layer and increase in global temperature
Methane	▨ Intensive farming of livestock ▨ Paddy rice farming	Increase in global temperature
Nitrogen oxides	▨ Agrochemicals, especially fertilisers	Increase in global temperature
Ozone	▨ Precursors formed from the combustion of fossils	Increase in global temperature
Particulates	▨ Combustion of fossil fuels	Increase in global temperature
Sulfur dioxide	▨ Combustion of fossil fuels	Acidification of rainwater

fluorocarbons (CFCs), some of which also contribute to increasing global temperatures; details of these pollutants are shown in Table 3.5.3.

When hydrocarbon fuels, such as oil and coal are burnt, carbon dioxide is produced, along with new hydrocarbons and nitrogen oxides. The increase of these gases in the atmosphere correlates with rapid increases in global temperatures. World-wide temperatures have increased by about 0.4°C during the last 140 years, the most rapid increase happening in the past 60 years (see Figure 3.5.5), and is predicted to increase by around 6°C by the year 2100.

Investigating the changing climate draws together scientists from different backgrounds. Some of the evidence that they examine is collected indirectly, for example records of average annual temperatures in different parts of the world, while others use proxy data. These are data sources which are used to *infer* changes in the temperature, for example:

- tree-ring samples which show when plants were growing faster (periods of higher temperature) and more slowly (periods of lower temperature);
- ice cores which have bubbles of oxygen gas trapped in them. The ratio of these different oxygen isotopes present can be used to determine temperature variation.
- marine corals which show different growth patterns, similar to tree-rings, depending upon the water temperature;
- pollen analysis which allows palaeobotanists to determine how plant distribution has changed as global temperatures have increased.

These data show that in recent history, over the past 1000 years, the Earth's temperature shows slight fluctuations in the mean global temperature. However, there has been a rapid increase in the mean temperature since 1860, the period when major parts of the world underwent their industrial revolutions. During this period, the concentration of carbon dioxide has increased by around 32 per cent, methane by 133 per cent and nitrous

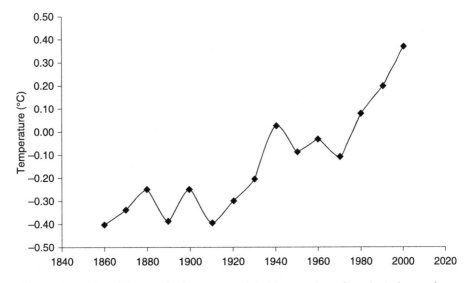

■ **Figure 3.5.5** The difference in the average global temperature, for selected years from 1860–2000, from the average global temperature in the period 1961–90

oxide by 16 per cent. These increases are closely correlated with the increase in global temperature.

The evidence for climate change does not rely solely on temperature changes but other, observable data:

- melting of polar ice caps, particularly sea-ice and mountain glaciers;
- changes in climate, for example, more 'extreme' weather such as unseasonal temperature fluctuations and rainfall;
- thawing of the permafrost layer;
- changes in the duration of growing seasons;
- early onset of flowering and animals coming out of hibernation;
- changes in migration patterns of animals.

The effects of climate change can be specific to different regions, and, in some cases beneficial. For example, in the UK, we have an extended growing season as well as the ability to grow crops that would normally be confined to Mediterranean countries. Of course, while beneficial to humans, there are often problems associated with introducing non-native plants for both the native plants and animals. However, set against the possible benefits, it is generally agreed that climate change is causing – and is set to cause – catastrophic problems for both humans and other living things. Examples of these are:

- raised sea levels which will cover lower-lying land or increase the salinity of the soil through more frequent flooding. This is a particular problem as deltas and land close to sea level are often very agriculturally rich.
- changing patterns in disease-causing insects, for both humans and non-human animals. For example the *Anopheles* mosquito which carries malaria is extending its current range.
- reduction in water supplies, particularly in areas which are already prone to periods of drought.

Further details about the effects of climate change can be found in Further Reading.

MECHANISMS OF CLIMATE CHANGE

The Earth receives radiation from the Sun, some of which is absorbed, while the rest is re-radiated out into space, the net result of which provides the average global temperature. The most important radiation responsible for increasing the temperature the Earth is infra-red, and it is radiation of this wavelength that is also re-radiated back out into space.

Water vapour in the atmosphere is essential to maintain a global temperature that supports life; without its presence, the Earth would be much cooler. Humans have little effect on the amount of water in the atmosphere, though they do interfere with the recycling of water (the water cycle, see below) through some of their activities. However, carbon dioxide, methane and oxides of nitrogen also contribute to the 'trapping' of radiation and prevent some of it escaping out into space. This is the so-called greenhouse effect (though different from the way that real greenhouses work) and the result is that the Earth's temperature increases.

The increase in global temperatures is becoming more rapid, and is now thought to be becoming self-sustaining primarily because, being white, snow was effectively reflecting much of the solar radiation. However, now much of this snow has melted from glaciers and the polar ice-caps, this is no longer happening and the radiation is absorbed by the dark-coloured underlying rock.

REDUCING CLIMATE CHANGE

The role of greenhouse gases in climate change is becoming better understood and almost all scientists agree that their increase in the atmosphere is causal with increased global temperatures. There is also general agreement about the important problems that the increase in global temperatures will bring, in terms of humanitarian crises, environmental disasters and economic breakdown. If climate change is to be slowed down, then the emission of greenhouse gases, particularly from industrial processes and transport must be reduced. However, like many aspects of pollution, this is not straightforward, first, because the effect of pollution caused by a particular country is not restricted to only that country, and, second, because it demands that developing countries that are currently undergoing their industrial revolution seek alternatives to carbon-based fuels: something which is expensive and will mean their development will be curtailed.

There are two major ways in which the concentration of greenhouse gases in the atmosphere can be reduced:

■ reduction in their production and release;
■ capture and removal from the atmosphere.

Reducing the amount of carbon dioxide that is released means reducing activities such as burning fossil fuels and changing farming practices, as well as changing our personal behaviour with relation to recycling and energy use. Governments can encourage these shifts through monetary incentives and penalties but it also requires a shift in perspectives about the relationship between humans and the planet and a worldwide initiative with countries working together and helping one another. This is both an exciting prospect and something which could help unite countries, but is also a major challenge (see Further Reading for details on how the UK Government is addressing some of these issues).

Carbon is naturally recycled in the environment through a series of processes described as the carbon cycle where it is exchanged between organic and inorganic forms. Carbon dioxide in the atmosphere is 'fixed' into organic forms (initially carbohydrate) through producers carrying out photosynthesis; it is then either released back into the atmosphere as the carbohydrates used in respiration, or it is trapped in carbon 'sinks'. This trapped carbon exists in the wood in trees, or in the formation of fossil fuels, where it can be released back into the atmosphere through burning. Another important sink is where carbon dioxide is dissolved in the oceans, and becomes incorporated into the shells of some marine organisms in the form of calcium carbonate.

Humans have also developed ways to capture carbon from when fossil fuels are burnt; this is most effectively carried out where the carbon dioxide is produced (at source). In post-combustion capture, the most commonly used method employs scrubbers that are situated in chimneys. Here amines react with the carbon dioxide, a process which can later be reversed, allowing the carbon dioxide to be transported elsewhere and the amines recycled for continued use in the scrubber. In other methods the carbon dioxide is streamed away for transportation. Once transported, the carbon dioxide must then be stored. There has been some success in injecting carbon dioxide into geological forma-tion, for example, oil fields or into rocks with high concentrations of minerals with which the carbon dioxide reacts. These storage methods can be problematic though, because of the risk of leakage. Increasingly, biological methods are being used to remove carbon dioxide directly from the atmosphere. The most successful of these involves using unicel-lular algae to trap the carbon dioxide as they carry out photosynthesis. The scale needed to make these 'algal farms' viable is massive, but advances in technology mean this is becoming an important method to lower the atmospheric concentration of carbon dioxide.

SUPPLYING POTABLE WATER

Water is essential for life and one of the key characteristics that we look for on other planets when considering life in other parts of the universe. A compound of an oxygen atom and two hydrogen atoms, hydrogen oxide exists as solid ice, liquid water and gaseous vapour, states with which we come into contact every day. The chemistry of water is complex but here we are concerned with its recycling and role in maintenance of life.

Water is recycled in the 'water cycle'. This involves a series of processes where water changes state through evaporation and condensation and freezing and, sometimes boiling, and moves between different parts of the atmosphere and the Earth's surface. This process involves both living and non-living things. Within the cycle are water stores, for example, oceans and snow in the polar regions where water may be trapped for long periods, meaning it is unhelpful to think of the recycling happening to all molecules at the same time. Describing the cycle in detail is beyond the scope of this book (for detailed discus-sions, see Further Reading). However, of particular importance is how water becomes available for human consumption.

Water that is safe enough for humans to drink is called potable. In this form it provides hydration, as well as essential elements, for example in the form of compounds of zinc, calcium and sodium. Water for drinking is obtained from a variety of sources:

▨   ground source, such as groundwater and aquifers;
▨   precipitation, including rain, snow, hail and fog;
▨   surface water, such as rivers and glaciers;
▨   biological sources from food;
▨   oceans through the removal of salt (desalination);
▨   the water supply network.

Unprocessed water can contain suspended solids, for example, clay particles, disease-causing organisms (pathogens), or organisms that carry disease (disease vectors) and pollutants, making it dangerous for human consumption. Obtaining a reliable supply of clean, safe drinking water is a major challenge for many developing countries where currently 780 million people live without any regular access to safe drinking water. The importance cannot be over-stated: every year hundreds of thousands of children under the age of 5 die in Sub-Saharan African countries because of dehydration caused by diarrhoea because of unsafe drinking water. Most industrialised nations use water supply networks to provide clean water through taps. The infrastructure needed to supply this is complex and extremely costly to set up and maintain. Typically water will be drawn from a ground source and then filtered, both physically, for example, through carbon filters, and chem-ically, to remove particulates. Chlorine and other disinfectants are added to kill pathogens and then the water is pumped to homes through underground pipes. Wastewater is then carried away from its point of use via sewer systems. From here it is taken to treatment works where bacteria are used to decompose organic material, for example, faeces, and chlorine is added before the water is safe to return to the distribution network.

THE FLUORIDATION OF WATER

In many parts of the world, as part of public health, fluoride is added to drinking water. This is normally accomplished through the addition of either sodium fluoride, fluorosilicic acid or sodium fluorosilicate. These compounds are both very soluble and cheap, making fluoridation a straightforward process. The presence of fluoride in the water helps prevent tooth decay because its helps suppress the production of saliva which, in turn, reduces the rate at which the tooth enamel surface is eroded.

The addition of fluoride to drinking water has been a great success in reducing the occurrence of tooth decay in both children and adults by around 40 per cent. The addition of fluoride to drinking water has not been readily accepted by everyone, however, both within the scientific community and in the wider population and is therefore a controversial issue. A small number of scientists deny its benefits to dental health, though this view is supported by very little scientific evidence. Some environmental groups are concerned about the possible harm that fluoride may cause to other living things. At present though there is no evidence that the presence of fluoride causes any environmental problems but research in this area is on-going. A particularly interesting issue surrounding the fluoridation of drinking water is that some people argue that it violates individual rights and that people should have greater choice over whether or not to drink water where fluoride has been purposefully added. On the other hand, there is an argument that, due to the benefits to health, it is unethical not to add fluoride to water and that to do so is a breach of rights. The arguments surrounding this issue are representative of the wider issues of socio-scientific issues which teachers of science are expected to address (see Unit 5.4), where the consideration of evidence and of individual versus public rights and responsibilities are central.

Task 3.5.2 requires you to consider opportunities to explore the themes of Earth and atmospheric science across the three sciences, as well as the wider curriculum.

Task 3.5.2 **Cross-science subjects and cross-curricular opportunities for teaching Earth and atmospheric science**

1 Look through the National Curriculum for Key Stages 3 and 4 (see Unit 2.1) sections of Earth Science and make a list of where in biology, chemistry and physics the key ideas are most obviously situated.
2 Discuss your findings with science teachers and find out which parts of Earth science they teach at KS4 and when this happens throughout the course. Does the sequencing of the teaching make sense in terms of the building up, and linking of ideas?
3 Discuss how Earth science is taught in the Geography department at your school and look for links with what is taught in science, particularly at KS3. Are there ways these links would be strengthened for pupils?

SUMMARY AND KEY POINTS

This unit has outlined the scope of Earth science and, in doing so, highlights the links that exist within biology, chemistry and physics within this topic. The structure of the Earth and the recycling of rocks have been considered, together with the formation of fossils and their importance in understanding the nature of the changes that have taken place throughout Earth's history. The Tectonic Plate Theory has provided a good example of how evidence is used in science to explain observations and the way that the accumulation of this over time can cause major changes in the way that the scientific community considers knowledge.

The unit has also considered changes that have taken place in the Earth's atmosphere and the significant role that humans play in altering its composition and the effects that this has on increasing global temperatures. Finally, it has introduced the importance of potable water and some of the processes that are used to provide safe drinking water; some of which are controversial.

FURTHER READING

Bates, B., Kundzewicz, Z. W., Wu, S. and Palutikof, J. (2008) *Climate Change and Water*, Geneva: Intergovernmental Panel on Climate Change (IPCC).

An academic book which looks at the effect of climate change on the hydrological cycle. It is an excellent resource for background information about potable water.

Clemitshaw, K. C. (2011) 'Measurement of air pollutants in the troposphere', *School Science Review*, 93(343): 59–65.

A readable article describing the principles and applications of methods used to measure air pollutants.

Flannery, T. F. (2006) *The Weather Makers: How Man Is Changing the Climate and What It Means for Life on Earth*. London: Grove Press.

A very readable account of climate change science. The sections on how climate change affects living things are useful for both Earth science and aspects of biology.

Francek, M. (2013) 'A compilation and review of over 500 geoscience misconceptions', *International Journal of Science Education*, 35(1): 31–64.
Frances, P. and Dise, N. (1997) *Atmosphere, Earth and Life*, Milton Keynes: Open University Press.

A book which provides a detailed account of Earth's changing atmosphere. It has an excellent section on the evidence for the evolution of the atmosphere.

Fries-Gaither, J. (2008) 'Common misconceptions about weathering, erosion, volcanoes, and earthquakes', in *Earth's Changing Surface*. Available at: http://beyondpenguins.nsdl.org/issue/column (accessed 6 February 2014).
Houghton, J. T. (2001) *Climate Change 2001: The Scientific Basis*, Third Assessment Report of the Intergovernmental Panel on Climate Change, Cambridge: Cambridge University Press.

Still an important work explaining in detail the evidence for climate change and our understanding of predictive models.

Intergovernment Panel on Climate Change (IPCC) (2013) *Fifth Assessment Report*. Available at: www.ipcc.ch/pdf/ar5/ar5-outline-compilation.pdf (accessed 6 February 2014).

King, C., Fleming, A., Kennett, P and Thompson, D. (2005) 'How effectively do science textbooks teach Earth science?' *School Science Review*, 87(318): 95104.

A useful review of how best to approach explaining Earth science in the classroom.

Rogers, N., Blake, S., Burton, K., Widdowson, M., Parkinson, I. and Harris, N. (2008) *An Introduction to Our Dynamic Planet*, Cambridge: Cambridge University Press.

A detailed resource explaining all aspects of geology with excellent information on volcanoes and tectonic plate theory.

School Science Review (2012) special issue, Earth Science. vol. 94.

A special issue of *School Science Review* with lots of information for teachers for Earth science.

Taylor, F.W. (2010) *Planetary Atmospheres*, Oxford: Oxford University Press.

Provides information on the atmospheres of planets in our solar system, a good resource for making comparisons between Earth and the other planets.

USEFUL WEBSITES

Earthquake patterns and tectonic plate distribution: www.earthquakes.bgs.ac.uk/ (accessed 6 February 2014).

Earth Science Teachers Association (ESTA): www.esta-uk.net/ (accessed 6 February 2014). *Life on Earth* **first episode showing the 'calendar' of life on Earth**: www.youtube.com/watch?v=HStl89NXdHQ
    The first episode from the BBC series *Life on Earth* where David Attenborough explains the arrival of important groups of living things through geological time using a 12-month calendar (accessed 6 February 2014).

Peck, D. The rock identification key: www.rockhounds.com/rockshop/rockkey/index.html~ate (accessed 6 February 2014).

Two excellent simulations that allow you to investigate radio dating and half-life are:

Radiodating activity: www.acad.carleton.edu/curricular/BIOL/classes/bio302/pages/half-life.html (accessed 6 February 2014).

Radioactive dating game: http://phet.colorado.edu/en/simulation/radioactive-dating-game (accessed 6 February 2014).

UNICEF 'Water, sanitation and hygiene': www.unicef.org/wash/ (accessed 6 February 2014).
    A detailed website that explores the impact of clean water on people's lives.

WHO/UNICEF Joint Monitoring Programme (JMP) for Water Supply and Sanitation: www.wssinfo.org/ (accessed 6 February 2014).
    The official website of the World Health Organisation and the UNICEF programme for future water supply.

PLANNING FOR TEACHING AND LEARNING SCIENCE

INTRODUCTION

Planning sequences of lessons, and individual lessons within those sequences is a complex activity: there are many variables to consider. This may appear rather daunting at first but does become easier with practice and some basic guidelines can make the process less problematic. Lesson planning needs to be carefully thought out and thought through and as a result, takes time. Be very wary of anyone who tries to suggest otherwise. It is a time-consuming process because of the many variables that need to be taken into consideration if you are to make the learning in the lesson an engaging, effective and worthwhile activity for all pupils. It is worth keeping in mind that it is pupils' learning that is the most important aspect of a lesson and that teaching is a way of effecting this learning. Although 'teaching and learning' is the usual phrase, it should probably be 'learning and teaching' as this puts an emphasis on learning as a priority.

There are numerous terms used in the teaching and learning process such as progression, differentiation, continuity and evaluation. These are addressed in the following Units. Although a single lesson may appear to be an important milestone at first, it is where, why and how this lesson is situated in a sequence of lessons on a topic that is an important aspect of planning that should not be overlooked. This places lesson planning within the perspective of medium and longer-term planning and is where the National Curriculum, examination specifications and a school's scheme of work play a part. However, it should not be forgotten that these cannot replace the need to plan a lesson and this planning involves the individual teacher's decisions about how an aspect of science is taught – and taught in a creative and engaging way.

UNIT 4.1

PLANNING FOR PROGRESSION IN SCIENCE

Ralph Levinson

INTRODUCTION

What is unique to learning science is that the learner comes across strange ideas that defy experiences of everyday life and common sense. Invisible charges drift through wires, invisible forces hold matter together, the massive trunks of oak trees are made up of building blocks that come predominantly from the apparently immaterial air, balls moving upwards have only a downward force acting on them, the invisible products of a combustion engine have a greater mass than the petrol that is burned, electrical impulses constantly surge through our body. Electrons, atoms, cells, fields, neurones are the invisible or microscopic stuff of nature. Osmosis, entropy change, and radiation are some of the processes that have to become real so that they have an explanatory power. Pupils can only start to understand these things if they are constructed on the back of experience and knowledge they already possess.

Progression 'describes the personal journey an individual pupil makes in moving through the educational system' (Asoko and Squires, 1998, p. 175). To understand how pupils' learning of science is structured, you need to understand progression. But what is involved in this personal journey? Do pupils move from simple to more complex ideas? Is there a pattern in the way all pupils progress which might help us organise their learning more systematically? How personal is the journey – what is the role of teachers? This chapter attempts to address these questions and to identify ways in which you can help pupils progress in their understanding of science.

OBJECTIVES

By the end of this unit, you should:

- be able to describe examples of progression;
- be aware of the complexity of progression;
- start planning for progression;
- identify the kinds of activities that enable progression.

DESCRIBING PROGRESSION

Imagine a 2-year-old at bath time playing with bath toys. Playing is hopefully a pleasurable experience for this infant though she is unlikely to make any distinction between toys which float and those which sink. Even if an adult intervenes and tries to draw the child's attention to these distinctions, they are likely to go unremarked. When the child is a little older, say, 4 or 5, she starts to categorise objects by certain properties, such as shape, size, colour, soft and hard. She begins to notice that shells, coins and pebbles sink to the bottom of the bath but other objects like polystyrene toys don't, even if they are pushed down – they bob back up to the surface. This might prompt the child, possibly with the support of a helpful older person, to see what happens when a further range of objects are dropped into the water, all of which might be characterised as 'floaters' or 'sinkers'. Once the child has had a range of experiences and has been able to talk about them, she might be able to generalise that 'sinkers' have attributes different from those of 'floaters' and to predict what happens when an object is dropped in water. According to the experiences from which the child generalises, 'sinkers' might be heavy, hard, compact, lacking air. It does not matter at this stage whether these generalisations are correct or not; the point about generalisations is that there are exceptions which might prompt the child to rethink the basis of her reasoning. Contradictions, for example, a hard heavy object like a boat that floats, might generate further trials either in the bathtub or, by this time, at primary school. The child might see what happens when she tries to submerge in water a bottle filled with air and then filled with water.

By this time the child's earlier generalisations are becoming refined, and through guided observations, the data collected is more directed. She begins to test certain things out, for example, to find out what happens when the bottle is half-filled with water. As well as being able to predict with some accuracy whether objects float or sink, she might notice now that water seems able to 'push up' on an object. She develops a language, with support, where the scientific meanings are very specific, that an object *weighs* less in water than it does in air, that there are *forces* acting on the object, that the upward force acting on the object is called *upthrust*. She begins to test whether the same objects float or sink when placed in different liquids and asks why some objects which sink in fresh water float in salty water. To test her ideas, she begins to make measurements, to use equipment to make the measurements (for example, a measuring cylinder to find out the volume occupied by the object in water), to record her data, make inferences and test these inferences further.

Of course, this is an idealised case. We have assumed that all the ideas follow on one from another, that the child does have baths in her early years, and has bath toys (some only have showers or don't always have the time to play), and that there's a helpful older other person who intervenes appropriately and knows the right kinds of questions to ask. Some children may have very particular experiences, interest in boats, for example, from an early age, while others might not have seen natural watercourses. Whatever the child's circumstances, the elaboration of one idea depends on an earlier idea. For example, a child cannot generalise about floating and sinking until she can recognise the difference and has thought about explanations for the differences. Children may go through these stages at different times and at different rates but the point is that all children go through the earlier stages. What we have described is progression, the child's developing ability to make increasing sense of the world, in this case, floating and sinking. This developing ability can be mapped through a number of different routes:

- an increasing sophistication of explanations, from the everyday to using scientific explanations (these objects float while these sink to how ships float when they weigh thousands of tonnes). This also includes argumentation in using relevant data and warrants to support claims (Simon and Maloney, 2007).
- moving from hands-on activities in familiar situations to applying ideas in less familiar contexts (observing things floating and sinking in a bath to testing ideas using laboratory equipment such as a measuring cylinder or 'Eureka' can);
- terminology becomes more precise and scientific ('water seems to be pushing on my hand' to 'water is exerting a force on my hand and my hand is exerting a force on the water');
- moving from qualitative to quantitative explanations (these objects float, these objects float in liquids above a certain density);
- developing practical and mathematical skills to underpin understanding.
- developing procedural skills (making simple observations, planning experiments to test hypotheses, using models as ideas).

Task 4.1.1 **Describing progression in different topics**

Find another context or topic, for example, photosynthesis, chemical reactions or light. Map the main stages in progression from Key Stage 1 to Key Stage 5 using about four main stages. For example, the more detailed account about floating and sinking above can be mapped:

Some objects float, others sink.
Light objects seem to float while heavy objects sink.
Objects denser than water sink, objects which are less dense float.
Whether objects float or sink depends on whether the force acting downwards is greater than the force acting upwards.

THEORISING PROGRESSION

From the previous section you would have a sense of progression of a moving forward from simple everyday ideas to more complex situations or to contexts requiring abstract concepts to explain them. Progression in all these situations may require the use of new scientific terminology and procedural concepts. But as a teacher you need to know how to enable and recognise this progression. Progression presupposes development, i.e. that, with maturity, the child can assimilate more experiences. Piaget produced the most widely recognised explanation of cognitive development as development through a number of age-related stages. In these stages knowledge is actively generated as the learner explores her world. In the first years of life the child understands the world through her senses and moves on to begin to categorise and describe objects through their characteristics. These first stages are known as the sensory-motor and pre-operational stages, respectively (see Burton, 2009) and correspond to the child's playing followed by categorising and classifying as described for floating and sinking in the previous section.

Two further stages were recognised by Piaget: the concrete operational and the formal operational. As the child moves from the stage of concrete operations to formal operations, she moves from a manipulation (both mental and physical) of specific experience to generalising and to logical, mathematical reasoning about events not seen. For example, pupils working at the concrete operational stage may be able to measure the time period of a pendulum and show that it is dependent on the length of the pendulum; the longer the pendulum, the slower the time period. If presented with the challenge of finding the effect of length and mass of the bob of a pendulum on the time period, pupils unaided may not be able to separate and control the two variables until they are working at the stage of formal operations. Furthermore, until they have progressed to this higher stage, they may not recognise the shortcomings of their approach and the validity, or otherwise, of their conclusions.

Piaget argued that children progress from one stage to the next as they encounter cognitive conflict and have to assimilate new explanatory models and more complex thinking. Although Donaldson has pointed to problems in Piaget's theory – because research shows that children can manipulate more complex variables than Piaget originally supposed – this was not a repudiation of the basis of general stage theory (Donaldson, 1978). (It is worth noting that there have been cogent critiques of the basis of developmental psychology from social constructivist (O'Loughlin, 1992) and feminist perspectives (Burman, 2008).) Intelligible and fruitful learning experiences assist this progression (Posner et al., 1982), hence the teacher has to be aware of the appropriate point to present material and explanations which will advance understanding.

The picture so far is one of the child constructing knowledge of the world about her with occasional facilitation by the teacher. However, the child lives in, and partakes of, a social world in which she is interpreting diverse forms of communication, mainly through talk (Vygotsky, 1978). The child, her peers and teachers generate meanings by interpreting what is said and co-construct new meanings together. The teacher, responding to detailed knowledge of the child's cognitive and social development, presents learning experiences which are beyond what the child already understands but gives enough support to move on to a 'higher rung of the ladder', a process teachers call 'scaffolding'. For further discussion of scaffolding, see Wood (1998).

A third explanatory model is that of the child as information processor. The mind acts to transform the information it receives but care needs to be paid to the capacity of the processor at any one time. Information overload inhibits learning and too little information results in lack of stimulation. Knowledge of how much information the child can process is crucial to effective teaching and learning (Kempa, 1992; Burton, 2009).

All three models of learning come under what is broadly termed 'constructivist' theory, because the learners are seen as actively constructing their knowledge. In the UK, there have been two particular developments in teaching related to progression in science based on constructivist theory:(1) the Children's Learning in Science Project (CLISP); and (2) the Cognitive Acceleration in Science project (CASE). The Children's Learning in Science Project takes as its basic assumption that many children have conceptions about scientific phenomena that are different from the scientifically accepted explanations (Driver et al., 1994). Thus, for example, younger children and some older children think that when you add a substance to a beaker of water and the substance dissolves, the mass of the beaker and water stays the same, clearly contravening the principle of the conservation of mass. You can't see it so it's not there. Many examples of children's everyday thinking have been identified, and a few are given below:

■ Heavier objects fall faster than light ones.
■ Electric current is used up as it passes through a circuit.

■ Whales are fish.
■ Plants get all their food from the soil.
■ When fossil fuels burn, there is no product.

Research into children's conceptions about scientific phenomena began in the 1980s, largely influenced by research work in New Zealand (Osborne and Freyberg, 1985). Since then, many articles have been written about children's explanations of events across the science curriculum. These explanations have been termed 'prior conceptions', 'misconceptions' or 'alternative frameworks' according to the viewpoint of the author. 'Prior conceptions' suggest that children have conceptions about nature before they are inducted into the accepted framework of science. 'Misconceptions' implies that children's ideas are often mistaken and need challenging and changing as they begin to understand correct scientific explanations. When children have 'alternative frameworks', the emphasis is that children have another way of explaining the world that is coherent to them and that science is another explanatory framework.

If children do have conceptions that do not accord with the accepted scientific explanation, how can teachers help them to understand something that challenges their way of thinking, particularly when many scientific explanations are counter-intuitive? Under normal circumstances we do not see the gases produced when fuels burn, so how can they be recognised as products? When an object rests on a table, how can the table be pushing up with an equal and opposite force? A table is a static object which doesn't appear to be doing anything, let alone exerting a force when an object is put on it. A whale lives in the sea and looks like a fish, so it is a fish. Mammals are hairy and live on land. It just doesn't make sense to say a whale is a mammal.

The challenge for the CLISP project was to provide a strategy, based on constructivist principles, which allows teachers to support pupils through these transitions in their thinking. To plan the learning tasks it is important to know what ideas pupils do have and how dissimilar they are to the accepted scientific ideas. Much of this information can now be accessed from the literature but the starting point is to provide opportunities for pupils to make their own ideas explicit (Driver *et al.*, 1985). Two stages are involved when children make their ideas explicit; the first is 'orientation' – setting the scene – where pupils are given stimulus material relating to the topic, recording what they already know; the next is to induce cognitive conflict by introducing students to discrepant events which may promote 'restructuring' of ideas. In doing so, the teacher is promoting in the learner an awareness that there is a difference between their ideas and the scientific idea and that there is a strategy for bridging the difference. Socratic questioning can be used where the teacher helps pupils to identify inconsistencies in their thinking. The last stage is that pupils try out these new ideas in a variety of contexts involving 'application' of ideas and they finally 'review' what they have learned. This strategy is by no means watertight because pupils have experiences which are consistent with their common-sense thinking and teachers are often exasperated to learn that pupils repeat their original conceptions when there was every reason to suppose they had assimilated the new scientific ideas. Think about the way people often say 'close the door or you'll let the cold in' rather than 'close the door otherwise the temperature gradient will mean that there will be a flow of heat from indoors to outdoors'. Everyday language is not very well suited to school science concepts. That is why these ideas are periodically revisited in different contexts. An example of this type of strategy is discussed in Task 4.1.2.

Task 4.1.2 **Understanding conservation of matter**

Context

Pupils are given a situation in which they are asked to choose between two possible explanations of an event, see Figure 4.1.1. In Figure 4.1.1 pupils have to decide whether the mass of the system changes or remains the same. This situation provides orientation by introducing a context and provides the second stage, elicitation, by asking questions. The third stage provides a situation where pupils are asked to carry out tasks which may challenge their preconceptions.

Your task

Go through this problem yourself identifying:

- concepts pupils might already hold (Driver *et al.*, 1994; Driver *et al.*, 1985);
- the scientifically acceptable conception;
- how the tasks might help restructure pupils' thinking about the topic;
- how you might run this activity in a Key Stage 3 classroom.

The CASE project has the aim of helping pupils to progress faster in their thinking skills by promoting cognitive conflict and through reflecting on their own thinking. The theoretical model for CASE is based on the learning theories of both Piaget and Vygotsky (see Burton, 2009). As we have seen in Piaget's work, children move through a sequence of stages as their understanding about the world develops. In Piaget's model, the child interacts with the environment where new stimuli are *assimilated* into the child's mental model. Where the child's cognitive structure has expanded so she becomes aware of discrepancies, there is cognitive conflict and the cognitive structure shifts to *accommodate* the new stimuli. The processes of assimilation and accommodation are intrinsic to Piaget's theory. For Vygotsky, the role of a peer or teacher (whom he calls an 'other') is crucial in enabling a child to complete a task successfully. Here the teacher becomes a

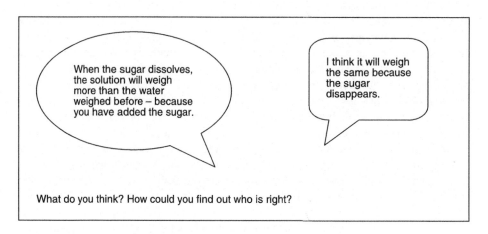

Figure 4.1.1 An orientation exercise

mediator in framing the task in such a way that the learner can make the necessary jump to success.

The CASE materials are based on the 'five pillar teaching model', which are stages in enabling progression (Adey and Yates, 2001). These pillars are:

1   *Concrete preparation*: pupils become familiar with the practical context of the task and the relevant terminology. The teacher and pupils develop a shared language through questioning and group work.
2   *Cognitive conflict*: pupils are led towards observations which occasion surprise and do not meet their expectations. The conditions have to be right for cognitive conflict to occur. Some children may simply not be ready for it, very able children may be able to assimilate and accommodate new observations with relative ease.
3   *Construction*: the pupil actively puts bits of information together to build new knowledge and make it her own.
4   *Metacognition*: the pupil not only solves a problem but can articulate how it was solved and can therefore use their thinking skills much more flexibly.
5   *Bridging*: applying the skills they have learned to a variety of contexts, for examples of bridging strategies, see Shayer and Gamble (2001).

Activities across all five stages encourage children towards formal operational thinking through such characteristic reasoning programmes as classification, probability, control of variables, equilibrium, and proportionality. The CASE project is aimed at developing scientific reasoning skills. Although CASE uses content and context to realise its objectives, the approach is not specifically designed to widen factual knowledge. Pupils may move more quickly through the Piagetian stages as a result of exposure to CASE activities but not all pupils may reach the level of formal operational thinking, or jump stages, such as from pre-operational thinking to formal operational thinking. Research shows that progress through CASE activities transfers across to progress in other subjects such as English and mathematics (Adey and Shayer, 1994).

As well as the main cognitive elements in progression, you should take into consideration other factors that may influence progression:

■   Pupils have different motivations.
■   Pupils learn in different ways.
■   Pupils learn at different rates.
■   Pupils have had different experiences.
■   Pupils have different language skills to help them.
■   Pupils have different emotional responses to the topic.

PLANNING FOR PROGRESSION

To support progression in learning in all your pupils, you should consider the following points:

1   What is it that you want the pupils to know, understand and do, i.e. to have learned, in this topic by the end of the course, module or lesson?
2   What is it that the pupils know, understand and can do at the start of the topic?

3   What sequence of learning activities will help pupils progress from their present understanding to the objective?
4   How will you know when pupils have reached where you want them to go?
5   Remember that pupils are individuals and will need a range of strategies to support learning.

One way to think about planning for progression is to consider points 1–5 in turn.

What do you want pupils to learn? Learning objectives and outcomes

What you want pupils to have learned by the end of an activity, lesson or topic is known as the learning objective. An objective at Key Stage 3, for example, could be 'pupils understand that chemical reactions can either be exothermic or endothermic' or 'pupils know how flowers help a plant to reproduce'. But stating objectives in this way begs a further question: How do you, as the teacher, *know* when pupils have achieved these objectives? How can you *tell* a pupil knows or understands something? To answer these questions, the pupils have to provide evidence of their understanding or knowledge. You need 'doing' words that describe this evidence, for example, 'sort these reactions into exothermic and endothermic', 'label the male and female parts of the flower', 'explain the differences between exothermic and endothermic reactions', 'draw what happens when pollen travels from one flower to another'. Statements like these are called learning outcomes, i.e. objectives that can be assessed. Outcomes contain terms like: *explain, design a poster, sort out, discuss, interpret, use the model to show (use the particle model to show the differences between solids and liquids).* Finding out if pupils do understand the differences between exothermic and endothermic reactions means they could do the following:

■   describe what happens in terms of temperature change in exothermic and endothermic reactions;
■   complete schematic diagrams showing where heat is being gained and lost;
■   interpret data from an experiment to show that a reaction is exothermic or endothermic;
■   identify the thermicity of a reaction from an energy diagram;
■   suggest ways of finding out how exothermic or endothermic a reaction is.

Most outcomes and objectives will only be partly achieved. Pupil A may answer a homework question by describing an exothermic reaction as one that gives out heat and an endothermic reaction as one that takes in heat. Pupil B might respond thus:

Exothermic reactions such as the burning of a candle and the reaction of magnesium with acid lose heat to the surroundings. We can tell it is an exothermic reaction because the temperature of the surroundings rises as a result of the reaction. If we put a thermometer in the reaction mixture of magnesium and acid, the temperature rises until the reaction is complete.

Clearly, pupil B has been able to meet the outcome more precisely than pupil A. You could therefore help pupil A to progress by giving a short exercise to help them identify instances of exothermic reactions and see if they can report what happens in terms of temperature change (see Unit 6.1 Assessment for Learning: A Formative Approach). Pupil B's answer can be superseded by pupil C's answer, who relates the temperature change to particle motion. Thus, there are opportunities for progression within a particular outcome.

Some teachers identify several levels of learning outcomes to cater for different levels of achievement in the class. They might state their outcomes as follows:

- All pupils will be able to recall that heat is lost to the surroundings in exothermic reactions and that heat is gained from the surroundings in endothermic reactions.
- Some pupils will be able to identify exothermic and endothermic reactions and to state what happens to the surrounding temperatures.
- A few pupils will be able to translate energy diagrams into exothermic and endothermic reactions.

Task 4.1.3 **Identifying three learning outcomes for one objective**

Take the following objectives and break each one down into three outcomes, i.e. what all, some and a few pupils can do:

1 Plan an investigation to find out the best anti-acid remedy.
2 Understand that light can travel through a vacuum but sound cannot.
3 Know that habitats support a variety of plants and animals that are interdependent.

What is it that pupils know, understand and can do at the start of the topic?

To help pupils to meet learning objectives you must have some idea of where the pupils are starting from. There are at least two reasons for this: first, pupils may have done much of the topic before and may become bored going over old ground. Second, you may assume knowledge which the pupils don't have, and if this is the case, they may become quickly disaffected. Of course, pupils won't all be starting from the same point, so you need a means of finding out what pupils do and don't know before starting a topic. The list below gives guidance on how you can find the relevant information:

1   Pupils ought to have covered something of the topic at Key Stages 1 and 2 if you are starting at Key Stage 3. Starting at Key Stage 4, there ought to have been some coverage at Key Stages 2 and 3. Find out from the National Curriculum what they are likely to have covered.
2   Ask more experienced teachers who can tell you about the kinds of things pupils know well and what gaps in knowledge to look out for.
3   Acquaint yourself with the literature on children's ideas (Driver *et al.*, 1985; Driver *et al.*, 1994) so you can anticipate ideas pupils may have on the topic.

4   Use diagnostic tasks and starter activities to find out what pupils know. These activities can be given at the beginning of a topic. They should be:

1   short;
2   easy to administer;
3   engaging for the pupils;
4   able to give you the information you want;
5   quick to mark.

What sequence of learning activities helps pupils to progress from their present understanding to the next learning objective?

Starter activities and diagnostic tasks not only tell you what pupils already know and don't know, they also reveal a wide range of understandings within the classroom. The instruction and learning opportunities you give pupils within the lesson must then have two characteristics:

1   They must offer sufficient challenge for all the pupils.
2   They must allow the pupils to develop scientific ideas, skills, terminology, etc. (this is likely to involve active instruction).

Whether you are teaching in a setted, streamed or mixed-ability class, there are always differences in knowledge and understanding, though the range of knowledge and understanding may be (but not necessarily) narrower in a streamed or setted class. Differences need not necessarily be vertical, i.e. one pupil knows more than another; they may simply be different and have knowledge in different types of context. Because all pupils are different, there is a tendency to think that the best way out would be to give each pupil individualised work. This approach is clearly impossible and probably undesirable; pupils can learn from each other, so devising activities for them which encourage discussion and exchange of ideas assists progression.

You need to ensure that you are starting from the appropriate level for those pupils who have clear misconceptions and that you are setting a sufficient challenge for those pupils who have clear understandings. Most departments have a bank of activities which you can adapt for your own purposes. You can support the lower attainers by giving them guided help. Suppose you ask pupils to explain how condensation appears on the outside of a cold, stoppered conical flask, which contains ice (a can taken out of the fridge rapidly gains condensation). Some pupils say that the water seeped through the flask. You might want to help them by showing them a flask containing water where condensation doesn't appear on the outside of the flask, or dyeing the ice red and demonstrating that the water on the outside is colourless.

Don't expect pupils to accept your explanations immediately because you are challenging beliefs they might hold quite strongly. When pupils come to realise that the explanations they have held up to now contradict new explanations which they are beginning to own intellectually, we call this situation cognitive conflict. Resolution of this cognitive conflict can take some time and needs reinforcement; this is why you need to revisit concepts and widen experience. Some pupils will need help to reinforce the concept to help them progress. For others, you will need to ensure that they have sufficient challenge.

Pupils are progressing through the topic but there are opportunities at various stages for reinforcement for some pupils and extra challenge for others.

Teachers rightly want to ensure that all their pupils are challenged but it is important not to be too ambitious and to devise too many activities. As a starting point, try the approaches listed below:

1   For each idea taught, devise three or four distinct activities, all of which underpin the understanding of the idea. For example, one activity might involve a short practical exercise such as finding out how quickly different liquids evaporate, another discussing a concept cartoon, a third answering questions on a short written piece and finally analysing a piece of data from a website.
2   Devise an activity which all pupils can do but at different levels. For example, it might be answering questions on a piece of data, or a short extract from a video, where successive questions become more demanding.
3   Ask pupils to plan an investigation where you set different demands.

Task 4.1.4 **Planning differentiated investigations**

If we take the example of evaporation, the following tasks could be set:

1 Find out the order in which four liquids evaporate. You will need a measuring cylinder, a stopwatch and an evaporating basin. Start off with the same volume of each liquid.
2 Plan an experiment to show how the surface area of a liquid influences the rate of evaporation.
3 Devise an experiment to find out if there is a relationship between particle size and rate of evaporation of a liquid.

Devise a set of similar graded investigations for the topic of seedling growth, electrical circuits or acids and bases.

How will you know when pupils have reached where you want them to go?

Pupils provide evidence of outcomes in the work they produce such as written exercises, drawings and analysis of practical work, but much of pupils' understanding is ephemeral, captured quickly in off-the-cuff remarks or contributing something to a discussion when they are not aware of being watched. It is important for the progress of individual pupils that you are able to record the necessary information. While you cannot record the progress in a single lesson of each and every pupil, focus on a sample of three pupils for each lesson and make any notes on points that they appear to have understood or that they find difficulty with. An example of how you can do this is given in Table 4.1.1. These notes should then be transferred to the register where you keep pupils' records.

Self-assessment is another way in which pupils can keep a record of their own progress. When the teacher makes explicit to pupils the stages in their learning, the pupils can

▣ **Table 4.1.1** Keeping notes of pupils' progress: context: comparing the rates of marble chips dissolving in acid

	Group 1 John, Paul and Mary	Group 2 Laura, Pamjit and Anwar
Making predictions	Paul could with reasons. John and Mary struggled.	Laura/Pamjit, good predictions but not sure why.
Devising procedure	All gave good response, but John not sure why.	Laura and Pamjit OK. Anwar only understood when told.

check how well they have understood each stage. This helps both the pupils and the teacher. Helping the pupil to develop the skills needed for self-assessment is discussed in Unit 6.1.

Remember that pupils are individuals and will need a range of strategies to support learning

Selecting teaching strategies to meet needs of individuals is explored in detail in Unit 4.4.

SUMMARY AND KEY POINTS

This chapter has discussed the ways in which progression may be described and the theories that underpin such discussion. Children do not always progress in the same way and effective teaching has to maintain a balance between challenge and support, pitching the work at just the right level of demand to encourage participation and success. The keys to enabling progression are two-fold: a sound knowledge of the topic in hand, and a sound knowledge and understanding of the pupils in your class. The first can be prepared for; the second develops over time, with increasing confidence and trust developing between you and your pupils. The main thrust of this chapter has focused on planning for progression and suggested the kinds of activities that you can try out in the classroom. The Key Stage 3 Strategy for Science (DCSF, 2009) has many useful ideas which complement the material in this unit.

REFERENCES

Adey, P. and Shayer, M. (1994) *Really Raising Standards*, London: Routledge, pp. 98–107.
Adey, P. and Yates, C. (2001) *Thinking Science: The Materials of the CASE Project*, Walton-on-Thames: Thomas Nelson.
Asoko, H. and Squires, A. (1998) 'Progression and continuity', in M. Ratcliffe (ed.) *ASE Guide to Secondary Science Education*, Cheltenham: Stanley Thornes, pp. 175–82.
Burman, E. (2008) *Deconstructing Developmental Psychology,* 2nd edn, Hove: Routledge.
Burton, D. (2009) 'Ways pupils learn', in S. Capel, M. Leask and T. Turner (eds) *Learning to Teach in the Secondary School: A Companion to School Experience*, 5th edn, London: RoutledgeFalmer, pp. 251–66.

DCSF (2009) *The National Strategies Framework for Teaching Science*, available at: http://webarchive.nationalarchives.gov.uk/20110809091832/http://teachingandlearningresources.org.uk/collection/22099 (accessed 30 December 2013).

Donaldson, M. (1978) *Children's Minds*, Glasgow: Collins.

Driver, R., Guesne, E. and Tinberghien, A. (1985) *Children's Ideas in Science*, Buckingham: Open University Press.

Driver, R., Squires, A., Rushworth, P. and Wood-Robinson, V. (1994) *Making Sense of Secondary Science*, London: Routledge.

Kempa, R. (1992) 'Research in chemical education: its role and potential', in M. Atlay, S. Bennet, S. Dutch, R. Levinson, P. Taylor, and D. West (eds) *Open Chemistry*, London: Hodder and Stoughton, pp. 45–67.

O'Loughlin, M. (1992) 'Rethinking science education: beyond Piagetian constructivism toward a sociocultural model of teaching and learning', *Journal of Research in Science Teaching*, 29(8): 791–820.

Osborne, R. and Freyberg, P. (1985) *Learning in Science*, Auckland, NZ: Heinemann.

Posner, G., Strike, K., Hewson, P. and Gerzog, W. (1982) 'Accommodation of a scientific conception: toward a theory of conceptual change', *Science Education*, 66(2): 211–27.

Shayer, M. and Gamble, R. (2001) *Bridging: From CASE to Core Science*, Hatfield: ASE.

Simon, S. and Maloney, J. (2007) 'Activities for promoting small group discussion and argumentation', *School Science Review*, 88(324): 49–57.

Vygotsky, L. (1978) *Mind in Society*, Cambridge, MA: Harvard University Press.

Wood, D. (1998) *How Children Think and Learn: The Social Contexts of Cognitive Development*, Oxford: Blackwell.

FURTHER READING

Harrison, C., Simon, S. and Watson, R. (2000) 'Progression and differentiation', in M. Monk and J. Osborne (eds) *Good Practice in Science Teaching. What Research Has to Say*, Buckingham: Open University Press.

This examination of progression draws on the research literature and helps the reader tease out several meanings of 'progression' that are appropriate to different contexts.

Jarman, R. (2000) 'Between the idea and the reality falls the shadow', in J. Sears and P. Sorensen (2000) *Issues in Science Teaching*, London: RoutledgeFalmer.

Ruth Jarman addresses continuity and progression across Key Stages 2 and 3 and raises important issues about acknowledging what prior learning pupils have and how that can be assessed and recognised.

Johnson, P. (2002) 'Progression in children's understanding of a "basic" particle theory: a longitudinal study', in S. Amos and R. Boohan (eds) *Teaching Science in Secondary Schools: A Reader*, London: RoutledgeFalmer for the Open University, pp. 236–49.

This is a report of a longitudinal study into secondary pupils' (aged 11–14) understanding of particle theory. Useful examples of strategies for discussing ideas with pupils and the types of understanding pupils display at different levels of progression.

Simon, S. and Maloney, J. (2007) 'Activities for promoting small group discussion and argumentation'. *School Science Review*, 88(324): 49–57.

UNIT 4.2

USING SCHEMES OF WORK TO SUPPORT PLANNING

Kevin Smith

INTRODUCTION

For a beginning teacher, the landscape of the science curriculum can seem quite daunting, a huge expanse of content, skills and processes ripe for exploration, but how to do it? Where to start? Often these are the fundamental questions that are asked. Fortunately the teacher has a guide through this landscape, a map if you like. This is the scheme of work (SOW). This chapter deals with the relationship between the curriculum and the scheme of work and how it can support you in your planning.

OBJECTIVES

By the end of this unit, you should:

- be aware of the levels of planning;
- understand the strengths and limitations of schemes of work;
- realise the need to gain an overview of the content of a topic prior to planning individual lessons;
- consider how you can make a contribution to developing the curriculum within a science department.

PLANNING AND SCHEMES OF WORK

Since the inception of the National Curriculum in 1989, the curriculum has undergone a number of changes. It is important to note that the National Curriculum when introduced provided some form of statutory guidance of what exactly should be taught, with few institutions being exempt. However, now we are in a situation where the National

Curriculum is now not the statutory guidance for all schools and there is increasing flexibility as to what might be taught. However, all schools must comply with statutory requirements on testing and assessment (DfE, 2013). Further information about some of these changes are provided in Unit 2.1.

The curriculum itself is a form of long-term planning; this focuses on the whole of the curriculum subject over the years. It does not specify how the subject is to be taught. Medium-term planning suggests to the teacher what is to be taught either in set time periods or for set year groups and provides guidance on how it can be taught. Short-term planning involves the interpretation of the medium-term plan into individual lessons.

The long-term plan for science for most state-funded schools is set out in the National Curriculum programme of study. However, it can just as easily be an independent set of curriculum statements devised by a school or an institution.

There is no prescription as to how the curriculum should be interpreted into a medium-term plan; however, most are developed into a *scheme of work*. You will find many different schemes and it is up to the school which scheme of work they will adopt. These schemes could have been bought in from a publisher or have been developed 'in house'. Often these schemes have their own particular underlying philosophy or assessment base which makes them distinct. Wherever the scheme has come from, it should meet the needs of the students and reflect the ethos of the school. An example of this is linear and spiral schemes. A linear scheme assumes a logical development of content and skills that builds on previous taught units, whereas a spiral scheme revisits key taught content and skills from previous units before teaching new content and skills. Another example of interpretation is a contextual curriculum, which uses themes or engaging contexts to deliver 'bundles' of content and skills clustered around the scheme.

It is also worth noting that at GCSE level there is sometimes an extra level of planning, that of the 'specification'. This is an examination board's particular interpretation of the curriculum, and this in turn is often (but not always) interpreted into a scheme of work.

Task 4.2.1 **What is the scheme for your school?**

Your first task is to find out what (if any) scheme of work they have. Work through the following questions (for published schemes you will find this in the first couple of pages, but sometimes you will need to ask).

- Name of scheme?
- Publisher, exam board or home-produced?
- Underlying principles: Is it content- or skills-focused? A combination? Or other?
- Underlying assessment base: Is it formative (ongoing) or summative (testing and assessment at key points)?
- How is it organised? In units of work? By subject?
- What does it provide you with? Lesson plans? Suggestions of activities? Key assessments?

Although there is in some cases considerable variance in just what is included in a scheme of work, all good schemes of work have certain features in common. Figure 4.2.1 indicates what a reliable scheme of work is likely (but not always) to include.

A scheme of work should:

■ Provide clear curriculum statements such as references to the National Curriculum

■ Meet externally set specifications related to an examination

■ Provide aims for science teaching at several levels (for the whole of pupils' schooling; for each Key Stage; for each year; for each topic)

■ Include learning intentions/objectives and/or learning outcomes (for topics and individual lessons)

■ Include assessment activities to provide evidence for learning and of learning

■ suggest lesson and, in some cases, topic timings

■ Provide options and guidance for activities and teaching techniques

■ Draw attention to safety practice, including risk assessment for lessons

■ Offer strategies and guidance for differentiation, including support for pupils with SEN/G+T

■ Give references to prior knowledge you may anticipate, e.g. previous teaching of relevant topics/concepts

■ Provide evidence of common barriers to learning associated with the topic

■ Give opportunities to explore and make progress in scientific enquiry

■ Give opportunities to explore the nature of evidence in science

■ Give opportunities for links to scientific enterprises, and global scientific activities

■ Provide opportunities and guidance on how to link into science, technology, engineering and mathematics

■ Give opportunity for developing functional skills (literacy, numeracy and ICT)

■ Suggest homework activities

■ Give references to books, resources and websites

■ **Figure 4.2.1** Some characteristics of an example of a scheme of work

Key message: a good scheme will interpret any statutory guidance for you and explore WHAT you need to teach and give you some ideas, but will not tell you HOW you are to teach it.

Different schemes give different levels of detail. Some provide the bare minimum and rely on interpretation by the teachers; others are extremely prescriptive and provide detailed lesson plans.

Schools will also vary as to how they expect teachers to use the scheme. A teacher's short-term planning directly relates to HOW the scheme is interpreted by the teacher into their planning for any individual lesson. Some schools will expect teachers to stick to it rigidly and others use it as a guide only and encourage teacher creativity. Whatever the expectation, the most important thing is for any teacher is to use the scheme wisely. If it is used too prescriptively, then there is a risk that the lessons would not be adapted to the needs of the pupils (and this is important for Teachers' Standard 5). If it is not used at all, there is a risk that the burden of planning becomes too much for any teacher and valuable resources and techniques are overlooked. Well-structured schemes of work reduce the anxiety about lesson planning, but do not remove the need for each teacher to undertake their own planning.

The now disbanded Qualifications and Curriculum Development Agency (QCDA) developed a set of exemplar schemes of work, which in their own way set the standard from which a plethora of published schemes sprung. These schemes have exemplified what aspects should be included in a scheme and these are outlined in Figure 4.2.2.

Even with a scheme of work as clear as this, mistakes and misinterpretations are made. A common example from the QCDA scheme is attempting to do every activity the scheme

---

Aspects and language found in the QCDA scheme of work

'**About this unit**': outlines the major content and skills.

'**Where the unit fits in**': explores links with other units in the scheme and schemes from previous Key Stages.

'**Expectations**': what knowledge, processes, skills and understanding you can expect most pupils to have acquired by the end of the unit.

'**Prior learning**': outlines what it is useful for the pupils to know or understand before studying this unit.

'**Language for learning**': explores the key vocabulary used in the unit.

'**Resources**': the resources needed to teach the unit.

'**Learning objectives**': these outline the small steps necessary to build up the knowledge and understanding that are the focus of the unit.

'**Learning outcomes**': these provide indications of progress for activities and lessons.

'**Health and safety**': essential; this gives guidance on the potential health and safety issues and how to control them.

'**Activities**': by no means exhaustive, these provide suggestions as to the activities that can be carried out with the pupils.

'**Out of school learning**': identifies key applications of the content in everyday learning and may make suggestions for projects and homework.

■ **Figure 4.2.2** Aspects and language found in the QCDA scheme of work

suggests even though it might not be necessary or indeed useful, this leads to stress regarding time and the teacher feeling they have not covered 'everything'.

Task 4.2.2 **Reviewing the scheme of work**

Now that you have an understanding of what to expect in a scheme, please look through the scheme you are to use or one you have available. You are now going to perform a form of SWOT analysis:

S = what are the STRENGTHS of the scheme of work?
W = what are the WEAKNESSES of the scheme of work?
O = what OPPORTUNITIES does the scheme provide you with?
T = is there anything about the scheme that may 'THREATEN' your progress as a teacher?

Key message: be aware of the level of guidance and prescription in the scheme of work in your own school, the good – and not so good – features of that scheme and how it is used in your department. It is always good to talk to teachers about how they use the scheme.

PREPARATION IS HALF THE BATTLE

So you have the scheme of work and you know what classes and topics you need to teach. Surely, if you follow the scheme, you will teach a good lesson? That's the point of it, isn't it? Not so.

A scheme only goes some way in helping you prepare for a lesson. A key feature of short term planning is to know your topic well. This includes having secure subject knowledge of what you are teaching AND the key steps in development of the subject. This in many ways is an essential first step and is related to Teachers' Standard (TS) 3 'Demonstrate good subject and curriculum knowledge', 'have a secure knowledge of the relevant subject(s) and curriculum areas, foster and maintain pupils' interest in the subject, and address 'misunderstandings'. This, in turn, will have a direct effect on other Teachers' Standards, for example, your ability to set high expectations (TS1) or your ability to 'promote good progress' (TS2), and therefore to 'plan and teach well-structured lessons' (TS4).

Once you have this secure subject knowledge, the second thing you need is the pedagogy (the approach) that works well at whatever particular stage you are teaching. I therefore suggest here you look at these two areas in preparation before you do any of the detailed planning of individual lessons, which is described in Unit 4.3.

KEY SCIENTIFIC CONTENT/KNOWLEDGE/PROCESSES AND SKILLS

It is impossible to plan sensibly, let alone teach, unless you have a clear understanding of the key science in a topic yourself. It is also wise to anticipate that unless you are only teaching within your subject specialism you might at some point in your career be called on to teach a subject outside of your specialism (e.g. a biologist teaching the principle of moments or a physicist teaching reproduction!).

You therefore need to develop your understanding of the key scientific knowledge, processes and skills you are teaching at a particular time and how they link with ideas that come later, and those learned earlier. For example, you might understand the idea of a food web, but what did the pupils learn in primary school that might be important for them to access? Do you understand how it relates to the more abstract concept of energy transfer in an ecosystem and where that comes in the scheme? Do you understand what difficulties and misconceptions the students might have? If you understand this, then it will help you pitch the lesson correctly.

Two sources of this information you might find useful are:

1   The schemes themselves provide just such guidance, in the case of the QCDA scheme it is found in the sections 'About this unit', 'Where this unit fits in', 'Prior knowledge' and 'Expectations'.
2   Progress guides such as the 'Yearly teaching objectives' found in the 'Framework for teaching science' in the National Strategy for Teaching Science 2002.

Task 4.2.3 **Identifying key ideas, processes and skills**

Look at the unit you will teach and, using the scheme of work or any key texts, identify the following in the unit you are currently teaching:

▪ key ideas covered in the unit: (includes misconceptions);
▪ key processes covered in the unit;
▪ key skills covered in the unit (this may not be so obvious).

Just by doing this you are preparing yourself for planning.

I suggest you now take this one stage further; now try organising your subject knowledge using an advance organiser such as a concept map (these are fantastic tools to have in your teaching repertoire and are great to use as consolidation activities or revision activities).

An activity like this will help you 'see' the big picture and identify any gaps in your knowledge and misconceptions you might have –and again you are preparing yourself for planning. An incomplete example is shown in Figure 4.2.3 for 'Circuits' (more examples of concept maps for other topics are given in Frost (2010, pp. 136–9). Use Task 4.2.4 to have a go for yourself.

Task 4.2.4 **Using a basic advance organiser to develop your scientific knowledge**

1 Choose a topic from the curriculum you wish to focus on.
2 Start with a blank piece of paper; place the topic title in the centre of the paper.
3 Subdivide your topic into a number of branches that help organise the topic into manageable chunks.
4 For each sub-branch further organise the topic into key ideas (if you are making a concept map, place a brief explanation as to the connection on the branch line).
5 Continue subdividing the branches until you have covered the whole of the topic.

Task 4.2.5 **Spotting how the idea progresses in the scheme of work**

1 Review your scheme of work looking at the unit titles and their key content throughout the units.
2 Start at the unit you will be teaching.
3 Now track back. Are there any related units? If so, what do they deal with?
4 Now look forward. Are there any related units. If so what do they deal with?
5 Try to complete a flow chart for the development of the idea within the scheme (an example is shown in Figure 4.2.4).

If you want to develop your skills, you can challenge yourself, extend and organize your concept map showing the progress in the key idea from year to year within the curriculum of your school (some schools may have already done this). You can also add in information about misconceptions.

Key message: make sure you understand your topic well. If necessary, support this process with the use of your own CPD time either enrolling on subject knowledge enhancement or by using online resources – and don't forget you can always ask the specialist teachers in your department.

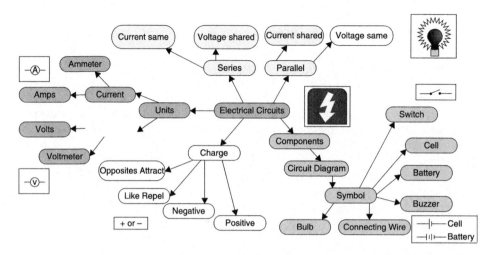

■ **Figure 4.2.3** Incomplete concept map for circuits

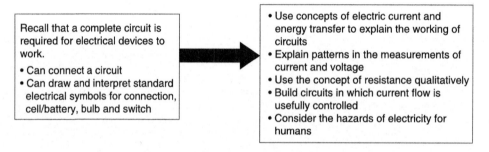

■ **Figure 4.2.4** A model of progress in circuits using the QCDA scheme of work

Developing your pedagogy

Again, an effective and well-written scheme of work will help you with ideas of activities and resources but it will only take you so far along the journey of planning using the scheme of work. More advanced lesson planning uses what is available and then adds to it or refines and adapts it.

Let us take the example of circuits and ask ourselves some key questions. A suggested activity might be to explore what happens to the current in series and parallel circuits. There is nothing wrong *per se* with this kind of activity, indeed, it is a nice exploratory activity. However, whether or not to use it will depend on the answer to these questions:

■ What year group/Key Stage are the pupils? Is it age-appropriate for the year group? Is it too easy? Is it too advanced?

■ What approach does your group engage well with? If a group struggles with, for example, written activities, it might not be the best approach to weight your lesson toward more written work. This is important, as some research suggests that boys respond better to more practical approaches to teaching science. So would you get the students to do the practical or do it as a written activity?

■ What familiar 'real-life' examples can you think of to illustrate the theory? This is particularly important for students when first approaching an 'abstract' theory and for those students who struggle with the 'abstract'. It is also more engaging.

■ What can they do or not do? Important if you have students with specific needs. For example, if a student struggles to read a particular type of ammeter, how could you adapt it?

■ Do I want to tell them the theory? Do I want them to find out for themselves? Do I want them to come up with ideas? This comes down to approaches to science teaching and can be greatly informed by the topic and the class you are teaching

■ What range of resources do you have available? How old are they? There is no point in planning an activity if you cannot resource it. For example, do I have a full set of circuit boards and ammeters? What type of ammeters do I have? What alternatives could I think of?

■ Will the resources I have available work well for my students? Are the resources inclusive and accessible? Again, very important for students with specific needs, but it goes further. Is there, for example, any point in giving a resource that is designed for degree-level students to a mixed ability class at KS3? So if I gave a worksheet with a set of instructions that is not accessible, what would the result be?

■ Finally, what approach do I have time to develop and then deliver? There would be no point in carrying out a full-blown investigation that is planned and then carried out and analysed by the students if there was not time to do this.

These are all important questions to answer and will inform your planning.

Task 4.2.6 **Developing your pedagogical content knowledge for a topic**

Start a collection of ideas to support your teaching of your current topic. This collection might include examples of:

■ everyday examples which are relevant: applications, related careers;
■ useful demonstrations;
■ helpful models and analogies to explain a concept;
■ real-life examples from scientific research;
■ activities that can be used to bridge from one Key Stage to the next or one topic or lesson to the next;
■ stories about how an idea or new understanding developed, e.g. the theory of genetics involving Mendel;
■ useful questions;
■ equipment lists and alternative practicals to carry out.

Plan a file to collect these resources and a reference system for easy access. Be on the lookout for ideas when you are watching other teachers in their classrooms.

SHARING

As a beginner teacher you may not feel you that you can contribute to curriculum development in a department. This is not true. Curriculum development is an ongoing process that relies on teachers sharing their successful ideas and incorporating them in the rewriting of the schemes of work. You may well have pedagogical content ideas that can be shared with teachers and that the department will, in the future, use in their schemes of work. If you get the opportunity and you feel you have the time, offer to help in curriculum development.

It might be that you have a particular interest in a topic and therefore have a wide subject knowledge base; this in turn can lead to you having a lot of 'soft' knowledge such as anecdotes and bizarre and interesting examples that can be used to engage students in the topic. If so, be willing to share them.

It might be that you have come fresh from university or industry where you have specialist knowledge and a specialist skill set that existing teachers do not have. As the curriculum develops, new content is added and old content is revised. You just might have something from your experience that others do not have. If so, be willing to share it (this can lead you into more formal CPD opportunities which enhance your own curriculum vitae).

It might be that you can be an ambassador for your subject. Most of you would have entered teaching because you want to share your passion for your subject. Offer to contribute to engagement and enhancement activities such as science clubs and careers and open evenings – all are valuable opportunities to contribute to the development of your subject.

Key message: you have a role to play in the department. You can contribute to curriculum development. The key is to identify if there is anything you can offer that is not included in the curriculum that would further enhance and engage the students in your school.

SUMMARY AND KEY POINTS

The curriculum, schemes of work and specifications provide you with guidance to start planning lessons. They provide you with an overview about the content and scientific knowledge needed. However, your own planning needs to respond to the needs of pupils, their understanding and your own creative approached to teaching.

REFERENCES

DfE (Department for Education) (2013) *The National Curriculum*, available at: www.education. gov.uk/schools/teachingandlearning/curriculum/secondary (accessed 9 February 2014).

Frost, J. (ed.) (2010) *Learning to Teach Science in the Secondary School: A Companion to School Experience*, 3rd edn, London: Routledge.

USEFUL WEBSITES

National Curriculum and its requirements: www.education.gov.uk/schools/teachingandlearning/curriculum/a00224489/further-info-stat-curric-req (accessed 9 February 2014).

QCDA schemes of work: http://webarchive.nationalarchives.gov.uk/20090608182316/standards.dfes.gov.uk/schemes3/ (accessed 9 February 2014).

UNIT 4.3

PLANNING AND EVALUATING LESSONS

Kevin Smith

INTRODUCTION

Both the Teachers' Standards (TS) (DfE, 2012), primarily TS4, and the current OFSTED grade descriptors for 'quality of teaching' specifically mention and require teachers to plan effective lessons. However, *how* this is done and in what format are down to the school or individual teachers.

The ideas discussed in Units 4.1 and 4.2 provided you with the basis for short-term lesson planning. Now we turn our attention to look in more detail at lesson design and planning.

OBJECTIVES

By the end of this unit, you should:

- be able to identify the main characteristics of lessons;
- be able to develop your understanding of pitch;
- understand why we have learning objectives and outcomes for pupils;
- reflect on the most appropriate approaches, activities and resources to help pupils;
- reflect on when, where and why we use assessment;
- begin to think about the impact of classroom and resource management, timing and pace and delivery on your lessons;
- explore different types of lesson plans;
- reflect on your lessons.

CHARACTERISTICS OF LESSONS

It is a complex task to do lesson design and planning, affected by any number of variables. All teachers need to consider these variables when planning a lesson. Examples of these variables are:

- what you want to/need to teach;
- what approach you want to take;
- what resources you have available;
- the class dynamics;
- you as the teacher.

It is acknowledged here that a slight change in any of these variables can lead to vastly different types of lessons and vastly different outcomes in the classroom and you will look at a variety of approaches in the rest of this book. However, which approach you decide to take, the activities you plan and whatever resources you use, an effective lesson needs to be planned. We therefore need to consider what we see in effective lessons and what to consider when planning lessons.

Task 4.3.1 **An effective science lesson?**

Write down everything you feel should be present in an effective science lesson.

Based loosely on the 'episodes' model produced by the DfES (2004) in *Pedagogy and Practice: Teaching and Learning in Secondary Schools*, I have outlined in Figure 4.3.1 the recognised characteristics found in an effective science lesson. In this unit, I do not want to get hung up on any particular structures, formats and terminologies as giving the impression that there is a set way or of planning lessons and language you need to use, as this reduces creativity and flexibility in lesson planning and can well cause more problems than there needs to be. You might see slightly different language and a different way of organising it depending on where you are teaching and if your school is using a particular support package.

It would follow therefore that these characteristics would be found in effective lesson plans.

Task 4.3.2 **Looking at other teachers' planning**

Ask to look at a range of different teachers' lesson plans in your school.

1 What do they look like?
2 Do they include all of the above characteristics?
3 Was it clear what they were doing and why they were doing it?
4 Was it clear what they wanted to do and how they would do it?
5 What else was in the plan that was not included above?

You probably noticed that there were many characteristics in the plans that were not included. They can be related to the pedagogy or the structure of the lesson. Some of these are summarized in Figure 4.3.2.

Characteristic	Purpose
Lesson objectives/intentions	Shares with pupils what they are to learn
Learning outcomes	Shares with pupils the standards expected of them
Approaches, activities and resources that help you assess learning.	Helps you: find out what the pupils have know and may have learnt find out any barriers to learning or misconceptions find out where to go next
Approaches, activities and resources that start the lesson, set the scene or establish the baseline	Provides a context Engages the pupils with learning Explores what they already know
Approaches, activities and resources that introduce new learning	Introduces new ideas and concepts to pupils Clarifying misconceptions Illustrates and models new learning Demonstrates new skills
Approaches, activities and resources that explore the new learning	Gives the pupils the chance to explore and investigate the new ideas and apply them Clarifies misconceptions Is an opportunity for independent learning Working with and practicing new skills
Approaches, activities and resources that consolidate the learning	Embeds the ideas Applies the learning Provides an opportunity to explore breadth of knowledge Is an opportunity for independent learning
Approaches, activities and resources that draw ideas together and finds out what progress has been made.	Summarises the learning Assesses the learning Provides a bridge or transition point

■ **Figure 4.3.1** Characteristics of an effective lesson

Characteristic	Purpose
Ability profile of class	Informs pitch and differentiation
Differentiation	Describes how you will adapt the approach, resources or activities for specific pupils or groups of pupils with specific needs such as EAL/IEP/EBD
Timings	Helps the teacher keep pace in lesson and informs resourcing and activities used
Teaching activities	Describes what the teacher will do
Pupil activities	Describes what the pupils will be doing
Assessment	Describes what the teacher will do to assess learning and progress
Health and safety	Identifies hazards and informs risk assessments
Use of support staff	Describe what role support staff will play in the lesson
Resources	Identifies the resources you will need for all activities
Homework	The tasks and resources you will use for homework
Cross-curricular skills	Identifies opportunities to support other areas of the curriculum and use those skills such as ICT/Literacy/Numeracy? PSHE/Citizenship/Thinking skills

■ **Figure 4.3.2** Other characteristics found in lesson plans

STARTING LESSON PLANNING

As you look at more plans and lessons, you will begin to appreciate just how much they can vary. I want to now look in more detail at these characteristics and other factors that you will need to consider when you are planning your lessons. I will guide you through a series of reflections but while we are doing this I want you always to keep in the back of your mind that the purpose of lesson plans is to produce a workable document that is fit for purpose.

Planning reflection point 1: Pitching it right

In Unit 4.2 we took you through the curriculum and schemes of work which show you what to teach. It is important to note once again that a new National Curriculum will be in effect from 2014 and that for all schools not exempt from this, it provides the statutory guidance of what to teach. Once you know what it is you are to teach and have an idea of what you want to do you can ask yourself this important question: 'Is what I am planning to do matched to the age/stage/level for the pupils I am teaching?' This is commonly called the 'pitch' of the lesson and Units 4.1 and 4.2 will help you gauge this with the profile of the class. Since pitch can have impact on engagement and progress, it is vital to get it right.

Task 4.3.3 **Planning at different Key Stages**

Look at our example from Unit 4.2 'Circuits' and ask yourself: would it ever be appropriate to use the content and skills from the previous Key Stage? When and how would you include it?

Pitch affects the phrasing of lesson objectives and outcomes as well as the activities and resources and vice versa.

Planning reflection point 2: Planning objectives and outcomes

Learning objectives are general statements of what you want the pupils to learn and learning outcomes, as explained in Unit 4.1, are assessable forms of objectives, These can be very powerful tools to help the teacher assess and the pupils learn but they are only powerful if they are user-friendly and are actually used! You will consider them in more detail in other parts of this book.

Task 4.3.4 **Lesson objective or outcome**

Take a lesson objective or outcome that you have seen in some of your observations. Reflect on the following questions:

1 Are they in an accessible form for the pupils? (Think about the language used.)
2 Are they useful to the teacher? To the pupils?
3 Are they shared with the pupils? If so, how?
4 Are they actually used as an assessment tool?

You will gain more experience in framing these in Units 4.1 and 4.4. Also do not assume they are the start of the beginning of the planning process, this is just one model of lesson planning.

Planning reflection point 3: Approaches, activities and resources that help you assess learning

Assessment is needed so the teacher is able to gain insight from the pupils about the extent to which they understand the science being taught and if they have made progress, and this is summarised in TS 6 (DfE, 2012). We also need it so that we can adjust and adapt our teaching and can plan the next lesson in the sequence. It is dealt with in more detail in Unit 6.1.

Ultimately what you assess and how you assess are linked to your learning outcomes and can take place at any point in the lesson.

One approach is to have assessment activities embedded during the lesson. I could choose to complete a short teaching sequence and then follow it by a short assessment activity where I could then judge if they can remember the names on a 'label a diagram' activity. If they could, I could assume they have met the outcome. At this point you could pause with the pupils and reflect with them the progress they have made.

Another approach is to use the end of the lesson as a time to assess if the outcomes have been met and therefore if your objective has been met. This is usually the purpose of the 'plenary'. It can be a very brief activity or a more substantial one but the purpose of this part of the lesson is to provide information for you and the pupils as to the progress made. It is useful for you as it can help you plan or adjust your planning for next lesson. It is also useful for the pupils as it helps them understand what they need to do next (it is also a good motivational tool!).

Task 4.3.5 **When does assessment take place?**

Observe a lesson taught by a teacher in your school:

1 List the opportunities taken by the teacher to assess the learning taking place, how frequent were they and how did the teacher organise it?
2 After the lesson discuss the kinds of activities and techniques the teacher used and ask why they chose those particular techniques/points in the lesson.

Planning reflection point 4: What approaches, activities and resources do I use in the lesson?

One of the biggest sources of angst I encounter with student teachers, and indeed qualified teachers is: *what approach/activities/resources do I use?*

There actually is no answer to this question (though you can use the suggested approach in the scheme of work, it may not be the best approach to take in your lesson. We looked at this in Unit 4.2 and it is further developed in Unit 4.4.) For example, I might decide to use an investigative approach to my lesson and as part of this I decide to focus my activities on planning an investigation and as a consequence I might need (depending on my group) a scaffold to help them plan their investigation. Thus, I would need to resource it. It doesn't help you that there is a huge range of different resources readily available for you to use as you still need to choose. To help you decide, I suggest you look at what you are considering in terms of these questions:

■ What is its purpose of the activity or resource?
■ Does it support the approach I want to take?
■ Will it help the pupil make progress?
■ Can all the pupils access it?
■ How long will it take to complete the activity?
■ How long will it take to resource the activity?
■ Does it work with or against the preferred learning styles of the learners?
■ How will I organise it?
■ Will it work if I adapt it?

For example, I have the objective 'to explain why we digest food'. I want the pupils to have a fun kinaesthetic way to start the lesson, to engage with an activity that informs me if they have any prior knowledge of names and locations of organs associated with digestion. If I found the activity in Figure 4.3.3 on the internet and it only took me 5 minutes to plan and will only take 5–10 minutes to run, I might judge that it is a good activity to start my lesson *but* only if I had considered all my variables and still found it worthwhile, could I consider it to be 'fit for purpose'.

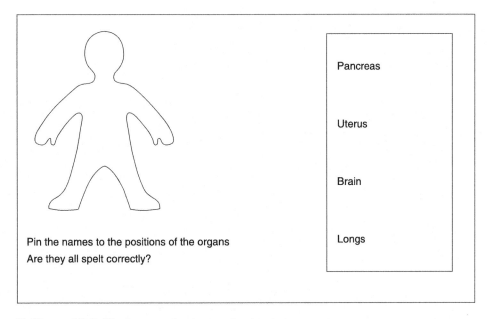

Pin the names to the positions of the organs
Are they all spelt correctly?

Pancreas

Uterus

Brain

Longs

■ **Figure 4.3.3** 'Pin the organ': an example of a starter

> ### Task 4.3.6 **Compare two activities that explore the same objective**
>
> Use the questions above to compare and contrast two different activities that could be used to explore the same objective.
>
> You can use one that you have already taught or you have seen taught and reflect if it is 'fit for purpose'.

Key message: An approach, activity or resource can only be considered to be effective if it is fit for purpose. If it isn't, do not use it.

Another question I am asked is: 'How many activities do I include?' Again, there is no set answer. However, the skilled teacher is always aware of the needs of the pupils. Some pupils work better with multiple simple activities to explore the ideas; others work well with complex activities that explore deeply the underlying concepts. Some approaches require open-ended activities, some require more focus and structure. You will need to make the decision.

> ### Task 4.3.7 **Practise the activity**
>
> Try out the activity you intend to use at home or give it to a friend. This will give you an idea of its pitch, a clue as to how to organise the activity and, finally, if there are any mistakes in the activity (always check activities and resources for accuracy and clarity).

Planning reflection point 5: Adapting and differentiation

An essential part of effective planning is how well what you plan is matched to the needs of all the pupils. This is a focus of TS 5 (DfE, 2012). This can sometimes be called 'differentiation' and in Unit 4.1 you looked at this.

Some of the needs you might encounter in a mixed ability classroom are: ability range, Statemented pupils, pupils with EAL, pupils with lower than average reading and writing ages, those with specific special needs, those with numeracy issues, Emotional and Behavioural Difficulties (EBD) pupils, gifted and talented pupils, and autism spectrum disorders (ASD) pupils.

Since the needs of the pupils you teach can vary considerably, you also need to adapt your planning to match their needs. Spillman (1991) explains it is more about being flexible with your approach and with your resources and I would add being creative as well. Hence, we also use the term 'adapt'.

You can adapt your planning in a number of ways and a few are mentioned below and throughout this unit.

- ▪ Adapting learning objectives or outcomes for different needs.
- ▪ Expecting different outcomes from tasks for different needs.
- ▪ Adapting tasks and activities for different needs.

■ Adapting resources for different needs.
■ Adapting groupings for different needs.
■ Expecting different rates of progress for different pupils.
■ Being flexible with your classroom organisation to address different needs.
■ Using additional adults to support those with different needs.
■ Giving different levels of independence for those with different needs.

Task 4.3.8 **Have a go . . .**

Look at a basic practical such as testing a leaf for starch. Try adapting it for the following needs:

■ You have two gifted and talented pupils in your class.
■ You have a group of EAL pupils.
■ You have a pupil with hearing impairment.

Planning reflection point 6: Organisation and management

If your lesson is organised and managed well, it is likely to be more successful. In fact, I would go as far to say this could make or break your lessons.

Task 4.3.9 **Am I organised?**

For a lesson you are preparing, reflect on the following questions:

1 Have I ordered the equipment (in advance!) and dealt with any issues with resources?
2 Have I tried out the activities myself?
3 Do I have a seating plan for the room and do the pupils know it?
4 How many copies/sets do I need or are available to me?
5 How can I organise the movement in the class?
6 How will the equipment be distributed? Will it already be set up?
7 How will the pupils be placed when practical work is being done?
8 If pupils are working in groups, what size of group? Are they self-selecting or do I decide?
9 How will I deal with health and safety?
10 How will I pack away?
11 Do I have enough time in my plan to do all of the activities?

These may seem very basic questions but you need to understand that disorganisation can have a serious impact on the delivery of a lesson (and health and safety). For example, if a piece of equipment is not working when you come to do a demonstration, how will you deal with it? How will you adapt? It is good practice to develop routines to help you organise yourself and avoid any issues.

There are no set timings for activities in lesson. However, timing and therefore the pace of the lesson are crucial. Too little time for activities and too fast a pace and you stand the risk of losing the pupils, they will not make progress and they will get frustrated and confused and therefore the potential for disruption arises. Give too much time for activities, and you stand the risk of losing the pupils, they do not make progress and they get bored, finding something else to do not related to learning and therefore the potential for disruption arises.

It is essential that you practise judging how long each activity takes and build this timing into your planning. In practice, it is fine to shorten and extend the time taken for activities but only if it is as a result of the insight you have gained from your lesson as it takes place. A good example of when it can go wrong is when you spend 25 minutes of a 50-minute lesson introducing the lesson.

Planning reflection point 7: Homework and planning

Does your school have a homework policy? Most will and you will need to find out what this is and plan accordingly.

Homework needs to be considered at the planning stage because: you will need to allow time in your plan to introduce it and for the pupils to record it; you will need to resource it; you will need to consider if it is an integral part of the unit of work or if it is adding breadth to it.

Another thing to consider is what to do if homework is *not* completed. If you have planned homework as an essential part of the lesson and it is not completed, what will you do so the pupil is not missing vital information and skills?

Task 4.3.10 **Homework**

Compare and contrast these two suggestions for homework for the topic *in-vitro* fertilisation (IVF). What would be the implications for planning for both of them?

1 Prepare an information leaflet for prospective users of IVF in a private clinic.
2 Is the use of IVF an appropriate use of NHS funding? Discuss.

Planning reflection point 8: Health and safety

Health and safety is a justifiably important topic all on its own and you can find much of what you need at CLEAPSS and the health and safety policy in your school. Suffice to say, it is absolutely essential for you to comply with the health and safety policy of your school, identify the hazards in your lesson and take appropriate measures to minimise the risks. Therefore this is an integral part of your planning.

A word about lesson plans and lesson plan pro-formas

Since there is no statutory requirement to have a written lesson plan, I have been asked: 'Is it necessary to have a written record of my lesson plan as I keep it in my head and I have taught this before . . .?' And, 'Surely it adds to the workload?' The answer I give is invariably, 'Yes', particularly for the student teacher for a number of reasons:

1   It provides evidence of what you intended to do which can inform anyone working with you.
2   It is a vital aide-mémoire for the busy teacher.
3   If something goes wrong, it is easier to adjust and adapt if a structure is in place already.
4   It can help with timing and pace.
5   It provides a record of what you have done and can be used again!

There are many ways to structure your lesson plans and some institutions provide their own templates and can insist that you use them. If you have freedom to choose your own, then you must choose one that is best for you, you will know what works for you and what doesn't.

A basic lesson plan needs to be fit for purpose, realistic and workable, it is often a good thing to imagine someone coming into your lesson and picking up the plan. It should be clear enough that they could understand what it is you are doing and how you will be doing it.

Figures 4.3.4 and 4.3.5 are two examples of pro-formas used for planning. Use them to complete Tasks 4.3.11 and 4.3.12.

SUBJECT	YEAR/GROUP	DAY/PERIOD/ROOM
TEACHER	DATE	NO. IN CLASS
ABILITY RANGE	TITLE OF UNIT OF WORK	LESSON No.
CONTEXT OF CLASS		
SUMMARY OF PREVIOUS LEARNING OUTCOMES (Pupils have previously experienced and achieved):		
INTENDED LEARNING OBJECTIVES AND LEARNING OUTCOMES (By the end of the lesson, all, most and some pupils will understand/know/be able to):		
DIFFERENTIATION (Most able, SEN, EAL learners):		
G&T		
SEN/EAL / FSM		
LEARNING RESOURCES:		
CONTENT OF LESSON: Starter: Main Activities: Opportunities for demonstrating progress. Plenary. Homework	T&L STYLES/ APPROACHES:	ASSESSMENT OPPORTUNITIES:

■ **Figure 4.3.4** Pro-forma example 1

Source: Reproduced by kind permission of Herschel Grammar School.

LESSON PLAN	Class:		Date:
	Subject:		Length: Timings should be included throughout the plan
PoS addressed/Key elements:	Previous experience:		
Specific learning intentions:			
Information from previous assessments			
Lesson format with approximate timings: Introduction: (Stimuli, learning intention, purpose, task) Development: (Activities, teacher/child roles) Conclusion: (Re-cap and evaluation: refer back to learning intentions) Extension activities:			Differentiation: (e.g. low attainers, more able and EAL)
Assessment of learning intentions: (Who, what and how? Be specific!)			ICT applications (please list and include any URLs)
Follow-up:			Resources needed (list all):

▪ **Figure 4.3.5** Pro-forma example 2

Source: Reproduced with kind permission of Brunel University.

Task 4.3.11 **Comparing lesson plan pro-formas**

Compare and contrast the two lesson plan pro-formas.

1 What do they have in common?
2 How are they different?
3 Is there anything in these plans you would like to include but have not?
4 Which one do you prefer and why?

Task 4.3.12 **Planning with pro-formas**

Now try planning the same lesson but using the two different pro-formas.

REFLECTIVE PRACTICE AND LESSON PLANNING

The final stage of lesson planning usually comes after the lesson. Reflection and evaluation of lessons are vital for a teacher as it is a way we learn and further develop. Reflective practice is the capacity to reflect on action as part of a continuous process of learning (Schön, 1983). We can do this 'in action' i.e. while we are in the process of planning. However, since the plan is about anticipating future events (our lesson), we will not learn about how effective our plan is but we might learn about our planning process (e.g. did I dwell too much on that particular activity?). To learn from our plans we need to evaluate them after the event or to reflect 'on action' and this is done in the process of lesson evaluation.

Evaluation is not just about making a value judgement, saying something was good or bad, or I liked it or did not like it, so it becomes a self-critical negative tool. It is far more effective to use it positively but is a very challenging thing to do (evaluation is, after all, very high up on Bloom's taxonomy of learning objectives (Bloom *et al.*, 1956)), yet TS4 (DfE, 2012) '*reflect systematically on the effectiveness of lessons and approaches to teaching*' requires you to do this.

There are different models available to help do this but a basic reflection and evaluation (based loosely on Gibbs, 1988) includes the following components:

- *A description* of what happened in the lesson without any value judgement attached to those descriptions. This is an important step as it will be the evidence on which to base your evaluation. If possible, jot down notes on your plan as you go along, e.g. note down timings, anything you did differently, or forgot to include, anything that didn't work, problems you encountered. Then after the lesson, note down anything that happened differently to what you expected.
- *Evaluation*: Here you can judge (or get others to help you) what went well and what didn't go so well, what was good or bad about the lesson.
- *Analysis of the lesson*: Why did it go the way it did? Why did I get those outcomes? For example, if your timings were out, why was this? It is important to be brutally honest with yourself at this stage even if it is uncomfortable.
- *A suggestion of further actions/action plan/self-improvement targets*: what could I do better/different next time? What can I learn from this experience? What actions do I need to take? Actions might include investigating new approaches, building up your subject knowledge, or attending training. This is especially important for people who are working with you, as self-reflection – if it is done well – helps those people (mentors and coaches) to support you.

You might encounter lesson plan templates that include evaluation templates with them. An example of this is seen in Figure: 4.4.6, taken from the Brunel University pro-forma.

Were the lesson aims/objectives/outcomes made clear to the pupils? (State how)

What assessments of pupil knowledge/understanding/skills took place during the lesson?

What evidence is there that the learning outcomes were achieved with relation to
(a) all pupils   (b) most pupils   (c) some pupils?

Which of *your* objectives were achieved and which, if any, were not?

What classroom management issues arose?

How were those issues dealt with?

How was literacy/numeracy/ICT addressed?

How will your assessments of pupil learning feed forward to the planning of your next lessons with the group?

■ **Figure 4.3.6** A lesson evaluation pro-forma

SUMMARY AND KEY POINTS

A number of different factors can affect lesson design and planning but, whatever the design of the lesson, all effective lessons have a structure and that structure requires a plan. Structures vary according to your approach. A lesson plan is populated by tasks, activities and resources that must be fit for purpose including matched to the needs of the pupils. It is useful to plan and record your lesson plans in templates provided for you by your HEI or school. After a lesson it is important that we reflect and evaluate so that we can continue to grow as a professional.

REFERENCES

Bloom, B. S., Engelhart, M. D., Furst, E. J., Hill, W. H. and Krathwohl, D. R. (1956) *Taxonomy of Educational Objectives: The Classification of Educational Goals*, New York: McKay.

DfE (Department for Education) (2012) *The Teachers' Standards.* Available at: www.education. gov.uk/schools/leadership/deployingstaff/a00205581/teachers-standards1-sep–2012 (accessed 5 April 2014).

DfES (Department for Education and Science) (2004) *Pedagogy and Practice Unit 1: Structuring Learning, Key Stage 3 National Strategy*, London: Department for Education and Science.

Gibbs, G. (1988) *Learning by Doing: A Guide to Teaching and Learning Methods*, Further Education Unit, Oxford: Oxford Polytechnic.

Ginnis, P. (2002) *The Teachers' Toolkit,* Carmarthen: Crown House.

Schön, D. (1983) *The Reflective Practitioner: How Professionals Think in Action*, London: Temple Smith.

Spillman, J. (1991) *Differentiation: An Approach to Teaching and Learning*, Cambridge: Pearson.

USEFUL WEBSITES

CLEAPSS: www.cleapss.org.uk/. This is an organisation, supported by subscription, that provides support for practical work in science and technology to schools and colleges (accessed 9 February 2014).

DfE (Department for Education) (2012) *The Teachers' Standards*: www.education.gov.uk/schools/leader-ship/deployingstaff/a00205581/teachers-standards1-sep–2012 (accessed 5 April 2014).

OFSTED (2013) Generic Grade Descriptors and Supplementary Subject-Specific Guidance for Inspectors on Making Judgements During Subject Survey Visits to Schools: www.ofsted.gov.uk/resources/generic-grade-descriptors-and-supplementary-subject-specific-guidance-for-inspectors-making-judgements (accessed 9 February 2014).

UNIT 4.4

TEACHING STRATEGIES AND ORGANISING LEARNING

Pete Sorensen

INTRODUCTION

The review of the science curriculum in Unit 2.1 highlights some of the key debates and concerns that have influenced changes to the Science National Curriculum in England since its inception. It shows that the aims and purposes of science education and the balance given to different objectives are contested and are likely to remain so. However, certain themes can be identified which have clear implications for the selection of teaching strategies and the way learning is organised. These themes include: a concern to ensure that science is seen as a relevant and exciting subject; to make science accessible to all; to support the supply of future scientists; to ensure all pupils have an understanding of the nature of science as a subject and what scientists do.

NOS

In contrast to the concerns of policy-makers, influential reports, such as those of the House of Commons Science and Technology Committee (2002), and *Beyond 2000: Science Education for the Future* (Millar and Osborne, 1998) noted pupils' perceptions of science as irrelevant and boring, with blame pointing to dull teaching methods, poor planning, lack of match to pupils' needs and little variety in teaching approaches. Other reports from across Europe have noted poor levels of the public understanding of science and scientific literacy, leading to recommendations to include this as a core emphasis within all pupils' experience of science (TLRP/ESRC, 2006; Osborne and Dillon, 2008).

NOS

At the same time difficulties faced by teachers in embracing such an emphasis, especially in relation to teaching the nature of science have been noted over many years (Lederman, 2007). Yet a crucial concern of the last change to the National Curriculum in England was that 'teachers should ensure that the knowledge, skills and understanding of how science works are integrated into the teaching of the breadth of study' (QCA/DfEE, 2007, p. 221) and similar considerations underpinned the focus on 'working scientifically' in the consultations leading to the latest version (DfE, 2013).

In contrast to some of the concerns outlined above, inspection reports have indicated that the quality of science teaching is high in many lessons. In reviewing the period 2004–10, OFSTED reports have noted many positive features, highlighting that 'the best teaching and highest standards were found in schools where staff drew on a rich range of resources to support a wide variety of activities. These were carefully planned to match pupils' needs and stimulate their interest' (OFSTED, 2008, p. 30). At the same time they expressed worries that:

> In too many primary and secondary schools, teachers were mainly concerned with meeting narrow test and examination requirements and course specifications. This led them to adopt methodologies which did not meet the needs of all pupils or promote independent learning.
>
> (OFSTED, 2008, p. 6)

The review of 2007–10 (OFSTED, 2011) noted that 'key factors in promoting students' engagement, learning and progress were more practical science lessons and the development of the skills of scientific enquiry' (OFSTED, 2011, p. 6) leading to a recommendation that teachers use 'practical work and scientific enquiry as the key stimulus to develop scientific knowledge understanding and skills' (OFSTED, 2011, p. 8).

It is against this background that we examine choice of teaching strategies and the manner in which these are implemented.

OBJECTIVES

By the end of this unit, you should:

- be able to identify a variety of teaching strategies for use in science;
- be able to select appropriate strategies to meet particular learning objectives and outcomes;
- be aware of how different teaching strategies and teacher behaviour can influence the motivation and interest of different pupils;
- be aware of ways of organising lessons to ensure that learning is maximised.

TEACHING STYLES

In Capel *et al.* (2013, p. 346, Unit 5.3), teaching style is defined as 'the combination of your underlying behaviours (personality plus characteristics), your microbehaviours (ways you communicate through speech and body language) and the teaching or pedagogical strategies you choose'. *Teacher behaviour* refers to the way that the teacher relates to the pupils. You may choose a very formal approach or a friendlier one; you may decide to use a more formal mode of behaviour in some instances (e.g. to give instructions for a practical) than in others (e.g. in facilitating class discussions). *Teaching strategy* concerns the actual teaching approach or method used. The teaching style chosen depends on particular views on how children learn, the group or individuals you are working with and the intended learning outcomes for a given teaching episode.

Task 4.4.1 **Analysing different teaching approaches**

Consider the three different approaches to teaching about corrosion outlined in Table 4.4.1.

1 List the strategies used by each teacher.
2 Identify possible strengths and weaknesses associated with each approach.
3 What differences in behaviour might be required of the teachers using each approach?
4 How do these approaches impact upon the requirements for the organisation of learning?
5 Which approach do you prefer and why?

The approaches in Table 4.4.1 roughly accord with the three broad bands of teaching strategies described in Capel *et al.* (2013, p. 349), with the first 'closed', the second 'framed' and the third 'negotiated'. You may have judged one particular approach to be more applicable to teaching specific aspects of the topic or particular pupils or classes and we consider these issues further within this unit. However, whatever the strategy used, there are aspects of your behaviour that are crucial to gaining the interest of the pupils. Thus an enthusiastic teacher, using the 'closed' approach, might start: 'Now, everyone! Look at this nail! Under water for 20 years and it still hasn't corroded! How can that be?' Compare this to a tired teacher, using the 'negotiated' approach: 'We're looking at corrosion over the next few lessons. You've done a bit of stuff on this before but we need to do some more. I know it's not very exciting but you need it for your exams. OK, let's brainstorm what you know to find out where the gaps are and together we can try and find a painless way to get the boring bits done.' I think you would agree that the first teacher is more likely to gain the pupils' interest. However, many would argue that the potential to stimulate interest and meet individual needs is higher in the negotiated approach. We return to such aspects of behaviour later in the chapter. In the next section we focus in more depth on teaching strategies, looking in particular at the range of methods available, their relationship to learning outcomes and the importance of using a range of strategies in your teaching.

TEACHING STRATEGIES

In deciding on which strategies to include within lessons there are a number of factors to consider. Here we look in particular at the need for variety, issues of concept development, enquiry and modelling.

The need for variety

There are a number of reasons why it is important to use a variety of strategies in teaching. These include the need to do the following:

■ meet a variety of learning objectives and outcomes;
■ cater for pupils' different backgrounds and attributes, including preferred modes of learning (drawing on evidence from learning theory and advances in neuroscience – see Chapter 5 of Capel *et al.*, 2013);
■ motivate and interest pupils.

■ Table 4.4.1 Three outline approaches to teaching the corrosion of metals

1	2	3
Four test tubes containing nails in different conditions present at start. Title: 'Corrosion' on board and diagram displayed on OHT. Class brought round front and teacher explains that each nail has been left for several weeks. Results explained to the class. Pupils return to seats and copy the diagrams and results from the board. Teacher explains nature of the processes taking place and dictates notes for the class to copy down. Class given some questions for homework as a preparation for a short test next lesson	Class given a brief introduction to the lesson, with an outline of the activities and objectives for the lesson. Worksheet distributed and discussed. This includes photographs of heavily corroded samples of 'iron' and others that have remained shiny and questions as prompts for suggesting hypotheses to explain differences. Class shown possible equipment that they might want to use and divided into small groups to suggest hypotheses and plan experiments. Plans shown to teacher and groups set up experiments to leave for next time. Class asked to complete plans for homework.	Question on board: 'Why does Mr Toplis's car have holes?' Class brought round front. Discussion of question linked to title of 'corrosion'. Task set: 'Investigate the factors that affect the corrosion of metals'. Class brainstorms possible factors and ideas to be investigated using flipchart. Class divided into small groups to investigate their chosen factors and prepare presentations. Some groups use the Internet; others decide to do a corrosion survey across the school; some opt for experiments. Class asked to gather information from home that might help as their homework.
Short test completed at start of lesson. Teacher goes over answers. Class given textbook showing results of corrosion experiments with different metals. Teacher explains results to group and writes notes on board to copy. Questions from book given to complete. Teacher concludes lesson by summarising work covered and relating to earlier work on the reactivity series. Second set of questions given for homework.	Short Q&A at start on last lesson. Objectives set. Group check nails. Changes noted. Teacher introduces idea of corrosion of different metals using video extract. Pupils set questions from book linking corrosion and the reactivity series. Lesson concludes with a Q&A to establish learning, and questions set for homework.	Teacher checks each group properly planned at start. Timings given. Support sheets provided to some pupils. Librarian and LSA work with groups who leave the classroom for surveys/research. Lesson finishes with group discussion of progress and further decisions on presentations. Some experiments shown to the whole class. Each pupil asked to write one thing they've learnt on posters stuck on wall by next time.

Homework questions discussed at start of lesson. Title 'methods of protecting against corrosion' given and slides of famous landmarks shown and discussed. Notes written on board for class to copy. Textbook with sections on 'factors that speed up/slow down corrosion' and 'uses of metals' discussed. Class asked to revise for test on corrosion next week as homework.

Past exam paper questions used for test. Last part of lesson used to discuss answers. Formal test signalled for end of year.

Pictures used for short Q&A at start, revising ideas covered so far. Nails checked. Teacher introduces set of nails left previously for longer period. Class discussion of findings. Pupils write conclusions based on class and teacher's results. Pupils' nails left set up to return to in 3 months time. Class set small group tasks to research 'factors that speed up/slow down corrosion' and 'uses of metals'. Class asked to research area for homework, to support posters for presentations

Class continue work on group tasks. Each group presents poster. Teacher summarises key points covered and pupils make notes. Q&A used to test understanding. Formal test to be given at end of year, with nails revisited part way through.

Posters on wall at start with 'things learnt'. Time limit set of first half of lesson to be ready to present. Teacher supports group preparation. 5-minute presentations given. Some involve rap, some posters, some plays, one a PowerPoint presentation. Teacher annotates flipchart from first lesson. Homework to prepare ready to teach others next time. Posters used to identify key areas for teaching: necessary factors; slowing/speeding up; nature of metal; link to uses all included.

Jigsaw activities used for pupils to teach each other the different aspects. Pupils asked to produce revision tools for their portfolio. Whole class concept map produced for display, updating flipchart. Some experiments left running. Signal that corrosion will be revisited later.

Let us examine the implications of each of these considerations for your practice.

Learning objectives and outcomes

There are many possible teaching strategies that can be used in a lesson. Thus, in seeking to teach the reactions of metals with acids, the teacher may choose to start with a demonstration, run a class practical in the main body of the lesson and conclude with a group discussion of the results and some note-taking. In deciding which methods to employ, it is important to identify the learning objectives and intended learning outcomes first, as indicated earlier in Unit 4.1 where there is a discussion of the differences between objectives and outcomes and the issues arising from particular emphases. Many schools have expectations of using learning outcomes rather than objectives. However, here we refer to objectives as well as outcomes as this recognises that there are some learning goals that cannot easily be reduced to outcomes that are simple, measurable and achievable in short time scales such as an individual lesson. The argument is that you need to have both objectives and outcomes in mind when selecting learning activities.

Task 4.4.2 **Activities and learning objectives or outcomes**

Table 4.4.2 contains a list of activities used by beginning science teachers on a range of courses. Add to this if you can think of other examples. Now, imagine that you have been asked to teach 'The eye'. Pick out a few examples of activities that you judge may be suitable for meeting each of the following learning objectives or outcomes:

- ▪ be able to name the parts of the eye;
- ▪ be able to research information about problems with sight;
- ▪ understand the role that creative thought processes and use of data played in developing our understanding of the eye;
- ▪ make accurate observations;
- ▪ work effectively with other people.

In each case explain why you have chosen the particular activities. Are any of them capable of being used to try and meet all five of these learning goals?

In completing Task 4.4.2 you may have noted:

- ▪ Some activities are better suited to meeting particular learning objectives (e.g. 'practical work' to the improvement of observational skills).
- ▪ Some objectives may be achieved just as well by different activities (e.g. knowledge of the parts of the eye may be equally well learnt through producing posters or writing notes).
- ▪ Some activities may only lead to superficial knowledge acquisition (e.g. recitation) while others may support deeper understanding and the attainment of higher cognitive goals (e.g. discussion or thought experiments).
- ▪ Some objectives *cannot* be met by certain activities (e.g. 'the ability to work with other people' through 'dictation').

■ **Table 4.4.2** Ways of learning: possible activities to use with pupils

1. Assessments	26. Experimenting	51. Presentations
2. Blogging	27. Fieldwork	52. Problem-solving
3. Brainstorming	28. Film	53. Projects
4. Card sorting	29. Flow diagrams	54. Quiz
5. Case studies	30. Games	55. Radio
6. Classifying	31. Group discussions	56. Reading
7. Concept cartoons	32. Inductive approaches	57. Recitation
8. Concept maps	33. Interactive whiteboard	58. Records
9. Creative writing	34. Internet searches	59. Reports
10. Critical incidents	35. Interviews	60. Role play
11. Crosswords	36. Investigations	61. Simulations
12. DARTS	37. Jig-saw activities	62. Slides
13. Data analysis	38 Lectures	63. Spider diagrams
14. Data bases	39. Mind maps	64. Spreadsheets
15. Data logging	40. Mobile learning	65. Surveys
16. Debate	41. Modelling	66. Tape work
17. Demonstrations	42. Multimedia	67. Thought experiments
18. Design tasks	43. Music	68. TV
19. Diaries	44. Mysteries	69. Video
20. Dictation	45. Note taking	70. Visitors
21. Discussion	46. Observation	71. Visits
22. Displays	47. Paired work	72. Web-page development
23. Drama	48. Photography	73. Word searches
24. Drawing	49. Posters	74. Workshops
25. Evaluation	50. Practical work	75. Writing

The need to link methods carefully to learning objectives is one reason why it is important for you to use a variety of strategies in your teaching. Moreover, some learning objectives may be missed altogether without careful thought about methods. For example, the learning objective which mentions the role of 'creative thought processes' reflects the aim of getting pupils to understand the importance of this in science. However, this is often given quite limited attention, hence leading to notions of 'creativity' being missing from pupils' understandings of the nature of science.

Pupil differences, learning styles, learning strategies and cognitive development

When selecting teaching strategies, it is clearly important to recognise the needs of the learners. Materials to support teachers produced at national level have been developed in the light of research suggesting that people have a range of preferences in the way they use their senses to explore ideas and construct their views of the world. Included in this are issues of cognitive development, learning styles, including visual, auditory and kinaesthetic learners, and multiple intelligences.

Task 4.4.3 **Learning styles and multiple intelligences**

Read the sections on learning styles and multiple intelligences from Units 4.3 and 5.1 of Capel *et al.* (2013). Consider the possible benefits for including learning styles and multiple intelligences as an important consideration in planning teaching and organising learning, together with critiques from those who counsel caution. Where do you stand in relation to this debate and why? Why do you think learning styles are so popular with a lot of teachers? This is an area of considerable controversy and it will be important for you to think carefully about your stance throughout your practice, as you seek to draw lessons from this field. Try out and evaluate strategies with your groups on teaching practice in the light of discussions with tutors and mentors.

Whatever your stance on issues of learning styles and multiple intelligences, the constructivist arguments examined in Unit 4.1 have clear implications for differentiation in the application of teaching strategies. The attendant organisational issues which arise are discussed later in this unit.

It is important to include a further reference here to pupils with additional needs. Thus, for example, various forms of physical impairment may make it difficult or impossible for some pupils to learn if a particular teaching strategy is used. In such cases it is also important that a variety of strategies are developed in order to meet such needs. There is also the need to seek to remove barriers to the inclusion of pupils with particular needs when planning teaching strategies, as has been made clear in National Curriculum documents (e.g. DfES/QCA, 2004). Difficulties can be overcome with the right support or modifications to course materials, equipment or buildings. In science practical work, this could include resizing and providing unbreakable apparatus (where sight impairment or dyspraxia is an issue), providing adjustable tables (for example, to assist wheelchair users) or supporting a pupil's upper arms (where pupils have weak muscular control). Unit 4.6 of Capel *et al.* (2013) gives sources of support for helping to meet particular additional needs. At the same time it is important to stress that ICT can often help overcome difficulties. For example, computer simulations of experiments which allow variables to be manipulated can enable a pupil to 'carry out' an experiment where the actual experiment is not possible.

Motivation and interest

Here we simply point out the importance of variety in maintaining interest and concentration. Psychological research shows that an individual's attention span on single tasks is limited, even when the motivation is there in the first place.

Concept development

One of the critiques of the modular organisation of the curriculum, a feature of many specifications in recent years, has been that less attention has been given to specific pedagogical approaches to teaching particular science concepts (see Unit 1.1 for a discussion of PCK). The CLISP project (see Unit 4.1) suggests an emphasis on constructivist approaches to learning, with the teacher selecting teaching strategies designed to overcome misconceptions and build deeper understanding. These issues have been recognised in some of the National Strategy materials designed to strengthen the teaching of concepts. The strategies finished in 2011 but a lot of excellent materials were created and can still be accessed through the National Archives (see Useful Websites).

Task 4.4.4 **Teaching strategies in using a constructivist approach**

Pick a science topic from the National Curriculum that you will be teaching at KS4 in your placement school and identify:

- progression in the concept across the Key Stages;
- common misconceptions (Driver *et al.*, 1994 and National Strategy materials will help here).

Plan and evaluate a lesson designed to use constructivist approaches to overcome likely misconceptions at earlier Key Stages.

Enquiry approaches

A number of arguments have been put forward for the use of enquiry strategies in science teaching and learning. These include: the potential to motivate and engage pupils; the potential for deepening learning; and the importance of explicitly modelling the way scientists work, hence supporting the teaching of aspects of the nature of science.

Task 4.4.5 **Enquiry-based learning**

Research the literature on enquiry-based learning in the science curriculum. Examine some materials designed to support teaching in this manner (you will find recently completed European projects such as PRIMAS, available at www.primas-project.eu, helpful in this regard). List the key components of enquiry teaching strategies. How is enquiry represented in the current science National Curriculum and examination specifications? What strategies would you use to ensure that enquiry is a strong feature of your teaching approach?

A key component of enquiry approaches is engagement with evidence and argumentation. The importance of using argumentation is taken up in Unit 5.1.

Modelling

The importance of using models and visualisations in science teaching and learning has been stressed for many years. Here we ask you to look in detail at the use of models in one area of science with considerable conceptual difficulties and then apply this in your teaching.

Task 4.4.6 **Modelling**

Work on misconceptions concerning electric current and voltage has led to the production of resources to support teachers in use of models to overcome such misconceptions. The scheme produced at Leeds University (available at www. education.leeds.ac.uk/assets/files/research/cssme/ElecCircuitsScheme.pdf) was at the forefront of thinking in this area and the 'Supermarket and Bakery' model was turned into an interactive model, currently available online through the National STEM Centre at www.nationalstemcentre.org.uk). Access and evaluate the model and its use.

Many other models can also be accessed online. Examine a range of these models. What are the characteristics of the effective use of different models? Pick out an area where you think models will be useful for teaching a particular concept in your placement school. Plan and evaluate a lesson using one or more models.

Researchers and curriculum designers have been seeking to develop approaches and resources that include modelling and visualisation in enquiry approaches. A very good example of this, now being used by teachers in many countries, is the web-based inquiry science environment (WISE) developed by Marcia Linn and colleagues at the University of California at Berkeley (www.wise.berkeley.edu).

THE ORGANISATION OF LEARNING AND TEACHER BEHAVIOUR

Thus far, we have concentrated mainly on teaching strategies. It is now important to bring in the second part of the teaching style definition mentioned at the start of the unit, that of teacher behaviour. This factor is crucial if interest is to be generated and maintained and learning is to be organised in an effective manner. In this section we incorporate aspects of teacher behaviour within the organisational aspects of implementing teaching strategies.

In considering the organisation of learning we focus on: (1) the different sections of a lesson, including transitions between sections; (2) questioning; (3) differentiation issues; and, finally, (4) 'awe and wonder'.

Different sections of lessons

The Science National Strategy, implemented from 2001 until 2011, sought to stress particular features and structures of effective lessons. This was interpreted by some as meaning that you must have a 'three-part', 'four-part' or even 'six-part' lesson for it to be effective. This is not the case. The key is to structure in a way that is flexible and geared to meeting the learning needs of the pupils. Thus, the subsections which follow are not intended to be read as fixed sections, rather as guides to approaches.

Start of lessons

The start of lessons is crucial (DCSF, 2009). It is here that expectations are established and the correct atmosphere for learning developed. Although this chapter does not focus on the organisation of the classroom *per se*, it is worth remembering that the learning environment itself is important (see Unit 1.3).

There are a number of actions to consider at the start of lessons:

- Seek to create a positive learning environment through the way you greet pupils. This means being at the door and being positive in the way you interact on arrival.
- Share the purpose of the lesson, indicating how it links to previous lessons and prior learning.
- Share the learning objectives or outcomes with the pupils *when this is appropriate* – you may wish to hide these until later, let them emerge over time or encourage individual pupils to make their own decisions about priorities. It is often a good idea to have objectives displayed somewhere in the room so they can be referred to at different points in the lesson. In some schools there is an expectation that outcomes are 'levelled', either in National Curriculum or examination grade terms. However, this is not a national expectation and OFSTED have made clear that they are not expecting to see this.
- Use formative assessment strategies to establish prior learning (see Unit 6.1 for examples of these as well as a discussion of broader assessment issues). It is here that you can also expose misconceptions and use this as a means to be explicit about the development of concepts or processes.
- Use techniques to help relax the class (e.g. closing eyes and focusing thoughts; repetition of instructions to relax at progressively lower and slower rates; breathing exercises). Share these explicitly with the class, explaining their purpose with groups unused to this sort of approach.
- Use music to help establish a positive working atmosphere. However, take care! For some people background music can be irritating and it is best to avoid more recent popular music as this can provoke off-task discussion and argument.
- Include physical activities (these can be incorporated from time to time during lessons). There is evidence that aerobic exercise can support aspects of brain function (see Capel *et al.*, 2013: Unit 5.6, for a more detailed discussion of the brain and learning). Others would simply say that activities such as this help create a good atmosphere in which to start work.

It is obviously not possible or sensible to use all of the different techniques each time. However, establishing routines that include scene setting and short activities to generate interest is important. It is also important that pupils are clear about *why* they are doing what they are doing. Further to this, you might want to consider putting pupils in the position of being scientists right from the start of your teaching with any group. Your start to individual lessons might then reference this, with particular aspects of being a scientists picked out within each lesson.

Starter activities

Aspects of many of the activities included in Table 4.4.2 can be drawn on to develop starter activities. A typical starter will last from five to ten minutes but there are no rules.

The one chosen depends on a number of factors, including the objectives of the lesson and the nature of the group. Examples of starters include:

■   visual cues to promote enquiry questions (e.g. picture of the Shard in London to prompt questions about materials and construction);
■   models to prompt thinking about concepts;
■   thought experiments – examples can be found in the CASE materials (Adey and Yates, 2001); for a discussion of some famous examples, see Brown (1991);
■   'science in the news' items (the Internet is very helpful here). Present an article or headline relevant to the topic and ask for opinions or explanations.
■   controversial statements – present and start the lesson by taking sides;
■   diagnostic tests using 'show me' strategies for answering questions (e.g. answers written on small white boards; yes/no cards; 'traffic light' cards to indicate confidence/ agreement (red indicates no idea/wrong, amber some idea/maybe and green sure/right);
■   short video clips, e.g. volcanic eruption; woman on chat show making her eyes pop out of their sockets!;
■   key word games, e.g. loop cards, word dominoes.

Many commercial books and web-based resources are available to support you in developing further ideas.

Main body of the lesson

The main body of the lesson can itself include a number of different parts which depend on the nature of the objectives and the activities being included. However, even if there is one main activity, such as a practical, it is important to ensure that this is broken down into parts to help maintain pace and check on learning. Thus short mini plenaries within lessons, with a focus back on objectives, may often be important. Other approaches, such as jigsaw activities, simulations and role-play may contain more natural breaks; for details of the thinking behind such approaches, see Joyce *et al.* (2002); there are many practical examples in this book. Strong arguments have been made for the inclusion of a lot of practical activities within the core of the lesson (see Unit 5.2). For some pupils it is helpful to use activities that last for relatively short periods in order to help maintain concentration, keep on task and generate pace. If you have the expected learning outcomes displayed in the room, you can refer individuals back to these without interrupting the main flow. This will help with approaches to AfL (see Unit 6.1). However, there are lessons where the intended learning is not easily broken down into specific chunks or measurable outcomes, so you should not always feel you have to do this as a matter of routine.

End of lesson

The end of a lesson is as important as the start. A plenary at the end of a lesson might typically last for five to ten minutes. It is here that you can have an overall check on whether or not learning objectives or outcomes have been met. You can also reinforce expectations, share achievement and set targets. Again, strategies that promote the active involvement of pupils are important. A whole range of activities may be included here as well, with a focus on determining the learning that has taken place. Examples include key word matches, sharing mnemonics, pupil presentations and concept map development.

Transitions between phases

A crucial point of lessons is the transition between activities. There are two important aspects of transitions: organisational issues and learning considerations.

Careful management and organisation of transitions are vital. To be effective in this respect, it is important to establish clear routines and ensure that expectations are met. Aim to develop signals to use with your group. These could involve a clap, count down, loud bang, particular snatch of music or an announcement of 'statues!' Such techniques can also be used to introduce breaks in activity (e.g. for aerobic or relaxation exercises) when pupils seem to be drifting off task. This is often important in longer lessons. There is also a need to give clear time warnings in advance of transitions, sometimes counting down ('five minutes left now!'; 'one more minute only!', etc.), so pupils are prepared for the point when you want everyone to stop. Such time warnings may also be accompanied by organisational instructions, such as: 'turn Bunsens off now!', 'return equipment to trays and clear up the bench' or 'discuss results with your partner ready to share with the class'. These again help to ensure pupils are ready for the change of activity or focus.

The second aspect of transitions focuses on intended learning outcomes and is equally important. This concerns the need to ensure that the links between possible learning outcomes from one activity and learning targets in the next part of the lesson are made explicit to the pupils. If this is not done, it is likely that many pupils may miss the point of the activities and simply remember what they *did* rather than what they were supposed to learn. It is also possible that they will not draw on earlier parts of the lesson appropriately in later tasks. The cues needed to help with this aspect of transition are provided by phrases such as: 'now we've got those two factors identified, we're going to find out why they're important', 'hold on to that idea, you are going to use it to try and solve the next problem' or 'keep those results in mind, we are going to see if they fit with Newton's ideas'. As mentioned earlier in the chapter, it is sometimes useful to focus back on any intended learning outcomes shared at the start of a lesson at key transitions.

Questioning

One generic aspect of teaching that is important to cross-reference here is that of questioning. This is a vital part of many teaching strategies. It is particularly important in science if targets associated with higher level thinking and enquiry are to be achieved.

Task 4.4.7 **Types of questions science teachers ask**

Read pages 135–9 of Capel *et al.* (2013) and the article on the types of questions asked by science teachers (Koufetta-Menicou and Scaife, 2000). Observe one or more questioning sequences used by teachers during your observations in your placement school and classify the questions according to the categories identified by Koufetta-Menicou and Scaife. Draw up a questioning sequence of your own for use while teaching objectives from the enquiry parts of the science curriculum. Ask your mentor to provide you with feedback about the sequence used.

Differentiation

The need to differentiate in order to meet individual needs is discussed in detail in Capel *et al.* (2013), Unit 4.1. The issues raised in the unit have considerable importance for the organisation and structuring of lessons. Complete the tasks associated with differentiation in Unit 4.1 of Capel *et al.* (2013) and Task 4.4.8.

Task 4.4.8 **Differentiation strategies**

During your early experiences in schools, keep a log of the differentiation strategies you observe being used by experienced teachers. Where possible, discuss these strategies with pupils and note their response. How effective are the strategies you noted?

   Keep a log of the differentiation strategies you make use of during the early part of your school experience and in the later part experiment with any strategies you have not already had the opportunity to trial. Ask experienced teachers to observe and give feedback. Again, seek to determine pupils' responses and use these to inform your future practice.

Awe and wonder

Awe and wonder cannot be taught but maybe they can be caught. How can you as a teacher convey a sense of the excitement of science to your pupils? This comes back to the enthusiastic teacher mentioned earlier. Is it really amazing (as well as counter-intuitive) that bulb after bulb can be placed in parallel and still shine as brightly as the previous one? Or is learning physics simply a list of equations to be learnt and calculations to be done? Can a dull grey rock really contain that shiny metal? Or is Earth science really boring? A tree – from thin air? Imagine journeying to Mars! On paper, it is hard to convey the behavioural attributes of a teacher who is seeking to generate such feelings of wonder without sounding crass or resorting to multiple exclamation marks. Yes, generating awe and wonder does require using a variety of teaching strategies, including those which allow feelings to be expressed and shared. Yes, appropriate use of ICT can help. Yes, it is important to know about the pupils' needs. However, it is your behaviour as a role model that is most important of all. Without showing that you are interested, you stand little chance of gaining the interest of many pupils. This is especially important in motivating pupils at the start of lessons, as noted earlier in the unit. Many of us were motivated to become scientists by either the subject, or the teacher, or possibly both. Richard Feynman attributes the influence of his father to his way of looking at the world and gives an example of such an encounter:

> I was playing with what we called an express wagon. It had a ball in it and I pulled the wagon and I noticed something about the way the ball moved, so I went to my father and I said, 'Say, Pop, I noticed something: when I pull the wagon the ball rolls to the back of the wagon and when I am pulling it along and I suddenly stop, the ball rolls to the front of the wagon' and I says, 'Why is that?' And he said 'That nobody knows ... this tendency is called inertia but nobody knows why it is true.' That's a

deep understanding, he doesn't give it a name, he knew the difference between giving it a name and knowing something. He went on: 'If you look close, you'll find the ball does not rush to the back of the wagon but it's the back of the wagon that you're pulling against the ball; that the ball stands still or as a matter of fact from the friction starts to move forward really and doesn't move back.'

(Feynman, 2000, pp. 4–5)

Feynman's father had no direct scientific training but appears to have had a sharp eye, an inquiring mind and a sense of wonder about the natural world.

METACOGNITION

In conclusion, let us return to the learners. There is growing evidence that when students are taught about how to learn, encouraged to think about their own learning and given choices about the strategies they use, then their learning is enhanced (see Unit 5.1 in Capel *et al.*, 2013)). The development of thinking skills was an important part of the Secondary National Strategy and the QCDA's (2009) Framework of Personal, Learning and Thinking Skills (PLTS) included the development of 'Reflective Learners' as a key goal for schools. In terms of the focus of this chapter, this means going further than simply selecting and implementing particular teaching strategies. It also means sharing with pupils the *reasons* why you are using the strategies chosen and the way you are implementing them. It also means sometimes giving *them* the opportunity to work in ways they choose themselves. You might like to look back now to Task 4.4.1 and the implications of ideas on metacognition for deciding between the three approaches outlined.

SUMMARY AND KEY POINTS

In this unit we have discussed different teaching strategies and the way that these can be used to achieve particular learning outcomes and meet the needs of different pupils. We have also considered the importance of teacher behaviour in generating interest and enthusiasm. The important stages of a lesson have been highlighted and strategies that can be employed to help maximise learning discussed. In employing such strategies it is suggested that you should seek to do these *with* pupils rather than *at* them.

REFERENCES

Adey, P. and Yates, C. (2001) *Thinking Science: The Materials of the CASE Project*, Walton-on-Thames: Thomas Nelson.

Brown, J. R. (1991) *Laboratory of the Mind: Thought Experiments in the Natural Sciences*, London: Routledge.

DCFS (2009) *The National Strategies Framework for Teaching Science*, available at: http://webarchive.nationalarchives.gov.uk/20110809091832/http://www.teachingandlearningresources.org.uk (accessed 10 February 2014).

DfE (2013) *The National Curriculum in England: Framework Document*, available at: www.education.gov.uk/schools/teachingandlearning/curriculum/nationalcurriculum2014/ (accessed 10 February 2014).

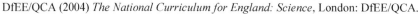

DfEE/QCA (2004) *The National Curriculum for England: Science*, London: DfEE/QCA.

Driver, R., Squires, A., Rushworth, P. and Wood-Robinson, V. (1994) *Making Sense of Secondary Science: Research into Children's Ideas*, London: Routledge.

Feynman, R. P. (2000) *The Pleasure of Finding Things Out*, London: Penguin, pp. 4–5.

House of Commons Science and Technology Committee (2002) *Science Education from 14 to 19. Third Report of Session 2001–02*, London: The Stationery Office Ltd.

Joyce, B., Calhoun, E. and Hopkins, D. (2002) *Models of Learning: Tools for Teaching*, Buckingham: Open University Press.

Koufetta-Menicou, C. and Scaife, J. (2000) 'The types of questions asked by science teachers and their importance for science teaching', *School Science Review*, 81(296): 79–84.

Lederman, N. G. (2007) 'Nature of science: past, present and future', in S. K. Abell and N. G. Lederman (eds), *Handbook of Research on Science Education*, Hillsdale, NJ: Lawrence Erlbaum Associates, pp. 31–79.

Millar, R. and Osborne, J. (eds) (1998) *Beyond 2000: Science Education for the Future: A Report with Ten Recommendations*, London: King's College London, School of Education.

OFSTED (2008) *Success in Science*, London: OFSTED.

OFSTED (2011) *Successful Science*, Manchester: OFSTED.

Osborne, J. and Dillon, J. (2008) *Science Education in Europe: Critical Reflections. A Report to the Nuffield Foundation*, London: King's College.

PRIMAS (2013) *Promoting Inquiry-Based Learning in Mathematics and Science Education*, available at: www.primas-project.eu (accessed 10 February 2014).

QCDA (2009) 'Framework of Personal, Learning and Thinking Skills (PLTS)'. Available at: http://webarchive.nationalarchives.gov.uk/20110223175304/ http://curriculum.qcda.gov.uk/uploads/PLTS_framework_tcm8-1811.pdf

QCA/DfEE (2007) *Programme of Study for Key Stage 4*, London: QCA.

TLRP/ESRC (2006) *Science Education in Schools: Issues, Evidence and Proposals,* London: University of London: TLRP/Institute of Education.

FURTHER READING

ASE Science Practice series.

For reading on specific strategies for teaching particular science concepts and aspects of the curriculum, the ASE Science Practice series has been designed to provide subject knowledge support for teachers. Here are some of the titles.

Kind, V. and Kind, P. M. (eds) (2008) *Teaching Secondary: How Science Works* (ASE John Murray Science Practice), London: Hodder Education.

Reiss, M. (ed.) (2011) *Teaching Secondary Biology* (ASE Science Practice), London: Hodder Education.

Sang, D. (ed.) (2011) *Teaching Secondary Physics* (ASE Science Practice), London: Hodder Education.

Taber, K. S. (ed.) (2012) *Teaching Secondary Chemistry* (ASE Science Practice), London: Hodder Education.

Ginnis, P. (2002) *The Teacher's Toolkit*, Carmarthen: Crown House Publishing.

A very useful generic book containing a wealth of strategies to support teaching and learning, together with their rationale.

USEFUL WEBSITES

In terms of national expectations and initiatives for the four home countries, government websites (e.g. DfE for England) provide important links.

National Strategy materials are available through the national archives: http://webarchive.nationalarchives.gov.uk and the National STEM Centre, www.nationalstemcentre.org.uk (accessed 9 April 2014).

A range of advice, support and materials for implementing teaching strategies are provided by the **subject associations** (ASE, IoP, SoB, RSC) and other supportive organisations such as Nuffield and Gatsby.

TEACHING SCIENCE
SPECIFIC CONTEXTS

INTRODUCTION

Teaching science is not just about the subject matter but is about ways and means, the contexts, of how the subject can be taught. Some of these contexts are specific to science, such as the use of practical work. Some are more general but nevertheless directly applicable to science such as language or the use of Information and Communication Technology (ICT). This chapter explores some of these contexts that need to be borne in mind when teaching and learning science, how science can be made accessible to pupils and how it connects to other areas of the school curriculum and beyond.

Unit 5.1 deals with the need for effective communication in science and lowering the language barrier if science is to be meaningful and comprehended by all pupils. It suggests some strategies for questioning, for dialogue and for managing discussions.

Unit 5.2 discusses the types, reasons and some issues around the uses of practical work in science, including the all-important areas of safety and organisation of work in the laboratory. Practical work brings with it many advantages for pupils but the need to anticipate management issues and to try all practical activities beforehand cannot be emphasised enough. All too many practical lessons or practical work in lessons have failed because the planning and preparation have not been sufficiently thought out or thought through.

Unit 5.3 addresses some uses of ICT in science and some advice about the contexts in which ICT can be used and how to evaluate its contribution to learning science.

Citizenship is a theme for Unit 5.4 that crosses the curriculum in secondary schools and deals with many of the issues that affect pupils' lives. Science education plays an important part in this theme and in this unit Marcus Grace explores some of the socio-scientific topics that arise and some ways these may be approached in the classroom.

Unit 5.5 discusses the sensitive and personal issues around sex and health education. It provides invaluable advice and guidance about how this area can be approached and the law relating to sex, sexuality and the use of drugs.

Unit 5.6 goes beyond the classroom and into what can be regarded as more authentic contexts. Again, planning is of vital importance here but the opportunities are very wide indeed and not only can go beyond the classroom but beyond the science curriculum.

LANGUAGE IN LEARNING SCIENCE

Rob Toplis

INTRODUCTION

The sciences have their unique languages. Just like other languages, these include specific vocabulary, grammar and constructions. A pupil coming into the science classroom has to become familiar with the language of science. It is hardly surprising therefore that scientific language is often seen as a barrier to learning science (Henderson and Wellington, 1998). In order to appreciate some of the problems, look at Task 5.1.1 and answer the questions.

Task 5.1.1 **Jabberwocky**

Read the following well-known poem and answer the questions at the end.

> 'Twas brillig, and the slithy toves
> Did gyre and gimble in the wabe;
> All mimsy were the borogoves,
> And the mome raths outgrabe.
> "Beware the Jabberwock, my son!
> The jaws that bite, the claws that catch!
> Beware the Jubjub bird, and shun
> The frumious Bandersnatch!"
> He took his vorpal sword in hand:
> Long time the manxome foe he sought –
> So rested he by the Tumtum tree.
> And stood awhile in thought.

(Carroll, *Jabberwocky*)

Questions:

1 Apart from the Jabberwock, what else must the son beware of?
2 What sort of sword was it?
3 What did the slithy toves do?

If you answered: 1. the Jubjub bird; 2. vorpal sword and 3. did gyre and gimble in the wabe, you can clearly comprehend the poem. But it's all nonsense; these things do not exist and the poem is pure fantasy. And yet you are able to answer the questions correctly. In a number of instances, science is like this for a number of pupils. It may not make any sense to them, but they can sometimes learn to answer the questions. They may *know* but they may not necessarily *understand*.

OBJECTIVES

By the end of this unit, you should:

- be aware of the range of language in science and the way it's used;
- appreciate that science has a distinct language that learners need to engage with;
- consider the diversity of speaking, reading and writing in science;
- be aware of the science teacher's role in developing language in science.

The poet Sylvia Plath explained her own response to some of the problems she encountered in school science:

> The day I went into a physics class it was death. A short, dark man with a high lisping voice, named Mr Manzi, stood in front of the class in a tight blue suit holding a little wooden ball. He put the ball on a steep grooved slide and let it run down to the bottom. Then he started talking about "let a equal acceleration and let t equal time" and suddenly he was scribbling letters and numbers and equals signs all over the blackboard and my mind went dead.
>
> (cited in Claxton, 1991, p. 21)

This description provides an example of one way in which the language of science blocks out understanding and enjoyment of science. One set of problems with the use of language in science is that it is not like the language used in everyday contexts. These problems may relate to how the language is used, the registers or how the language is expressed in science, and the different meanings of words. Science has a number of different groups of words.

TYPES OF WORDS

Technical words

'Technical' words are those that are specific to science. These are often the names given to chemicals, animals, plants or pieces of apparatus. Pupils may be familiar with that icon of school science, the Bunsen burner, but will be less familiar with words such as alkali, condenser, van der Graaf generator or Toricellian barometer.

Concept words

These words convey meaning around concepts such as energy, reaction or homeostasis. These concepts are often quite difficult for pupils to grasp and frequently depend on their cognitive level, that is, their level of understanding related to their age and progress. The Swiss psychologist, Jean Piaget, proposed two levels that are relevant to the secondary age range: concrete and formal operational, and stated that these roughly equate to moving from a descriptive level of understanding to an abstract level at around the age of 11 years. Although there is some debate about the ages that pupils can move between these levels, Piaget's work does help us to understand some of the problems that pupils may have at different stages. Many scientific concepts are abstract ideas and therefore pose difficulties for pupils at certain ages and stages. The concepts around the meanings of these words usually have to be taught explicitly, using models, analogies and examples, and reinforced at intervals.

Process words

These words bear some similarity to concept words but represent distinct scientific processes. The first problem, as with concept words, is that these processes are often abstract in nature and difficult to understand. Processes such as respiration, photosynthesis and decomposition involve ideas that are beyond easy description and require higher level functioning to understand. If we use the process of *excretion* as an example, the abstract ideas associated with absorption, transport and with removal of waste, as well as dealing with any misconceptions about excretion and faeces, all require some very abstract thought. Second, these processes are often complex in having numerous steps or stages that need to be understood. The *synthesis* of ammonia in the Haber process to then produce fertilisers has a number of stages and is further complicated by the temperature, pressure and catalyst conditions in the process. Third, there is a risk that these words will be misconceived by pupils who will take the meaning of the process as something entirely different. There are a number of processes that produce misconceptions in the minds of school-age pupils (and also undergraduates and even scientists themselves!). If we take the example of *respiration*, scientists have a very specific understanding about this complex biochemical process. However, pupils may come to science lessons with an entirely different understanding, often assuming respiration is the process of breathing and sometimes even confusing it with 'perspiration'.

Science words and everyday words

Further confusion may arise in pupils' minds where scientific words are identical to everyday words but where the meaning in science and meaning in everyday language are very different. A word such as 'volatile' has a very specific meaning in chemistry as a liquid with a low boiling point that evaporates easily. However, its everyday meaning indicates a person who may be quick-tempered and liable to rapid changes of emotion. Similarly 'work' has a defined meaning in physics but may be seen by pupils as associated with employment.

TYPES OF AUDIENCE

The language of teachers and the language of pupils may differ considerably. If you listen into the pupil talk in playgrounds and corridors and compare it with talk in staffrooms and school offices, there are very noticeable differences in the words chosen, the length of spoken sentences and responses, and in the use of local or regional words. The latter may not be limited to local dialect words but may be words derived from the current media or sub-culture: it has been estimated that only 23 per cent of 15-year-olds use Standard English as their common parlance (Hudson and Holmes, 1995). Against this background it is important for teachers to 'mind their language'.

Task 5.1.2 **Unfamiliar words**

Consider the following extract:

Today we are going to review our findings from last lesson and extend these by changing a second **variable**. Analysis of the data should show a relationship between the **voltage** and **resistance** and the **current** and **resistance**.

The words in bold are those associated with science but what about the others? Which of the other words might be unfamiliar?

This is not to suggest that a teacher's own language should become stilted or adopt slang terms. It is rather to suggest that certain words used in a teacher's everyday speech may not be those adopted by the pupils in the class and that a teacher needs to be aware and offer explanations where necessary, rather than take it for granted that everything he or she says is understood.

TYPES OF REGISTER

Science has a number of registers, or varieties of formal language and vocabulary, which are not used often in everyday language and are therefore uncommon. The registers contain unfamiliar tenses and constructions that indicate the tentative nature of scientific data or conclusions such as: *could, may, seem* or *is said to be*. They include logical connectives such as *thus* and *therefore* and verbs converted into nouns (nominalizations), for example, *growth, respiration* and *excretion*.

The writing styles in science can be very unfamiliar; the personal or active (*We did*), compared with the traditional passive (*It was done*). These two styles of writing in science are the subject of a continuing debate. Supporters of the traditional passive voice in science reports claim that this style is how science has always been reported and that it makes the report more impersonal, more objective. The belief that a passive voice is expected by scientific convention and by journals poses a number of questions. Do all scientists write like this? If this is a convention, why are we imposing it on the vast majority of school science pupils who will never go on to use it? What styles of writing do scientists really use? It is worth remembering the opening sentence of the Watson and Crick letter published in *Nature* in 1953, 'We wish to suggest a structure for the salt of deoxyribose nucleic acid (D.N.A.)' (Watson and Crick, 1953, p. 737). The writing style in science reports is further compounded by the format of Apparatus, Method, Results, Conclusions, and the use of the terms 'experiment' and 'investigation' when we all know what the answers will be! These continue to be some of the idiosyncrasies peculiar to school science but do these enhance the image of science?

USING THE VOICE

The voice is the main tool for teachers and science teachers are no exception. It is used to introduce, direct, organise, maintain attention, question and summarise. It is important to use it effectively – and to look after it. In the first few days of term, particularly after the longer summer break, the voice can suffer. It is at this time that it can become strained, hoarse and the teacher is prone to sore throats and aching neck muscles as voices adapt to new volumes and directions. Volume is not usually the answer to being heard: clarity, variations in tone and voice projection are. Volume usually means a high volume or shouting. This is not often effective and is wearing for both the class and you. A higher volume needs to be reserved for those few occasions when it is really necessary. Clarity means speaking clearly without mumbling and involves directing your voice towards the class or individuals rather than speaking to your notes or lesson plan. A variation in tone is needed to avoid a monotone which will very quickly fail to engage pupils. Voice projection is something that is important and can be learned; it may involve directing the voice to an imaginary row of pupils behind the back row of the class. It is a good idea to practise and ask someone to listen from a suitable distance. If your voice projection needs more help, the drama teacher will be the expert in school.

Task 5.1.3 **Using the voice**

As part of your secondary school experience, observe and note drama lessons:

1 How does the drama teacher make their voice carry across the drama studio or space?
2 How does the voice vary when the teacher is reading, giving instructions or inviting responses?
3 Does the voice change for different groupings of pupils? How?
4 What kinds of phrases does the teacher use to move, group and change pupils' activities?

ASKING QUESTIONS

Science teachers ask a lot of questions: what do we call the centre of an atom? What process does a green plant use to make food? How are snow hares camouflaged? Why does a satellite stay in orbit? What would happen if an astronaut mending the outside of a space station lost his lifeline? Why is the theory of evolution important? Some of these questions can elicit simple one-word or one-phrase answers; others require more detailed answers, thought and consideration. In other words, some are closed questions – for which there is a short and simple answer – and others are more open questions that require extended answers. It is probably not as simple as this, as there is a spectrum with different kinds of questions and answers that vary in their description and reasoning.

Closed, one answer questions   Open, extended answer questions

There are advantages and disadvantages of closed and open questions. Short, directed questions can be used effectively to maintain the pace of lessons, to provide a quick check on understanding by different individuals at various points of the lesson and to ensure that pupils know what they have to do in practical sessions. However, a broad range of questioning techniques is needed to ascertain the level of pupils' understanding and open questions provide opportunities to reason, to uncover misconceptions and to provide some thinking behind the science.

A useful typology of questions has been suggested by Koufetta-Menicou and Scaife (2000) (see Unit 4.4) that is hierarchical in moving from lower cognitive levels to higher ones:

■   *Recall*: A simple recall of facts, definitions or events of the type, 'Do you remember last lesson when we . . .?'
■   *Describing*: Relatively simple descriptive or comparative judgements such as 'Which leaf is longer?', 'Which flask has the darker colour?'
■   *'How' questions*: Using procedures for justification. For example, 'How would you make this a fair test?'
■   *Evidence seeking*: Questions that seek proof or use evidence such as, 'How do you know smoking is linked to lung cancer?'
■   *Pattern recognition and questioning* pupils about patterns that may show a trend in data.
■   *'Why' questions*: These questions are possibly some of the most useful as they represent deeper levels of thinking and using scientific knowledge. They are also valuable in diagnosing misconceptions in science.
■   *'What if . . .?'* questions that take the problem further and allow extrapolation.
■   *Prediction*: These questions are also able to extend pupils' ideas and draw upon their scientific knowledge.
■   *Concluding questions* such as 'What can we say about the results of this practical?'. These questions may allow pattern recognition, the use of scientific knowledge and evaluative suggestions about data and future work.

Task 5.1.4 **Categorising questions**

As part of your secondary school experience, observe and note some of the questions used in lessons:

1 How many of the questions were closed? How many were open?
2 How were the questions directed? To boys? To girls? To individual pupils by name? To the whole class?
3 How many questions started with 'Why? How many with 'What?'

4 How many questions were asked by pupils themselves? Were these open or closed?

It is important to keep in mind what questioning is really for; what are you trying to do as a teacher? Are your questions assessing? Diagnosing misconceptions? Are you using them as a link to another section of the lesson? Are you checking your learning outcomes or objectives have been met for the lesson?

Problems can arise with verbal questioning in the classroom. The first is the 'Can you guess what I'm thinking' question, the one where the teacher knows the answers and yet asks questions in an attempt to get the pupils to somehow arrive at the same answer. Invariably, they don't. The process then becomes time-consuming and frustrating for both the teacher and the pupils. What is more important is that it is not about pupil learning. Questions therefore need to be thought about carefully, with consideration of what you are trying to achieve. You may want the class to arrive at a particular answer, key word or item of understanding but need to consider how they will get there and even if questioning is an appropriate way of getting there. In other words, you will need to *scaffold* your classroom strategies to achieve your final aim.

A second problem relates to your own questioning behaviour. Are you questioning or interrogating? Quick-fire, short-answer, yes or no answers may maintain a degree of attention and pace for a while but they may not be very conducive to learning. A situation where all sensible contributions are accepted and wrong or partial answers are used to pick up misconceptions, rather than being simply classed as right or wrong, are more likely to provide you with information for adapting the lesson or planning the next. Associated with quick-fire styles of questioning is a third problem, that of not allowing thinking and answering time. Classroom assessment is more effective when pupils are given time to think about answers, rather than any delay in answering being followed by an easier question. This may seem one of those ideas that is fine in theory but in practice may lead to opportunities for disturbance and draw the focus of pupils away from the teacher and their objectives of the questioning. However, using suitable strategies such as timed paired peer talk or very short written answers may allow thinking time to be built into a lesson without the risk of 'off-task' behaviour. Whatever the types of questioning used, a variety of styles that involve interaction will be more constructive than a limited number of approaches.

USING TALK

Dialogic teaching

Dialogic teaching refers to using talk to encourage pupils to participate actively in extended dialogues that help them articulate, reflect upon and modify their own understanding. It involves ongoing talk between teacher and pupil, rather than teacher presentation, and it is through this dialogue that pupils can develop their understanding, adopt new concepts and help them to address misconceptions (Scott *et al.*, 2007). Dialogic teaching relies on a communicative approach on how a teacher works with pupils to develop their ideas where there is an attempt to acknowledge the views of others and to attend to them through dialogue. The extensive work of the late Phil Scott characterised this approach along the dimensions of *interactive–non-interactive* and *dialogic–authoritative* which, when combined, give four ways a teacher can communicate with pupils in science lessons:

Interactive/dialogic
Non-interactive/dialogic
Interactive/authoritative
Non-interactive/authoritative

A teacher may not always use a dialogic approach but its value lies in developing scientific ideas in the classroom (Scott *et al.*, 2007). The suggested reading of Mortimer and Scott (2003) will allow you to explore dialogic teaching further.

Task 5.1.5 **Observing classroom talk**

As part of your school experience, observe what sort of discussion work takes place in a variety of lessons:

1 How is the class arranged for discussions?
2 How much time is used for discussion?
3 What is the teacher's role?
4 Which of the dialogic categories above (interactive/dialogic; non-interactive/ dialogic; interactive/authoritative and non-interactive/authoritative) were evident?
5 What were the outcomes of the discussions?

Managing discussions

Science teachers tend to use discussion approaches with their classes less often than in some other school subjects such as English or the Humanities. However, pupils often enjoy discussion activities (Cerini *et al.*, 2003) and this approach is often fruitful when dealing with more controversial issues in the classroom (see Unit 5.4). The following four categories suggest ways that discussions can be managed in a science classroom – and some questions about the approaches suggested:

1 *The Open Forum Model*: Ask two questions, for example, 'What adaptations do giraffes show? How did they get like this?' If you nominate respondents with their hands up, some pertinent questions might be: How did I select respondents? Why did I select those respondents? What would have happened without the 'hands up' rule? What did I do about the wrong answer or the controversial answer? Who is this discussion for?
2 *The Pair Model*: Ask the question, for example, 'What adaptations do badgers have to survive in their habitats?' Allow pupils to discuss this question in pairs and ask some pairs to volunteer answers. Some questions to consider might be: What does the non-speaking member of the pair do? What do some of the pairs do when a pupil is answering? Is there a way this can be improved? In what ways is this approach better than the first model?

3   *Group Discussion Model*: The pupils are in groups of three or four. The teacher asks: 'In your groups, suggest ways you could conduct a practical inquiry to find out if a urine sample is from a patient with diabetes.' Some evaluative questions for you might be: What knowledge is needed for this? What are you looking for with this discussion? Who provides a summary of the discussion? How is this discussion recorded for everyone?

4   *Combined Group Discussion Record Model*: In pupil groups, outline all the ideas associated with metal reactivity on the poster sheets. After two minutes, pass these on to the next group to add their ideas. After one minute, pass these to the next group to add their idea. After 30 seconds, pass the poster on. At the end, one person from each group summarises to the whole class.

These models are suggestions, ideas for carrying out class discussions. Clearly some models are more appropriate for different contexts that will vary with groups, times, age and prior experience but provide some ideas for the ordered organisation of discussion activities and – in the fourth model – a tangible outcome.

Using evidence: argumentation

Science is about evidence. Unfortunately many pupils (and adults) are subjected to anecdote, opinion and hearsay in everyday life. It is one of the responsibilities of the science teacher to reinforce the need for evidence to support statements or assertions, not only in science but in many other aspects of life. Argumentation refers to the process of arguing, between two or more people, which involves the construction, justification and refutation of arguments. When pupils work together with argumentation activities, they develop experience of constructing arguments, justifying arguments with evidence, evaluating alternatives and reflecting on the outcomes of argumentation. As Shirley Simon points out:

> Experience of argumentation in different contexts can equip students with the skills to make decisions about controversial issues in science, to understand how evidence is used to construct explanations and to understand the criteria that are used in science to evaluate evidence.

> (2011, p. 71)

With these aims in mind, argumentation activities need to engage interest, stimulate pupil discussion, provide resources that can be used in the classroom for constructing and evaluating arguments and provide alternative positions as well as solutions that may not be immediately obvious (Simon, 2011). Furthermore, these activities need to be manageable for teachers. Some of the research on argumentation and strategies that have been developed to enhance the practice of argumentation in school science are discussed by Simon (2011) in the suggested further reading.

USING WRITING

What is writing for?

The Key Stage 3 National Strategy has identified three main functions of writing: (1) using writing as a tool for thought; (2) structuring and organising writing; and

(3) developing clear and appropriate expression (DfES, 2004). Clearly these are important aims for learning science and ones that can be encouraged through writing activities and support. The skills include the ability to write formally and informally in order to plan, collect, develop and evaluate; to organise writing so that it is presented clearly and logically, and to express ideas clearly in writing using appropriate vocabulary, grammar and punctuation. This does not mean to say that the pupils' writing need be dull, lifeless non-fiction; there is space for imagination and creativity in science (as long as it is accurate) as well as in English lessons.

Task 5.1.6 **Comparing textbooks**

Look through a modern school science textbook and compare it with one from about 30 years ago:

1 How is the text arranged? Are there large blocks of text? Are these broken up? If so, how?
2 How much use is made of diagrams? What sort of diagrams? Simple or complex?
3 Are bullet points used? Are there summaries?
4 What are the styles of writing? Are they 'distant'? Impersonal? Engaging?

Supporting writing

What appears to be obvious to those with science degrees and qualifications is not necessarily obvious to pupils. Writing for particular purposes therefore has to be explicitly taught, modelled and supported. An example might be writing a good conclusion to practical work that includes the main points such as what was found, what patterns emerged and the scientific reasoning behind it, as well as a possible evaluation. These are not obvious to pupils and therefore cannot be assumed. Pupils need to be guided and the type of writing modelled. This needs to be explicit with pupils given the chance to criticise different examples. This is the subject of Task 5.1.7.

Task 5.1.7 **Writing a good conclusion**

One way of encouraging pupils to write for meaning in science is to allow them the opportunity to look at different models of writing conclusions, to criticise them and to use this as a way of writing a good conclusion. For this activity, aimed at Key Stage 3 pupils, you will need to do the following:

1 Present some results or data from a practical activity.
2 Write three possible conclusions that have some shortcomings.
3 Draft part of a lesson to address writing good conclusions.
4 Discuss this with your mentor.

---

5 Plan part of a lesson that asks pupils to criticise these conclusions and suggest improvements.
6 Get pupils to write a good conclusion, based on their criticisms and suggestions.

A number of science teachers use 'fill in the missing word' or cloze activities. These are often worksheets that pupils read and fill in. They have the advantage that in many cases they can be adapted to a particular class and different individuals in the class: they can be *differentiated*. For example, different worksheets can be constructed that allow for different amounts of reading, different levels of answers, different use of words or ideas and, for some pupils, cues to help them with the answers. Many of these worksheets are produced by educational publishers and are available in schools (see Further Reading). However, it is important to make sure they are in a format that you can tailor to your particular classes and contexts. How you actually do this will depend on your knowledge of the class and the work you are doing, that is, your beginning professional judgement. Equally important is to avoid the over-use of worksheets, the 'death by worksheet' syndrome.

When faced with a writing task and a blank sheet of paper, many pupils simply do not know how to get started. This may be compounded further by their lack of understanding of different writing styles and conventions. Writing frames are a way of helping structure pupils' writing. These are resources – often worksheets – that highlight the key features that need to be considered. In many cases they help to structure investigative activities but can also help to support report writing, writing explanations, writing up practical work and helping to construct an argument. Wellington and Osborne (2001) provide further information and guidance, with examples, on the use of writing frames in science (see Further Reading).

Narrative and extended writing in science

So far, the discussion has been about non-fiction writing and 'writing up' in science. What about story writing? Pupils' own voices, their narratives, can add much to writing in science. They may be familiar with this form of expression from their English lessons but when they walk through the door of the science laboratory, they suddenly have to switch to a less personal, less engaging style of writing. It may be no surprise then that seeing science as an impersonal and distant subject in school contributes to reducing pupils' engagement with science as they move through the secondary years. Pupils' own stories such as 'Journey to the centre of the Earth' (structure of the Earth) or 'A day in the life of a bacterium' (bacterial growth and destruction) may add new interest to science as well as enhancing literacy. Added to this is the tremendous wealth and popularity of science fiction and related literature that can be used critically to interest pupils and enliven their science diet. Fiction and fantasy in science may have distinct advantages for pupil interest as long as it is scientifically accurate. A review of some science fiction may even help to unearth misconceptions and provide opportunities for pupils to critically evaluate the science involved.

SUMMARY AND KEY POINTS

In this unit we have explored some of the language barriers with learning science, involving not just the specialist language of science but some of the ways that language is used that may lead to confusion and misunderstandings. A number of aspects of science teaching and learning have been considered that include questions and questioning, approaches to pupil talk and ways of organising discussions in classrooms, using your own voice, and the role of writing and how pupils can be supported with their own writing. Reflection on these issues and experiences are important ways of widening your own repertoire of classroom strategies for teaching for pupils' understanding of science.

REFERENCES

Carroll, L. (2001) *Jabberwocky*, New York: Dover.

Cerini, B., Murray, I. and Reiss, M. (2003) *Student Review of the Science Curriculum*, London: Planet Science, Institute of Education and the Science Museum.

Claxton, G. (1991) *Educating the Enquiring Mind*, Hemel Hempstead: Harvester Wheatsheaf.

DfES (Department for Education and Skills) (2004) *Key Stage 3 National Strategy Literacy and Guidance for Senior Leaders*, London: DfES Publications.

Henderson, J. and Wellington, J. (1998) 'Lowering the language barrier in learning and teaching science', *School Science Review*, 79(288): 35–46.

Hudson, R. and Holmes, J. (1995) *Children's Use of Spoken English. A Short Report Prepared for the School Curriculum and Assessment Authority*, London: University College London. Available at: www.phon.ucl.ac.uk/home/dick/papers/texts/scaa.pdf (accessed 26 December 2012).

Koufetta-Menicou, C. and Scaife, J. (2000) 'Teachers' questions', *School Science Review*, 81(296): 79–84.

Mortimer, E. F. and Scott, P. H. (2003) *Meaning Making in Science Classrooms*, Milton Keynes: Open University Press.

Scott, P., Ametler, J., Mercer, N., Kleine Staarman, J. and Dawes, L. (2007) 'An investigation of dialogic teaching in science classrooms', paper presented at the NARST conference: New Orleans, April.

Simon, S. (2011) 'Argumentation', in R. Toplis (ed.) *How Science Works: Exploring Effective Pedagogy and Practice*, London: Routledge, pp. 71–84.

Watson, J. D. and Crick, F. H. C. (1953) 'Molecular structure of nucleic acids', *Nature*, 171: 737–8.

Wellington, J. and Osborne, J. (2001) *Language and Literacy in Science Education*, Buckingham: Open University Press.

FURTHER READING

Mortimer, E. F. and Scott, P. H. (2003) *Meaning Making in Science Classrooms*, Milton Keynes: Open University Press.

This reports extensive research into how dialogue does and doesn't take place in the classroom. It is underpinned by theoretical principles and provides a framework for considering effective talk for the development of concepts in science.

Naylor, S. and Keogh, N. (2000) *Concept Cartoons in Science Education*, Cheshire: Millgate House Publishers.

This popular book, ideal for Key Stage 3 classes, provides a range of accessible cartoons on many scientific topics. These can be used to promote pupil discussion and address a number of widely held misconceptions.

Simon, S. (2011) 'Argumentation', in R. Toplis (ed.) *How Science Works: Exploring Effective Pedagogy and Practice*, London: Routledge, pp. 71–84.

This book chapter gives an overview of the importance of argumentation for developing scientific literacy that uses evidence-based work. It provides examples and approaches to scaffolding argumentation in the classroom.

Staples, R. and Heselden, R. (2001) 'Science teaching and literacy, part 1: Writing', *School Science Review*, 83(303): 35–46.

This article is the first of three that gives suggested contexts and guidelines for potential teaching approaches to writing in science. It is readable, suggests teaching approaches for the classroom and answers a number of questions.

Wellington, J. and Osborne, J. (2001) *Language and Literacy in Science Education*, Buckingham: Open University Press.

This valuable book provides a wide coverage of many aspects of this somewhat neglected area of science education. The discussions are thoroughly informed by research evidence, are comprehensive, readable and provide a wide range of examples and ideas for adaptation and use in the science classroom.

PRACTICAL WORK

Rob Toplis

INTRODUCTION

What do many pupils think when they enter a school science laboratory? 'Are we doing a practical today?' may be one of their frequent questions. Often they associate practical work with that icon of school science, the Bunsen burner, but also with exotic glassware, microscopes, flashes, bangs and hair standing on end. This chapter examines the role of practical work in teaching science: what it's for, the types of practical work and how it can be carried out effectively.

OBJECTIVES

By the end of this section you should:

- be aware of the background to practical work in science and the types of practical work used in secondary science;
- appreciate some of the reasons why practical work science is carried out;
- know how practical work can be carried out effectively in the laboratory;
- know how it can be carried out more effectively for learning science.

Practical work in science education has had something of a varied past. In the nineteenth and early twentieth centuries, science in schools was essentially teacher-led, a legacy we see today in a number of older schools with hardwood demonstration benches on a raised platform at the front of the class, seen then, to be a good way of illustrating the theory of some classic experiments. An important – and sometimes regarded as a radical figure – during the second half of the nineteenth and into the twentieth century was H. E. Armstrong. His philosophy of 'heurism', of learning by discovery, involved hands-on practical activity. Despite his critics and later moves away from heuristic approaches, Armstrong's contribution to practical science education was important at the time and later during the Nuffield projects of the 1960s and 1970s that exemplified the discovery approach. Despite some criticisms about the courses being aimed at the upper ability range of pupils and the degree of guidance they received (Wellington, 1981), Nuffield courses raised the profile of practical work in schools and provided a level of new equipment and resources rarely seen before. The process approach of the 1980s placed emphasis on scientific process skills such as classifying, observing and inferring, rather than science content such as facts, laws and principles (Gott and Duggan, 1995). This approach has been criticised (Millar and Driver, 1987) as a limited view of science education where there is not necessarily a split between process and content but that the two are integral to learning science. Furthermore, Millar and Driver argue that though scientists may have characteristic ways of working, the 'scientific method' cannot be rendered into set of rules for the way that science is carried out.

One important area of practical work, investigative science, was included in scientific enquiry (Sc1) within the National Curriculum for England from 1989. This made investigations a mandatory part of the school science curriculum. Scientific enquiry later formed part of the 'How Science Works' strand of the 2004 National Curriculum, together with the use of scientific evidence, applications and implications and communication, and now 'Working Scientifically' in the latest National Curriculum.

Practical work is seen by many science teachers to be an integral part of their teaching, a belief that 'doing' helps learning: 'I do and I understand'. A lot of time, money and effort have been devoted to practical work in school science, so why is it carried out?

REASONS FOR INCLUDING PRACTICAL WORK

Wellington (1998) provides three main arguments for carrying out practical work in school science: (1) the skills argument such as those of observation, prediction and inference, as well as manipulative skills; (2) the cognitive arguments for improving understanding and conceptual development; and (3) affective arguments for generating interest, motivation and enthusiasm. These divisions may not be this simple, as affect, such as the enjoyment of science, may be linked to cognitive development, the understanding of science (Alsop, 2005). An early questionnaire survey of teachers' reasons for doing practical work (Kerr, 1964) indicates that observation and scientific thinking were ranked highly, as was encouraging accurate observation and careful recording for the 16–18 age group. However, a later comment (Ormerod and Duckworth, 1975) indicates somewhat conflicting views about practical work; teachers placed promotion of 'interest' low on their list whereas pupils placed it at the top of their value list.

For skills

The skills argument appears to be a straightforward one at first, that of allowing pupils to develop the skills of handling apparatus, and making measurements. However, there must be cognitive dimensions to this as decisions need to be made about which apparatus to use, which measuring device to choose and the degree of accuracy or precision of the measurement. Skills are more than just the manipulative aspects of practical work which pupils acquire and draw upon at a later date (Gott and Duggan, 1995, p. 26). They may extend to those processes of predicting, observing and interpreting and may be transferable to new contexts (Wellington, 1998). However, the skill of observation in science depends on prior expectations in order to decide what is or is not relevant; that we bring our own set of 'spectacles' to an observation (Millar, 1998, p. 18). Recent work (Allen, 2009) shows that the spectacles may be clouded to the extent that observations may be a result of expectations, that pupils actually see what they think they are supposed to see – they really do think a heavier object falls faster than a light one because they expect it to. We may even need to consider whether some of the traditional skills of measuring, such as reading a thermometer or reading an ammeter, are as relevant as they once were now that there are digital alternatives, or that they will be used at all after an individual leaves school. Nevertheless it can be argued that an appreciation of accuracy and precision are important generic skills.

Task 5.2.1 **Observing practical skills**

During your observation of science classrooms, focus on pupils' skills with the following suggested examples:

▨ Year 7 pouring a liquid from a bottle into a test tube;
▨ a Key Stage 3 class reading a thermometer;
▨ a Year 9 or 10 pupil making a correct reading from an ammeter scale;
▨ a Key Stage 4 pupil using a microscope.

What do you notice about their abilities with the skills needed? Did they need help? Consider how their skills could be improved.

Affect

It appears that practical work features highly in pupils' attitudes towards, and enjoyment of, school science. When I asked small groups of pupils about their experiences of science at secondary school, they mentioned feelings and comparison with other aspects of science lessons such as 'fun to do something, not just writing', 'all working together' and 'more interesting than reading or listening to teachers' (reported in Wellington, 2005, p. 103). Jarman's survey (1993) reports that when pupils transfer from primary to secondary school they note that there is more practical work and with different equipment, including . . . the Bunsen burner.

A number of attitude studies make specific mention of practical work in school science. One wide-ranging survey (Bennett and Hogarth, 2005) covered attitudes to science where a number of secondary school pupils' comments made reference to the fun, exciting, interesting or enjoyable aspects of science lessons, with some specifying experimental and practical activities. Another survey, this time using a web-based format, produced 1,450 responses to questions about effective and enjoyable ways of learning. Although the item on discussions and debates in class scored the highest (48 per cent) for being useful and effective, 'doing a science experiment in class' came within the top three of 11 items for being enjoyable (Murray and Reiss, 2005, p. 86). Parkinson *et al.* (1998, p. 172) show that practical work was high on the list of 'likes' by both boys and girls aged 11–14 and note that many of the responses indicated pupils enjoyed the opportunity of working with others during experimental work.

Although questionnaire surveys provide detailed numerical data and are useful for identifying the nature of the problem, they provide little information about *why* pupils have preferences for practical work (an exception being where free response items are included, as with the survey by Bennett and Hogarth, 2005). Qualitative studies can therefore provide further information. Osborne and Collin's (2000) interviews found that pupils expressed great interest in practical work, enjoyed the personal autonomy, the fun (for example, dissection) and found practical work made science more accessible and more easily retained. Abrahams (2009) indicates that practical work provides situational interest, an interest that is stimulated in an individual as a result of being in a particular environment or situation and that, unlike a personal interest, can be stimulated by teachers. The pupils in Abraham's study had a *relative* preference for practical work, where they claim to like practical work in preference to alternative methods of teaching.

For improving understanding

The web-based survey of pupils (Murray and Reiss, 2005, p. 86) showed that of the 1,450 responses to the question, 'How does practical work help learning', 47 per cent thought practical work made understanding theory easier and 12 per cent believed it provided a deeper understanding.

Task 5.2.2 **Observing understanding with practical work**

During your observation of science classrooms, focus on pupils' understanding with either one physics concept (such as force, motion, electric current), one chemistry concept (such as chemical change, particles, structure and bonding) or biology (such as photosynthesis, respiration or feeding relationships).

■ What are the main misconceptions in these areas?
■ How was the practical work used to address these misconceptions or develop ideas?
■ Consider how you can tell if the practical work was effective in addressing these.

Is the cognitive argument for improving understanding and conceptual development of science limited solely to understanding substantive ideas – the facts, laws and theories of science? It has been argued (Gott and Duggan, 1995) that procedural understanding – the thinking behind the doing – involves a set of ideas that are complementary to conceptual understanding and include a cognitive demand. This procedural understanding requires 'concepts of evidence' which refer to, for example, the design, measurement, data handling and evaluation of practical work (Gott and Duggan, 1995, p. 30), the thinking needed to solve problems as part of scientific enquiry. Recent findings (Abrahams and Millar, 2008) indicate that teachers' focus on practical lessons was predominantly one of developing scientific knowledge rather than scientific enquiry but that practical work was generally effective at getting pupils to do what was intended with physical objects rather than use scientific ideas and reflect on the data. They note that there was little evidence of a cognitive challenge in linking observables to ideas, and that practical tasks rarely incorporated explicit strategies to help pupils make these links. This indicates that the cognitive argument for practical work in school science is not as clear as it appears, that learning science with practical work is successful when it is incorporated as an explicit strategy to help pupils make links.

Task 5.2.3 **Hands on, minds on**

Use the Practical Activity Analysis Inventory (PAAI) to carry out an analysis of a practical activity you plan to use with a class. This is found in the book by R. Millar (2009) *Analysing Practical Activities to Assess and Improve Effectiveness: The Practical Activity Analysis Inventory (PAAI)*. This can also be downloaded from the University of York website.

TYPES OF PRACTICAL WORK

It is not easy to develop a typology of practical work in science, partly because the use of one particular practical task may have several purposes but also because there may be a number of skills or reasons for the practical work in mind. However, the following categories may help to classify practical work according to its purpose, based on those from Woolnough and Allsop (1985).

Illustrative practicals

Illustrative practical work can be achieved in two ways. The first is the classic demonstration to the whole class. It is a tried and tested approach to practical work and one that generally illustrates what it is supposed to. If it does fail, it is usually possible for the teacher to offer some explanation that may rely on questions and answers to and from pupils. As with any practical work – and probably more so with the teacher demonstration – is the need for two things: preparation and good subject knowledge. Preparation does not just mean giving the laboratory technician a list of apparatus and chemicals three days before but relies on carrying out a trial run first. What the textbook says will not necessarily always work in practice and there may be things that need to be tried and even adjusted beforehand. It is worth remembering that the science teacher is very much the centre of pupils' attention here and the performance must be one that is rehearsed, even down to what the questions are and when they are asked. Like all performances, the timing needs to be rehearsed as well. Demonstrations have the added advantage that they allow a low risk use of fragile or expensive equipment or those practical activities deemed too dangerous for pupils to carry out themselves. We only have to remember the Royal Institution Christmas lectures to realise that well-organised and timed demonstrations can be valuable learning opportunities and are one part of the science teacher's range of strategies.

The second way of using illustrative practical work is to allow pupils to carry it out themselves. These may appear to be rather like cookery book exercises that involve following recipes of procedures with precise amounts, times and order but can lead to learning advantages and can provide episodes that can aid recall at a later date (White, 1988). Examples might include practical work around gas exchange, testing a leaf for starch, food tests or electrostatics. Often they are very visual and it is this aspect that can lead to their recall. However, there remains the nagging question: what you do when it doesn't work?

Let's take the example of oxygen production from the Canadian pondweed, *Elodea*. This is a classic practical which illustrates oxygen production during photosynthesis where oxygen is collected in an upturned funnel and test tube over a 24-hour period. What do you do if there is no oxygen the next day? Wellington (2000, p. 230) discusses some of the responses to these sorts of incidents based on the work of Nott and Smith (1995) that include 'talking your way out of it', 'conjuring' and 'rigging'. Talking you way out of it, or rather through it, is one way to allow pupils to be critical about scientific work and to experience the nature of science. 'Conjuring' is carried out but is probably a highly dubious practice: adding acid at the end of a yoghurt-making practical to adjust the pH because you could only get pasteurised yoghurt instead of a live culture for the starter is plainly fraudulent. 'Rigging' relies almost on a craft knowledge based on experience with practical work and one area where it is always useful to have a good rapport with the science technician who will have seen a practical *not* work before. Before we leave this area of practical work, the Canadian pond weed 'failure' has been 'rigged' in the past using a grow light or adding sodium hydrogen carbonate to the water.

Practical exercises

Practical work exercises can provide opportunities for teaching skills. Typically these are carried more often in Year 7 at the start of the secondary school when teachers want their classes to become familiar with the apparatus and techniques of handling; with some pupils, this still may need to be revised at a later stage of science teaching. Very often these skills are taught in context of a lesson covering some aspect of science content. However, it is important not to underestimate how long it will take for pupils to acquire new skills. One lesson to introduce the use of the microscope and make a slide of onion cells may simply be expecting too much. It may take one lesson to set up and use a micro-scope correctly, possibly using it to simply look at a few everyday items such as cloth fibres or hairs, and another lesson to revise using the microscope, prepare and draw a slide of onion cells. You cannot assume that something that is easy and quick for you to do will be as simple for pupils unfamiliar with the apparatus or materials. Explicit teaching of skills may be needed. You will need to make it clear in your lesson planning exactly what your objectives and outcomes are for the acquisition of science skills and techniques.

Task 5.2.4 **Using the Bunsen burner**

Use this task to plan an outline of how you would teach a new Year 7 class the skills of how to set up and use a Bunsen burner. You may need to consider safety rules, where and if you will demonstrate part of this procedure, checking the gas flow, checking the type of flame and even packing away. You will very probably draw on this task in your first year of teaching.

Practical investigations

There is some debate about the definition of an investigation: they may be hypothesis testing or problem solving (Woolnough, 1994) but a suggested definition is that they are a task for which the pupil cannot immediately see an answer or recall a routine method for finding it (Gott and Duggan, 1995). In reality, they may be far from this. Nott and Wellington (1999) found that most teachers used 'set' investigations that had been developed over the years and saw them primarily as assessment exercises. This aspect of investigative work that suggests that the outcomes of pupil investigations are unknown at the start is something of a myth.

Investigations have a tendency to take on a summative assessment rather than form-ative assessment role for pupils that involves being able to 'jump through hoops' (Nott and Wellington 1999, p. 14; Toplis and Cleaves, 2006). This situation is illustrated vividly in Keiler's work (Keiler and Woolnough 2002) where gaining marks – even to the extent of falsifying practical results – was seen to be important by pupils for the examinations. This is hardly surprising given the high stakes requirements of examinations and the need to complete investigative activities within certain windows of available time. Nevertheless, it is important to consider the formative nature of investigations and whether or not they involve authentic activities; a pertinent question might be, 'who poses the investigation?'

Many investigative activities have also been limited to a 'control of variables' or 'fair test' model where one variable – the independent one – is changed and all others kept the same. These activities tend to be laboratory-based and use an essentially linear model of: predict–plan–collect data–analyse and present data–evaluate. However, do all scientists work like this all the time? Can biologists studying meerkat behaviour use this experi-mental method of scientific enquiry? Do cosmologists work in this way? Is this linear approach a reflection of the 'messy' way in which scientists work? A fair test model as the only way of conducting a scientific investigation has its limitations with the way that science is portrayed and many teachers disagree with this narrow approach. Work carried out as part of the AKSIS Project (Association for Science Education and Kings College London Science Investigations in Schools) (Watson *et al.*, 1999) opened up investigative approaches to include:

▨ classifying and identifying: managing and arranging data and identifying unknowns;
▨ fair testing: relationships between variables and controlling variables;
▨ pattern seeking: observing and recording natural events and identifying patterns;
▨ investigating models: deciding on and collecting evidence to test ideas and models;
▨ exploring: observing and making decisions about exactly what to observe and how many;
▨ making things or developing systems: technological investigations involving design and need.

In practice, investigative work has become increasingly prescribed with, for example, examination boards setting the problems and with some school science departments carrying out very controlled activities. Investigative work in science does not have to be reliant on a set of tried and tested examination or summative assessment activities but can involve work that is incorporated into normal day-to-day teaching as an integral part of a scheme of work or, more flexibly, in response to pupils' questions of the type, 'what would happen if . . .?'

MANAGING PRACTICAL WORK IN THE CLASSROOM

It is easy to overestimate the level of organisation that pupils may show in the lab. As a beginning teacher of a practical subject, you cannot assume that all the pupils will know exactly what to do, how to do it and when to do it. You are, essentially, like the conductor of an orchestra where you have to direct exactly which pupils move, what they do, how they carry out the tasks and when they do so. It is in this way that they will produce a final result and will learn. Using the same analogy of the conductor and the orchestra, your score is your lesson plan, including any additional notes. At early stages this may even resemble a script of precisely what you and the pupils will do at any particular moment. In writing this script, you will have thought through exactly what they will do and have planned for all eventualities, have reduced risk to an absolute minimum and have gained confidence in planning and teaching a practical lesson. Importantly, the pupils in the class will have the maximum opportunity of gaining skills, obtaining and analysing results, discussing those results and learning science through practical work.

Starting to plan practical work

You will need to plan for practical work in detail. A suitable starting point is knowing what pupils have done before, followed by your lesson objectives and outcomes. What can they do already? What do you want the pupils to do in the lesson? What do you want them to have achieved by the end of the lesson? Answers to these questions will then determine how you are going to plan the time, what activities you will decide to use, and how pupils will carry out the work. When planning practical work at first, it may be useful to draft a timeline for each step of the work. This may provide time for an introduction, instructions about the procedures – including movement and safety as well as the practical procedures – clearing away, discussion of results, summarising and a plenary.

Risk

Risk needs to be assessed at an early stage of planning any piece of practical work; you must know what pupils are allowed to do, at what age and with which apparatus. There may be times when pupils of certain ages can only work with some concentrations of chemicals such as sodium hydroxide. There may be practical activities that only you can demonstrate. You will find all the information about risks by using the CLEAPSS handbook and the set of 'Hazcards' which will be in the main preparation room. Again, the technicians will be a source of valuable information about risks. You will also need to be aware of where items such as fire extinguishers, safety spectacles or goggles, eye-wash bottles and safety screens are in the laboratories and will need to check these in advance. The article by Peter Borrows (2002) is recommended as providing a measured response to risk and safety in practical science.

Pupil working groups

Who pupils work with and how they are allocated to groups can be a difficult issue for beginning teachers. One argument is to allow pupils to choose themselves. This, however, can be fraught with difficulties, depending on the nature of the class. A situation can arise where a free choice allows larger working groups than anticipated, lone pupils, inappropriate arrangements of pupils and groups dominated by certain individuals. Another reason for allowing a free choice of groupings is that a beginning teacher may want to appear sympathetic to pupils' wishes. Going back to the analogy of an orchestra, you as the teacher will need to conduct all the players in the class and directing the arrangements of the working groups is part of this if you want to maximise the effectiveness of the planned practical activities. In the first instance, it may well be appropriate to go with the plans of the class teacher but you may need to consider a number of questions. How many sets of apparatus do you have? What size groups do you want for the available apparatus? Do you want to avoid some combinations of individuals? Do you want some individuals to help others? Do you want the mix boys and girls in the same group? Whatever your decisions about these groupings, it is important to plan for these arrangements and to communicate this clearly to pupils. Showing group names on a slide is one way that pupils will know exactly who they are expected to work with during the lesson and later lessons; furthermore, they will know that you know! Additionally, the TAs and technicians will also be aware of these groupings from your plans so they are in a position to provide the support needed (see Unit 1.3).

Managing movement (and apparatus) in the laboratory

With as many as 30 pupils moving around a practical class there is the potential for problems but the majority of these can be avoided with careful planning for movement. You will want to avoid the scenario where, on asking a class to collect Bunsen burners, there is a scrum around one cupboard. You might consider placing apparatus at several stations around the room, directing one member of the working group to collect different apparatus, asking the technician to set up trays of apparatus for each working group and have careful sight of certain equipment or chemicals. You, as the teacher, will be in a position to know the layout of the room and how best to make the practical work run smoothly. Again, considering where and what the TA can do is an important part of this planning. Task 5.2.5 provides some opportunity to plan the details of a practical activity.

Giving instructions

During the practical work you have carefully planned and organised, you will want the pupils to know what they are supposed to be doing and to act safely. Instructions are therefore an important part of the activity. And can be built into planning. Very often, too many different instructions are given and some pupils will only remember the first and the last points. In other cases, the thought of doing a practical may lead to a selective block on listening to instructions and result in a lot of unnecessary questions and time-wasting. It is therefore worth considering how you will give instructions, how many points to instructions, whether or not you present these as 'chunks' for some work, if you want to provide a written sheet, if pupils will read all the written sheet and if you need to ask individuals to summarise instructions. Some pupils will remember better by seeing the procedure and a short demonstration will often be a good use of time as you talk your way through it.

Task 5.2.5 **Organising practical work**

This task allows you to plan the organisation of a practical lesson and to think about, and through, some of the many factors that need to be considered during the planning stage. Consider a class of 28 Year 8 pupils (16 boys, 12 girls) who are doing a practical on heating metals in air. The metals available are: copper, magnesium, calcium, steel wool (iron) and lead. The class contains: a visually

---

impaired pupil (girl), a pupil with an attention deficit disorder(boy) and two pupils with reading problems (one boy, one girl). There is one LSA (TA) for the two pupils with reading problems. The lesson is 50 minutes.

Draw a plan of the layout of a laboratory you have observed. Mark on it: the main cupboards where apparatus is kept; where the seats are located; the front bench; the whiteboard and/or screen; the gas and water taps; the side benches; the door; the fire extinguisher, fire blanket and eye wash. You need to consider:

■ seating and grouping;
■ distribution of apparatus;
■ health and safety;
■ how instructions are given;
■ your rules;
■ timing for starter, instructions, doing, clearing up and summarising, plenary.

Where does practical work go from here? There are certainly strong indications that practical work is to be encouraged for a number of reasons and purposes. What is important is that it is effective in terms of the clarity of the learning outcomes it provides, its impact on learning and the quality of the practical activities. It may be very difficult to imagine the class waiting at the door *not* asking if they are going to do a practical today.

SUMMARY AND KEY POINTS

This section has covered a very brief background to the emergence of practical work in school science and the arguments for it being part of the science curriculum. It has reviewed some of the types of practical activities, both as teacher demonstrations and hands-on pupil approaches and has taken a critical look at the use of – and potential for – investigative work. The section has emphasised the importance of careful planning for managing practical work, including the safety aspects, for effective use of laboratories for learning science.

REFERENCES

Abrahams, I. (2009) 'Does practical work really motivate? A study of the affective value of practical work in secondary school science' International Journal of Science Education, 31(17): 2335–353.

Abrahams, I. and Millar, R. (2008) 'Does practical work really work? A study of the effectiveness of practical work as a teaching and learning method in school science', International Journal of Science Education, 30(14): 1945–69.

Allen, M. (2009) 'Learner error, affectual stimulation, and conceptual change', *Journal of Research in Science Teaching*, 47(2).

Alsop, S. (2005) 'Bridging the Cartesian divide: science education and affect', in S. Alsop *Beyond Cartesian Dualism*, Dordrecht: Springer, pp. 3–16.

Bennett, J. and Hogarth, S. (2005) *Would You Want to Talk to a Scientist at a Party?: Students' Attitudes to School Science and Science*, York: Department of Educational Studies, University of York.

Borrows, P. (2002) 'Managing health and safety in science departments', *School Science Review*, 84(306): 33–8.

Gott, R. and Duggan, S. (1995) *Investigative Work in the Science Curriculum*, Buckingham: Open University Press.

Jarman, R. (1993) 'Real experiments with Bunsen burners: pupils' perceptions of the similarities and differences between primary science and secondary science', *School Science Review*, 74(268): 19–29.

Keiler, L. S. and Woolnough, B. E. (2002) 'Practical work in school science: the dominance of assessment', *School Science Review*, 83(304): 83–8.

Kerr, J. F. (1964) *Practical Work in School Science*, Leicester: Leicester University Press.

Millar, R. (1998) 'Rhetoric and reality', in J. Wellington (ed.) *Practical Work in School Science: Which Way Now?* London: Routledge, pp. 16–31.

Millar, R. (2009) *Analysing Practical Activities to Assess and Improve Effectiveness: The Practical Activity Analysis Inventory (PAAI)*, York: Centre for Innovation and Research in Science Education/ Department of Educational Studies, University of York

Millar, R. and Driver, R. (1987) 'Beyond processes', *Studies in Science Education*, 14: 33–59.

Murray, I. and Reiss, M. (2005) 'The student review of the science curriculum', *School Science Review*, 87(318): 83–93.

Nott, M. and Smith, R. (1995) 'Talking your way out of it, "rigging" and "conjuring": what science teachers do when practicals go wrong', *International Journal of Science Education*, 17: 399–410.

Nott, M. and Wellington, J. (1999) 'The state we're in: issues in Key Stage 3 and 4 Science', *School Science Review*, 81(294): 13–18.

Ormerod, M. B. and Duckworth, D. (1975) *Pupils' Attitudes to Science. A Review of Research*, Windsor: NFER Publishing Company.

Osborne, J. and Collins, S. (2000) *Pupils' and Parents' Views of the School Science Curriculum*, London: Kings College London.

Parkinson, J., Hendley, D., Tanner, H. and Stables, A. (1998) 'Pupils' attitudes to science in Key Stage 3 of the National Curriculum: a study of pupils in South Wales', *Research in Science and Technological Education*, 16(1): 165–76.

Toplis, R. and Cleaves, A. (2006) 'Science investigation: the views of fourteen to sixteen year-old pupils', *Research in Science and Technological Education*, 24(1): 69–84.

Watson, R., Goldsworthy, A. and Wood-Robinson, V. (1999) 'What's not fair with investigations?' *School Science Review*, 80(292): 101–6.

Wellington, J. (1981) 'What's supposed to happen, Sir?' *School Science Review*, 63: 167–73.

Wellington, J. (ed.) (1998) *Practical Work in School Science: Which Way Now?* London: Routledge.

Wellington, J. (2000) *Teaching and Learning Secondary Science*, London: Routledge.

Wellington, J. (2005) 'Practical work and the affective domain: what do we know, what should we ask, and what is worth exploring further?' in S. Alsop (ed.) *Beyond Cartesian Dualism*, Dordrecht: Springer, pp. 99–109.

White, R. (1988) *Learning Science*, Oxford: Basil Blackwell.

Woolnough, B. E. (1994) *Effective Science Teaching*, Buckingham: Open University Press.

Woolnough, B. E. and Allsop, T. (1985) *Practical Work in Science*, Cambridge: Cambridge University Press.

FURTHER READING

Abrahams, I. (2011) *Practical Work in Secondary Science*, London: Continuum.

This book provides a research-based critical view about aspects of practical work in science and how practical work can be used to support pupils with a 'minds on' as well as a 'hands on' approach to learning.

ASE Safeguards Committee (2006) *Safeguards in the School Laboratory*, 11th edn, Hatfield: Association for Science Education.

Simply, essential reading.

Borrows, P. (2002) 'Managing health and safety in science departments', *School Science Review*, 84(306): 33–8.

This valuable short article emphasises the importance of assessing risk and the value of departmental health and safety policies, how they are implemented and how they are monitored.

CLEAPSS (2004) *Hazcards*. Uxbridge: CLEAPSS School Science Service.

A set of easy reference cards for checking the safety implications of apparatus and chemicals.

Millar, R. (2009) *Analysing Practical Activities to Assess and Improve Effectiveness: The Practical Activity Analysis Inventory (PAAI)*, York: Centre for Innovation and Research in Science Education, Department of Educational Studies, University of York.

This book provides background to the purposes of practical work and an inventory that allows a particular practical activity to be analysed and evaluated.

Wellington, J. (ed.) (1998) *Practical Work in School Science. Which Way Now?* London: Routledge.

This edited book provides a range of valuable chapters on different perspectives on the development, knowledge, influences, authentic nature, contexts and use of ICT for practical work in schools.

USEFUL WEBSITE

AstraZeneca Science Teaching Trust: www.azteachscience.co.uk/resources/curriculum-materials/getting-practical-asecleapss.aspx (accessed 17 February 2014).

USING TECHNOLOGIES TO SUPPORT LEARNING SCIENCE

Ruth Amos

INTRODUCTION

Computer-aided drug design, nanotechnology and DNA machines, twenty-first-century scientific developments and day-to-day science activity happen more and more courtesy of the technology revolution (Tan and Koh, 2008). Recent estimates predict that by 2020, 95 per cent of all jobs will involve an element of computer technology. And so this revolution continues at an alarming rate, but do not panic! This unit encourages you to build confidence in using new and not-so-new technologies purposely with your pupils as effective learning tools. New technologies allow pupils to learn in new ways (Hammond, 2013) and, importantly, pupils can readily lead their own learning. As science teachers, we need to reflect upon how best to support pupils preparing for a contemporary world heavily influenced by new technologies.

Exploring the provision of technologies across a range of secondary schools reveals increasing diversity beyond the traditional bookable suites of computers and class sets of laptops in the science department. Many schools continue to house data projectors, interactive screens and whiteboards (IWBs) in science labs and classrooms. Visualisers, digital microscopes and CCTV cameras may also form part of a science department's suite of resources. Schools have also been investing in mobile technologies such as 'smart' phones, portable media players and tablets so that a whole new range of online resources and tools for learning and teaching become ever more accessible within the classroom. This has caused some controversy in as much as some schools have asked parents/carers for financial contributions to either hire or buy mobile technologies.

Social networking is having an increasing impact on learning. Pupils are emailing homework to teachers; teachers are hosting online learning platforms for posting practice questions, and subsequent self-assessment using teachers' mark schemes. Questioning and dialogue which previously only happened if pupils stayed behind at the end of the lesson are now possible beyond the school gate. Think about the degree to which you want to establish online communications with your pupils.

Technologies are increasingly present in young people's everyday lives. Davis and Good (2009) found through a survey in the UK that 87 per cent of 8–17-year-olds live in a house with at least one computer, and 82 per cent have access to the Internet at home. Young people are playing games and using simple 'apps' (mobile applications) almost as soon as they can touch a screen these days! In typical schools, however, pupils report using technologies mostly still for undertaking research or making presentations (Condie and Munro, 2007; Morris, 2010), which are rather limited applications, given what is now possible. Your own motivation, and confidence and ability to create technology-supported learning will influence your pupils' understanding of their potential. In your training year and beyond try to invest time in understanding which technologies make a positive difference to pupils' learning experience and developing twenty-first-century skills. These skills include collaborative learning, self-led learning and making choices about technology tools for a purpose. Learning how to use hardware and software you are not already familiar with, how to access appropriate resources efficiently and transform them into effective learning tools, can be time-consuming. However, when you create an effective learning activity using new technologies, the rewards in terms of the quality of pupils' learning can be high. Technologies provide the means to create an inclusive classroom very effectively (McKeown and McGlashon, 2012).

There is a vast array of software available for supporting learning ideas and skills inside and outside the science classroom. Discovering and evaluating animations, simulations, video clips and images which have the potential to enhance learning for your pupils require a clear focus on desired learning outcomes for an activity. Arguably, one of the key features of an effective science department is a commitment to actively research, evaluate, store and share online and created technology-supported learning resources. Collaborative, well-structured strategies situated regularly within schemes of work (SoW) can make important contributions to the learning and teaching experience. Online forums for sharing good resources exist and provide you with some assistance as a busy teacher. There is a danger that you may 'grab' an online resource without fully exploring the value that may bring to the learning experience, or establishing clear learning objectives and outcomes linked to the technology. Of course, your approach to planning a lesson incorporating technologies is no different to planning a lesson of any kind (see Unit 4.3). Ask yourself the questions:

1   What can the technology-supported strategy bring to learning objectives and outcomes that another approach cannot?
2   Do learners need to develop specific technology-related skills during the activity or are you confident that they are already skilled enough to focus on the science ideas/skills through the use the technology?

Always have a non-technology back-up activity prepared as well, just in case technical support is not available when you need it most!

OBJECTIVES

By the end of this unit, you should:

■ be aware of the range of technologies available for learning and teaching science, and their underlying rationale alongside other strategies;
■ establish your own developmental targets for incorporating technology-supported learning in your science lessons;

> ■ be able to identify those technology-supported strategies which involve the pupils in active learning.

PLANNING LESSONS INCORPORATING TECHNOLOGY TOOLS

Before we consider the various new and not-so-new technology tools and applications that you can use in developing effective learning experiences, review the skills you need as a teacher to include such activities in your teaching repertoire. We all have differing confidence and ability in using new technologies; in terms of online learning, some of you will create your own web pages, blogs and apps, whereas others will rely on what is already available. However, as teachers, we need to understand how to use technologies, and how to adopt and adapt resources effectively. Developing such pedagogical skills takes time so it may be helpful to think about your growing repertoire in terms of 'frequency' of use. In other words, you will naturally focus on using certain technologies more often than others. The danger is that you will become focused only on the 'ordinary' and miss great opportunities to enhance your pupils' learning with the 'extra-ordinary'. This does mean taking some risks in the classroom, and you will need good technical support, but those risks are usually very worthwhile. Set yourself a goal to work on using a different technologies strategy on a regular basis in your first years of teaching. Be realistic and balanced in terms of other demands on your time. Once you get into the swing of using technologies, you and your pupils will benefit.

There is an ever-growing number of activities in which technology-supported learning can be appropriate aids. Table 5.3.1 gives an overview of some activities and supportive tools frequently used. Table 5.3.2 suggests more 'adventurous' activities. The term 'adventurous' is used here in the sense that perhaps specialised hardware is needed, high speed online facility is required, it may be challenging to set them up, more time is required, or higher levels of technical support are required. Use both tables to construct your developmental goals.

■ **Table 5.3.1** Basic technology-supported learning activities for school science

Activity focus	Examples and resources
Communication and presentation	Simple slide presentational packages (e.g. PowerPoint), word processing packages (e.g. Word), desktop publishing (e.g. Publisher), emailing, digital capture of photographic images
Information gathering and examining evidence	Internet browsers, websites displaying 'static' data and information
Simulations and animations	Modelling to help understand and explain abstract phenomena, virtual experiments, educational apps (assuming availability of smart technologies)

■ **Table 5.3.2** Adventurous technology-supported learning activities for school science

Adventurous communication and presentation	Online collaborative writing/discussion (e.g. Google Docs, VoiceThread, Wikispaces), creation of simple stop motion digital films, complex presentation packages (e.g. Prezi), web authoring, video-conferencing, micro-blogging, email contact with 'real' scientists
Adventurous information gathering and sharing, examining evidence	Education apps,[1] online learning platforms (e.g. Edmodo, ShowMe), real time data monitoring
Practical work[2]	Sensors, interfaces, data logging, visualisers, CCTV cameras, video (including time lapse films), educational apps[1]
Data handling	Spreadsheets and graphing software (e.g. Excel), database searching
Building conceptual links and understanding	Mind mapping (e.g. Exploratree, mindmeister, Visio), interactive whiteboard (IWB) applications, online video tutorials, electronic voting systems (EVS)
Use of mathematical models, exploring relationships, predicting and testing theories	Spreadsheets and graphing software
Assessment for learning (AfL)	Electronic voting systems (EVS)

Notes:[1] Assuming availability of smart technologies.
[2] Data logging does not need to be classified as 'adventurous' but can be perceived as such.

So, familiar software applications for producing text and worksheets, spreadsheets and databases or slide presentations can facilitate some of your central preparation for lessons. What are the current requirements in the National Curriculum for science in terms of embedding technology-supported learning?

TECHNOLOGY-SUPPORTED STRATEGIES FOR LEARNING SCIENCE

The current Science National Curriculum (NC) programme of study for Key Stage 3 (KS3) (DfE, 2013) makes no direct mention of using technology-supported approaches in science. In the 'Working Scientifically' strand, learners having access to technologies is implied (see Table 5.3.3).

At the time of writing, the notion of ICT as a curriculum subject is changing; 'ICT' is to be replaced in September 2014 by 'computing' (with a focus on coding and programming in contrast to using software applications, as has been the case since the late 1980s). This change comes about as a result of the digital literacy for all debate (similar to debate about the need for scientific literacy) and is somewhat controversial. There is a perceived need to develop future citizens' digital literacy, as well as to cater for the smaller number who will become specialist computer scientists. Perhaps we shall see an even greater role

▪ **Table 5.3.3** Extracts from 'Working Scientifically' strand in the Key Stage 3 (DfE, 2013) and draft Key Stage 4 National Curriculum for Science*

Key Stage	Experimental skills and investigations	Handling information and problem solving
3 and 4	'using appropriate techniques, apparatus . . .'	'present observations and data using appropriate methods'
3 and 4	'making and recording . . . measurements using a range of methods'	'interpret observations and data'
4		'communicate . . . using electronic presentations'

Note: *Available at time of writing.

for teachers of all subjects to embed technology-supported learning. One important aspect of using online facilities is e-safety. Useful documents which remind teachers of important considerations are given at the end of the unit.

The next section looks at using a selection of technology tools effectively in your teaching to support learning.

COMMUNICATION AND PRESENTATION

Teacher slide presentations

Slide presentations provide an easily accessible, potentially powerful means of structuring lessons. Slides can be created to convey learning objectives, making the return to these at key points in a learning sequence more purposeful. Objectives and intentions can be transformed into possible outcomes which can then be used as checkpoints for pupils' actual progress, initiating links to your assessment tools and strategies. How proficient can you become in creating simple easily understood slides, such that the *production* of your presentation does not become the main focus of precious planning time? The optimal number of slides for an hour's lesson is open to debate but try to be minimalist. Create a reusable 'lesson presentation' with *six* key slide templates which you can easily amend each lesson to include:

1   an engaging image which captures attention and ignites curiosity as pupils arrive;
2   the rules for productive learning/signals for attention/safety, etc.;
3   the learning objectives;
4   clear 'what, how, how long' instructions for the main activity, to support modelling of what pupils need to do;
5   a small number of key questions linking to the learning outcomes;
6   the checkpoints for intended learning outcomes.

Try not to fall into the trap of preparing so many slides that you are giving a lecture (the term 'PowerPointism' has been coined, alluding to its over-use by teachers and pupils!). If you plan quizzes or a series of linked images, see them as separate, interwoven presentations. Embed movement to rouse interest, or perhaps sounds to use as signals for attention. It can be helpful to use a slide presentation in conjunction with an 'old-fashioned' write-on whiteboard if you have access to one. You can then authentically record and build upon pupils' ideas and you are more open to unanticipated points as they emerge. If you structure the lesson so tightly through prepared slides, it can lead to pupils 'waiting for the answer', rather than thinking for themselves.

Used appropriately, therefore, slide presentations can help to structure the organisation and pace of your lessons. Include reminders (for you too!) about tasks like homework and deadlines, and what is coming in the next lesson, to support the learning journey for pupils beyond the lesson.

Word processing and desktop publishing

You will probably create many worksheets over the coming months and years. Worksheets can be devised as excellent sources of information, question/assessment tools and interactive learning tools (for example, card sorts for organising ideas or flow diagrams for ordering steps in a sequence such as a practical method). Make worksheets attractive and clear, avoiding dense text. Who is reading the worksheet? Have you taken into account your pupils' current reading ages? Do you want several different versions of the worksheet, some with more hints and support than others or more images for students with English as an additional language (EAL) and so forth (see Units 5.1 and 4.4)? Or do you want all students to see the same information, the same questions (which might get progressively more challenging, with a 'red hot' challenge at the end!)?

Desktop publishing software can be a useful tool for you and your pupils if you use templates to present text and images in engaging and organised ways.

Pupil digital photography, video and slide presentation

Communication technologies give pupils the opportunity to prepare both colourful and imaginative presentations, whether for personal work, or for posters and whole class talks. Adding images to illustrate ideas and concepts can increase appeal. Pupils can capture their own digital photographs or videos of an event to include. They can easily experiment with ideas by writing, reviewing and changing, and this can be a great support for the overall writing process. Collaborative work is achievable. If you are providing 'writing frames' these can be put onto the computers. Pupils do need structured guidance about what to include in a presentation. Give them a clear remit, for example:

■ maximum number of slides (keep this low – five or six);
■ one image only per slide;
■ key questions to answer;
■ everyone must contribute.

Slide presentations should encourage the audience to actively participate as well. Have evaluation frames for pupils so that when they are watching each presentation they know what to record, and they can also peer-assess one another using agreed criteria. Ask everyone to assess scientific accuracy closely – pupils often copy and paste information into presentations without actually reading/checking it. The presentation itself is not the only final outcome.

Digital video can support pupils' learning. Schools are recording experiments / discussions which can be viewed online to follow up ideas and tasks. The advent of online learning platforms has made a wealth of video tutorial material available.

Pupils can also link up with their peers in other countries to take part in joint projects/ discussions. Exciting opportunities for role-play and 'real-life' interactions are possible using video-conferencing. Pupils can talk 'live' to scientists across the world and take part in simulations of global events. For example, the National Space Agency in Leicester runs a 'Montserrat' disaster simulation in which pupils try to respond to the eruption of a volcano which began in July 1995. They have to make decisions about what to do as scientists relay information about what is happening at that moment.

INFORMATION GATHERING AND EXAMINING EVIDENCE

Using websites effectively

Pupils need carefully constructed tasks, with specific prompts, to guide them productively through websites when gathering information. Most sites are heavily text-based, so select ones which are suitable for your pupils and access particular learning objectives. Find sites which are easy to navigate, and which perhaps include video clips, good animations, search facilities and quizzes to assess what has been learnt. Check the level of interaction of a site using the checkpoints here as a simple guide:

▪ low interaction – browsing and reading only;
▪ medium interaction – with some tasks but mainly 'click and reveal';
▪ high interaction – tasks involve forms/multiple-choice with answers, email access to authors;
▪ very high – communication, active participation.

A small number of interactive sites are included at the end of this unit. If *you* find them difficult to use, then so will pupils. At the end of an activity, set up an evaluation of the site in which the pupils give feedback on key aspects so that you can build upon the original activity. Always evaluate the use of a website compared with a more traditional paper-based resource and decide whether using technology will enhance learning. The main challenge is to keep up with the latest and most effective web-based resources so think and plan carefully how you keep an updatable record of your favourite sites.

You will also find an ever-growing range of online resources for supporting your day-to-day planning, teaching and assessment of learners' progress. Again, keeping up with online resource banks and ideas for teaching or online continuing professional development (CPD) sites which model effective pedagogical approaches requires high levels of commitment and organisation.

Using educational apps

We are in the throes of an explosion in the creation of educational 'apps' – mobile applications which are designed to run on smart phones, tablets and other mobile devices. If schools continue to invest in the hardware for downloading and running apps, their use may well outpace more traditional online technologies, as even young pupils find them easy (and enjoyable) to use. Once again you need to have a clear, organised strategy for finding and using apps for pupils' learning. Spend some time defining the difference between a 'fun' activity and an 'engaging' activity – the distinction between these two is very important for purposeful learning. Apps have the potential to transform learning experiences in terms of introducing digital mechanisms, such as augmented reality, which pupils report supporting their learning well through a sense of being 'right in there'. Engaging apps currently exist for dissecting a frog, exploring cells and molecules in 3D and establishing which celestial bodies are right above your head. Making your own apps, and having pupils make their own (see the end of the unit for supporting organisations) can be very fruitful in terms of relevance and sense of achievement, as with any created resource.

Online learning platforms

A number of useful online learning platforms have been created by teachers for teachers over recent years. Two kinds of platform have become popular. Online video tutorials can support your ongoing development of school subject knowledge and confidence in science explanations. For your pupils, you can set up online learning groups for communicating tasks, uploading and sharing pupils' work, posting online assessments, and so forth. You can create a closed group for your class so that e-safety can be maintained.

You could upload your own short science explanations to share among your peers during your training year, and with teachers in your department, as well as for your pupils as a record of ideas in a lesson. These tutorials can be particularly effective for older pupils to reinforce explanations explored in class or during homework. Pupils often prefer the teacher to 'appear' in the online video which is worth bearing in mind. A short selection of online learning platforms is given at the end of the unit, which inevitably need updating very regularly.

PRACTICAL WORK: DATA LOGGING AND CONTROL

Data logging involves replacing traditional measuring devices, such as thermometers, by a sensor, and replacing manual results recording and graph drawing by an interface and then usually a computer. Data loggers log (collect and store) data remotely, away from a computer. The data can be downloaded onto the computer at a later time. This can be useful, say, for recording temperature fluctuations over an extended period out in the field. A single sensor and data logger can be used either for demonstration (projecting the digital or graphical display on the big screen so that everyone can see) or as a component in a circus of activities. Building pupils' understanding of types of variables can be well supported through data logging – the technology allows them to focus on ideas about dependent and independent variables, rather than worrying about taking an accurate measurement themselves. Once you are familiar with the hardware and software, data logging provides authentic opportunities for pupils to engage in the work of 'real' scientists. It is useful to have technical support at hand during the first few sessions you use a data logging activity, as sensors and interfaces can often stop linking with each other for no apparent reason. Try to become familiar with some of the easy-to-solve issues to ensure your data logging lessons run smoothly.

There is a wide range of sensors available, from a number of suppliers, and a selection of some useful ones and their applications are given in Table 5.3.4.

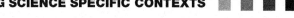

■ **Table 5.3.4** List of commonly found sensors and examples of use in practical work

Sensors	Examples of application/practical activities
Temperature	Exothermic and endothermic reactions (e.g. ammonium chloride and barium hydroxide crystals) Temperature changes over a day (in a building, in a greenhouse, outside) Investigating why some animals huddle in the winter
Light	Monitoring light levels in different environments Monitoring the rate of a reaction in which a precipitate is formed Investigating light reflected from different materials
Pulse	Investigating fluctuations in resting pulse rate Investigating how quickly pulse returns to normal after exercise
Light gates	Measuring speed using an air track and 'floating' trolleys Measuring reaction times (e.g. the disappearing cross experiment)
Voltage and current	Investigating the voltage current relationships of resistors, thermistors, diodes Charging and discharging a capacitor
Pressure	Pressure change with depth of water Pressure change with altitude (within tall buildings, out on field trips in hilly country)
pH	Investigating acidity in ponds, streams, soil Monitoring acid-base reactions
Oxygen	Monitoring oxygen levels in a yeast culture to indicate microbial growth Monitoring oxygen levels in streams
Position	Investigating whether plants grow faster during the day than at night Measuring distortion of elastic material Monitoring the oscillations in a spring Monitoring the rate of a gaseous reaction, with a gas syringe
Mass (electronic balance)	Monitoring the rate of a gaseous reaction

The guidance given about practical work in Unit 5.2 applies here, especially trying things out beforehand. For instance, do your temperature sensors give the same readings as a conventional thermometer for the temperature of boiling water? Trialling data logging equipment, particularly alongside non-data logging methods, can create useful evaluative investigations for pupils (Dixon, 2008). Encouraging pupils to choose appropriate apparatus from their own perspective in crafting a plan works well. They can then discuss the benefits of the sensor method versus the non-sensor method, try out the different approaches and suggest improvements based upon reliability and precision.

There are four main advantages to using data logging for learning science, namely:

■ Simultaneous graphing offers the opportunity for discussion of what is happening *while* it is happening, and of identifying how the graph relates to the phenomenon, i.e. the phenomenon and the visual representation of the phenomenon are happening together.

- Both fast and slow changes can be monitored which would be difficult or tedious if done manually.
- Less time is spent on plotting graphs, which releases more time for interpretation of the graph, a skill which pupils often find difficult (see Data Handling below);
- Pupils can have a more realistic understanding of how data might be collected by real scientists. 'Real-time' monitoring of changing situations can be followed online.

DATA HANDLING

Data handling packages handle numerical data and can be useful in a number of ways. Pupils can prepare relatively simple databases incorporating maybe only five or six fields. Try using data about themselves, selecting aspects which are not too sensitive (possible fields: hand span, arm length, size of foot, length of forearm, eye colour, hair colour). You can then use the software to create bar charts and pie charts to review the data (e.g. distribution of people with different colour eyes; use search facilities to find those people, say, with blue eyes and large hands; correlation graphs to review whether people with long arms also have large hands; you can test the theory that the size of your foot is the same as the length of your forearm, etc.). Similar activities on using data, for example, on the planets or elements in the Periodic Table can help pupils to look for patterns/characteristics and to exercise higher-order thinking skills. The ability to interrogate a database is an important skill. This is where discussion comes in and the time saved not having to draw all the charts and graphs can be used on interpretation. Some applications do not plot lines of best fit very well.

A spreadsheet allows pupils to manipulate numerical data in two main ways. First, you can do routine calculations by putting a formula in (e.g. if you are measuring mass and volume, then you can set it to calculate density automatically in the next column). This can allow a whole class set of results to be processed and discussion can focus on their reliability. Pupils investigating rates of reaction can input gradient calculations, or explore the effects of different orders of reactants on rate very easily at KS5. Second, it is possible to graph results, again if class sets are being collected, and to keep an eye on the graph which is building up.

Interactive whiteboard (IWB) software may have the facility to 'drag' graph paper and axes on screen, thereby giving pupils opportunities to actively practise building scales and plotting data (Beauchamp and Parkinson, 2005).

Task 5.3.1 **Developing graphical skills**

Investigate the assertion that producing graphs manually can take some pupils 'three to four times longer' than producing computer-aided equivalents (Barton, 2004, p. 32).

1 Talk with colleagues in your maths/computing departments about the timing and extent of graphical learning that pupils will have gone through prior to your lessons. Develop a guide for both manual and spreadsheet graph-plotting which your pupils can use.
2 Choose two lessons in which pupils either collect or are given data, which requires them to understand the concepts of dependent and independent variables.

---

3 In the first lesson, set the task of manual graph plotting. In the second, book a computer room or the science department laptops and ask pupils to create graphs using a spreadsheet. (Be prepared to devote an entire lesson to both activities, with extra material ready if a whole lesson is not needed.)

4 Reflect upon and evaluate the successes and drawbacks of both approaches and re-develop your guides to graph-plotting in the light of what you learn about your learners. How much variation was there in times needed for successful graph production? Which skills did students develop successfully during each activity? What was most challenging?

SIMULATIONS AND ANIMATIONS

Simulations are virtual experiments such as building electric circuits, altering pressure and temperature in the Haber process and studying changes in a predator–prey relationship. They allow pupils to investigate a phenomenon, focusing on conceptual understanding, without the messiness and clutter of reality slowing them down. They are interactive and provide feedback to pupils about what is happening. They must not be confused, however, with reality and unless pupils have experience of handling the appropriate equipment, they will lose sight of what the simulation relates to. Simulations can also provide virtual experiences like journeys to the planets, or through the blood system or models, say, of the human body or molecules which can be manipulated in some way. Some simulations add 'conceptual labels'; for instance, in showing the movement of a bouncing ball force and velocity arrows will be added so that it is possible to watch what is happening to these parameters as the ball moves.

Software companies and educational app designers have produced a wide variety of animations designed to contribute to pupils' understanding of abstract scientific theories. Moving images of particles in solids, liquids and gases dance before pupils' eyes but beware! Animations may contain inherent errors and over-simplifications (often as a result of unavoidable limitations in graphic capability). Particles in a liquid are inevitably displayed with spaces in between them, thereby reinforcing a commonly held misconception. Therefore, you should critique, and encourage pupils to do so, the limitations of this kind of model as you explore the ideas which it is intended to support (see Useful Websites).

BUILDING CONCEPTUAL LINKS AND UNDERSTANDING

Concept mapping

Brainstorming ideas at the start of a new topic and creating summary concept maps using concept mapping software give students opportunities to organise and store their ideas electronically.

Interactive whiteboards

Using interactive whiteboards (IWBs) to help build explanations and to assess pupils' progress in understanding ideas can be very effective. Flipcharts can be designed easily once you are familiar with the software. The following features are most useful when getting started (don't try to become an expert on all the interactive features at once!):

- covering up images fully or partly to ignite curiosity or to initiate thinking;
- uncovering key words gradually during assessment activities (but beware of the 'wait for the answers' response);
- labelling scientific diagrams in stages using layering techniques (an electronic version of the OHT);
- interactive 'drag and drop' sorting and assessments;
- saving pupils' ideas and following them up in later lessons.

The software comes with instructions on how to build these kinds of interactive activities. Engaging contexts can be used. Figure 5.3.1 shows a sketch diagram (originally with a famous cartoon character as the top layer) to show how a layering technique can be used to 'reveal' the underlying digestive system. The apple is the 'rubber', allowing pupils to see beneath the skin. Figure 5.3.2 shows an IWB reflection.

What happens to the apple?

■ **Figure 5.3.1** IWB cartoon

Source: Adapted from and reproduced with kind permission from Nick O'Brien. Sketch reproduced with kind permission from Satomi Saki.

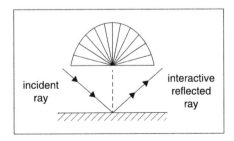

■ **Figure 5.3.2** IWB reflection. Sketch diagram to show how demonstrations such as judging the angle of the reflected ray when investigating reflection can be facilitated

Source: Adapted from and reproduced with kind permission from Jamie Styles.

MATHEMATICAL MODELS

There are commercially available mathematical models, such as on predator–prey relationships in ecology, or breeding rates of rabbits in a restricted environment. It is helpful, too, if pupils can set up their own models, however simple, as they then know what the model is that they are experimenting with. They could set up a model of the energy consumption in a house, with columns for 'appliance', 'wattage', 'time it is run', 'cost'. They can allocate a box for total cost over a week, another for budget which they must not exceed, and another for the difference between expenditure and budget. The model allows them to monitor their energy consumption against budget.

ASSESSMENT FOR LEARNING/EXPLORING IDEAS

Electronic voting systems (EVS) are tools for assessment. There are a number of possible applications of the technology, in which individual pupils have a 'pod' or 'clicker' through which they can interact with questions driven through specific software. Multiple choice and 'dilemma-style' questions can be created easily, and capturing answers immediately allows pupils to see individual and whole class answers on the big screen. The same questions can be revisited after a learning activity and pupils can see their own progression very quickly. In class, users can be anonymous between themselves but each 'pod' can have an identifier, and assessment data can be exported to a spreadsheet. The capture of individual performance data is an advantage of EVS over the non-technology equivalents (thumbs up, thumbs down or traffic light cards, for example). You could use the initial assessment results to put pupils into groups where at least one person has a good (accurate) idea and acts as the 'expert' in peer teaching. You might have a series of questions, which depending upon the categories of understanding into which pupils' answers fall initially, you give different interventions to different groups. The tool is also helpful in accurately gauging pupils' confidence in their answers, alongside the answers themselves, which can reveal important aspects of their development to you.

Task 5.3.2 **Evaluating the effectiveness of technology-supported resources, M-level**

At some point in your training year, try to use and evaluate the effectiveness of as many of the technology resources described in this unit as you realistically can. Your task here is to do the following:

1 Choose two resources that have conventional, non-technology equivalents (for example, using data logging versus a non-technology measuring device; using a drag-and-drop interactive activity versus a card sort, etc.).
2 Read at least two of the texts recommended below to make some inferences about why the technology method may enhance pupils' learning about science or process skills.
3 Run the technology and non-technology activities side-by-side (using half the class for one and half for the other, trying to balance higher and lower achievers in each half).

---

4 Critically reflect upon your assessed learning outcomes for the lessons which you focused on, and attempt to diagnose the different contributions of the technology and non-technology approaches to pupils' development of ideas and skills.

5 Use what you learn to develop your next approaches to activities for promoting learning.

SUMMARY AND KEY POINTS

Using technology tools and resources to support the learning and teaching of science is a well-established strategy, but new opportunities are emerging all the time. Specific resources and activities need to be trialled and evaluated thoroughly and technical support needs to be strong to ensure that lesson time is effective. Be very clear about the differences between using technology-supported resources to structure a lesson, as opposed to directly supporting pupils' active learning.

REFERENCES

Beauchamp, G. and Parkinson, J. (2005) 'Beyond the "wow" factor: developing interactivity with interactive whiteboards', *School Science Review*, 86(316): 97–103.

Condie, R. and Munro, B. (2007) *The Impact of ICT in Schools: A Landscape Review*, Coventry: Becta.

Davis, C. and Good, J. (2009) *Harnessing Technology: The Learner and Their Context Choosing to Use Technology: How Learners Construct Their Learning Lives in Their Own Contexts*, Coventry: Becta.

Dixon, N. (2008) 'Can data logging improve the quality of interpretation and evaluation in chemistry lessons?' *School Science Review*, 89(329): 55–62.

Frost, R. (2002a) *Data Logging in Practice*, London: IT in Science.

Frost, R. (2002b) *Data Logging and Control*, London: IT in Science.

Hammond, M. (2013) 'Introducing ICT in schools in England: rationale and consequences', *British Journal of Educational Technology*, doi:10.1111/bjet.12033.

McKeown, S. and McGlashon, A. (2012) *Brilliant Ideas for Using ICT in the Inclusive Classroom*, London: Routledge.

Morris, D. (2010) 'Are teachers technophobes? Investigating professional competency in the use of ICT to support teaching and learning', *Proceeding of Social and Behavioral Sciences*, 2(2): 4010–15.

Tan, K. and Koh, T. (2008) 'The use of Web 2.0 technologies in school science', *School Science Review*, 90(330): 113–17.

FURTHER READING

Brechin, K. (2006) *Exciting ICT in Science*, London: Network Continuum Education.

Practical ideas for the science classroom.

Condie, R. and Munro, B. (2007) *The Impact of ICT in Schools: A Landscape Review*, Coventry: Becta.

A good overview of the developing issues with ICT in the classroom.

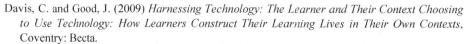

Davis, C. and Good, J. (2009) *Harnessing Technology: The Learner and Their Context Choosing to Use Technology: How Learners Construct Their Learning Lives in Their Own Contexts*, Coventry: Becta.

Dixon, N. (2008) 'Can data logging improve the quality of interpretation and evaluation in chemistry lessons?' *School Science Review*, 89(329): 55–62.

A useful article showing how A-level students developed data analysis skills through data logging.

McKeown, S. and McGlashon, A. (2012) *Brilliant Ideas for Using ICT in the Inclusive Classroom*, London: Routledge.

Practical ideas for the science (and any) classroom. Includes very clear 'getting started' tips on each approach for teachers.

USEFUL WEBSITES

Online learning platforms

Here is a selection of popular platforms (current at the time of writing) for supporting your school subject knowledge development and for setting up online learning:

https://www.edmodo.com/
www.khanacademy.org/
www.scoop.it/t/science-education-secondary
www.showme.com/

Some online resources for learning science

www.aerospaceguide.net/nationalcentre.html is the National Space Centre, Leicester website.

www.nasa.gov/ is the official website for the American Space Agency, NASA. It is an excellent example of one in which pupils can have a high level of interaction. Current space shuttle missions can be followed and the latest projects at NASA explored.

www.absorblearning.com/en/Free_online_Absorb_resources/ is an online library of simple simulations, animations and other useful resources. It remains (at the time of writing) free to use online.

www.beep.ac.uk/ is the website for the BioEthics Evaluation Project (BEEP) which can be used for online debating of socio-scientific issues for A-level biology.

www.thenakedscientists.com/ includes an online science radio show, podcasts, discussion forum, science, medicine and technology news, interviews, medical and health advice, educational resources and articles, experiments, projects and book reviews. It was set up with support from, among others, the Royal Society and Cambridge University.

http://revealproject.org/ reports on a two-year study into the use of electronic voting systems (or learner response systems) in educational settings and has many useful examples for science and tips on how to make the most of the assessment opportunities.

Science teachers' resources and CPD sites

www.ase.org.uk/resources/becta-legacy-science-resources/ is a repository within the ASE website for BECTA ICT resources. Lots of the examples and ideas for activities are still useful. The ASE also includes reviews of useful websites and educational apps in its journal, *School Science Review*.

www.gettingpractical.org.uk/ is the website for this ASE-supported practical to promote confidence in teaching and learning through practical work in science.

Nuffield websites

The following three websites are the Nuffield-supported teaching through practical work sites. They include printable practical worksheets and advice on risk assessment.

www.nuffieldfoundation.org/practical-biology
www.nuffieldfoundation.org/practical-chemistry
www.nuffieldfoundation.org/practical-physics

www.iop.org/resources/index.html is the Institute of Physics resources webpage. It gives ideas for teaching and learning physics at all levels.

www.rsc.org/learn-chemistry is the Learn Chemistry area of the Royal Society of Chemistry website. It gives access to lots of ideas for practical and non-practical chemistry resources.

www.education.gov.uk/schools/teachingandlearning/curriculum/nationalcurriculum2014 gives details of the National Curriculum for science for 2014 onwards.

www.education.gov.uk/schools/pupilsupport/pastoralcare/b00198456/principles-of-e-safety gives current details about how to promote e-safety with your pupils when using the Internet or storing pupil data, etc.

http://webarchive.nationalarchives.gov.uk/20130401151715/https://www.education.gov.uk/publications/standard/publicationDetail/Page1/DCSF-00290-2010 details the progress made with e-safety since the 2008 Byron Report.

All websites accessed 3 March 2014.

UNIT 5.4

SCIENCE FOR CITIZENSHIP

Marcus Grace

INTRODUCTION

The place of Citizenship in the curriculum has been under dispute for many years – whether it should be statutory, whether it should be cross-curricular, whether it should be distinct from Personal Social Health and Economic Education (PSHE), and whether indeed it should be part of Science. However, it is generally agreed that the school curriculum has a fundamental part to play in helping young people learn how to become citizens within our democratic society. The breadth of definition of citizenship expands and contracts with successive governments, but this chapter uses a broad definition in line with the aims of the Citizenship Foundation (2013):

> We want young people to leave school or college with an understanding of the political, legal and economic functions of adult society, and with the social and moral awareness to thrive in it. Citizenship education is about **enabling** people to **make their own decisions** and to **take responsibility** for their own lives and their communities.
>
> (original emphases)

It is worth noting here that the science for citizenship discussed in this chapter is not the same as what is now commonly known as 'citizen science', which generally refers to public participation (including schools) in scientific research, i.e. collecting and analysing data by amateurs and non-professionals (Hand, 2010).

The current National Curriculum in England states the purpose of study of Citizenship as:

> A high-quality citizenship education helps to provide pupils with knowledge, skills and understanding to prepare them to play a full and active part in society. In particular, citizenship education should foster pupils' keen awareness of how the United Kingdom is governed and how its laws are made and upheld. It should also prepare pupils to take their place in society as responsible citizens by providing them with the skills and knowledge to manage their money well and make sound financial decisions.
>
> (DfE, 2013, p. 3)

The document lists the aims of Citizenship as being to ensure that all pupils:

- acquire a sound knowledge and understanding of how the United Kingdom is governed, its political system and how citizens participate actively in its democratic systems of government;
- develop a sound knowledge and understanding of the role of law in our society and how laws are shaped and enforced;
- develop an interest in, and commitment to, volunteering that they will take with them into adulthood;
- are equipped with the financial skills to enable them to manage their money on a day-to-day basis as well as to plan for future financial needs.

(DfE, 2013, p. 3)

As practising, caring and professional teachers we obviously have an important role to play in promoting these concepts among our pupils. Through our everyday interactions with pupils, we demonstrate 'democratic' values such as working together, listening to each other, respecting other viewpoints, trying to reconcile conflicting differences, and appreciating and celebrating that we are all equal yet different. To take the principles of citizenship seriously, we need to acknowledge the importance of pupil 'voice' by giving them opportunities to explain their ideas and views. Discussing how they plan to carry out an investigation or why they disagree with someone else's findings is part of science, but it is also part of citizenship.

As teachers, we have a job to do in introducing and nurturing democratic values among our pupils. Although in the UK we have the luxury of living in a relatively wealthy and democratically stable country, there is considerable evidence that this does not necessarily result in democratically engaged youngsters. In fact, positive attitudes towards citizenship values and participation are more evident in relatively poorer countries with a less democratic profile (Hoskins *et al.*, 2012).

OBJECTIVES

By the end of this unit you should be able to:

- identify opportunities for teaching citizenship through science;
- use a range of strategies to teach about controversial socio-scientific issues;
- assess citizenship in science;
- locate appropriate resources.

WHAT IS CITIZENSHIP?

Citizenship has two common interconnected meanings. It can refer to the status of being *a citizen*, i.e. *belonging to* a certain community or country, which brings with it certain rights and responsibilities defined in law, or it can imply the expected behaviour associated with being a citizen.

Whether citizenship is delivered as a separate curriculum subject or integrated into other curriculum subjects, it should link very closely with pupils' spiritual, moral, social and cultural (SMSC) development, which is an aspect of Ofsted school inspections. Ofsted refers to:

> the opportunities created by the school for pupils to take part in a range of artistic, cultural, sporting, dramatic, musical, mathematical, scientific, technological and, where appropriate, international events and activities that promote aspects of pupils' SMSC development.
>
> (Ofsted, 2013, paragraph 97)

So citizenship can help give pupils a secure learning environment which is required to tackle the controversial issues that will continue to confront them through their lives (Crick, 2001).

WHAT IS THE CONNECTION BETWEEN SCIENCE AND CITIZENSHIP?

Citizenship could be seen as an overarching theme linking all other subjects together. As science teachers, it is initially probably advisable to stick to what we know best and concentrate on the science-related components. Science teachers have a specific contribution to make to help develop pupils' ways of thinking and behaving as active citizens of the future. Science lessons provide an opportunity for pupils to learn about the applications of science and about socio-scientific issues, i.e. issues which have a basis in science and have a potentially large impact on society (Ratcliffe and Grace, 2003). There are questions raised in the media every day relating to controversial socio-scientific issues which impact on us all: How conclusive is DNA evidence in a murder trial? Is climate change really as big a threat to humanity as scientists tell us? Should our country invest in fracking?

With the advancement of science, the knowledge base of education for socio-scientific issues is becoming increasingly complex, and making decisions about the issues involves a difficult compromise between many conflicting values. So socio-scientific issues are not purely scientific, but also include social, moral, spiritual, political and economic values, which fall within the citizenship education remit.

HOW DO SCIENCE AND CITIZENSHIP FIT TOGETHER AT SCHOOL?

Sir Martin Taylor, Chair of the Royal Society's Vision Committee, introduced the Society's 'Vision for Science and Mathematics Education' by stating: 'We want an inspirational education system that will deliver both scientifically and technologically informed, engaged citizens and appropriate numbers of qualified people who wish to take up science and technology-based careers' (The Royal Society, 2013).

The science curriculum therefore has twin goals: (1) for all pupils to develop a certain level of scientific literacy; and (2) for some pupils to begin training as future scientists. Millar (2012) makes the point that these are not two separate groups of pupils, and we should remember that the future scientists are themselves future citizens (Figure 5.4.1). Teaching science for citizenship therefore also has this dual purpose, i.e. to develop generically scientifically literate citizens, and to additionally develop a subset of these citizens to become future scientists.

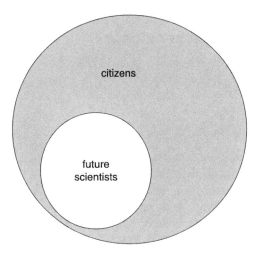

■ **Figure 5.4.1** The relationship between citizens and future scientists
Source: Millar (2012).

The science curriculum contributes to citizenship by providing the background subject knowledge which we should all have in order to function as citizens. Of course, views will differ about exactly which concepts should be considered essential, but Harlen (2010), for example, identified ten 'big ideas' about the material world (Table 5.4.1).

■ **Table 5.4.1** Ten 'big ideas' in science

1. All material in the Universe is made of very small particles.
2. Objects can affect other objects at a distance.
3. Changing the movement of an object requires a net force to be acting on it.
4. The total amount of energy in the Universe is always the same but energy can be transformed when things change or are made to happen.
5. The composition of the Earth and its atmosphere and the processes occurring within them shape the Earth's surface and its climate.
6. The solar system is a very small part of one of millions of galaxies in the Universe.
7. Organisms are organised on a cellular basis.
8. Organisms require a supply of energy and materials for which they are often dependent on or in competition with other organisms.
9. Genetic information is passed down from one generation of organisms to another.
10. The diversity of organisms, living and extinct, is the result of evolution.

Source: Harlen (2010).

Task 5.4.1 **Big ideas in science**

Look at Harlen's list of 'big ideas' in science in Table 5.4.1. Are there any other big ideas you would consider adding to the list which all people should know about to function as citizens? Would you consider removing any of Harlen's big ideas from the list?

So science contributes subject knowledge, which enables people to make more scientifically informed judgements about socio-scientific issues. However, as citizens, it is also important for pupils to communicate and exchange their views about these issues. Pupils should be encouraged to engage with debate and decision-making about contemporary controversial issues, and ultimately become informed and active citizens. Science teachers have a particularly important part to play when these issues are underpinned by science.

There are many different ways in which you can teach citizenship through science. The examples given below are linked to three aspects of citizenship: (1) enquiry and decision-making; (2) communication; and (3) taking informed and responsible action.

Enquiry and decision-making

Pupils could do the following:

▪ investigate the accuracy of science stories (socio-scientific issues) presented in the media and the extent to which they influence public opinion. Examples might include 'designer babies', 'superbugs', genetically modified ('Frankenstein') foods, and risks from vaccinations or mobile phones. They could examine the reliability of the sources of information upon which the stories are based.

▪ access and evaluate sources of information about the use of electricity or water by the school, to consider how valid and reliable the data is. This could involve consulting utility companies over prices, and surveying related patterns of behaviour among pupils and staff.

▪ analyse and evaluate the variety of opinions surrounding a socio-scientific issue. Issues could range from complex and emotional ones such as the need to cull badgers to prevent the spread of bovine TB, to decision-making about the school's energy management plan.

Communication

Pupils could do the following:

▪ consider how different people express themselves when putting forward their point of view;

▪ practise communicating with different audiences, such as writing a letter to the local MP or newspaper, to attempt to get their message across as persuasively as possible;

▪ give a presentation about a socio-scientific issue, representing the views of others with which they do not agree.

Taking informed and responsible action

Pupils could do the following:

- create or review the school policy on purchasing environmentally-friendly products by carrying out research on the life cycle of materials;
- plan how to collaborate as a class to communicate their collective view about a socio-scientific issue to a relevant local or national organisation;
- teach younger children about, for example, the value of reusing and recycling of waste materials.

Task 5.4.2 **Citizenship and science in your school**

Find out how aspects of science for citizenship are taught in your school.

1 Why has the school decided to take this approach?
2 Look through your department's schemes of work. What opportunities can you identify for teaching citizenship in science lessons?

HOW DO SCHOOLS TEACH SCIENCE FOR CITIZENSHIP?

It is up to individual schools how they deliver the citizenship curriculum. The Mountbatten School and Hounsdown School in Hampshire run particularly motivating citizenship programmes. The Mountbatten programme is combined with PSHE as three whole days ('collapsed days') annually for pupils in all year groups. Most teachers are involved and pupils generally remain in their tutor groups. There are sometimes themes for certain age groups (e.g. the global community, community cohesion, fair trade, drugs and alcohol), and external groups ranging from the police to citizenship-oriented theatre groups are invited to give talks and workshops. Pupils also follow a 'job trail' around the school and are involved in Skyping about citizenship issues with pupils from other schools. In addition, there is an annual 'work enrichment day' which gives pupils an opportunity to engage with the world of work in local businesses and colleges. The school leavers (Year 11) also have the opportunity to engage in activities alongside other youngsters they would not normally encounter through the National Citizens Service Hampshire (NCS, 2013, see Useful Websites).

The Hounsdown programme links with all other curriculum subjects. The school has three Citizenship Focus Days and three Citizenship Theme Days during the course of the school year. On Focus Days, subject teachers teach whatever was already on their timetable, but modify the lessons to focus on key content and processes in the citizenship curriculum as well as those in the science curriculum. An example of a Focus Day science lesson is shown in Figure 5.4.2.

On the Theme Days, the whole school comes off the normal timetable and different citizenship themes are arranged for each year group. All pupils work their way through a series of activities through the day, some run by teachers and others by external organisations. Many of the activities consider socio-scientific issues such as Junk Food, Fire Safety, Fair Trade, Race and Human Rights, Consequences of Vandalism, Sexual Health, Drugs Awareness, and Being a Global Citizen.

Lesson title: The problems with polymers
Aims: To understand the environmental impact of making and using polymers
Citizenship content: ▧ Critical thinking and enquiry: research, plan and undertake an enquiry into issues and problems using a range of information and sources ▧ To discuss the environmental aspects of making and disposing of polymers ▧ To carry out research to identify these issues ▧ To present the findings to the public
Science content: ▧ Polymer manufacture from non-renewable fossil fuels ▧ The environmental effect of alternative methods of polymer disposal – excessive landfill, toxic combustion, waste of valuable resources
Key vocabulary: polymer, environment, non-renewable resource, combustion, toxic fumes
Starter: short videos made by pupils on recycling to promote ideas about waste management
Development: Pupils to research and discuss the problems of plastics from manufacture to disposal. Pupil groups choose which issue to investigate – manufacture, combustion, landfill, reusing and recycling
Plenary: pupils present their work to the class (in the role of a public audience)
Evidence produced: Group posters showing ideas used for their presentation
Resources required: camcorders, science textbooks, A3 paper, coloured pens
Assessment: Pupils level themselves against citizenship attainment target levels

▧ **Figure 5.4.2** Outline of a Year 9 lesson on polymers

TEACHING ABOUT CONTROVERSIAL ISSUES

Effective teaching of citizenship in science involves the discussion of pupils' ideas in the classroom. Many of these ideas are controversial, i.e. significant numbers of people argue about them without reaching a conclusion (Oulton *et al.*, 2004b). Stradling defined controversial issues as: 'issues on which our society is clearly divided and significant groups within society advocate conflicting explanations or solutions based on alternative values' (1985, p. 9).

Pupils will encounter moral dilemmas before and after they leave school, and we as teachers therefore have to help them develop the means to make properly informed decisions.

Class discussion

Class discussion is widely recognized as an effective way to encourage pupils to explore issues. However, pupils are sometimes rushed into making up their minds on the issue, and there is a danger that they might form their opinions too soon, possibly based on the personality of the protagonist rather than the validity and reliability of the evidence being presented.

It is useful to decide what we mean by the terms *discussion*, *debate* and *argument*. All these terms can be used synonymously generally to mean verbal interaction aimed at resolving a controversy (Newton *et al.*, 1999).

However, we need to be clear that we are talking about the kind of verbal interaction in which all participants respectfully listen to each other's viewpoints, involving self-reflection and a clarification of values (Solomon, 2001), not the scenario of frequent heckling as witnessed in the House of Commons, or argument without structure or reasoning akin to that often found in television programmes such as *EastEnders*.

The very process of discussing socio-scientific issues requires pupils to act and behave in a way expected of good citizens, and it is important that they understand basic ground rules for discussion, such as respecting and listening sensitively to each other's points of view. Although the activity may be carried out within a science lesson, pupils should also be considering personal and social values; when dealing with real issues the emotional aspects need to be handled sensitively. This involves finding out (if you can) if there are pupils in the class who might be deeply affected by the issue. Some pupils may prefer not to be present and this is of course their prerogative; on the other hand, they may want to talk about their experiences. If pupils have questions, they would prefer not to ask in front of their peers, you could use a question box where they can post questions anonymously for discussion in the next lesson.

Managing discussion

In chairing a discussion about controversial issues, we need to consider some main principles – which themselves can be controversial! (QCA, 1998):

- *Neutrality*: Some teachers prefer to act as a neutral chairperson, not declaring their own view while encouraging pupils to express theirs. However, neutrality is difficult to sustain and can undermine the rapport that the teacher has built up with the pupils (Stradling, 1985). Other teachers have a 'stated commitment' approach, where they declare their views from the start, and encourage pupils to agree or disagree on the basis of their reasoning. Oulton *et al* (2004b) argue that if we really want pupils to be open about what they feel and think, then the teacher should reciprocate to engender trust and transparency among all concerned.
- *Balance*: A 'balanced' approach is where the teacher tries to ensure that all different views of the issue are covered, and one-sided arguments are countered by playing 'devil's advocate'. The difficulty is knowing how to achieve balance. The teacher will need to have some understanding of all viewpoints. The QCA (1998) point out that it is impossible, and in some cases undesirable, to be completely unbiased, but we need to avoid indoctrination.
- *Reason*: We must guard against giving pupils the impression that real-life issues can always be resolved through reason (Ashton and Watson, 1998), and oversimplifying moral dilemmas, which renders them unrealistic (Kibble, 1998).

The QCA (1998, p. 56) suggests that:

[We] teach pupils how to recognize bias, how to evaluate evidence put before them and how to look at alternative interpretations, viewpoints and sources of evidence, above all to give good reasons for everything they say or do, and to expect good reasons to be given by others.

Task 5.4.3 **Teaching about different controversial issues, M-level**

Write down your definition of a controversial issue. If possible, ask someone else to do the same and compare your definitions. Then compare them with Stradling's definition above. List some current controversial socio-scientific issues and note whether Stradling's definition holds true for each. Comment critically on the approaches to neutrality, balance and reason advocated by the authors in the section above. Look at the survey questions in Table 5.4.2 about two controversial issues. To begin with, cover up the figures given in the table and complete the survey yourself. Then compare your responses with the figures given. These are results from a survey of over 200 teachers showing the approaches that they would adopt when teaching the two different controversial issues. There are clear differences among the teachers. Think about why these might both be considered socio-scientific issues, and write down why you think teachers hold a range of opinions about the teaching of different topics (see Oulton *et al.*, 2004a, for further discussion of this data).

▨ **Table 5.4.2** Approaches teachers would adopt when teaching two different controversial issues

If I was teaching these topics I would:	Racism	Factory farming
1 (a) Present a balanced view	62	83
(b) Present a biased view	21	12
(c) Explain to pupils that balance is impossible to achieve	17	05
2 (a) Not give my opinion	29	33
(b) Only give my opinion if asked	29	53
(c) Make my opinion clear to pupils	42	14
3 (a) Encourage pupils to make up their own mind on the issue	41	82
(b) Try to influence pupils to adopt a particular attitude to the issue	34	07
(c) Discourage pupils from making up their mind at this stage of their development	02	11

Note: Figures show percentages of respondents indicating their choice.

Source: Oulton *et al.* (2004a).

USING AND DEVELOPING PUPILS' KNOWLEDGE OF SOCIO-SCIENTIFIC ISSUES

Before the class discusses an issue, you should ensure that the pupils have sufficient understanding of the underlying science and social aspects. To establish that pupils have the required knowledge base, you will have to find out what they know already, what they need to know for the discussion, and how they will access this knowledge. With the proliferation of sources of information all purporting to be accurate and based on scientific evidence, it can be extremely difficult to gauge the reliability of the information. This is even more difficult for pupils to disentangle. In their attempts to engage us with issues, journalists may sometimes unintentionally dilute the scientific evidence due to editing, restricted space, their own interpretation of the data, and their use of emotive language. But before we go rushing to scientific reports for reliable data, we should also remember that scientists themselves may also be prone to bias. They are only human, with their own priorities, values, beliefs and role in society. Fortunately there are now a number of well-established and reliable education sites with excellent resources, enabling teachers to conduct informed discussion about a range of socio-scientific issues. The added value of restricting your pupils to such resources is that you are more able to control the direction the discussion is likely to take.

Task 5.4.4 Observing an experienced teacher

New teachers will have fundamental concerns about teaching controversial issues. Pupils might ask 'non-scientific' questions which you are unable to answer or feel uneasy about answering. A good way to learn how to organise and facilitate a discussion is to ask to observe experienced teachers, including English and humanities teachers, who tend to use this approach more readily than science teachers. Observe a discussion lesson and try to note down answers to the following questions:

1   How is the dilemma presented?
2   Does the teacher draw on pupils' knowledge and experiences?
3   Does the teacher use a carefully selected set of information and resources for discussion? How are they distributed?
4   Are media reports being used? What kind?
5   Is this a whole-class discussion, or a collection of small group discussions, or a mixture of both?
6   If pupils are grouped, how does the teacher organise the groups? Do the pupils have stimuli to provoke discussion? Does the grouping occur spontaneously or does the teacher allocate groups? Does the teacher allocate roles within the groups?
7   What are the aims of the discussion? Are these made clear to pupils?
8   Are there expectations/ground rules? What are the intended learning outcomes?
9   Do all pupils contribute equally?
10 What is the role of the teacher during discussion?
11 What is the level of noise? Are pupils overly noisy? Are there uncomfortable silences?
12 Do pupils have enough time to think about the issues before and during the discussion?

---

13 How does the teacher manage obstinate, sensitive, emotional or unaccept-
   able viewpoints? How does the teacher deal with dominant or 'opinionated'
   pupils? Does the teacher press for consensus? Does the teacher try to highlight differences?
14 How does the teacher deal with questions he/she is unable to answer?
15 How much time is devoted to teacher talk and pupil talk?
16 How are the results of the discussion presented?
17 Do the pupils seem content or frustrated with the activity and the overall
   outcomes?

TEACHING STRATEGIES

As in all teaching situations, the approach you use will depend on factors such as the age, ability, and group dynamics of the class, the space available and the general situation at that time. The following is a brief introduction to a range of teaching strategies you may wish to use.

Role play

Role play is one of the most frequently used approaches for teaching about controversial issues among secondary school teachers (Oulton *et al.*, 2004a); it offers pupils the oppor-tunity to explore other people's perspectives. However, simply putting a pupil in role does not necessarily mean that they can empathise with the viewpoints of others (Lynch and McKenna, 1990), so we should be cautious about its universal effectiveness.

Heads and hearts

This activity (Ratcliffe and Grace, 2003) encourages pupils to recognise the existence of an emotional reaction and a rational response to a controversial issue. Pupils are asked to immediately react to a question, for which you give them up to four choices. Depending on their choice, they move to the relevant corner of the room. Pose a question such as: 'Should we have genetic testing to eliminate serious genetic disorders from our society in future generations?'

Designate each corner of the room as: not at all; compulsory for everyone; compulsory for those who have relatives with the disorder; only for those who want to be tested. Some pupils may want to stand mid-way between corners. Then ask them to put their hand on the head if they had made the decision by thinking rationally, or on their heart if it was an immediate emotional response. Ask some to explain their views.

Consequence mapping

This allows pupils to explore a 'What if . . .' scenario, by considering the consequences of an action. Get pupils working in small groups to write the proposed action in the middle of a large sheet of paper, and then map the possible primary and secondary consequences of this action. For example, the proposal might be: 'What if fishing in the North Sea is completely banned?' Other groups could map the opposing view: 'What if fishing in the North Sea is completely unrestricted?' The maps could be displayed on the walls for comparison. The activity encourages pupils to identify their own values and those of others in relation to the issue, and appreciate that socio-scientific issues involve considering values as well as scientific evidence.

Evaluating media reports

Media reports (from tabloid and broadsheet newspapers, TV, radio, the Internet, etc.) can demonstrate the relevance of science to everyday issues. They can be used to identify scientific terms, the underpinning science concepts, the values and opinions of people involved, and the evidence that is being used to support or challenge claims being made. Pupils can also learn about the nature of media reporting itself by looking at the role of an editor, or by concentrating on 'hooks' which draw in the audience. These might include surprise elements, exciting visual or audio presentation, or emotional triggers such as sadness, humour, fighting against almost unbelievable odds, incredible coincidences and so on. One systematic way of evaluating science-related media reports is to get pupils to answer the following questions:

■ What are the scientists/researchers claiming? (i.e. what are their conclusions?)
■ What scientific knowledge did the researchers use to support their conclusions?
■ What evidence is provided to support their conclusions?
■ Does the evidence provided here convince you that the conclusion is correct?
■ What extra evidence is needed?
■ How might this be collected?

To highlight the socially-framed nature of scientific research, additional questions could be posed:

■ Who did the research?
■ Who do they work for?
■ How certain are they about their conclusions?
■ Do other scientists agree with their conclusions?

Probability and risk

In analysing risk, pupils need to understand probability and to recognise that nothing we do is completely risk-free. Risk is a combination of the probability of something going wrong, and the cost to you if something does go wrong. Individuals will have different views. You could ask pupils how willing they would be to engage in a range of potentially dangerous activities, and compare their perceptions with risk statistics from the Health and Safety Executive website, or the government's UK National Statistics website. Pupils could rate the danger by discussing in small groups how much money (or other benefit) they would require to take the risk. This kind of activity promotes discussion about science and society:

■ how risk statistics are derived;
■ how the risks associated with the issues are presented to the public;
■ why scientists are unable to state categorically the risks associated with certain issues;
■ how we decide whether or not to carry out risky activities. Do we always calculate the risk first?

The Mind Tools website also provides some useful resources and ideas about probability and risk.

Decision-making frameworks

A way to promote systematic and critical risk-benefit discussions among pupils is to provide them with a decision-making framework of the kind shown in Figure 5.4.3.

Present pupils with some background on a real socio-scientific issue, maybe as brief text with some visual stimulus. Here is an example:

Follow these steps, consider the questions and complete the table as you go.

1. OPTIONS
   - What are the options?
   - Discuss the possible solutions to the problem and list them in a table.

2. IMPORTANT THINGS TO CONSIDER
   - How are you going to choose between these options?
   - Discuss the **important** things to consider when you look at each option, and add them to the table.

3. INFORMATION
   - Do you have enough information about each option?
   - Discuss what **science** is involved in the problem.
   - Discuss what **extra scientific information** you need to help you make the decision.

4. ADVANTAGES/ DISADVANTAGES
   Discuss the advantages and disadvantages of each option, and add them to the table.

5. CHOICE
   Which option does your group choose?

6. REVIEW
   What do you think of the decision you have made?
   How could you improve the way you made the decision?

OPTIONS (possible solutions) *[as many as you think of]*	IMPORTANT THINGS TO CONSIDER *[for each option]*	ADVANTAGES *[for each option]*	DISADVANTAGES *[for each option]*
1.			
2.			
3.			

Figure 5.4.3 A decision-making framework for learning about socio-scientific issues

Source: After Ratcliffe and Grace (2003).

About 30 per cent of teenage boys and girls in England are overweight or obese. Unhealthy fast foods are convenient and relatively cheap, which suits busy people and disadvantaged people. A recent Government report has estimated that £6 billion could be saved and 70,000 early deaths could be avoided if people improved their diets. We have strict regulations on sewers, clean drinking water, car seat belts, and smoking in public places, but the Government believes that people should have the right and responsibility to decide on their own diets. The Government's plan is to work with the food and soft drinks companies to spread healthy messages, have health campaigns and projects, which encourage people to eat more healthily. But teenage obesity continues to rise.

What should be done about the problem, *why* and *how*?

Pupils then spend five minutes alone thinking quietly about how and why the problem should be solved. This enables them to start forming their own views to draw on in the subsequent discussion. Then pupils discuss the issue in small groups using the decision-making framework as a guide towards making a decision. Meanwhile you can circulate among the groups observing the group interaction, though you need to decide in advance how much to intervene, bearing in mind that your presence could alter their discussion and even stifle their creative ideas! If handled carefully, this is an excellent means of demonstrating to pupils that an active citizen needs to develop the skill to balance human values and science knowledge to take part in informed decision-making about social issues. At the end of the discussion, some groups may have reached a decision, others may remain undecided. The important purpose of this activity is not to force pupils into making a decision, but to take the pupils through the decision-making process.

ASSESSMENT METHODS

Useful types of assessment in teaching about controversial issues include observation, written open responses, listening to discussions, self-assessment, a portfolio of evidence, and active, participatory approaches. Evaluation of learning from the activities above is perhaps not as straightforward as for the recall of scientific 'facts', development of practical skills, or explanation of science concepts and processes. Our main educational aim of education for citizenship is for pupils to develop informed and responsible attitudes and actions when confronted with real issues. Research has shown that there is not a strong correlation between knowledge and attitudes (e.g. Gayford and Dillon, 1995), and attitudes may be modified without corresponding behavioural change. It might therefore not be realistic to expect changes in behaviour, and the best we can do is evaluate opinions and decision-making. Furthermore, we are not necessarily aiming to change pupils' attitudes. Two pupils might have strongly opposing views on using animals in medical research. We are not in a position to judge that one view is better than the other, what we want to assess is pupils' reasoning in reaching this view.

Assessing pupils' understanding of socio-scientific issues can be attempted by constructing a hierarchical scoring system of the kind shown in Table 5.4.3. Give pupils the outline of a controversial issue, and then ask them to make a decision about it, explaining their answer as fully as possible. It is, of course, important to make the marking criteria clear to the pupils from the start.

There are also ways of assessing pupil interaction while they are discussing issues in small groups. For example, Hogan (2002) identified roles that promoted the group's reasoning processes:

Table 5.4.3 A possible scoring system for assessing decision-making

Score	Pupil response
0	No response given
1	Decision stated but lacking any supporting reasons
2	Evidence used for one side of the issue
3	Evidence used for at least two perspectives
4	Pros and cons of the perspectives are weighed
5	Perspectives weighed and limitations of the evidence highlighted

- promoters of reflection;
- contributors to content knowledge;
- mediators of group interactions and ideas.

Other roles inhibited the group's reasoning process:

- promoters of acrimony (outwardly hostile to fellow group members);
- promoters of distraction;
- participants reluctant to collaborate.

This approach obviously requires the teacher to know the pupils well and can only be conducted in a trusting environment. It is also important that the pupils are aware of the learning goals from the start, and they should have opportunities to self-assess or peer assess their work (Black and Wiliam, 1998).

AVAILABLE HELP AND RESOURCES

Many outside organisations will readily help with citizenship days, although you should look out for possible bias in messages being promoted. Excellent help can be sought from local police and fire safety services, NHS sexual health nurses, environmental organisations, fair trade organisations, etc.

Teaching resources on socio-scientific issues can be accessed through websites associated with the Association for Science Education (ASE), the Science Museum, the Wellcome Trust, the Society of Biology, the Institute of Physics, and the Royal Society of Chemistry. Several national newspapers have good websites for accessing information on contemporary issues in science. See also the list of resources at the end of this unit.

Task 5.4.5 **Evaluating a resource**

Access information about a specific issue from an organisation's website or pamphlet.

1 What views does the organisation advocate?
2 What might be the opposite viewpoint?
3 Are images used appropriately to support the message?
4 Do they give sources of their information?

SUMMARY AND KEY POINTS

This chapter has highlighted the challenges facing teachers when dealing with socio-scientific issues as part of the citizenship curriculum. Unfamiliar approaches, like engaging pupils in discussion, can be a daunting prospect for a new teacher. However, when handled well, such approaches can be hugely motivating to pupils of all ages and abilities. When starting out teaching, observe experienced teachers dealing with these issues, look for overlap between the science and citizenship programmes of study, and see where controversial issues occur in your schemes of work.

ACKNOWLEDGEMENTS

I am very grateful to Jackie Smith, Personal Development Learning Coordinator and Careers Coordinator at The Mountbatten School, and to Maxine Farmer, Citizenship Coordinator at Hounsdown School, for their very helpful advice and discussion.

REFERENCES

Ashton, E. and Watson, B. (1998) 'Values education: a fresh look at procedural neutrality', *Educational Studies*, 24(2): 183–93.

Black, P. and Wiliam, D. (1998) *Inside the Black Box: Raising Standards through Classroom Assessment*, London: Kings College.

Crick, B. (2001) 'Citizenship and science; science and citizenship', *School Science Review*, 83(302): 33–8.

Department for Education (2013) *Citizenship: Programmes of Study for Key Stages 3–4*. Available at: www.education.gov.uk/schools/teachingandlearning/curriculum/secondary/b00199157/citizenship/ks3/programme (accessed 17 February 2014).

Gayford, C. G. and Dillon, P. J. (1995) 'Policy and the practice of environmental education in England: a dilemma for teachers', *Environmental Education Research*, 1: 173–84.

Hand, E. (2010) 'Citizen science: people power', *Nature*, 466: 685–7.

Harlen, W. (2010) *Principles and Big Ideas of Science Education*, Hatfield: Association for Science Education.

Hogan, K. (2002) 'Small groups' ecological reasoning while making an environmental management decision', *Journal of Research in Science Teaching*, 39(4): 341–68.

Hoskins, B., Villalba, C.M.H. and Saisana, M. (2012) *The 2011 Civic Competence Composite Indicator (CCCI-2)*, Ispra, Italy: European Commission. Available at: http://eprints.soton.ac.uk/208115 (accessed 17 February 2014).

Kibble, D. (1998) 'Moral education dilemmas for the teacher', *Curriculum Journal*, 9(1): 51–61.

Lynch, D. and McKenna, M. (1990) 'Teaching controversial material: new issues for teachers', *Social Education*, 54: 317–19.

Millar, R. (2012) 'The Presidential Address 2012: rethinking science education: meeting the challenge of "science for all"', *School Science Review*, 93(345): 21–30.

Newton, P., Driver, R. and Osborne, J. (1999) 'The place of argumentation in pedagogy of school science', *International Journal of Science Education*, 21(5): 553–76.

Nott, M. and Wellington, J. (1997) 'Critical incidents in the science classroom and the nature of science', *School Science Review*, 76 (276): 41–6.

Ofsted (2013) *Subsidiary Guidance: Supporting the Inspection of Maintained Schools and Academies*. Reference no: 110166. London: Ofsted.

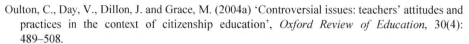

Oulton, C., Day, V., Dillon, J. and Grace, M. (2004a) 'Controversial issues: teachers' attitudes and practices in the context of citizenship education', *Oxford Review of Education*, 30(4): 489–508.

Oulton, C., Dillon, J. and Grace, M. (2004b) 'Reconceptualizing the teaching of controversial issues', *International Journal of Science Education*, 26(4): 411–23.

QCA (1998) *Education for Citizenship and the Teaching of Democracy in Schools*, London: QCA.

Ratcliffe, M. and Grace, M. (2003) *Science Education for Citizenship*, Maidenhead: Open University Press.

Royal Society (2013) 'Vision for science and mathematics education', available at: http://royalsociety. org/education/policy/vision/ (accessed 17 February 2014).

Solomon, J. (2001) 'A response to Bernard Crick', *School Science Review*, 83: 39–40.

Stradling, R. (1985) 'Controversial issues in the curriculum', *Bulletin of Environmental Education*, 170: 9–13.

FURTHER READING

Ajegbo, K., Kiwan, D. and Sharma, S. (2007) *Diversity and Citizenship Curriculum Review*, London: DfES.

Levinson, R. and Reiss, M. (eds) (2003) *Key Issues in Bioethics*, London: RoutledgeFalmer.

Nott, M. and Wellington, J. (1997) 'Critical incidents in the science classroom and the nature of science', *School Science Review*, 76(276): 41–6.

School Science Review Three special issues of *School Science Review* below are particularly useful and relevant to science for citizenship:

Grace, M. (ed.) (2010) 'Education for sustainable development', *School Science Review*, 92(338).

Levinson, R. and Reiss, M. (eds) (2004) 'Ethics in science education', *School Science Review*, 86(315).

Nott, M. (ed.) (2001) 'Science and citizenship', *School Science Review*, 83(302).

USEFUL WEBSITES

Among the best websites for secondary schools are:

Association for Citizenship Teaching (ACT): www.teachingcitizenship.org.uk/about-citizenship (accessed 13 April 2014).

Resources but only for paying members.

BBC: www.bbc.co.uk/schools/teachers/ (accessed 13 April 2014).

Resources and teachers' packs for all subjects.

Citizenship Foundation: www.citizenshipfoundation.org.uk/ (accessed 13 April 2014).

Resources include free downloadable lesson plans.

Health and Safety Executive: www.hse.gov.uk/education/index.htm (accessed 13 April 2014).

UK statistics for education – particularly about risk education.

Kudos: www.cascaid.co.uk/kudos/ (accessed 13 April 2014).

'an impartial online careers guidance and information program that helps young people plan their future and make informed decisions.'

Mind Tools: www.mindtools.com/ (accessed 13 April 2014).

Useful resources and ideas about probability and risk.

National Citizens Service Hampshire: www.ncshants.co.uk/ (accessed 13 April 2014).

Activities to broaden the horizons of Year 11 and 12 students. Participants 'meet new people, learn lessons that can't be learned in a classroom and put their energy and enthusiasm into projects that matter to them.'

STEM Ambassadors scheme: www.stemnet.org.uk/ambassadors/ (accessed 13 April 2014).

Links schools with professional scientists and engineers.

Teachers TV archive: www.education.gov.uk/schools/toolsandinitiatives/teacherstv/ (accessed 13 April 2014).

Archived downloadable videos, podcasts and classroom resources.

Theatre of Debate: www.theatreofdebate.com (accessed 13 April 2014)

A theatre company that presents dramas on contemporary issues for young people.

UK National Statistics: www.statistics.gov.uk/hub/index.html (accessed 13 April 2014)

Useful UK Government statistics.

UNIT 5.5

SEX AND HEALTH EDUCATION

Sandra Campbell

INTRODUCTION

Since the implementation of the National Curriculum in 1989 schools have been expected to provide pupils with sex education within the science curriculum and the Personal, Social, Health and Economic Education (PHSEe) curriculum. At the time of writing, the status of sex and relationship education has not changed and guidance for the provision of sex education in schools can be found in a document entitled *Sex and Relationship Education Guidance* (DfEE, 2000); this guidance makes it clear that sex education needs to be set in a wider context and that the focus should be on sex *and* relationships.

Although *Sex and Relationship Education Guidance* provided clear guidance for Sex and Relationship Education (SRE) in schools, the debate about how SRE should be approached in schools continues. It is important for you to know how dynamic the SRE situation is and to be alert to any new guidance and changes in legislation that may affect your teaching. PSHEe is not, at the time of writing, a statutory subject and the programme of study for PSHEe is not due to be updated in the new curricula due for implementation in 2014 and 2015. Schools do, however, have a legal responsibility to promote the well-being of pupils and provide sex and relationship and drugs education. You will be expected to teach those sex and health education topics that come under the remit of the science curriculum and during these science lessons pupils often ask questions that go beyond the curriculum. Additionally, in fulfilling your wider role in school life, such as form tutoring, you need to be aware of issues and opportunities regarding health and sex education.

Pupils will have had some age-appropriate sex and relationship education and health education in primary school, for example, learning about where babies come from, puberty, and keeping healthy. During their secondary education they learn more details of, for instance, adolescence, fertilisation, foetal development and childbirth, contraception, HIV/AIDS, sexually transmitted infections and the effects of drugs, volatile solvents, smoking and alcohol. Depending on which examination syllabus your school is following for GCSE, you may need to teach across a wide range of topics including the menstrual cycle, oral contraceptives, in vitro fertilisation, the use and misuse of drugs, and drug addiction. It is also worth noting that the subjects taught as a part of a school's sex education programme may differ across England, Wales, Scotland and Northern Ireland.

Although this unit is about sex and health education, the main focus will be on preparing you to teach sensitive issues in general and most teachers would agree that teaching pupils about sexual matters is one of the most sensitive issues on the curriculum. At least you can be assured of pupils' interest and cannot be accused of teaching a topic that is irrelevant. The separation of 'sex education' from 'health education' is an artificial one, but, as the two are subject to different constraints they will be discussed separately.

OBJECTIVES

By the end of this unit, you should:

■ appreciate how science topics related to sex and health education fit in with the whole school policy on SRE, and PSHEe;
■ understand the legal aspects of health-related matters and the teacher's responsibilities in teaching sex education;
■ recognise your own concerns about teaching sex and health education;
■ identify teaching strategies that are appropriate for teaching about sensitive issues.

SEX AND RELATIONSHIP EDUCATION

State schools are legally required to have a Sex and Relationship Education Policy that should describe how SRE is provided within the school and who is responsible for providing it. SRE is defined as:

> learning about the emotional, social and physical aspects of growing up, relationships, sex, human sexuality and sexual health. It should equip children and young people with the information, skills and values to have safe, fulfilling and enjoyable relationships and to take responsibility for their sexual health and well-being.
>
> (Sex Education Forum)

Children and young people should be able to access confidential advice and support in relation to their well-being, relationships and sexual health and teachers need to aware of the range of advice and support services that are available (see Useful Websites).

Although SRE cannot be taught entirely by the science department, clearly some aspects of SRE can be provided within the science curriculum. It is important to be clear about the responsibilities of different departments in the school so that pupils receive a coherent and coordinated SRE. In this unit, we focus mainly on the responsibilities of the science department in the provision of SRE and highlight some links with the PSHEe curriculum.

The need to teach about sexual health

Ask secondary school pupils who they feel will give them accurate and useful information about sex and relationships and sexual health and though they value a number of sources, such as parents and teen magazines, they place high importance on learning about these topics in school. In your teaching you may wish to draw on current data and statistics related to sexual health in your region.

It is worth checking the statistics on sexual health each year; for example, the number of teenage pregnancies, of under-16 abortions and rates of sexually transmitted infections (STIs) in young people. The Office for National Statistics provides this information or you may access the summary documents produced by Brook, a well-regarded charity for advice for young people on sexual health and contraception. Another source of statistics on sexual health is produced by the Medical Foundation for AIDS & Sexual Health (MedFASH). Such statistics can help to provide a context for young people learning about sexual health or may help build your confidence in teaching SRE. Examples of relevant statistics include:

■   Teenagers are far less likely to get pregnant today than they were in the early 1970s. The conception rate in 1970 was 82.4 per 1000 15–19-year-olds, compared with 54.6 in 2010.
■   69 per cent of 14-year-olds who become pregnant have abortions.
■   Young people aged less than 25 experience the highest rates of Sexually Transmitted Infections (STIs) in the UK; this age group accounts for nearly half of all STIs diagnosed in GUM (Genito-urinary Medicine) clinics.
■   The Gay Men's Sex Survey in 2006 found that 25 per cent of men aged 14–19 had had one male sexual partner in the last year, 41 per cent had had two to four, and 34 per cent had had five or more.

Secondary school pupils receive considerable information about aspects of human reproduction but research shows that this can result in patchy understanding. A report on the provision of SRE in schools (DCSF, 2008) indicated that the *science* part of SRE was taught well; in fact the survey of young people's views suggested that SRE is *too biological*. The 2013 Ofsted report into teaching of PSHEe would appear to support this view. It stated that there was too little emphasis placed on relationships, sexuality, and the influence of pornography on students' understanding of healthy sexual relationships. It is the broader aspects of SRE that cause concern, i.e. teaching about the skills for coping with relationships including pressurising, abusive and exploitative relationships and the feelings and emotions experienced during relationships.

You may be expected to teach an SRE-related topic, so it is important that you are aware of which topics are taught in science.

Task 5.5.1 **Sex and health-related topics in the science curriculum**

Obtain copies of the science department's schemes of work for KS3 and the examination syllabus taught at KS4 and identify which sex and health topics are in the curriculum:

1   What topics are related specifically to sex and health education?
2   In which year group are these topics covered?
3   Are any of the topics re-visited as the pupils get older?

This task should help you to appreciate your responsibilities for teaching aspects of sex and health education. Make a note of any topics you need to revise before you teach them. Note also any resources available in your school that you need to review to assess their suitability for your classes.

Whole school policy

Before you plan your approach to teaching these topics you need to appreciate how the teaching of sex and health-related issues in science lessons fits in with the school SRE policy. The guidance given to schools by the Department for Education makes it clear that effective sex and relationship education is to be firmly rooted in the framework for PHSEe. The aim of SRE is to equip pupils with the skills, knowledge and understanding and in this respect it is much like any other part of the curriculum. However, sex and health-related issues are often controversial and need sensitive handling at an individual and group level.

The pupils in your classes may well represent a wide range of divergent views on sex and contraception. They may have very different interpretations of what 'family' means. They or their parents or carers may be heterosexual, bisexual or homosexual. A recent report commissioned by the Office of the Children's Commissioner for England (Horvath, 2013) states that a significant number of children are accidentally or intentionally viewing pornography and other sexually explicit material on- and off-line. This can lead to a distorted view of what constitutes normal sexual relationships. Being able to talk with young people about pornography can open up useful conversations about, for instance, self-esteem, body image, boundaries, pleasure, consent, feminism, masculine norms and relationships. Bish UK provide training materials that can help you think about the issues involved. Differences regarding sexual morality and religious views on sexual behaviour have to be taken into account unless we plan to teach pupils merely the biological facts about sex and reproduction. For a summary of the moral perspectives of six religious groups on aspects of sex education, refer to Jennifer Harrison's (2000) *Sex Education in Secondary School*.

While a small number of new science teachers feel confident about teaching sex and relationship education, for many, it is a daunting prospect. Talking to other teachers about their experiences in teaching SRE is often reassuring. Many teachers will have some very funny stories to tell you as well as helpful hints to help you cope with any feelings of embarrassment you might anticipate when using words such as 'clitoris' or 'penis' in front of a class for the first time. Experienced teachers in your school are likely to have a clear idea about the questions that you may be asked and how you might answer them sensitively. While it is important to understand how to teach the 'plumbing' of sexual reproduction, it is through eliciting and discussing the pupils' questions that the 'relationship' part of SRE is best covered.

The most helpful guidance is to be well prepared, not just in your subject knowledge, (and any good biology textbook will help in this respect), but also in the way you intend to handle questions that are not appropriate for you to answer in a science lesson or questions you do not feel capable of answering. It is important therefore that you understand in which parts of the curriculum aspects of health and sex education are taught in your school. Task 5.5.2 helps you to identify which aspects of the SRE and Health Education curricula come within the remit of the science department. It should also reassure you that even if you feel your teaching in science seems divorced from the discussion and reflection that pupils need to develop a fuller understanding of their sexual health, this need is being addressed elsewhere in the curriculum. It also gives you the confidence to avoid such discussion should you feel ill equipped to cope with this style of teaching in your class.

Task 5.5.2 **Two aspects of teaching SRE, M-level**

For a review of SRE (DCFS, 2008) teachers were asked to comment on current SRE delivery. One of the key findings was that most teachers 'considered that the factual aspects of SRE and contraception – were taught well. But that the teaching on the relationship aspects – sexuality, feelings and emotions, skills for coping with relationships and making decisions about sexual activity was weak.'

Find the school's documentation for PHSEe and select some of the resources used in science and PHSEe for one aspect of SRE.

1 Interview a teacher of PHSEe and a teacher of science to find out about the approaches used in these lessons.
2 Does what you have found out support the views reported in the survey? Analyse the responses from the teachers to ascertain how much emphasis there is on providing factual information, and how much discussion of feelings and emotions. Does this vary between PHSEe and science? Why do you think this might be?
3 Do you think that parents should have the right to withdraw their children from SRE? Justify your answer with reference to both the science and the PSHEe curriculum.

The legal aspects

You need to be aware of legal aspects about sex and the law. The Sexual Offences Act 2003 introduced new laws to protect children under 16 from sexual abuse. The law is not intended to prosecute mutually agreed teenage sexual activity between two people of a similar age, provided that this does not involve exploitation or abuse. Specific laws protect children under 13, who cannot legally give their consent to any sexual activity. There is no defence of mistaken belief about the age of the child as there is in cases involving 13–15-year-olds. Below are those that are most pertinent to young people of secondary school age. In England and Wales and Northern Ireland, the same laws apply to heterosexual and homosexual activity and offences can be committed by anyone, male or female, over the age of 10, which is the age of criminal responsibility. In Scotland, the age of criminal responsibility is 8.

▨ The age of consent to sexual activity is 16.
▨ Children under the age of 16 do not commit an offence if they take part in sexual activity with an adult.
▨ It is an offence to intentionally engage in sexual touching with a young person aged 13, 14 or 15. 'Touching' covers all physical contact, including touching with any

part of the body, with anything else and through anything, for example, through clothing. It includes penetration.

- It is an offence of strict liability for an adult to take part in sexual activity with a child under 13 years. If the offender is under 18 there is a lesser maximum penalty.
- An adult is not guilty of an offence because he takes part in sexual activity with a girl under the age of 16 but not under the age of 13, if he has reasonable grounds to believe the woman to be aged 16 or over.
- A boy aged 13 could be liable for offences of sexual activity with a child.

As legislation changes regularly, you need to keep up to date with any changes in the law. For further information concerning sex and the law, the FPA website is very helpful (see Useful Websites). The inclusion of these aspects of the law in this unit is not to suggest that you should be teaching them to your classes but to raise your awareness of their existence and to give you confidence should you be asked by your pupils about such matters.

It is worth noting the guidance on sexual orientation provided by the DfEE:

The Secretary of State for Education and Employment is clear that teachers should be able to deal honestly and sensitively with sexual orientation, answer appropriate questions and offer support. There should be no direct promotion of sexual orientation.

(2000, p. 13)

Textbooks and many teaching materials assume intercourse is heterosexual and you need to think about how your use of language might expose your own views on sexual orientation. For instance, are you using language that makes an assumption that all the children you teach are heterosexual or come from heterosexual families? It is important that you consider this point for all matters related to sex and health education.

Unit 12 of the PHSE Key Stage 4 curriculum contains a true or false quiz which you may find helpful. It is reproduced in Figure 5.5.1.

Young people and the law
Mark each statement true or false

1. Parents have a legal right to withdraw a pupil at secondary school from any sex education that is not part of the science national curriculum.
2. It is illegal for a school to teach about homosexuality.
3. A 16-year-old can get married with the permission of their parent(s)/carer(s).
4. A pharmacist/chemist is allowed to refuse to sell emergency contraception to a pupil under 16.
5. A girl under the age of 16 cannot legally have an abortion.
6. People of all ages can buy condoms.
7. If a 14-year-old goes to a family planning clinic or their GP for contraceptive services their parent(s)/carer(s) have to be told.
8. Schools may display information about local and national contraceptive services.
9. The age of consent for gay men is 18.
10. If a 15-year-old pupil tells a teacher in confidence that they are having a sexual relationship, that teacher is legally bound to keep what has been said confidential.

(Adapted from de Meza and de Silva 2004)

Answers: True (T) and False (F) are below:
1. T, 2. F, 3. T, 4. T, 5. F, 6. T, 7. F, 8. T 9. F, 10. F

■ **Figure 5.5.1** True/false quiz

It is wise to establish ground rules for any classroom discussions, but this is of particular importance when talking about potentially sensitive topics. Pupils sometimes ask their teachers personal questions because they trust their advice and want the benefit of their teachers' experience, but keeping discussions to a theoretical level avoids a number of pitfalls.

Task 5.5.3 **The need for ground rules**

This task requires you to reflect on how much of your personal details you are willing to reveal to your class and to plan the 'ground rules' you expect your class to follow in your lessons.

1 Consider the implications of answering these pupils' questions.

- Are you married?
- Do you have a girl friend/boy friend?
- Do you have children?
- Do you smoke?
- How much do you drink?
- Have you ever taken drugs?

2 Consider which questions you would definitely not answer.
3 What does it imply to the pupils if you are prepared to answer some personal questions and yet not others?

Some of the answers to the questions may be obvious to pupils if you are an established teacher in a school. However, pupils are unlikely to know personal details of a student teacher on school experience except that they will probably know whether you smoke or not, and they may feel uncomfortable being told about the hazards of cigarette smoking to their health by someone who is obviously ignoring the advice themselves.

Task 5.5.4 **Developing ground rules**

This task enables you to plan the ground rules to use with your classes. Although you probably want to ask your classes to suggest the rules themselves it is a good idea to have some idea of what you want beforehand. Consider this list and identify the rules that you think the pupils may suggest and the rules you may have to introduce yourself.

1 We must listen to each other's opinions.
2 We must respect different points of view.
3 We must be able to change our minds.
4 We should use the correct biological words whenever possible.
5 We won't ask personal questions.

What other rules do you think should be added?

HEALTH EDUCATION

Ask pupils to draw a healthy person and they are likely to draw someone who has a big smile and looks happy. They appreciate that being healthy is not just about an absence of illness but is also about the state of mind and social well-being of a person. Being healthy is about being confident to make informed decisions and being able to function within your own community. It is worth considering a little further what you mean by 'healthy'.

Task 5.5.5 **What does 'being healthy' mean?**

This task helps you clarify your thoughts on what being healthy means. It is also a useful introductory activity to use with your pupils as it engenders a lot of discussion, always a good start to a topic.

Indicate on the list of statements below whether you agree or disagree with each one.

Being healthy is. . . .	Agree	Disagree
Enjoying being with people		
Hardly ever taking medicine		
Being able to run for a bus		
Not smoking		
Being the ideal weight		
Being able to adapt to changes in my life		
Eating the 'right foods'		
Being able to touch my toes		
Not being ill very often		

If possible, share your decisions with other science teachers or student teachers. Can you suggest how your science teaching can promote the skills pupils need in order that they can choose a healthy lifestyle for themselves?

Teaching about a balanced diet, drugs and alcohol abuse

Although children spend only one-fifth of their time in schools, the contribution of schools to their well-being can be highly significant. Many primary and secondary schools have achieved National Healthy Schools Status (NHSS) and have strengthened their policies relating to PSHEe education, healthy eating, physical activity and emotional well-being. A Healthy School provides a supportive environment, including policies on smoking and healthy and nutritious food, with time and facilities for physical activity and sport both within and beyond the curriculum; and 'comprehensive PHSEe which includes education on relationships, sex, drugs and alcohol as well as other issues that can affect young people's lives such as emotional difficulties and bereavement' (*The Lancet*, UK Policy Matters, 2014).

A key issue here for secondary teachers is that the work covered in these topics needs to *build on* what pupils have covered at KS2. In the primary school they learn about the importance of an adequate and varied diet, the effects on the human body of tobacco, alcohol and other drugs. They may have drawn posters to promote giving up smoking, drawn meals on paper plates that promote healthy eating and the work at KS3 must take this into account.

Legal aspects

Information about the effects and associated risks of drugs and alcohol, including relevant street names for different illegal drugs or controlled substances can be found on the website www.talktofrank.com. This website also contains clear guidelines as to the law relating to individual drugs and as such laws can be changed you will need to check the following information is still current:

- Illegal drugs are classified Class A, B or C with Class A considered to be most harmful.
- Class A drugs include ecstasy, LSD, heroin, cocaine, crack, and magic mushrooms (whether prepared or fresh).
- The penalties for possession of a Class A drug are up to seven years in prison and/or an unlimited fine.
- Dealing in a Class A drug, which includes giving it to friends for no charge, can result in a life prison sentence and/or an unlimited fine.
- Class B drugs include cannabis and amphetamines.
- Being caught in possession of Class B drugs can result in a five-year prison sentence and an unlimited fine. The actual penalty is likely to depend on the amount of drug that is in someone's possession, their age and whether or not it is their first offence.
- Someone caught dealing in Class B drugs can go to prison for up to 14 years.
- Class C drugs include ketamine, tranquillizers like temazepam and some painkillers.
- Possessing Class C drugs can result in a two-year prison sentence, while the penalty for dealing is up to 14 years.
- Dealing in drugs on or near school premises, at or around the time when young people are present there, is a very serious offence known as aggravated supply.
- Cigarettes and other tobacco products cannot be legally sold to anyone under the age of 18.

The Talk to Frank website also gives the complicated details as to the legality of sale and consumption of alcohol, on and off licensed premises.

Teaching strategies

There is a range of teaching strategies you could adopt when teaching sex and health education but many science teachers avoid the more creative teaching methods. There is no reason to leave the more innovative methods to PHSE/Citizenship teachers; science teachers need to select appropriate methods for the topic and age of the pupils.

As so much of sex and health education involves pupils engaging in discussion and making decisions about their own personal life, it can make lessons uncomfortable for them. To avoid pupils having to give details about their own lifestyle or information that is too personal, you can use 'distancing techniques'.

These techniques enable pupils to question and discuss topics that are of interest to them without having to disclose personal details. For example, they could watch a video where the characters act out a situation that raises questions that the class can discuss. The pupils can talk about the issues regarding the characters and at the same time raise issues that concern them. You may find the Channel Four sex education programme website 'Let's Talk Sex' useful in this respect (see Useful Websites).

Case studies with invented characters, theatre productions and role-plays are other examples of distancing techniques. Pupils are able to introduce issues into the discussions without exposing their own ignorance or experiences; they can explore the consequences of certain behaviours without indicating what they would do, or have done, themselves. Nevertheless, pupils need to be able to get the answers to specific questions that trouble them but how this is facilitated requires careful consideration. Imagine the potential result should a teacher invite pupils to ask *any* questions during a lesson. A common technique used to address pupils' queries is the 'Question Box' where pupils are allowed to write down any questions they have (without their names on) and place them in a box.

Task 5.5.6 **The 'Question Box' technique**

This task enables you to reflect on using the 'Question Box' technique and to consider how you would ensure its successful use in the classroom. Ideally you should be carrying out this activity with a class you teach. However, if you are not scheduled to teach this topic with one of your classes you can still obtain pupils' questions but you will have to agree with the teacher beforehand how the pupils' questions will be answered.

1 Negotiate with the science department to find a class where you can set up a 'Question Box' at the beginning of the topic on Human Reproduction. Alternatively, negotiate with the PHSE/Citizenship coordinator to set up the box at the beginning of the topic Sex Education.

2 Explain the activity to the pupils and leave the box in a place that is accessible.

3 Empty the box and sort the questions out into these categories:

(a) Questions that should be answered in the science lessons and questions that you think would be addressed better in PHSEe lessons (see Task 5.5.1).

(b) Questions that you don't know the answers to but do think should be answered (consider whether science or PHSEe).

(c) Questions you don't think are suitable to be answered in class.

4 Discuss with the class teacher how departments need to liaise with one another to answer pupils' questions. How will you deal with questions in category (b)?

5 What resources are available in the school to help you answer questions in category (c)?

6 Consider how you would have dealt with all these questions had you opened the box and read the questions out for the first time in front of the class.

Another important aim when teaching SRE is to give pupils the opportunity to rehearse forms of language using technical terminology. They will certainly be able to appreciate the difference between forms of language when comparing slang names and scientific names for the parts of the body.

Task 5.5.7 **Technical language used in science**

Collect the resources used by the science teachers when teaching sex and health. Look at the materials studied and the language used. Consider how many of these terms the pupils might be meeting for the first time, for example, *uterus*, *menstruation*, *ovulation*, *placenta*, *testis*, *scrotal sac*. Pupils may well have an understanding of the concepts but may not use these biological terms in their explanations.

Some teachers adopt a technique known as the 'Graffiti board' where the pupils put forward words that they know are commonly used to describe the human reproductive parts and processes and these are written on the board. Then the correct terms are identified and pupils are subsequently expected to use these in lessons. You might feel that this is inappropriate but it is important that we acknowledge that pupils are familiar with a rather different vocabulary from the one we would wish them to use in the classroom.

We must ensure that the pupils can use the correct terminology, for example, by having clearly labelled diagrams readily available and having key words on the board or around the room. Familiarity with the new words may help to reduce their embarrassment and enable them to use the terms in the correct way, thereby also reinforcing the correct spellings of the words.

A typical activity used in school is to ask pupils to label the diagrams of the human reproductive systems, copying from a book or from an image on the interactive whiteboard, and then finding out the function of each part. Alternatively they could be asked to describe, draw the shape or make models of each part so they have to consider the relative size of the various parts, how many there are and where they are located in relation to each other. If pupils then find out the function of the parts, it may help them to make associations between structure and function.

Task 5.5.8 **Devising activities for the classroom**

This task requires you to devise an activity that develops pupils' literacy skills. Select a health topic taught in KS3 and devise an activity using one of the following tasks:

1 Analysing teenage letters pages; what knowledge and attitudes are portrayed in the letters?
2 Analysing two newspaper articles on the same topic; which one has the more detailed and accurate scientific content?
3 Role play – make a video of a discussion between two people of opposing views.
4 Using ICT – make a PowerPoint presentation presenting alternative views.
5 Write an article for a school magazine presenting an argument for and against an issue.

An important idea in discussions of health is the concept of risk. Pupils need to understand how health risks can be affected by lifestyle choices, such as the risk of getting lung cancer from smoking.

Using data which helps pupils assess the risks to their health if they smoke, drink alcohol or take drugs (that are not medicines) makes the topic more relevant to them and also involves them using numeracy skills. Causes of death statistics for different age groups can be obtained from the Office for National Statistics. You may find it helpful to liaise with the mathematics department to find out when the pupils study probability so that they can appreciate how to estimate risk.

RESOURCES

Some of the topics that come under the umbrella of 'Health and Sex education' are controversial and/or the subject of ongoing research. To keep abreast of these developments, you can find up-to-date information, resources and materials supplied by a number of organisations. Among these are:

- the Wellcome Trust;
- the Society of Biology;
- the Department of Health;
- Health Education Authorities;
- television programmes for schools;
- Teachers TV.

See Useful Websites.

SUMMARY AND KEY POINTS

Teaching pupils about keeping healthy is a topic that will, hopefully, always be a part of the science curriculum. However, the issues included under this title will naturally always be subject to change.

What changes can you look forward to in the future? The substances identified as commonly used drugs are likely to alter as new drugs become available and the legal status of existing drugs may also change. Links between certain diseases and lifestyle may become more evident.

Of course, not everything is subject to change. The bodily changes at the onset of puberty are unlikely to alter (although the average age at which they begin may). The 'natural way' for conceiving a baby will not change although new techniques for promoting fertility may well be developed.

Our role as science teachers is to ensure that we keep abreast of changes and work with other departments to develop the knowledge and skills of pupils in order that they can become informed and responsible citizens, able to understand issues of risk and to make decisions about their own lives, taking into account how these decisions affect other people.

REFERENCES

DCSF (2008) *National Strategies: Assessment for Learning*, available at: http://nationalstrategies. standards.dcsf.gov.uk/node/154056?uc=force_uj (accessed 6 June 2009).

De Silva, S. and De Meza, L. (2004) *More About Life: Sex and Relationship Education in Secondary School*, London: Forbes Publications Ltd.

DfEE (2000) *Sex and Relationship Guidance*, London: DfEE.

Harrison, J. (2000) *Sex Education in Secondary Schools*, Buckingham: Open University Press.

Horvath, M. A. H., Alys, L., Massey, K., Pina, A, Scally, M. and Adler, J. R. (2013) "*Basically . . . Porn Is Everywhere": A Rapid Evidence Assessment on the Effect that Access and Exposure to Pornography Has in Children and Young People*, London: Office of the Children's Commissioner for England.

Ofsted (2013) *Not yet good enough: personal, social, health and economic education on schools*. Manchester; Ofsted.

The Lancet UK Policy Matters (2014) *National Healthy Schools Programme*. Available at: http:// ukpolicymatters.thelancet.com/policy-summary-national-healthy-schools-programme/ (accessed 14 September 2014).

The Sex Education Forum. Available at: http://www.sexeducationforum.org.uk (accessed 2 November 2014).

FURTHER READING

De Silva, S. and De Meza, L. (2004) *More About Life: Sex and Relationship Education in Secondary School*, London: Forbes Publications Ltd.

This is a comprehensive teaching pack for teaching about sex and relationship education in secondary schools within the context of PSHE.

DfEE (2000) *Sex and Relationship Guidance*, London: DfEE.

This document clarifies what schools are required to do by law but the most useful section for students teachers is the section on practical strategies for teaching some of the sensitive issues which may need to be tackled. It is also worth noting the guidance concerning confidentiality.

Harrison, J. (2000) *Sex Education in Secondary Schools*, Buckingham: Open University Press.

This book contains a comprehensive background to policies on sex education together with practical guidelines and resources that are particularly helpful for student teachers.

USEFUL WEBSITES

BISHUK: http://bishuk.com/
> The BISHUK website has many interesting ideas and materials for Sex and Relationship teaching including ways on which student questions about pornography could be answered (accessed 17 April 2014).

Brook: www.brook.org.uk
> This is a long-established charity offering free and confidential advice specifically to the under-25s. Its website contains quizzes and games and gives teachers and young people access to a wide range of relevant publications (accessed 17 April 2014).

Channel 4 websites: www.channel4.com/learning/microsites/L/lifestuff/content/up_close/letstalksex/stories.html and http://sexperienceuk.channel4.com/

The Channel 4 websites Let's talk sex and Sexperience both can be used for a range of materials that are useful for distancing techniques or for developing your own knowledge and understanding of young people's experiences of sex and relationships (accessed 17 April 2014).

FPA. www.fpa.org.uk (accessed 2 November 2014).

Medical Foundation for HIV and Sexual Health: www.medfash.org.uk

This website contains useful statistical and other information for teaching about HIV/AIDS and sexual health (accessed 17 April 2014).

NHS Change for Life: www.nhs.uk/change4life/Pages/change-for-life.aspx

This government website offers advice and relevant resources on exercising more and eating well (accessed 17 April 2014).

Office for National Statistics: www.ons.gov.uk

Recent government statistics on, for example, teenage pregnancy and abortion rates can be accessed through the website of the Office for National Statistics (accessed 17 April 2014).

Professional organisations and healthcare workers: www.healthtalkonline.org/ (accessed 17 April 2014).

Talk to Frank: www.talktofrank.com

This is an independent government-funded website where young people can access information about drugs and can also ask questions and seek advice on drug-related matters (accessed 17 April 2014).

Young people: www.youthhealthtalk.org/Home

A website about young people's real-life experiences of health and lifestyle (accessed 17 April 2014).

23 and a half hours: www.youtube.com/watch?v=aUaInS6HIGo

An engaging, 10-minute, animated talk by Dr Mike Evans on preventative health research related to exercise, health and well-being (accessed 17 April 2014).

UNIT 5.6

BEYOND THE CLASSROOM

Ruth Amos

INTRODUCTION

This unit encourages you to be actively open to using and creating out-of-classroom learning opportunities. Learning outside the classroom as informal learning is often seen as totally separate from formal (in-class) learning but approaches associated with the two contexts can be blended to create what is more accurately 'non-formal' learning. For example, in-class learning in secondary school is usually characterised by inflexible teaching periods throughout the day, whereas non-formal learning allows for longer, structured learning activity.

Learning outside the classroom can give reality and purpose to science learning (Braund and Reiss, 2006), helping pupils to contextualise their world within school science. Science concepts take on relevance while actually examining plants' adaptations in a particular habitat, observing folding in rock strata or discussing objects and artefacts in a museum. Pupils may develop a sense of wonder about the world (Goodwin, 2001). There is growing evidence that 'fieldwork . . . offers learners opportunities to develop their knowledge and skills in ways that add value to their everyday experiences in the classroom' (Dillon *et al.*, 2006: 107). Pupils (and teachers) will often act differently when away from the constraints of school boundaries, and learning can be more pupil-led, playful and hopefully spontaneous.

The National Curriculum for Key Stage 3 (DfE, 2013, p. 4) states that pupils should be taught to 'use appropriate techniques, apparatus, and materials during fieldwork and laboratory work, paying attention to health and safety'. Fieldwork, visiting industry, universities and other sites of scientific interest can support that goal. There is also a requirement for pupils to be able to 'assess risk and work safely . . . in the field'. Working with pupils outside the classroom can also open up a wealth of opportunities to explore sustainable development, environmental issues, cultures and customs.

At KS4, the draft National Curriculum for science (DfE, 2013, p. 4) requires fieldwork to contribute to the 'Working Scientifically' strand. Table 5.6.1 shows what is intended (and see also Unit 2.1).

■ **Table 5.6.1.** Curriculum intentions related to fieldwork

Key Stage	Experimental skills and investigations	Handling information and problem solving
Key Stage 3 Key Processes (2007)	'assess risk and work safely . . . in the field . . .	'present observations and data using appropriate methods'
Key Stage 3 Curriculum opportunities (2007)	'experience science outside the school environment'	'interpret observations and data'
Draft Key Stage 4 (2014)	'use knowledge of techniques, apparatus, and materials, during fieldwork and laboratory work, select those that are appropriate to the investigation, and use them appropriately, adapting apparatus and strategy flexibly when problems arise and paying attention to health and safety'	

OBJECTIVES

By the end of this unit, you should:

■ be open to exploring the importance of relating science beyond the classroom to the science curriculum;
■ be aware of the range of resources which enable you to place science in interesting contexts, including fieldwork;
■ be able to plan and carry out some teaching outside the classroom;
■ be aware of the advantages of residential fieldwork for teaching science;
■ be alert to safety and legal factors when undertaking fieldwork.

INSPIRING OPPORTUNITIES OUTSIDE THE CLASSROOM

Why fieldwork?

Fieldwork has traditionally supported and enriched the learning of science and may be carried out during lesson time, on one-day excursions or longer residential sessions. Fieldwork encompasses investigations located outside, seeing the effects of science or technology on our lives or visiting a site of special interest such as a museum, local graveyard or field centre. Some courses at KS5, such as Salters' Chemistry and Salters' Horners Physics (SHAP, 2003), require pupils to carry out a case study or visit to a site of industrial and scientific importance (the physics visit may be used as part of AS coursework assessment).

Fieldwork can also help to raise awareness of the interactions between science, technology and the natural and made environment. However, many schools have excellent in-house resources; digital video and the Internet can now bring a wealth of images and information into the classroom (see Unit 5.3, Using ICT for Learning Science), so why undertake fieldwork when it can be more time-consuming and challenging to organise than standard laboratory work? Plants and animals in the wild do not perform to order and successful visits to most sites depend on advanced planning involving a pre-visit.

The broad educational benefits of fieldwork can include:

▨ promoting enthusiasm for science and the natural and made environment;
▨ encouraging a lifelong interest in those environments;
▨ allowing pupils to 'become' biologists, chemists, geologists, physicists out in the real world;
▨ broadening understanding of how science and technology interact with, and are part of, our lives;
▨ promoting awareness of issues around environmental damage and protection;
▨ revealing human impacts on the environment;
▨ developing positive attitudes towards the environment;
▨ encouraging speculation and discussion.

Fieldwork is important because it is, sometimes, the only way for pupils to truly experience some phenomena, e.g. the diversity of living things, the motion of the stars and planets or the effects of pollution (Figure 5.6.1).

In relation to the science curriculum, fieldwork can allow pupils to do the following:

▨ increase their knowledge of science across biology, chemistry, physics, earth science and astronomy;
▨ develop process skills, e.g. plan and practise whole investigations;
▨ understand how numerical and other data are collected in the field;

▨ **Figure 5.6.1** Inner city KS3 pupils exploring a rocky shore, Pembrokeshire, Wales

- use data logging equipment (Fearn, 2006);
- develop collaborative skills;
- bring recordings/observations back into school for further study, using digital technologies;
- prepare and give presentations.

From a management point of view, pupils have greater freedom to discuss, interact and move outside the classroom. This enhanced freedom can be daunting to inexperienced teachers but usually has a beneficial effect on behaviour and general motivation to learn. However, a successful visit does need to be carefully organised.

Task 5.6.1 **Joining in a field visit or excursion**

Discuss opportunities with your mentor for taking part in a school visit or excursion during your placement. If appropriate, offer to supervise one or more activities planned for the trip or, with support, plan an activity. Taking part in a science-based field visit would be ideal but taking part in an outdoor activity in another subject area can also be beneficial.

Keep a record of how the trip was planned and carried out; the checklist in Figure 5.6.2 may help you. Collect your (and their if possible) impressions of the pupils you worked with. The headings below may help you structure your records:

- *knowledge*: what pupils knew about the visit and intended learning before and what they gained from the task;
- *understanding*: could pupils explain what they were doing and why? Could pupils explain how the data and observations they collected would help them meet the learning outcomes for the activity?
- *attitudes*: were pupils motivated to tackle the task(s)? Did they enjoy the experience and consider the activity worthwhile? Were there any other outcomes (e.g. affective or social impacts) of the visit?
- *science in the real world*: how did pupils have a sense they were being 'real scientists' in the field?

Working outside the classroom can involve working in the school grounds or nearby, but more ambitious activities may require a half day or whole day visit. Occasionally a residential field visit may be planned. We turn first to the use of regular classroom time, such as a timetabled period.

FIELDWORK IN LESSON TIME

Most schools have playgrounds, which are a source of habitats, materials and structures. Others have playing fields or access to open spaces. If planned carefully, an hour's science lesson can be taught outside the classroom. Some activities are taught outside because they need space to be effective; others can only be taught outside. Ideas for activities and a discussion of associated planning are discussed below.

Aims

▪ What are the learning objectives for, and proposed outcomes of, the activity?

▪ How are the objectives achieved by working outside?

▪ Are there guidelines for the activity in the SoW or elsewhere?

Legal and safety issues

Have you:

▪ discussed the proposal with your class teacher?

▪ carried out a risk assessment on the site?

▪ identified any special safety issues to be observed?

▪ planned your briefing to pupils to cover behavioural and safety issues?

▪ planned adequate supervision by you and the class teacher?

▪ checked that your pupils can work outside without risk, e.g. none have allergies?

Preparation and planning

▪ Try out the activity yourself and check that it can be carried out on the chosen site in the time available.

▪ Check that data obtained can be used to meet your objectives and achieve your learning outcomes.

▪ Prepare briefing for pupils, including instructions and any record sheets as well as safety and behavioural matters.

▪ Check the availability of equipment for the number of pupils in your class; discuss your requirements with technical staff.

▪ Plan how the equipment is to be distributed and returned (use pupils as monitors, for example).

▪ Check whether pupils need instruction about how to use the equipment you select.

▪ Plan timings for briefing, departure, work and return.

▪ Ensure that pupils know what to do with data on return to the classroom. Are the data to be followed up immediately or later?

▪ Where are the data to be kept between now and the next lesson?

▪ Plan, as needed, an appropriate homework task.

▪ Prior to the activity, remind pupils to bring sun/rain protection as necessary.

▪ **Figure 5.6.2** Checklist for planning a short outside activity

Activities

A variety of data can be collected in the school grounds, or in local sites of interest, for example:

▪ measuring the length of a shadow as part of estimating the Earth's size (Ogborn *et al.*, 1996);

▪ identifying building materials;

▪ estimating animal populations. Some pupils may regard small animals such as insects as insignificant, or be unaware of the diversity of insect populations or that some small animals are important for productive soil, e.g. worms.

▪ reading instruments in a weather station. Helping pupils to connect physical measurements, such as pressure, humidity, etc. to the changing weather patterns and to national weather forecasting.

- sampling soils to relate, e.g. differences in plant populations to soil profile;
- studying leaves to reveal variation in one plant (Bebbington, 2006), within a species or as part of a wider study of diversity;
- following a science trail to identify areas for study (Borrows, 1999; Murphy *et al.*, 2002a);
- examining headstones for evidence of weathering;
- monitoring river pollution levels (Sanderson, 2006).

The March 2006 special issue of *School Science Review* was dedicated to outdoor science and gives ten good examples of out-of-classroom activities across the sciences. There is also a growing number of online resource banks for activities in rural and urban locations (Glackin and Jones, 2012) mentioned at the end of this unit.

Task 5.6.2 **Planning a science trail**

Explore the school buildings and grounds to identify sites of interest to include in a science trail that could be experienced, or indeed devised, by pupils within a single period. The sites could have a common focus (see collection of data above). Asking pupils to create a trail for younger peers, for example, visitors from the local primary school gives a good sense of purpose. Identify a topic or short sequence of lessons you expect to teach, or choose a topic of personal interest. Identify four or five 'sites' that would provide interest and contribute to understanding of the topic. For each site, identify the locality and what pupils are expected to look for and record:

- explain for yourself the science involved;
- prepare an explanation of the science for the pupils, or better still, construct a series of questions which allows them to explore the station and then to explain observed phenomena;
- link the pupils' experiences to the topic and hence to the SoW.

Draft a record sheet for pupils to use on the trail. Discuss your notes and record sheet with your class teacher or mentor. Where possible, try out the trail with a group of pupils. Creating clues involving digital photographs to lead pupils from one station to another can improve engagement and adds an element of challenge. Evaluate the learning outcomes for the activity and build upon these for your next attempts.

Demonstrating phenomena

Examples of activities that may work well outside include:

- developing a timeline for the age of the universe (Murphy *et al.* 2002b);
- comparing the speed of sound with the speed of light (needs a very large playing field!);

- modelling states of matter using pupils as molecules;
- the Doppler effect (Weaver, 2006);
- launching a water rocket.

Planning

Working outside the laboratory depends on your own preferences and experience, but also on departmental policy. As a teacher in training you should not take a group of pupils outside on your own, the class teacher or another qualified person must be with you. Your school will have an Educational Visits Coordinator (EVC) who will be able to guide you as well.

Successful outcomes depend on checking out the proposed site in advance (not too far ahead though, as local activity can change sites rather suddenly). When planning your lesson, consider factors such as:

- the length of a period and what is possible;
- the class size and your ability to supervise the activities safely;
- whether another colleague might like to co-teach the session, bringing their class along too;
- guidelines and routines to emphasise to ensure safe and sensible behaviour;
- the suitability of sites for outside study;
- safety factors, e.g. road traffic, local ponds, unpleasant plants or pupils susceptible to hay fever;
- the role of the regular class teacher in your activity.

The checklist in Figure 5.6.2 may help you plan such an activity.

The weather can adversely affect plans so have a non-fieldwork activity ready in case it really is too challenging to go outside! Some activities can interestingly be done by looking through the window. For example, the Earth Science Education Unit (ESEU) based at Keele University has an excellent range of resources on its website, including various 'through the window' activities (see Useful Websites).

GOING OFF-SITE

One-day excursions or residential courses allow opportunities for activities which cannot be carried out in lessons or in school. The new environment often stimulates motivation and greater engagement (Amos and Reiss, 2006; 2012). You may get to know your colleagues better and see pupils in a different light. Parental permission is required for all activities outside the school grounds, even if you are only walking to a local site down the road. Be alert to the opportunity to join a field visit and offer to help with planning and preparation. The EVC in your school should have a plan and checklist for fieldwork to which you should refer (see Task 5.6.3).

Pupils need explicit guidance and advice about behaving appropriately in outdoor areas frequented by members of the public. In addition, farm animals or dogs out for a walk can elicit a surprising amount of curiosity, and occasionally unease, amongst pupils who normally reside in urban areas. Clear guidelines are vital to ensure the wearing of sensible outdoor clothing and shoes (not their £100 trainers!), sunhats and sunscreen (or woolly hats and gloves), and so on. Some of the potential problems can be alleviated by preparing a 'kit' checklist for parents/carers. Recommend that pupils bring only small amounts of money on a day/residential field visit, and that electronic equipment as much as possible stays at home. Most schools have clear policies on whether pupils can take mobile phones on field visits (this may be different from the usual in-school 'no mobiles' policy as some parents/carers are keen to be in mobile communication with their offspring whil they are away). Any pupils who have to take regular medication need to have it available; often a member of staff will look after all medical treatments but some pupils may need to carry their own so always double check that everyone has whatever they need with them before you leave school.

SITES OF SPECIAL INTEREST

Many schools arrange activities at a variety of sites. Examples include:

- hands-on science centres;
- local or national museums;
- a neighbourhood industry;
- waste disposal, recycling and water treatment sites;
- waterways, ponds and bridges.

Museums and hands-on centres

Planning a visit to a museum or hands-on centre can be challenging. Falk and Dierking (2000) advise paying attention to three contexts for learning in informal settings: the personal, social and physical. Most museums require pre-booking for school groups so be sure to check, and book ahead in plenty of time. In addition, specific galleries (such as the Launch Pad at the Science Museum in London, Figure 5.6.3) allow groups specifically allocated time. Demonstration shows may be on offer, so ask in advance. Where possible, allowing pupils to freely explore a museum gallery first, then bringing them back to the same gallery later in the visit can help to overcome the initial 'novelty value' (DeWitt and Osborne, 2007). Naturally, adequate supervision has to be in place for all activities but as long as galleries are a manageable size, it is possible for teachers to position themselves strategically to allow pupils to explore freely. Ask pupils to choose a 'buddy' with whom they spend the day (checking that they are in the appropriate place, etc.). When planning a museum or centre visit, the guidance for organising fieldwork is broadly applicable and, in addition, think about the following:

- a pre-task at school to help orientate pupils to what they will explore;
- a mix of free choice exploration and semi-structured learning in the gallery/centre ('who am I?' photographs showing part of an object/artefact can help to engage pupils on a trail, but avoid worksheets unless you want the visit to be labelled as being 'just like school'!);
- build in peer discussion, or collaborative approaches, where possible;
- a post-visit activity to build upon the learning opportunities.

Field centres

Many field centres organise teaching programmes for groups of pupils. Pupils generally respond well to a combination of adventure activity and subject-focused work, especially

■ **Figure 5.6.3** A science student teacher working with a group in the Space Gallery at
    the Science Museum, London

when the latter is subtly woven in. Measuring your heart rate while climbing, learning
about forces while canoeing or examining geological features while abseiling alongside a
waterfall can create memorable moments, to which learning can be linked in the longer
term. While AS-level or A-level coursework has often been the goal of traditional field
centre visits in science, younger pupils can also benefit from a residential experience.
Sites of special interest such at the historical copper mine at Ecton in the Peak District
(see Useful Websites) can bring ideas to life in unique ways – the large-scale outdoor
chemistry lab at Ecton has unrivalled views across the landscape! In addition to learning
science, being away from home contributes to pupils' growth in independence and self-
confidence. Opportunities for problem-solving and team building can give a tremendous
boost to pupil–pupil, and pupil–teacher relationships back at school.

Task 5.6.3 **Planning a field visit**

If the opportunity arises join in with a field visit. Use the checklist below to guide
you through the approaches needed. Much of the guidance in Figure 5.6.2 is also
pertinent here.

Educational objectives

Identify:

1 the purposes of the trip and links with the SoW;
2 the facilities at the field centre;
3 how fieldwork is to be initiated and followed up in school;
4 the contribution of fieldwork to preparation for coursework and possibly public examinations;
5 the suitability of the field centre resources.

Legal responsibilities

You should:

1 read the school (and LA) regulations which apply to field trips;
2 identify how the Health and Safety at Work Act applies;
3 carry out risk assessments for travel and fieldwork;
4 identify the responsibilities and rights of parents while their children are on residential courses;
5 collect medical requirement data for all participating pupils;
6 collect contact details for parents/carers during the visit;
7 know the agreement to which parents consent when they sanction a field visit for their child and how that consent is obtained;
8 know the adult–pupil ratio which applies to travel and working in the field;
9 know how insurance is effected for the trip;
10 know how pupils can be helped financially to attend the course.

Advance planning

Find out:

1 how pupils are briefed and prepared for the trip, including the Country Code of Practice;
2 the equipment needed from the school and how that is identified, collected and delivered to the site;
3 what pupils need to bring with them, and prepare the checklist for parents/carers;
4 who prepares the written course materials;
5 the domestic arrangements during the course;
6 how to cost the trip and the parental contribution;
7 the transport arrangements.

Safety

Obtain copies of documents which identify:

1 guidelines for working and behaving at the field centre;
2 special precautions/hazards associated with the particular field centre;

3 arrangements made for pupils and parents to contact each other in an emergency;
4 staff responsibilities, including responding to injured or unwell pupils.
5 guidance on health and safety given by the Health and Safety Executive (www. hse.gov.uk/services/education/school-trips.htm).

What happens while you are away? Find out what you do about your teaching responsibilities; normally you will set cover work for all your classes and leave it with your Head of Science or subject mentor.

OTHER OPPORTUNITIES

People with knowledge or expertise

It is highly motivating for pupils to listen to and talk with people whose specialist knowledge enriches the science curriculum. Outside speakers are particularly useful for controversial issues. Many professional and learned societies provide speakers, e.g. the Institute of Biology, the Institute of Electrical Engineers and the Medical Research Council. Parents and governors of the school may be a source of expertise. The Widening Participation initiative created useful links between higher education institutions (HEIs) and schools. Many HEI science departments provide ambassadors (often research students) who go out to school to give demonstration lectures, master classes and careers advice. Also, as part of your teacher training course, you may be involved in out-of-classroom learning projects with pupils from partnership schools.

SUMMARY AND KEY POINTS

Whatever your circumstances, there are often opportunities to go beyond the classroom when planning science lessons for your pupils. Some schools promote cross-curricular field studies, e.g. geography and science, which can be very effective. What is possible depends on the local environment, your ability to identify opportunities and the support you get. In this chapter we have made suggestions of ways to go beyond the classroom and suggest you regularly monitor the publications of your professional associations (for example, the ASE) for further ideas.

REFERENCES

Amos, R. and Reiss, M. (2006) 'What contribution can residential field courses make to the education of 11–14 year olds?' *School Science Review*, 88(322): 37–44.

Amos, R. and Reiss, M. (2012) 'The benefits of residential fieldwork for school science: insights from a five-year initiative for inner-city students in the UK', *International Journal of Science Education*, 34(4): 485–511.

Bebbington, A. (2006) 'Some prickly thoughts: does holly become more prickly when it's grazed?' *School Science Review*, 87(320): 83–90.

Borrows, P. (1999) 'Chemistry trails', *Education in Chemistry*, 6, 158–9.

Braund, M. and Reiss, M. (2006) 'Towards a more authentic science curriculum: the contribution of out-of-school learning', *International Journal of Science Education*, 28(12): 1373–88.

DeWitt, J. and Osborne, J. (2007) 'Supporting teachers on science-focused school trips: towards an integrated framework of theory and practice', *International Journal of Science Education*, 29(6): 685–710.

Dillon, J., Rickinson, M., Tearney, K., Morris, M., Choi, M.Y., Sanders, D. and Benefield, P. (2006) 'The value of outdoor learning: evidence from research in the UK and elsewhere', *School Science Review*, 87(320): 107–11.

Falk, J. and Dierking, L. (2000) *Learning from Museums*, Walnut Creek, CA: AltaMira Press.

Fearn, F. (2006) 'Data-loggers in ecological enquiry in school grounds and beyond', *School Science Review*, 87(320): 69–73.

Glackin, M. and Jones, B. (2012) 'Park and learn: improving opportunities for learning in local open spaces', *School Science Review*, 93(344): 105–13.

Goodwin, A. (2001) 'Wonder in science teaching and learning: an update', *School Science Review*, 83(302): 69–73.

Griffin, J. (2002) 'Look! No hands! Practical science experiments in museums', in S. Amos and R. Boohan (eds) *Teaching Science in Secondary Schools: A Reader*, London: Routledge Falmer.

Murphy, P. J. and Murphy, E. (2002a) 'Urban geology trails', *School Science Review*, 83(305): 140–3.

Murphy, P. J. and Murphy, E. (2002b) 'A timeline for geological time', *School Science Review*, 84(306): 125–6.

Ogborn, J., Kouladis, V. and Papadotretrakis, E. (1996) 'We measured the Earth by telephone', *School Science Review*, 77(281): 88–90.

Sanderson. P. (2006) 'Twenty-first century pollution detectives', *School Science Review*, 87(320): 33–40.

Weaver, N. (2006) 'Physics outdoors: from the Doppler effect to F = ma', *School Science Review*, 87(320): 65–8.

FURTHER READING

Braund, M. and Reiss, M. (2004) *Learning Science Outside the Classroom*, London: RoutledgeFalmer.

A practical guide to using a wide range of informal, non-classroom-based contexts for science education. Risk assessment and safety issues are addressed.

DfES (2006) *The Learning Outside the Classroom Manifesto*, London: Department for Education and Skills.

The manifesto was launched by the DfES (now the Department for Education, DfE) to demonstrate renewed commitment to outdoor experiences. The website developed from the manifesto is now managed by the Council for Learning Outside the Classroom and can be found at www.lotc.org.uk/. It contains contemporary advice and guidance on a whole range of issues (accessed 3 March 2014).

Glackin, M. (2007) 'Using urban green space to teach science', *School Science Review*, 89(327): 26–9.

A very useful article for teachers in urban areas.

Lock, R., Slingsby, D. and Tilling, S. (eds) (2006) (special edition) 'Outdoor science', *School Science Review*, 87(320): 23–111.

A very good collection of ideas and activities for outdoor learning in science.

Reiss, M. (ed.) (1999) *Teaching Secondary Biology*, London: John Murray for the ASE.

An excellent resource addressing many important topics in the teaching of biology. Chapter 9 discusses ecology and provides valuable advice about using the environment and undertaking field work.

SHAP (Salters Horners Advanced Physics) (2003) *Exemplar Coursework: Visits*.
Available at: www.edexcel.com/migrationdocuments/GCE%20New%20GCE/UA026741_GCE_ Lin_Physics_Issue_5.pdf (accessed 24 December 2013).

USEFUL WEBSITES

ASE: www.ase.org.uk/resources/outdoor-science/ (accessed 3 March 2014).

> The Association for Science Education (ASE) Outdoor Learning Group webpage. This includes evidence for what works well outside the classroom and ideas for activities

Earth Science Education Unit (ESEU): www.earthscienceeducation.com/ (accessed 3 March 2014).

> The Earth Science Education Unit (ESEU) is based at Keele University. This has an excellent range of online resources and ideas for teaching earth sciences.

Ecton Hill copper mine field: www.ectonhillfsa.org.uk/ (accessed 3 March 2014).

> The large-scale outdoor chemistry lab has views across the Peak District and gives KS4 and KS5 chemistry pupils an excellent, hands-on historical story of the mining, extraction and uses of copper (and other metals).

Health and Safety Executive: http://www.hse.gov.uk/services/education/school-trips.htm (accessed 3 March 2014).

> The Health and Safety Executive provides advice and guidance on risk assessment for fieldwork and out-of-school visits.

The National Curriculum: www.education.gov.uk/schools/teachingandlearning/curriculum (accessed 3 March 2014).

Salters Chemistry: www.york.ac.uk/org/seg/salters/chemistry/ (accessed 3 March 2014). The website for Salters Chemistry.

Salters Horners Physics: www.york.ac.uk/org/seg/salters/physics/ (accessed 3 March 2014).

> The website for Salters Horners Physics.

Thinking Beyond the Classroom: www.pstt.org.uk/resources/continuing-professional-development/thinking-beyond-the-classroom.aspx (accessed 3 March 2014).

6 ASSESSMENT IN SCIENCE

INTRODUCTION

Assessment is a vital part of teachers' lives in providing information for pupils, for parents, for teachers themselves and to provide data for school improvement. Formative assessment, or assessment *for* learning (AFL) and summative assessment, or assessment *of* learning are essential parts of teaching and assessment has been a strong theme in previous units. Essentially, assessment *of* or *for* learning seeks to answer questions about how you know and how pupils know about teaching and learning so do not be led into thinking you can leave worrying about assessment until after you have mastered teaching.

In Unit 6.1, Christine Harrison describes a range of assessment strategies that you can adopt as part of your day-to-day teaching and explains the underlying rationale. The unit is based on research and her in-service work with teachers.

Another important task for teachers is to prepare pupils for external assessments and examinations such as GCSE and A-levels, and this aspect of assessment is addressed by Christine in Unit 6.2. Examination results are high-stakes assessment; they can provide pupils and their parents with a sense of achievement and influence future action. Examination results affect the standing of a school locally and nationally and influence the popularity of the school to prospective parents. For these reasons, preparing pupils for external assessments and examinations receives high priority in schools. Finding out about the scheme of assessment associated with any course you teach has to be done as soon as possible and Unit 6.2 discusses some of the processes involved.

ASSESSMENT FOR LEARNING
A FORMATIVE APPROACH

Christine Harrison

INTRODUCTION

In recent years, assessment in England, and elsewhere in the UK, has seen many changes, including a shift in the focus of attention away from the technicalities of test construction towards approaches that focus on pupil learning (Black and Wiliam, 1998; Mansell and James, 2009). Part of this has arisen from criticism of high stakes testing (Harlen and Deakin-Crick, 2004; Brooks and Tough, 2006), while the influence of several research programmes on formative assessment indicates alternative perceptions of pedagogy and learning (Bell and Cowie, 1999, Stiggins, 2002; Black *et al.*, 2003; Harrison, 2005; Cowie, 2005; Hutchinson and Hayward, 2005).

Assessment covers a wide range of activities in education from marking books, setting tests and asking questions and has a number of purposes, the most important of which is Assessment for Learning. When assessment is used to advance learning, the focus is on improvement and teachers and learners work together to plan and work on next steps in learning and this is formative in nature. It is therefore a forward-looking process as opposed to many tests and examinations whose purpose is to measure the previous learning. Currently, science teachers use a mix or formative and summative assessment practices in UK schools to meet the demands of accountability at school and government level alongside using assessment to promote and support learning.

OBJECTIVES

By the end of this unit, you should:

- recognise what AfL looks like in the classroom;
- know some of the assessment strategies that support learning;
- begin to see how formative assessment fits alongside summative assessment;
- be aware of the importance of involving the learner in the assessment process.

High stakes testing remains a priority for schools in England at both primary and secondary high school level, and yet the growth and development of formative assessment practices under the banner of Assessment for Learning are evident in almost every school nationwide. This has stemmed mainly from the review on formative assessment published by Black and Wiliam in 1998. While there had been previous reviews in this area, this review caught the attention of researchers, teachers and politicians because it posed three questions:

■   Is there evidence that improving formative assessment raises standards?
■   Is there evidence that there is room for improvement?
■   Is there evidence about how to improve formative assessment?

In 1998, the answers to these questions was YES, YES and NOT REALLY and, over the last decade and a half, many have tried to explore formative practices more fully by providing evidence of what this looks like in classrooms and why it works (Black *et al.*, 2003; Marshall and Drummond, 2006; Brookhart, 2001; Harrison and Howard, 2009).

Black and Wiliam's review was commissioned by the Assessment Reform Group (ARG), which originated in 1989 as a voluntary group of researchers on the BERA Policy Task Group on Assessment. ARG's aim was to ensure that assessment policy and practice at all levels took account of relevant research evidence. In its early years, ARG was particularly concerned to study the introduction of national testing in the four countries of the UK and to stimulate discussion of their impact on schools and classroom practices. Subsequently the focus has broadened to the use of assessment to advance learning as well as to summarise and report it.

In 2000, ARG set up the Assessment and Learning Research Synthesis Group (ALRSG) to review research relating to the practice, processes and outcomes of assessment in schools. The ALRSG was registered as a Collaborative Review Group of the DfES-funded Evidence for Policy and Practice Information Co-ordinating (EPPI) Centre. Five reviews have now been completed and published in the EPPI Centre's online Research Evidence in Education Library. These reviews explain the implementation of assessment policies and practices that happened with the introduction of the National Curriculum in England and Wales and of assessment for learning across all four countries in the UK and provide an interesting backdrop for the state of current assessment practices in all four regions.

HOW DOES ASSESSMENT FOR LEARNING WORK IN CLASSROOMS?

Assessment for learning focuses on where pupils are in their learning and how they might be helped in moving that learning forward. In Assessment for Learning, teachers need to use a variety of tools to find where pupils are in their learning; these might be questions or activities that encourage learners to talk and express their understanding. The successful teacher is:

able to ask the right questions at the right time, anticipate conceptual pitfalls, and have at the ready a repertoire of tasks that will help students take the next steps requires deep knowledge of subject matter.

(Shephard, 2000, p. 12)

From what learners say and do in classrooms, teachers can make judgements that can help the pupil move on to the most appropriate next step in learning, and so guide them towards improvement. This process is known as formative assessment and at its heart is effective feedback. For feedback to function in a formative way, there are a number of prerequisites:

- ▨ a need for teachers to create regular opportunities in the classroom for pupils to discuss and communicate their perception of their evolving learning;
- ▨ a willingness by teachers to develop or adapt future learning activities in response to learning needs and development;
- ▨ an awareness of the skills, ideas and concepts needed to produce quality pieces of work that recognises misconceptions, likely reasoning errors and mistakes as the beginning of developing better understanding;
- ▨ the capability of teachers to give and model descriptive feedback that encourages learners to make improvements to their work;
- ▨ an acceptance that learners need to be involved in decisions about their learning and are given time and helped to develop the skills to do this.

If all these factors are at work in the classroom, then communications about where pupils are in their learning and the vision of where teachers hope to take them through the next set of activities become a shared mission for both teacher and learner. So the teacher does not just plan activities with the curriculum in mind but considers how tackling the activities will challenge the learning of each of their pupils and how the opportunities to engage with the activities and with other learners will reveal pupils' strengths and weaknesses. This approach allows the teacher and the learners to pinpoint the pupils' leading edge of learning – the place where pupils start to waiver in their understanding and begin to lack confidence in their answers. This is usually the place in the lesson where pupils may need support in expressing their understanding or where they may need to reconsider their reasoning so far. As such, it requires a teacher who is willing to set up situations where pupils feel comfortable expressing their views and ideas and where listening to pupil talk takes priority over correcting ideas in the first instance.

Task 6.1.1 **Observing and collecting questions**

Begin work on this by observing experienced teachers working with their classes. Note down the questions that seem to prompt and promote dialogue and reflect on how the teacher handles the answers. Good teachers often manage questioning effectively without realising the skilled way in which they do this. It may be useful to ask them afterwards what they were trying to achieve with specific questions and how such questions have worked with other classes. Sort, sift and collect useful questions on different topics as well as collecting generic ones that you can use to develop and support classroom discourse.

Deciding when to intervene and when to allow talk to continue is a key skill in the formative classroom because the formative process requires a rich source of data for judgments to be made about next steps in learning. Stopping the talk too soon might mean that the teacher does not fully understand the problem that pupils are having with a particular concept, while allowing the talk to continue for too long may leave insufficient time in the lesson for ideas to be challenged and problems sorted out. The important point here is that learning does take time and a teacher simply restating an incorrect statement by a pupil is unlikely to change that pupil's understanding and also the understanding of the other pupils listening in. Such an approach also requires pupils being open to advice about what they should do next, and being motivated to develop their understanding and improve their work. Clearly pupils are more likely to be willing to make improvements during the production of their work rather than returning to what they considered a finished piece completed several days earlier. This therefore requires the teacher to run the assessment process alongside the learning process. In other words, it is the 'process used by teachers and students to recognize and respond to student learning in order to enhance the learning during the learning' (Bell and Cowie, 1999, p. 32).

Creating the classroom culture where pupils feel they can reveal current understanding and be helped to firmer understanding is an essential ingredient to making formative assessment function in the classroom. Talk is vital in enabling pupils to develop their ideas and thinking and so make progress, because, through active discussion, ideas may be shaped and restructured. This is only possible, however, if classroom discussion develops beyond a series of rapid-fire closed questions to an environment where the activities are so presented and steered that they offer real opportunities for thinking and reflection. The dialogic classroom also serves as a feedback mechanism to the teacher about current and developing understanding of their various learners and so the teacher has up-to-date evidence on which to base both short-term and long-term planning.

If pupils are to benefit from feedback through classroom discussion, then the teacher's role is to promote, sustain and develop the talk. This is not an easy skill for the teacher, since their good understanding of the topic tempts them to correct pupils, or to only respond positively to correct answers, avoiding comment on incorrect ideas. So, imagine the classroom where the pupils are asked to watch a video on recycling. Afterwards, the teacher asks the class to discuss with their partner what they believe recycling is and why it is necessary to recycle some materials. The skill of the teacher is then to take ideas from the pupils without closing down the talk. It is tempting to take some statements they offer, and to use it to explain to the class what a text book explanation of recycling would be. However, taking such steps would provide minimal feedback to the many ideas that the individual pupils offer as the incorrect, unusual and sometimes weird ideas that pupils have are often more important to discuss and work out the reasoning behind them than providing a correct explanation on the board.

For assessment to function formatively, teachers need to make teaching programmes, lessons and activities flexible and responsive. This involves collecting evidence of how well pupils have understood part of a lesson or topic and refining future activities to remediate any problems that have arisen. Sometimes this requires a change in pace or direction, and sometimes it requires jettisoning lesson plans and moving ahead in the curriculum, if the class has mastered ideas quickly, and so require more challenge in their learning. So teachers need to become both more proactive in creating opportunities for pupils to demonstrate what they know, what they partly know and what they don't know and reactive in deciding to focus on the partly and unknown parts of learning, rather than rehearsing what is already achieved. In some classrooms, elaborate PowerPoint presentations make an Assessment for Learning approach difficult because the reasoning and flow of the lesson are determined by the material on the slides rather than the pupils' responses and thinking.

USING FEEDBACK TO PROMOTE LEARNING

Receiving feedback will only lead to improvement if the pupil is provided with an opportunity to try out an idea on another occasion or in a different context. Each time they try out a similar activity they can hone their approach and gradually progress towards competency. In other words, they are gradually 'closing the gap' and moving towards the next stage in their understanding. Helping pupils develop the learning behaviours where they are confident and eager to respond to feedback is an important part of Assessment for Learning. This starts with allowing pupils time to sort out and rehearse their ideas through discussion in groups. It is strengthened by valuing pupils' responses and giving pupils time to explain or justify their thoughts, rather than selecting those pupils whom you expect to get an answer right or only considering some answers when taking several responses from the class. Many classrooms use strategies such as 'think, pair, share' to help foster this approach and often incorporate the use of mini-whiteboards or selecting pupils to answer using names on lolly sticks to encourage all pupils to have a go at an answer. Making it clear that you are interested in their current thinking rather than the correct answer helps pupils realise their role in the learning process.

While feedback can help all learners, it gives particularly good results with low attainers, where it concentrates on specific problems with their work. Often high attainers have already cued into teacher expectations about the quality of work that the teacher hopes for, but low attainers find it difficult to focus on the next step without help and encouragement. When teachers share, with pupils, suggestions for the next steps in learning and how they might take them, they are more likely to understand what they need to do to improve. Each step, however small, and a means of achieving them in the short term, is what moves the learning forward and prevents such learners losing sight of their long-term goal or being inhibited from attempting it because of overtones of comparison and competition. Assessment for learning is a pedagogy that has the flexibility for the teacher to differentiate while at the same time helping learners take a more active role in their own learning, and this winning combination can help all learners distinguish where to focus their effort in order to make progress. This approach might well be thinking about and discussing work and varied ideas need to be 'aired', so that individual pupils can compare their ideas with those of their peers. It is therefore essential that teachers think about how to deal with children's responses and contributions to the discussion, because it is this response that will shape each learner's understanding and the way that learners value themselves and others within the learning environment.

Pupils also receive feedback when their work is marked and here again it is important that the feedback is used to improve the piece of work or to understand what could be done to produce a similar piece of work of higher quality. Feedback by comments provides the information for improvement in a more detailed way than marks or grades could achieve. Comments also are more likely to encourage the learner to think again about the work, particularly if the feedback asks questions or requires the learner to add something or change part of the assessed piece. Working with feedback helps learners develop a sense of what quality means in a particular area of work and this is what they need both to understand their current understanding but also to aspire to better achievement in the future. Research by Ruth Butler (1987, 1988) demonstrates that acquiring this approach to improving work can be inhibited if grades or marks are involved during the learning process because these take the focus away from improvement and centre on attainment. Research by Carol Dweck (2000) on 'growth mindset' complements this approach as it ensures that both teacher and learner are more aware of making learning a challenging but supportive endeavour that is not shaped by predetermined views of teaching and learning.

Task 6.1.2 **Planning for quality feedback**

1 Look through a sequence of lessons that you have taught or the scheme of work for a topic and decide which activities will produce work that needs checking and which will need more careful thought when marking in order to give quality feedback.
2 Decide which features of the activity, or product from the activity, suggest that more time should be devoted to giving detailed feedback.

The learner needs to see improvement as a journey, and the feedback comments provide sections of a map for them to use to move towards their goal. Peer assessment and encouraging peer support during the learning process further help develop this approach. In classrooms where teachers regularly give good written feedback, the development of peer assessment exercises is relatively easy since the teacher feedback serves as a good model for peer feedback. This, in turn, leads to better self-assessment and ultimately self-regulation of learning. In strongly developed formative classrooms, learners are able to take charge of their learning and to use teacher and peer feedback to shape their own self-assessment of their current progress, which enables and equips them with the confidence and wherewithal to take their learning forward. Pupils come to realise that the role of school is to help them learn, rather than simply provide them with things to learn, and that the responsibility to move their learning forward requires them to be active and collaborative in the classroom.

Task 6.1.3 **Understanding your school's assessment policy**

1 Obtain a copy of your school's assessment/marking policy and any information that the science department produces on these issues.
2 Read the documents carefully and check with your mentor any ambiguities, such as what 'marked regularly' means.

---

3 Ask experienced teachers how they interpret the policies on a day-to-day basis and ask them to show you evidence of what they do in the pupils' work and in their mark books.

4 Ensure that you know:
- ▨ when and how to set and mark work for your classes;
- ▨ how to store assessment evidence for your purposes and for the usual teacher of that class;
- ▨ what the assessment evidence is used for.

THE CURRENT STATE OF ASSESSMENT FOR LEARNING IN UK SCHOOLS

Despite the very positive response from teachers and schools to developing a more formative approach to assessment, many have not yet achieved this, as indicated in reports from school inspectors (OfSTED,1998, 2004, 2007), government agencies (DCSF, 2007) and research (Gorard and Smith, 2010). Several of these report that implementation of Assessment for Learning is sporadic and underdeveloped. In 2004, AfL was adopted by the National Strategies as one of its policies for whole-school improvement and considerable funding and professional development were aimed at implementing AfL across schools in England. According to recent research (James and Pedder, 2006; Keppell and Carless, 2006), the practical implementation of AfL as a pedagogical practice is complex because the way that a teacher approaches assessment reflects the teacher's beliefs and assumptions about what it means to know or understand, which, in turn, shapes the learner's own beliefs about learning.

Part of the problem is that Assessment for Learning is sometimes wrongly portrayed. In the USA, some publishers provide AfL materials which are no more than sets of progress tests, while in England the DCSF (2008) statement of AfL emphasises a similar mis-interpretation. The emphasis is on judgment of learning achievement, not on helping the learning itself, whereas the whole point of AfL is to enhance the quality of those formative interactions which help learners to grasp what they are finding hard to understand. Indeed, the frequent testing approach is deeply flawed for a number of reasons. It seems to rest on the evidence that AfL can improve learning, whereas in fact the balance of research evidence on frequent testing is that, on its own, it produces very little gain (Hattie and Temperley, 2007). Second, it diverts teachers' attention away from the AfL activities which actually help pupils to learn, and third, it can damage the learners' attitude to their own learning (Harlen and Deakin-Crick, 2003).

Sometimes assessment practices within a school are out of step with teaching and learning approaches (James, 2006) and can limit the realisation of AfL This was evident in the government's own action research project – Assessment for Learning 8 Schools Project – which categorised the factors that schools needed to ensure are in place for AfL to function. Thirteen messages emerged from this research for the successful implementation of AfL across a school; four of these focused on what went on in the classroom while the remaining nine involved how whole school support, implementation and development needed to be done.

There are many reasons why teachers have found it difficult to incorporate AfL within their classroom practice but perhaps the most fundamental one is that they cannot conceptualise AfL fully before they begin to develop it in their classrooms and so are unable to perceive the types of changes they need to make in their day-to-day practice (Harrison, 2013). The problem here is that changes of this size and complexity are sometimes difficult to achieve. There already exists a substantial tome of literature that explores how the beliefs of teachers affects the decisions they make in practice for both experienced (Nespar, 1987) and inexperienced teachers (Pajares, 1992). Much of this focuses on how teachers use their previous experience of classrooms to make sense of new situations and dilemmas as these arise. So, for both novice and experienced teachers, beliefs about lesson planning, assessment and evaluation influence the actions and decisions made in the classroom scenario (Enyedy *et al.*, 2005). If context and experience strongly influence practice, then this suggests that it may be difficult to bring about change in practice as the 'status quo' of teachers' existence confines the interpretation of any new pedagogic ideas within the realms of previous ideas. This suggests that radical change in practice may be difficult to achieve.

For teachers new to the profession, Assessment for Learning is slightly easier to master if they begin by using assessment to support learning and work on developing classrooms where dialogue is the main means of learning. Building assessment into planning and working on questioning technique is a useful start to building a teaching repertoire that leads to formative practice.

Task 6.1.4 **Finding research evidence for an interdependent relationship between teachers and pupils, M-level**

Read the following review and suggest why and how teachers and schools need to focus on an interdependent relationship between teachers and pupils rather than a dependency model, as found in many schools at the present time: Sebba, J., Crick, R.D., Yu, G., Lawson, H., Harlen, W. and Durant, K. (2008) 'Systematic review of research evidence of the impact on students in secondary schools of self- and peer-assessment: technical report', in *Research Evidence in Education Library*. London: EPPI-Centre, Social Science Research Unit, Institute of Education, University of London (see Useful Websites).

SUMMARY AND KEY POINTS

This chapter has addressed the role of formative assessment in the science classroom and outlined ways of working that allow you to collect a rich source of assessment evidence about your pupils. Assessment prioritises classroom dialogue, written work and tests as sources of evidence of learning and understanding and suggests how each of these might be used to make judgements about the next steps in the teaching and learning. Your school will undoubtedly have systems in place for monitoring and accountability and part of your development will be making sense of how the formative and summative assessment systems can work together. At this stage of your teaching career it is essential that you try out and practise a range of assessment strategies and that you regularly discuss the implications of these on both teaching and learning with your mentor and peers.

REFERENCES

Black, P., Harrison, C., Lee, C., Marshall, B. and Wiliam, D. (2003) *Assessment for Learning: Putting It into Practice*, Buckingham: Open University Press.

Black, P. and Wiliam, D. (1998) *Inside the Black Box: Raising Standards Through Classroom Assessment*, London: GL Assessment.

Bell, B. and Cowie, B. (1999) 'Researching formative assessment', in J. Loughran (ed.) *Researching Teaching*, London: Falmer Press.

Brookhart, S. (2001) 'Successful students: formative and summative uses of assessment information', *Assessment in Education; Principles, Policies and Practice*, 8(2): 153–69.

Brooks, R. and Tough, S. (2006) *Assessment and Testing: Making Space for Teaching and Learning*, London: IPPR.

Butler, R. (1987) 'Task-involving and ego-involving properties of evaluation: effects of different feedback conditions on motivational perceptions, interest and performance', *Journal of Educational Psychology*, 79(4): 474–82.

Butler, R. (1988) 'Enhancing and undermining intrinsic motivation: the effects of task-involving and ego-involving evaluation of interest and performance', *British Journal of Educational Psychology*, 58: 1–14.

Cowie, B. (2005) 'Student commentary on classroom assessment in science: a sociocultural interpretation', *International Journal of Science Education*, 27(2): 199–214.

DCSF (2007) *Assessment for Learning (AfL) 8 Schools Project*, available at: http://national-strategies.standards.dcsf.gov.uk/node/97897 (accessed 29 August 2010).

DCSF (2008) *National Strategies: Assessment for Learning*, available at: http://nationalstrategies.standards.dcsf.gov.uk/node/154056?uc=force_uj (accessed 6 June 2009).

Dweck, C. S. (2000) *Self-Theories: Their Role in Motivation, Personality and Development*, Philadelphia, PA: Psychology Press.

Enyedy, N., Goldberg, J. and Welsh, K. (2005) 'Complex dilemmas of identity and practice', *Science Education*, 90(1): 68–93.

Gorard, S. and Smith, E. (2010) *Equity in Education: An International Comparison of Pupil Perspectives*, Basingstoke: Palgrave.

Harlen, W. and Deakin-Crick, R. (2003) 'Testing and motivation for learning', *Assessment in Education*, 10(2): 169–208.

Harlen, W. and Deakin-Crick, R (2004) *Testing, Learning and Motivation*, Cambridge: Assessment Reform Group.

Harrison, C. (2005) 'Teachers developing assessment for learning: mapping teacher change', *Teacher Development*, 9(2): 255–63.

Harrison, C. (2013) 'Collaborative action research as a tool for generating formative feedback on teachers' classroom assessment practice: the KREST project', *Teachers and Teaching: Theory and Practice*, 19(2): 202–13.

Harrison, C. and Howard, S. (2009) *Inside the Primary Black Box*, London: GL Assessment.

Hattie, J. and Temperley, H. (2007) 'The power of feedback', *Review of Educational Research*, 77(1): 81–112.

Hutchinson, C. and Hayward, L. (2005) 'The journey so far: assessment for learning in Scotland', *Curriculum Journal*, 16(2): 225–48.

James, M. (2006) 'Assessment, teaching and theories of learning', in J. Gardner (ed.) *Assessment and Learning*, London: Sage, pp. 47–60.

James, M. and Pedder, D. (2006) 'Professional learning as a condition for assessment for learning', in J. Gardner (ed.) *Assessment for Learning: Theory, Policy and Practice*, London: Sage, pp. 27–43.

Keppell, M. and Carless, D. (2006) 'Learning-oriented assessment: a technology-based case study', *Assessment in Education*, 13(2): 179–91.

Mansell, W., James, M. and the Assessment Reform Group (2009) *Assessment in Schools. Fit for Purpose? A Commentary by the Teaching and Learning Research Programme*, London: Economic and Social Research Council, Teaching and Learning Research Programme.

Marshall, B. and Drummond, M. (2006) 'How teachers engage with Assessment for Learning: lessons from the classroom', *Research Papers in Education*, 21(2): 133–49.

Nespar, J. (1987) 'The role of beliefs in the practice of teaching', *Journal of Curriculum Studies*, 19: 317–28.

OFSTED (1998) *Secondary Education 1993–7: A Review of Secondary Schools in England*, London: Her Majesty's Stationery Office.

OFSTED (2004) *Standards and Quality 2002/03: The Annual Report of Her Majesty's Chief Inspector of Schools*, London: The Stationery Office.

OFSTED (2007) *Annual Report of Her Majesty's Chief Inspector, 2006–2007*, London: Her Majesty's Stationery Office.

Pajares, M. F. (1992) 'Teachers' beliefs and educational research: cleaning up a messy construct', *Review of Educational Research*, 62(3): 307–33.

Shephard, L.A. (2000) 'The role of assessment in a learning culture', *Educational Researcher*, 29(7): 4–14.

Stiggins, R. (2002) 'Assessment crisis: the absence of Assessment for Learning', *Phi Delta Kappan*, June: 758–65.

USEFUL WEBSITES

Assessment Reform Group: www.aaia.org.uk/afl/assessment-reform-group/ (accessed 7 June 2014).
Contains links to many documents about Assessment for Learning, performance data and examinations.
Evidence for Policy and Practice Information and Co-ordinating Centre (EPPI): http://eppi.ioe.ac.uk/cms/ (accessed 7 June 2014).
This contains a number of reviews on assessment matters. Follow the links to 'Assessment'.

UNIT 6.2

SUMMATIVE ASSESSMENT AND EXAMINATIONS IN SCIENCE

Christine Harrison

INTRODUCTION

Public examinations are part of *summative* assessment, and must be distinguished from the *formative* assessment for learning described in Unit 6.1. They lead to accreditation for nationally recognised qualifications and involve different tasks and tests to provide an opportunity for pupils to demonstrate the range of skills, knowledge and understanding that they have gained. Nationally recognised qualifications serve several purposes: they credit individuals' achievements; they contribute to selection procedures for further study or employment; and are used as accountability measures for judging schools' performances. As a result, they become 'high stakes' events for teachers and schools as well as the pupils who take the examinations.

OBJECTIVES

By the end of this unit, you should:

- have an overview of how assessments can be valid and reliable;
- be familiar with schemes of assessment in public examinations in science;
- understand the place of teacher assessment in science qualifications and know about the ways in which teachers' own marking is moderated;
- understand the implications of assessment arrangements.

SUMMATIVE ASSESSMENT

The reason why we assess in education is to use our understanding of the teaching and learning provided in that school or that classroom to make a judgement, then draw a conclusion and then act on it. The decision might be about entry into a school or course and so we need to assess for selection purposes, or to inform parents about their child's progress and so assessment aids reporting, or about how well a class has understood a topic and so the purpose is for future learning. As Cronbach (1971) pointed out, an assessment is really just a procedure for making inferences and the richer and greater the data, the easier it is to be confident in the decision taken.

Tests and examinations are often used by teachers to check on the learning that has taken place over a period of time. In science, teachers regularly check pupil knowledge and understanding at the end of a topic with a test and this provides information on how the individual pupils are progressing and also on the teaching quality for the topic concerned. While tests are the most widely used assessment tool for providing summative assessment, they are not the only tools that can be used for this purpose. It is just as valid to provide a task for pupils to complete as long as the task incorporates the skills and concepts that formed the main learning goals in the topic being assessed. Tests tend to be used as they generally are more capable of covering the breath of the topic as separate questions can focus on different aspects of the topic. The problem with most tests is that they do not always require in-depth answers and so recall, comprehension and low-level data analysis tend to dominate science tests.

Clearly one aspect that is key to good assessment practices is confidence in the outcome of the assessment. Confidence usually refers to 'reliability' and 'validity' and these are normally features of educational testing and in particular classical test theory. Reliability refers to the reproducibility of the assessment and so asks the question whether a different set of questions or completing the task on a different day might alter the score achieved by the learner. Validity refers to the extent to which the assessment measures what it is expected to measure. It therefore requires the test to have covered all the skills and content that formed the curriculum that was taught. Both reliability and validity are context-dependent measures.

In general, we expect that reliability will increase with the number of assessments made. Teachers make professional judgements about the performance of their pupils every day as they engage in classroom activities, ask questions and mark work. In fact, because teacher assessment is based on observations occurring on a number of occasions over a period of time, this would lead to an expectation that assessment judgements based on these observations would be more reliable than assessments made on the basis of a one-off test. However, concerns are often expressed about how to ensure the reliability and validity of teacher assessment, especially in an era of performance management of education systems. As a consequence, in recent years, many education systems have relied on external testing to chart pupil progress with teacher assessment only accounting for a small proportion of the final marks or grade. External testing regimes are often considered to be more reliable and independent, even though there is little research to support this claim, even if they are seen to be limiting the scope of what is taken as evidence of pupil achievement. In other words, currently, confidence in assessment is focused primarily on reliability rather than validity.

One of the main problems with threats to validity is subject under-representation. An extreme example of this would be an integrated science test that had only biology and chemistry questions because the omission of physics questions challenges the test's validity as an integrated science assessment. Some people argue that construct under-representation is not generally as big a problem as is claimed because often performance on an aspect that is not included in the test correlates reasonably well with performance on the aspects of the subject that are tested. Such an argument is sometimes used, for example, to justify the removal of practical assessments in science. While it is true that the correlation between scores on assessment of practical skills in science correlate quite highly with scores on written tests, there is no reason to expect such correlations to persist if we stop assessing practical skills in science. When practical skills are assessed alongside scientific knowledge, there is a strong incentive for teachers to ensure that pupils are taught practical skills, and for pupils to take this aspect of their studies seriously. However, if the assessment of practical skills is removed from the examination, the incentives to ensure pupils are learning practical skills are reduced. Teachers may give less emphasis to practical work and pupils may give less attention to these aspects of science in their revision, so that the written assessment is no longer a good indication of the level of the pupils' practical skills. In such a situation, using the scores on written tests to make inferences about pupils' practical skills would no longer be warranted.

WHAT KIND OF EXTERNAL ASSESSMENTS ARE DONE IN SCHOOLS?

You will already be familiar with the range of external examinations in science available generally, and in your school, from your study of the curriculum in Unit 2.3 of this book. If you have not already done so, you should, together with this unit, read Unit 6.2 of Capel *et al.* (2013) *Learning to Teach in the Secondary School*, which gives background information about the development and structures of GCSE and GCE examinations and diplomas. It provides information on the use of external examination results for public accountability of schools, and describes what systems are in place to ensure validity and reliability in external assessments and examinations are. It also explains how comparability between the different awarding bodies is achieved.

Recently Ofqual, the Office of Qualifications and Examination Regulation, has altered the assessment arrangements at A-level. The reform will separate a pupil's final A-level grade in the sciences from their performance in the practical competence assessment. The Science Community Representing Education (SCORE) is extremely concerned that the decision to separate practical marks in science from the overall A-level grade has not been properly discussed within the education community and with UCAS and university admissions officers. It seems that the proposals present an ill-thought-through solution to the recognised problem of how to assess practical skills in the sciences with reforms being rushed into implementation. While the drive in schools has been to increase the amount and value of practical work in science, this reform mitigates against this. In particular, extended investigations are specifically prohibited from being included as a contribution to the A-level grade, which means that skills needed for these are less likely to be taught and topics that fit well with this approach, such as ecology, may receive less emphasis in the curriculum. The possible consequence of separating out the grade for practical work is that schools may reduce the opportunities for pupils to do practical work if this element is viewed as less important than the A-level grade

UNDERSTANDING THE SCHEME OF ASSESSMENT IN A SPECIFICATION

Details of schemes of assessment for any course are contained in a range of publications from the awarding body, such as:

■   the specification;
■   the teacher's guide;

■ exemplar material for internally assessed tasks and their assessment (often in the teacher's guide);

■ specimen question papers and answers, or (better) a set of recent past papers;

■ a recent examiner's report, which gives information about how candidates tackled questions and where the main problems lay.

Your school may be able to lend you these; alternatively, download them from the awarding body websites (see Useful Websites in Unit 2.3).

The specification contains most of the basic information about the scheme of assessment. In it you will find information about:

■ units of assessment;
■ assessment objectives;
■ weighting of the objectives;
■ internal assessment;
■ mark schemes and criteria for marking internally assessed work;
■ help and support that teachers can give for internally assessed work;
■ moderation procedures;
■ administration.

Assessment objectives and weighting of objectives

The assessment objectives are derived from the aims of the course. Not all aims are assessable (aims about enjoyment of science, for instance). Assessment objectives for GCSE and GCE sciences are concerned with knowledge and understanding of science and of *How Science Works*; with the application of that knowledge and understanding, and with skills related to evidence and practical skills. All assessment objectives are subdivided into more specific sub-objectives. Assessment objectives are not necessarily given the same weighting; the marks allocated to each objective may be different. Schemes of assessment give the weightings of the objectives and show how the testing of the objectives is distributed through the different units of assessment.

Internal and external assessment

Internal assessment refers to assessments where work is undertaken in class or homework time, where teachers support part of the work, and where teachers undertake the marking. 'Internal assessment', 'centre assessment' and 'teacher assessment' all mean the same thing (a 'centre' being a school or college offering the examination). The centre-assessed unit of assessment might well include more than one task. External assessment refers to elements of the examination set and marked by the awarding body, usually through written examination papers.

Over the last 25 years, there has been a marked change in the way internally assessed work has been approached in England. When the National Curriculum was introduced in 1989, the Task Group on Assessment and Testing (TGAT) suggested a model of assessment, which incorporated teacher assessment as a key component of the system. While some initial work was done to incorporate the TGAT approach, the government quickly changed tack and reduced the position of teacher assessment in determining attainment. One of the problems of focusing assessment on examinations rather than teacher assessment is that some areas of the curriculum are difficult to assess by written papers, for example, practical work, problem solving and inquiry. Trying to assess aspects like these through written papers is difficult because the skills and knowledge involved are not easy to capture in the short answer-type questions that form the majority of our examination papers. If questions can be devised in these areas, research by the Assessment of Performance Unit (APU, 1984) suggests that performance on written questions does not necessarily correlate with performance in authentic settings.

Internal assessments for GCSE, previously referred to as 'coursework' are now 'controlled assessments', in that the awarding body retains control over the setting of the task, develops the criteria for marking, and stipulates the conditions under which the tasks should be carried out. For example, OCR currently has a task for the GCSE 21st Century Science course that involves candidates having an article to read two or three weeks in advance. For the assessment, fresh copies of the article are provided and candidates answer a set of previously unseen questions about it. The awarding body chooses the article and sets the questions. The teacher supports the candidates in researching the topic, and marks the final script. In another task, candidates carry out data collection in a practical activity in normal lesson time, in preparation for questions about data interpretation and evaluation answered under examination conditions. Guidance on appropriate practical tasks is specified by the awarding body. Again teachers mark the scripts. In the related GCSE additional science course, the internal assessment consists of a research study, data interpretation and practical skills, each with varying degrees of control from the awarding body. (Look out for acronyms; AQA, for instance, uses ISAs (Investigations Skills Assignments) and PSAs (Practical Skills Assessments) for CAUs (Centre Assessed Units)).

While specific mark schemes are suitable for some of the internally assessed tasks, other tasks require the use of criteria by which teachers can judge the level of attainment; this is particularly true for assessment of practical skills. Criteria may seem precise on first reading, but both judgement and experience play a large part in deciding reliably whether a candidate has reached a particular level or not. In schools, teachers carry out moderation exercises to ensure that they are interpreting the assessment criteria in similar ways and this serves as useful professional development for staff. Criteria can be found in the schemes of assessment within the specifications and you will need to refer to them later, for the Tasks. Task 6.2.1 is a short exercise intended to extract the basic information about the schemes of assessment for courses in your school. For this, you need to use only the specification. Later tasks (Tasks 6.2.2 and 6.2.3) analyse the assessment in greater depth.

Task 6.2.1 **Understanding schemes of assessment for GCSE and GCE**

Use the specification only for the GCSE *science* course in your school.

1 Find:

- ▪ the units of assessment, the time for each and the marks allocated to each unit;
- ▪ the tasks for the teacher-assessed component;

> ▓ the assessment objectives and the sub-objectives;
> ▓ the weighting of the assessment objectives and their distribution through the different units of assessment;
> ▓ the marks allocated for quality of written work or quality of communication.
>
> 2 Do the same for the GCSE *additional science* and GCSE *additional applied science* and for a GCE A-level in your specialism.
> 3 Talk with your mentor about when the tasks and tests are done, and the opportunities that pupils have to retake units of assessment.
>
> Keep notes in your professional portfolio, particularly of the features with which you are unfamiliar.

Marking criteria for internally assessed work

The specification is the 'rule book' for a public examination, and equally importantly, the question papers and the internally assessed tasks form the 'case law'. The question papers and internally assessed tasks show the depth of treatment expected in teaching the course, and the relative emphasis given to different parts of the content. You should therefore study them carefully at an early stage (see Tasks 6.2.2 and 6.2.3).

Task 6.2.2 **Analysing question papers**

This task involves answering and analysing examination papers. Using the same specifications that you used in Task 6.2.1, do the questions yourself and check against model answers. Then analyse the papers as follows:

1 Identify which assessment objectives are examined by the written papers.
2 Match the individual questions (or parts of questions) to the more detailed 'sub-objectives'.
3 Identify the questions that test different aspects of *How Science Works* or *Working Scientifically.*
4 For GCSE, identify the difference in demand between the foundation and higher tier papers.
5 For the GCE A-level papers, find the questions that are synoptic (i.e. the questions which link different sections of the course) and those questions that are the 'stretch and challenge' questions, which distinguish the A* candidates from the A candidates.
6 Think what kind of guidance you would give to pupils taking these papers and make a list of your main suggestions.

Keep records of this task in your portfolio. Discuss with other student teachers, your tutor or mentor any questions that you found difficult. Share your list of guidance suggestions with mentors; they may well be able to confirm your selection and add points from their experience.

Task 6.2.3 **Analysing the internally assessed components**

Using the same specifications that you used in Task 6.2.1, look at the guidance and examples for the internally assessed components. Decide how you would tackle the tasks yourself before answering the questions below:

1 Which assessment objectives are tested?
2 For GCSE, are the tasks the same for foundation and higher tier?
3 Do teachers and/or pupils have any choice? Is there guidance given about how to choose?
4 Can any of the work be done outside lesson time?
5 Can any work be done collectively (e.g. collecting data from a practical investigation)?
6 What is the nature of the final product? Answers to questions? A written report? A presentation? A set of laboratory skills? Other?
7 Are the tasks marked using criteria or a marking scheme?
8 Has the awarding body produced an explanation of the tasks and criteria specifically for pupils? If so, ask mentors how they use it.

Write a brief summary of the key points related to the centre-assessed units of assessment and put this in your PDP. Talk with teachers about how they fit these assessments into the normal rhythm of their teaching, and which tasks present the greatest challenge to them and to the pupils.

Examination rules and professional judgement

It is the job of the department's teaching team to end up with *valid* and *reliable* marks for the internally assessed tasks to submit to awarding bodies. Do the pupils' marks reward success in skills in line with the expectations of the syllabus and the mark scheme? If they do, they are valid. Is the standard of marking fair and consistent across different pieces of coursework from any one pupil, and across different teachers' marking? This is a further test of reliability–inter-marker reliability. Both issues are addressed by the awarding body's rules, and both are serious professional challenges.

VALIDITY AND 'AUTHENTICATION' OF COURSEWORK

As with tasks of any kind, what pupils achieve in their coursework depends on what they are asked to do, how it is introduced to them and the help and support available to them whilst doing it. Where there is choice (more likely in GCE than GCSE), this can be difficult for teachers and pupils, but guidance and exemplar material provided by the awarding body can be helpful.

The awarding bodies usually ask teachers to report the help given to pupils. 'Help.' includes advice given to the class as a whole, for example, through help sheets, as well as to individuals. The teacher may be required to make a note on the pupils' scripts of help given to individuals. The awarding body gives strong guidance in the specification on help that can be given. In addition, you should be learning from your schools about how to support pupils undertaking these assessments.

RELIABLE MARKING AND MODERATION OF INTERNALLY ASSESSED WORK

Moderation is the process through which marks for internally assessed work are brought in line with a common standard, thus making them reliable. 'Internal' moderation seeks to establish a common standard within the school. 'External' moderation makes the comparisons across schools and nationally. Internal moderation may be carried out in various ways. In science, teachers generally aim to establish the correct standard of marking as early as possible. Usually, they look together at the awarding body's guidance and interpret it for their own circumstances; they may produce marking guidelines for particular internally assessed tasks, illustrating pupils' responses for different marks, and they will exchange scripts, mark them separately and then discuss them to resolve differences. The latter may be organised annually at a formal moderation meeting in the department. Even when teachers have become familiar with applying the awarding body's criteria, any marks reported to pupils or their parents are provisional since they will still be subject to external moderation. Feedback to pupils is valuable especially if there will be opportunities for them to improve their performance, but schools and departments may set their own rules about what feedback is allowed.

Task 6.2.4 **Internal moderation**

Compare your own judgements in marking an internally assessed task with another teacher's judgements. If possible, do this first with the teacher of a class you are working with and for a task you have seen them do.

  Both you and the class teacher should mark the same scripts independently, without access to the other's marks. This approach is sometimes referred to as 'blind marking'. Mark at least six pupils' work, selected from the top, middle and lower ranges of achievement in the class. The first marker will need to annotate the script in line with the awarding body's guidance. Then compare the marks each of you has given; discuss the reasons for any differences and note how these are resolved. You may be able to follow this up by attending a moderation meeting in your science department.

Science departments work out the marks for internally assessed tasks. A number of sample scripts are supplied to an external moderator appointed by the awarding body, selected from across the range of pupil achievement and from different classes and teachers. The moderator has the right to ask for additional scripts if necessary, so the department must keep all the pupils' scripts that contribute to their final marks until after the external moderation is completed. It is not uncommon for moderators to make adjustments to the school's marks, if they feel a school has been too lenient or too harsh in their interpretation of the criteria. The adjustments are made to all pupils' marks from the school, even though based on a small sample. It is assumed that the sample is representative of the whole.

External moderators write a short report on their decisions, a copy of which is returned to the school.

PREPARING PUPILS FOR THEIR PUBLIC EXAMINATIONS

Schools and science departments pay increasing attention to preparing pupils for examinations by:

- developing pupils' study skills for revision;
- teaching 'examination techniques' for answering questions effectively;
- providing specific resources to help revise course content;
- actively supporting pupils during the revision process;
- building up their confidence and motivation (most important of all).

Most schools make use of one or more of the published revision guides, some of which are exactly matched to each specification. There are usually also accompanying workbooks. However, only a minority of pupils are likely to find guides and workbooks helpful since they require a text-based learning style (and a good deal of persistence). There are lots of ways to revise, just as there are lots of ways to learn. Teachers need to introduce different techniques to pupils using, for example, mind mapping, key fact summaries, problem-solving exercises, quizzes, paired testing as well as practice examination questions. Software packages for revision are also popular with many pupils. They include online revision, for example the well-established BBC Bitesize, and reasonably priced CD-based packages, some of which incorporate sophisticated tools for pupils to track their individual progress through the material.

SUMMARY AND KEY POINTS

As well as helping children to learn, one key element of your job is preparing pupils for their examinations. Examination success is a highly visible and rewarding aspect of your teaching; good results are a source of professional satisfaction and pride. The annual set of results is one way in which individual teachers, subject departments and schools as a whole assess their performance, as well as an important basis on which they are judged, not least by their local communities. Understanding the nature of this summative assessment, so that you can prepare pupils adequately for it, is of paramount importance. You are strongly advised to try out the examination questions, to learn about the internal assessment tasks, to understand marking processes and to learn how to prepare pupils as soon as possible. Work with teachers on moderation procedures and learn what you can about the administration of the assessments and examinations.

REFERENCES

Assessment of Performance Unit (1984) *Science at Age 13*, London: Department of Education and Science.
Cronbach, L. J. (1971) 'Test validation', in R. L. Thorndike (ed.) *Educational Measurement*, 2nd edn, Washington, DC: American Council on Education, pp. 443–507.

FURTHER READING

Capel, S., Leask, M. and Turner, T. (2013) *Learning to Teach in the Secondary School*, 5th edn, London: Routledge
Lambert, D. and Lines, D. (2000) *Understanding Assessment: Purposes, Perceptions and Practice*, London: RoutledgeFalmer.

The first half of this book provides a deeper guide to examination principles. The second half is devoted to formative assessment and is applicable to Unit 6.1.

USEFUL WEBSITES

Specifications, exemplar examination material and mark schemes are available online from the awarding bodies AQA, Edexcel, OCR, CCEA, WJEC (see Useful Websites in Unit 2.3).
BBC Bitesize science: www.bbc.co.uk/schools/gcsebitesize/science/ (accessed 7 June 2014).
Ofqual: www.ofqual.gov.uk (accessed 7 June 2014).

UNIT 7

IS EDUCATION RESEARCH VALUABLE FOR TEACHERS OF SCIENCE?

John Oversby

INTRODUCTION

'Is education research valuable for teachers of science?' seems like a simple and obvious question to which the simple answer should be yes. To produce a unit in response suggests that the answer must be complex, and therefore potentially interesting.

OBJECTIVES

By the end of this unit, you should be able to:

- develop an understanding of research and scholarship;
- report specific research and scholarship that indicates how to improve teaching and learning;
- explore how the contribution of research and scholarship to being a professional works;
- provide guidance on how to engage with research and scholarship as an active teacher.

UNDERSTANDING RESEARCH AND SCHOLARSHIP

Almost like knowledge and understanding, research and scholarship have become two concepts that almost always appear together. Many universities have in their mission statements phrases about encouraging research and scholarship as enterprises of the higher education community that mark out the status of that community. Interestingly, the UK Research Excellence Framework (REF) for universities gives no real clue as to its meaning of research, often moving into tautology, i.e. research is that which is funded by

Table 7.1 Qualities of research and scholarship

Research	Scholarship
• Empirical systematic and rigorous enquiry into an area of knowledge to produce new knowledge claims • Open to scrutiny among peers	• Engagement with scholarly contributions of others, both research and scholarship • Reflection on personal practice • Communication and dissemination of ideas about aspects of theory and practice • Open to scrutiny among peers

a Research Council. It is as though the meaning of research is obvious. However, the juxtaposition of research and scholarship does provoke questions about their distinctive meanings, and of the relationship between the two.

Although the REF does admit that there are different forms of research output for some disciplines, such as musical performance and the creation of a piece of art, its focus on scholarship is that of research scholarship. However, 'scholarship' remains ill-defined. The greater and explicit emphasis on research leads to the notion of two hierarchical concepts, of research and scholarship, with research held in higher esteem.

In the absence of an official consensus about the meanings, I suggest qualities of research and scholarship elements of writing created by science educators in Table 7.1.

Most so-called research papers contain some elements of both research and scholarship features. Their references to prior literature are clearly scholarship in intent and realisation. In most cases, construction of a concluding section involves integrating analysis of collected data (research feature) and associated published knowledge (scholarship feature). Other writings probably owe more to their scholarship features than empirical research. Nevertheless, it is my view that they represent a proper output of a university, that is knowledge transfer, not just the content at a high level but the methods employed, based on a reflection of scholarly contributions by others and self-reflection.

The distinction, therefore, between research and scholarship features, in my view, is one of empirical against secondary evidence. Both qualities are capable of producing new knowledge claims and both must be subject to scrutiny among peers, as a measure of the level of quality.

In the UK, it seems that that there are fewer active 'researchers' in science pedagogy as time passes. Science educators, by which I mean those working in higher education, must take responsibility for teaching the skills of creating scholarship and researching, as appropriate. Mentoring on university-based and school-based courses will be an important component in developing this capacity. It could also do much to reduce the separation between empirical research and teaching. Education researchers often place impact in the classroom a low second in their writings. Greater focus on scholarship by teachers could achieve this.

I believe that an essential characteristic of good professional teachers is to engage in scholarship. Negotiation of access to the vast range of published work might also be a significant contribution to professional development courses for teachers. Formal recognition of their achievements can come through the extensive network of university-based

Master's programmes and through the Chartered Science Teacher status available through the Association for Science Education (ASE). A valuable outcome of teachers engaging with small-scale research in their own classrooms is that they become sensitised to existing research, and skilled in evaluating this research. They also develop skills in using the research as one influence on their own teaching. Especially for those new to teaching, I know that there are many influences on gaining teaching skills. These include, but are not limited to, observing and copying other teachers, explanations in text books, thoughtful advice from school-based mentors and university tutors, theoretical textbooks, as well as ideas from research such as trying out interventions or using assessment methods.

SPECIFIC RESEARCH AND SCHOLARSHIP THAT INDICATE HOW TO IMPROVE TEACHING AND LEARNING

The *ASE Guide to Research in Science Education* (Oversby, 2012) provides a systematic review of a range of robust research evidence across a range of topics such as the Nature of Science, the role of ICT, what do teachers and children know and understand, inquiry, and modelling. A third of the book is devoted to a substantial guide for teachers carrying out Practitioner Research in their classroom. It is recommended for early career teachers in primary and secondary schools, for students in pre-service education courses, and for those starting out as teacher educators in Higher Education and as advisers.

Intervention evidence

Hattie (online, see Useful Websites) provided a range of metastudies (reviews and syntheses of other studies) to produce a quantitative value (effect size) of the impact of a wide variety of interventions. He showed that Teacher–Student Relationships, Mastery Learning, Challenge of Goals, Peer Tutoring and Feedback had positive to very positive effects on learning, in some cases worth up to two years' advancement, while Ability Grouping was hardly valuable at all. Much of this work has been interpreted by Petty (1998) for the UK context. These studies have provided much useful evidence for teachers to improve teaching and learning in their classrooms but, obviously, they are limited to those studies where the samples are large enough to be statistically valid, where the variables are sufficiently controlled, and where the pre- and post-intervention assessments are valid.

Large-scale programmes

In 1975, the UK Government set up a sampling system for assessment of student attainment at 11, 13 and 15 years old, in science and mathematics, under the Assessment of Performance Unit (e.g. Brian, 1976). It was based on a random, yet sufficiently representative, sample of students carrying out pencil and paper, and practical tests, the latter by trained assessors who also marked the responses. It provided a national snapshot of student attainment in carefully selected aspects of science (and mathematics) learning in England. Its questions and methodology, some of it based on research about interviews about concepts (e.g. Gilbert *et al.*, 1985), and the style of questions have influenced writing of examination questions and class discussions over the years (see below).

The Learning in Science Project (LISP) in New Zealand was concerned with exploring ideas that children have about scientific concepts and processes. This was at the start of the alternative conceptions movement. It gave rise to some innovative methods for exploring children's ideas such as Interviews About Concepts and Interviews About Instances (Gilbert *et al.*, 1985).

The Cognitive Acceleration in Science Education (CASE) devoted to faster learning through specially created tasks, with books (*Thinking Science*) and research papers. When I was teaching in a secondary school, I attended a workshop by Michael Shayer and Philip Adey at one of the annual ASE conferences. I went straight back to school, tried out some of the activities, and could not stop sharing with colleagues the successes I was having!

The Relevance of Science Education (ROSE) is an international Norwegian project. Svein Sjoberg and colleagues initiated the ROSE project as a way of finding out what turned on interested adolescents and what did not. Apart from boys' strong interest in explosives and taking things apart, and girls' well-developed interest in well-being, this research has led to many teachers trying to find out about their own classes.

International assessment programmes such as Programme for International Student Assessment (PISA) and Trend in International Mathematics and Science Survey (TIMSS) with their coterie of researchers in science education acting as consultants and item writers are instrumental in charting national achievements with consequent impact on what is taught as teachers work on improving their national rankings.

Action Research

Bennett (2003) has written an illuminating account of the value of Action Research in projects in which she has collaborated with teachers. From the USA, Roberts *et al.* (2007) is a treasure trove of the positive impacts of Action Research in 14 areas of science learning at all levels. Chapters 19–25 in Oversby (2012) give clear guidance on how to conduct such research.

The messages from studies such as these are that practising classroom teachers can engage in carrying out valuable research that makes a contribution to knowledge in the field, that this process enhances and sharpens their personal evaluations, and that the process facilitates understanding published research, including its strengths and limitations.

Policy messages

Much of the influence of research on policy is obscured by the opaque nature of much of policy-making. The two examples below owe much to the transparency of the researchers in sharing their work at the professional level.

1 Research into the role of assessment was a springboard for the highly influential Assessment for Learning framework, spearheaded by Paul Black and Christine Harrison, among others.
2 Research into the Nature of Science (e.g. Taber, 2012) led to the inclusion of the How Science Works strand in the National Curriculum in England.

Case study examples

Case study 1: Grouping

In this case study, I will share an experience I had with secondary pre-service teachers to illuminate some thinking about working in groups with Year 10 (15 years old) pupils. My aim was to differentiate the class with pupil-chosen tasks. The lesson was concerned with looking at mass changes when magnesium is burned in oxygen. This is a traditional experiment but the Year 10 class had pupils working at quite different levels. One aim, for some, was to examine the relationship between the mass of oxygen and mass of magnesium. We were using two methods: (1) measuring the percentage of magnesium in the final product for consistency; and (2) a graph of the two variables to check for proportionality. The percentage proportion was aimed at illuminating the Law of Constant Composition, a historical idea. For a third group, noticing that there was an increase in mass and understanding that an invisible gas in air was, perhaps, quite a reasonable achievement, and this aim could be shared with the other groups. A bonus was that their mass measurements would also be available to the other groups, providing a larger data set. For a few, in this lesson, moving to a sub-microscopic interpretation based on different relative masses of component particles would be an excellent achievement. The experiment consists of weighing a crucible, with lid, with and without a roll of magnesium. I would ensure that the rolls had a range of masses. They heated the magnesium, cautiously, and reweighed the cooled crucible, now containing magnesium oxide. They then calculated the mass of oxygen added. In terms of manipulation, this is a delicate procedure, and a test of their dexterity.

How to differentiate the group was a challenge. On each bench I taped a card with a problem: 'A piece of iron chloride has x g of iron and y g of oxygen. Calculate the % proportion of oxygen in the iron oxide.' This was to be done individually. At this point I asked each table to un-tape the card, which had a question on it: 'Did you find this calculation: (a) easy; (b) manageable; or (c) difficult?' All those responding (a) were to collect a blue worksheet and work with two others with the same colour. Those responding (b) collected a yellow worksheet, and (c) responders collected a green worksheet. I did not interfere with the choice but noted those perhaps choosing inappropriately from my knowledge of them for later discussions. This method of self-grouping has been used before.

With the Year 10 pupils there seemed to be no angst about this form of grouping, and the outcomes were suitably differentiated for my purpose. The differentiated worksheets provided appropriate support. The response of the secondary pre-service science teachers was very different. They became discomfited or even angry about what had happened, and started to complain. However, to them (but not the Year 10 pupils), I suggested working with mixed colour groups, and then they discovered that all the worksheets were the same except for the colour!

Case study 2: Cognitive structure

Having a clear and well-organised cognitive structure, Ausubel (1968, p.130) believes, 'is also in its own right the most significant independent variable influencing the learner's capacity for acquiring more new knowledge in the same field', and 'Existing cognitive structure, that is an individual's organization, stability, and clarity of knowledge in a particular subject matter field at any given time, is the principal factor influencing the learning and retention of meaningful new material' (1968, p. 217).

In this case study, I focus on learners working together in mixed ability classes, and how they can be inclusive yet differentiated. I had an opportunity to take a group of pupils to a fluorite mine in Weardale in the north-east of England. Fluorite was being used as a refractory component of blast furnace lining bricks because of its high melting point. The pupils were studying a chemical engineering module involving froth flotation to separate the fluorite from galena (a lead sulphide ore) that was also present. On the spoil heap were lumps of almost pure galena, silvery grey, weighing a few kilos each. We took a number of samples, for which I was sure to find a use, I thought. My Year 8 class was to find out. They arrived and entered the laboratory and noticed the lumps of the silvery-grey rock on each bench. Their curiosity soon got the better of them and they picked up the lumps, passing them round each bench. They remarked on its weight for its size, and its colour. Eventually one said: 'I wonder what it is made of?' I spoke for the first time, suggesting that this would be a good topic for the lesson, some minutes after they had first arrived. On my request they talked about how they would find out (focused talk involving technical language). I had kept my equipment trolley out of sight since I did not wish to influence their thinking. When they began to run out of new ideas, I asked someone from one group to make a suggestion. 'Filter it.' I brought out filter papers, filter funnels and funnel holders. They were adept at folding the filter paper and setting up the equipment, working collaboratively. Almost all at the same time, they realised that the lump would not fit! 'What should we do?' I gave them some small ground-up pieces I had broken off earlier, and they placed them into the paper. We waited, until one said that she remembered that water was necessary. I provided water bottles and they placed a beaker under the funnel and poured water into the funnel. Clear and colourless liquid dripped out of the funnel. They watched, rather crestfallen that their idea had not worked. Nevertheless, I had treated their ideas seriously, and let them try things out. We had spent about 20 minutes exploring their previous knowledge. However, the time had not been wasted since we had reviewed a method of analysis, treated their knowledge seriously, and let them test the validity of their idea. The rest of the lesson progressed through other methods they had tried until they came upon the idea of heating the galena (either in a fume cupboard or next to an open window). After consolidating their existing knowledge, it was time to invoke some historical knowledge and share the craft experience of smelters in metal extraction.

THE CONTRIBUTION OF RESEARCH AND SCHOLARSHIP TO BEING A PROFESSIONAL

In Roberts *et al.* (2007), the editors have produced an insightful compilation of individual teachers who have had 'opportunities to learn and use the skills of research to generate new knowledge about science and the teaching and learning of science' (NRC, 1996, p. 68). Roberts *et al.* (2007) mention Duckworth (1987) who notes that some teachers find the time to be interested in research and to write about it, and to contribute to theoretical and pedagogical discussions. Their introductory chapter notes the many terms that are used to identify inquiring into one's own teaching practices and pupil learning, characterising the many varied approaches to this kind of research. Teacher researchers are frequently engaged with professional researchers who adopt the role of facilitating the teachers' explorations rather than initiating them and controlling them. Often they work in collaborative groups valuing the solidarity and critical perspectives that colleagues provide. For many, this is in contrast to their normal teaching practice which is often an isolated activity as an adult. Much of the research methodology is qualitative. Communication of their findings occurs at professional meetings and in publications for teachers and researchers. However, it is very challenging for busy teachers with full timetables to continue with research. Such groups have provided access to funding that gives them space to develop their work and their collaborations with others in the teacher-researcher groups that often form. They report that teacher-researchers promote public conversation about teaching and learning through documentary websites. The book presents 13 case studies in three sections: integrating science and literacy learning; ongoing studies of learning and teaching in science contexts; and reflections on researching while teaching. This exemplary source of evidence demonstrates remarkably professional development through being researchers. Kathleen Hogan focused on her study of literacy when her Grade 1 elementary class were playing with a motion sensor (Chapter 1 in Roberts *et al.*, 2007). She used a computer to generate position-time graphs, and focused on their writing. After she spoke of her study at a teacher-researcher conference, she wrote:

> Someone said to me adamantly, 'But we don't need these [motion detectors] to help students learn about graphs or to learn to write clear directions.' My response to this person was, 'No, we don't, but I do.' My students needed it too. And that is what we should do as educators – find ways to help our students. Likewise, if we share our experiences, we can help motivate each other to continue finding ways to present material to our students, ensuring every student is given the opportunity to be successful.

Hogan had used her enquiry into student engagement to understand a method of linking scientific action to literacy, and to share this with colleagues. Her confidence, perhaps promoted by her enquiry, was strong enough to react positively to the put-down she encountered.

Trish Boswell worked with fourth grade students on an electric circuits' investigation. She describes this in Chapter 3 in Roberts *et al.* (2007). Her interest was in modelling an authentic scientific inquiry through her students' creation of science journals and presenting their work at a Science conference. Her data included her students' writings about what it meant to become scientists. Her focus was quite different from the usual activity which gives a recipe for the students to follow and 'discover' the conventional circuits. The students had a myriad of questions of many different kinds, some beginning with 'How many different ways . . .?' to 'How does a switch work?' to 'Can electricity hurt you?' Some had heard that a light bulb could be lit from citrus fruits or a potato and wanted to know more about it. They presented their inquiries on posters at the conference. She had learned how to provide a wide variety of opportunities for conducting different inquiries in one class by following the students' questions, and then to share the learning outcomes in a conference where the students were the teachers. Her idea came from her college physics teacher who modelled authentic inquiry with prospective teachers, and she was able to show that adoption of a facilitating and guiding stance made it work for these very young learners.

Matthew Ronfeldt taught eighth grade math and science in a school in San Francisco, He writes in Chapter 7 in Roberts *et al.* (2007). He was concerned with ethical perspectives on doing experiments on animals or humans. He used video recordings of class discussions, interviews, student work, and his own reflections in his year-long study. The study arises from his own values of becoming a teacher for moral and spiritual reasons. His study was challenging, from finding a school that would encourage such a study, to the lack of time available to explore the ideas that came out. His work was embedded in the existing curriculum, not an added extra, and fitted in well with the *Brain and Learning* Unit. He was aware that the students within one class would exhibit widely different stages in ethical development. His interest was in all of them as they developed their ethical stances. It was a rich and complex investigation which is worth reading for its documentation of case studies of some students as they progress through the year, and his interventions to support them. His work prompts him to read about existing literature on findings on conflict and to connect his data to that body of knowledge. His personal expertise improves during the study, which discovered that the students became more aware of their changing ethical stances, and were more willing to admit uncertainty in their positions. He notes that the curricular battle is often between coverage and quality and those worthwhile outcomes can often take more time than is allowed. He wrote:

> One of the most significant data sets for my research came on March 8, when I decided to show my students footage of themselves from a videotaped conversation that had occurred about four months prior . . . After reviewing this earlier conversation, I asked them to discuss together their reactions to watching it and to share any thoughts about the ethical issues involved.
>
> (Roberts *et al.*, 2007, p. 63)

How thoughtful and how brave of Matt to share this recording with his students to help them become more self-aware, and how mature of these students to learn from it. Although, the report does not provide any evidence of the impact in the school, the general evidence is that Matt would be sharing his material with his teacher colleagues. However, to look at how they changed would also be a separate doctoral investigation.

The examples chosen indicate very clearly the contribution of these three teachers to their personal professionalism. They also took part in sharing their ideas with colleagues, thus improving the professionalism of the community.

BRIDGING THE GAP BETWEEN TEACHERS AND RESEARCHERS: A UK EXAMPLE

The perception of a gap between education practitioners and researchers has been a source of commentary for over 100 years (e.g. Korthagen, 2007). More recently, this has been more tightly described in terms of impact on practice, especially in teacher education programmes.

What do we already know?

Most of the literature investigating a perceived gap between practice and research is to be found in the medical field, especially nursing. It seems that this issue is a more generic one, rather than simply for science education, from the existing literature. Korthagen (2007) notes existing dissatisfaction expressed by teachers, parents and politicians, though it is not clear exactly what they mean by research (published outcomes or the process). Embedded in his paper is an assumption that attending to research outcomes can improve teaching. Disseminating research appears to be conflated with implementing research, but again he does not provide a clear explanation of what either means. He concludes that there is a gap between two professional cultures (research and practice), and proposes 'communities of practice' that will bind the practice and research aspects. He points to the complexity of teaching, as one barrier to a simple implementation of research, and also cites the role of affect in mediating change, often to provide resistance.

The research on becoming a teacher (Hobson *et al.*, 2009) showed that most teachers had a sceptical view of research prior to their training:

> Prior to starting their ITT, most trainees reported that they had held a practical, classroom-orientated approach to learning to teach and had been sceptical about the value of the more 'theoretical' aspects of ITT provision.
>
> (Hobson *et al.*, 2009, p. 18)

Case study data indicate that HEI-based aspects of ITT were considered most valuable where they were perceived to have clear practical utility for trainees' work in schools and, specifically, where they related to:

- lesson planning;
- classroom management;
- differentiation; and
- educational policy and legal obligations.

(Hobson *et al.*, 2009, p. 19)

Thus, the research/theory element of their training was not highly regarded by the majority from the outset. This was even more so for school-based training students. Since most teacher education students had very little exposure to education research before they started their courses, it seems that there is something more innately negative in those who choose to become teachers. For teachers in their first few years, this research does not mention theory as a significant component of interest or CPD.

Dissemination

This is a well-tried method, but, unfortunately, not very successful unless it is well-resourced, over a period of time, with feedback sessions for planning the following stages. Dissemination can also be embedded in a course, with pointers to the influence of research outcomes. The PGCE science programme at the University of Reading from 1992 to 2008 was an example of this type. Latterly, each session was preceded by a detailed tutor's lesson plan. The plans had elements to promote reflection on research, linking theoretical approaches with practice, such as:

- Directed reading tasks, either from readily accessible research papers, but more usually from scholarly and available textbooks taking the approach of a review of research related to themes.
- Transparent identification of intended outcomes that might otherwise remain hidden. For example, in a session where the student teachers might carry out a practical

exercise to reduce copper (II) oxide with natural gas, they had the task of considering how they might use this to build a symbolic chemical equation as an interpretation of the process of reduction, relating this to research on modelling in chemistry at the symbolic level, and its counterpart in the macroscopic observations.

■ The lesson plans had explicit discussion of the various roles of the tutor, such as exposition, giving practical instructions, monitoring completion of activity, organising cleaning up, gaining assessment evidence through listening to student talk, managing whole class discussion, and dealing with misconceptions.

These elements were, by and large, not as successful as they might have been. The directed reading was abandoned by most students in the light of their motivation and large workload (see Hobson *et al.*, 2009). Many students reverted to their own successful methods for creating chemical equations that they had been taught. They appeared to be unaware of the difficulties children might have, even to the point of denying the research that indicated this challenge was substantial, not surprisingly since the procedures for setting in schools would mean they would hardly come into contact with such children. For the last point, they adopted the role of children (even, sometimes, to the point of minor misbehaviour) and not being metacognitive about their learning about becoming a teacher. It seems that embedding research in a concrete context is not as easy as some might think. For a more thorough discussion of this course, see Hedderly (2005).

Vanderlinde and van Braak (2010) investigated views of teachers, school leaders, intermediaries, and researchers concerning the gap between research and practice in Belgium. They noted:

> The gap between research and practice was acknowledged by all participants, but was perceived more strongly by teachers compared to school leaders and intermediaries. Overall, teachers were sceptical about the value of educational research and argued that educational researchers do not ask questions of practical relevance. The main factor facilitating the use of research by practitioners is the nature of the research question. Descriptive research was not deemed useful by practitioners. On the other hand, practitioners expressed an appreciation for design-based research or research that leads to practical applications. In this context, the main barrier was thought to be the technical and complex language used by researchers.
>
> (2010, p. 312)

On the other hand:

> Researchers stated that they mainly disseminate their results through publications in practitioner journals. However, we found that these journals are not well known by school leaders and even unknown by teachers. This compelled researchers to discuss the effectiveness of their dissemination activities and to rethink the nature of their dissemination activities. Researchers remarked that as their work is primarily assessed in terms of output in scientific journals and their impact factor, a supportive context in which to disseminate their results to practitioners is absent.
>
> (2010, p. 312)

■ **Table 7.2** Factors influencing the use of research by practitioners

Barriers	Facilitators
Lack of applicability and ambiguity	Research with practical applications
Ambiguity of research material	Providing evidence of the benefits
Technical and complex language usage	Time to read and use research
Descriptive research	Intermediary at the school level
	Pressure from the government to use specific research

Source: Vanderlinde and van Braak (2010).

Vanderlinde and van Braak identified some barriers between researchers and practitioners and Table 7.2 is taken from their published work.

They suggest:

> During the focus group interviews, suggestions were made concerning how to bridge the gap between research and practice. The overall recommendation made by all participants was the need for more cooperation. A plea for more evidence-based research and design-based research was also made during the interviews. Evidence-based research involves gathering empirical evidence about which teaching methods are effective and should inform practitioners about what they should do in practice. Design-based research involves the study of situated learning or learning in context through systematic design. It functions to create and extend knowledge about the development, enactment and sustenance of innovative learning environments.
>
> (2010, p. 312)

They express surprise at a proposal to create a database of research in Flanders to facilitate a flow of research information, particularly in the light of comments that teachers wish to engage with the researchers directly. This is not surprising to me as teaching is a human, not a technical, activity.

Teachers engaged as collaborators in the research enterprise

The PALAVA teacher researcher group is one example of a collaborative activity that has been quite successful. It began in 1996 when a small group of graduating student teachers asked the author how they might continue to engage with research, since they had been invigorated by thinking at a higher level. At first, it was concerned only with chemistry but has developed across the sciences with time. It is, first, voluntary, with free membership for those who wish to engage with science education research. This can range from discussing scholarly and empirical papers, to carrying out joint research. The group has been convened by the author throughout this time.

The report below is largely based on the contents of the group's website (see Useful Websites) containing agendas and reports of meetings, emails, and responses to a questionnaire sent to existing and previous members. Although the website is in the public domain, the contributions have been anonymised for the purpose of this section.

The first meeting was attended by teachers, who were mentors for the PGCE course, and past students, and the Convenor, a university education tutor. At this first meeting, those present chose to investigate a range of issues on chemical equations and symbols. This was their choice and set the tone of the group as dealing with practical issues. The Convenor provided input from his own work in the area of chemical modelling. The group set up provisional research questions, such as:

- Can learners recognise details of chemical symbols and formulae, such as the significance of upper and lower case in symbols, and the significance of coefficients and subscripts?
- Do learners understand the significance of different parts of chemical equations?
- How do learners go about balancing chemical equations?
- What sense do learners make of chemical word equations?
- Do learners appreciate the significance of signs in chemical equations, such as $\rightarrow$ and $+$ signs?
- What is the history of chemical symbols, formulae and chemical equations?

Members accepted the challenges of finding out what was already known from research investigations by the next meeting. They were very clear that the Convenor must collaborate, with his own task decided by the group! He was allocated the last question.

When the group met again, members shared their findings. The Convenor shared his experience of searching for the origin of chemical signs and symbols in the form of a paper, including his sources. He was a learner, alongside the others. The meeting moved to an anecdotal form, with discussion of practical difficulties of teaching these ideas in their classes. In time for the next meeting, they resolved to think about how they would investigate their questions, what methods would they use. Inevitably, they were influenced by the methods they had discovered in their reading.

The third meeting discussed, sometimes robustly, suggested methods to explore understanding among the learners. These included multiple choice questions on element and formulae symbols with the various responses influenced by known and expected misconceptions, creating word equations from a demonstration of a chemical reaction, labelling a given symbol equation with a response box linked to the part being investigated, learners creating a narrative description of how they were balancing an equation, and semi-structured recorded interviews of the meanings of chemical equations. In this, and future meetings, much time was given to refining the methodology. We discovered that it was very difficult to separate the role of teaching, where prompts and interventions to promote learning would be normal, from the role of the researcher, where a neutral position might be more helpful.

All agreed that one member would take responsibility for a particular method, but that all members would be invited to collect data from classes to be sent to that one member for collation. Not all members agreed to take part in data collection, but all would discuss at the meetings. The coordinating member would send out the research instruments by email.

At subsequent meetings, members tackled analysis of the data collected, a kind of methods course arising from practice. Since the group had committed to this joint action research (as it rapidly became), they had a strong group motivation to deliver their contributions. It was clear that all members were developing their understanding of data collection and analysis, even those who were not directly involved.

The group faced the issue of what to do with their discoveries, especially where this challenged their initial ideas. A first step for many was to change some aspect of their teaching, and then collect more data to share with the group. One teacher, for example, chose to use a physical analogy for formulae in equations, and tally each element until the numbers were identical on both sides. One teacher said at the group: 'I hope you don't mind but I have given the (15-year-old) students the history of symbols and equations paper. They have much appreciated it, especially now they have some specific details of their origins.' There was much delight at this comment. The group chose to have a dissemination conference for a day. Each section of research was allocated a slot for presentation, often as a workshop, with following questions. The conference was well attended, with other teachers, some student teachers, other researchers, and colleagues from the government Department for Education and Science (DFES). Advertising was mediated by the Royal Society of Chemistry and the Association for Science Education (ASE) as well as the normal university contacts. Discussion focused on method and impact as much as on data and interpretation. One research outcome was that chemical word equations appeared not to be a helpful intermediary on the way to formulae equations, and this was agreed by the DFES representative. To date, this outcome, disseminated at a number of conferences with a recommendation to delete its teaching, has not had any further effect, despite its wide acceptance by those hearing it.

The group has continued its work, partly funded by the DFES Best Practice Research Scholarships, dealing with themes such as particle models, revision in science lessons, and the value of making notes in exercise books. Learning about methods has expanded, partly by instituting a journal club. A journal club adopts a published paper (scholarly or, more usually, empirical research) and subjects it to intense scrutiny in the group. Its research output is subject to scrutiny through presentations at Local Authority meetings, regional ASE workshops, and international presentations by the Convenor.

It is difficult to be entirely clear about the positive effects of working in such a group, especially when the group work is live. Nevertheless, the descriptive account given provides some evidence for its success. What has not transpired is writing for practitioner journals by group members, or even research journals. However, what has been a great success is the increased respect for science education research, and its effect on the members' everyday teaching.

The role of professional development providers

In England, advisers and independent consultants who provide so much professional development are drawn mainly from the ranks of practising teachers, with little or no direct experience of research. They could have important roles as mediators but, in practice, are unable to fulfil these roles because of this lack of experience. They may well be one of the important sustainers of the gap between researchers and practitioners.

Discussion

No doubt, the perception that there is a gap will continue. I see no gap but different ways of thinking and working in the same profession. I have some recommendations:

1   Research into teachers' and practitioners' beliefs must continue.
2   Teachers and researchers must work together more as equally valued partners, principally to understand each other and generate more respect.
3   Those who provide professional development must have a foot in the researcher ethos, as well as a foot in the practitioner ethos.
4   Mediators, such as teacher educators, must be supported in their efforts to bridge the gap.

HOW TO ENGAGE WITH RESEARCH AND SCHOLARSHIP AS AN ACTIVE TEACHER

Although the place of education research for teachers is not always a requirement, many teachers still wish to take part and enjoy the experience. There is much anecdotal evidence for personal cognitive improvement as well as motivational strengthening among practitioners. What are the barriers for active teachers engaging with research, and how might they be overcome?

1   *Teachers have such a big workload already that they cannot take on extra tasks.* In addition, teachers have the professionalism to choose to give some extra time to planning, or giving feedback to their students. Nevertheless, some choose to undertake Action Research or to study for an education Masters degree that requires carrying out some research. A very few take on the challenge of a doctorate. It is important to recognise all choices as valid and professional.

2   *There is no reward for engaging with research.* Researching for a higher degree provides a higher qualification, a reward itself. For some leadership posts, this is a distinct advantage. Promotion can be gained through a variety of experiences, one of which is demonstrating clearly an interest in personal professional development. In some cases, undertaking research may involve working with teachers in other schools, which seems to be highly valued in education. Working with others is, indeed, a rewarding experience. Finally, here, gaining higher qualifications can lead to work outside the formal school system, a rewarding experience for some.

3   *Accessing the research literature is too difficult.* There are many mediating publications for those who wish to make a start on engaging with the research literature. The *ASE Guide to Research in Science Education* (Oversby, 2012) is one written especially for this purpose and there are others as the reference section attests. Studying a formal higher degree course brings access to the research literature, which is usually required anyway. For a modest fee, many universities encourage local teachers to register for library access, a pathway to the whole of the literature.

4   *Teachers do not have the skills to be academic.* Many pre-service HEI-schools partnership courses demand some work at M-level, an academic level that requires students to engage with research. Undergraduate courses often involve a dissertation. It used to be thought that teachers did not have these skills but the recent changes of standards in courses involving HEIs is evidence enough to counteract this.

5   *Teachers are not used to being researchers in education.* Point 4 above is an indication that this does not need to be true. For those who took a teacher education course some time ago, there are many successful examples of teachers who have taken up carrying out research later in their career.

5   *Schools make it too difficult for busy teachers to carry out research.* Many schools record the achievements of their teachers as indicators of their professional status and so of value to their schools. In an atmosphere where funding and time can be in short supply, the contribution of successful research outcomes can be beneficial to many aspects of school life. Effective schools recognise that a motivated and active environment promotes higher standards of learning and teaching. Ultimately, this translates into a more expert staff and higher achievements for the students.

REFERENCES

Ausubel, D. P. (1968) *Educational Psychology: A Cognitive View*, New York: Holt, Rinehart & Winston.

Bennett, J. (2003) *Teaching and Learning Science: A Guide to Recent Research and Its Applications*, London: Continuum.

Brian, K. (1976) 'The assessment of performance unit: its task and rationale', *Education 3–13*, 4(2): 108–12.

Duckworth, E. (1987) *The Having of Wonderful Ideas and Other Essays on Teaching and Learning*, New York: Teachers College Press.

Elton, L. (2001) 'Research and teaching: what are the real relationships?' *Teaching in Higher Education*, 6(1): 43–56.

Gilbert, J. K., Watts, D. M. and Osborne, R. J. (1985) 'Eliciting student views using an interview-about-instances technique', in *Constructing Worlds through Science Education: The Selected Works of John K. Gilbert*, London: Routledge.

Hedderly, A. (2005) 'How do secondary science student teachers approach knowledge? An investigation into cognition and affect', unpublished PhD thesis, University of Reading, Reading.

Hobson, A. J., Malderez, A., Tracey, L., Homer, M. S., Ashby, P., Mitchell, N., McIntyre, J., Cooper, D., Roper, T., Chambers, G. N. and Tomlinson, P. D. (2009) *Becoming a Teacher*, Final report, Nottingham, England. Available at: www.gtce.org.uk/research/commissioned_research/ (accessed 30 December 2012).

Korthagen, F. A. J. (2007) 'The gap between research and practice revisited', *Educational Research and Evaluation*, 13(3): 303–10.

McGregor, D. (2012) 'Group work: what does research say about its effect on learning?' In J. Oversby (ed.) *ASE Guide to Research in Science Education*, Hatfield: Association for Science Education.

National Research Council (NRC) (1996) *National Science Education Standards*, Washington, DC: National Academy Press.

Oversby, J. (ed.) (2012) *ASE Guide to Research in Science Education*, Hatfield: Association for Science Education.

Petty, G. (1998) *Teaching Today*, 2nd edn, Cheltenham: Nelson Thornes.

Roberts, D., Bove, C. and van Zee, E. (eds) (2007) *Teacher Research. Stories of Learning and Growing*, Arlington, VA: NSTA Press.

Taber, K. S. (2012) 'Teaching and learning about the nature of science', in J. Oversby (ed.) *ASE Guide to Research in Science Education*, Hatfield: Association for Science Education.

Vanderlinde, R. and van Braak, J. (2010) 'The gap between educational research and practice: views of teachers, school leaders, intermediaries and researchers', *British Educational Research Journal*, 36(2): 299–316.

USEFUL WEBSITES

Hattie: http://growthmindseteaz.org/johnhattie.html (accessed 3 March 2014).
Work on intervention evidence for teaching and learning.
PALAVA teacher researcher group: www.palava.wikispaces.com (accessed 3 March 2014).

INDEX

INDEX ■ ■ ■ ■

materials (teaching resources) *see* equipment and apparatus; resources
mathematical modelling 216
Mathematics 50
Matthews, B. 73
McKenna, M. 230
measurement skills 194
media reports, using in class 229, 231
medicine 83
Mendel, Gregor 82
Mendeleev, 91
mentors 12, 14–15, 19, 287
Merton, Robert 68, 72
metacognition 131, 175
metastudies on interventions 288
middle management posts 24, 30–1
Millar, R. 40, 57, 161, 193, 195, 222
mini-plenaries 172
Miodownik, M. 88, 89, 99
misconceptions, pupils': beware of education apps 214; cognitive explanations for 129; enabling understanding 134; making pupils' ideas explicit 129; and questioning strategies 184–5; and scientific language 181; teachers must know about 5, 17, 104; teaching strategies 169, 184–5; using modelling to overcome 169–70
modelling 104, 169–70
moderation 280, 283
modular assessment (vs linear) 59, 61–2
molecular structures 91–2, 97–9
moles 93–4
moral dilemmas *see* controversial issues
Mortimer, E. F. 186
motivation (pupils'): and off-site visits 258; and teacher enthusiasm 174; and varied tasks 168
Mountbatten School 225
movement, classroom 200
MRS GREN 77
multiple intelligences 167–8
Murray, L. 194, 195
museums and hands-on centres, visiting 259
music in the classroom 171

nanochemistry 98
narrative writing 189
National Curriculum: changes to 5–6, 34, 35, 40–1, 161–2, 238; and Citizenship 220–1; history of 36–7; and inclusion 168; and internal assessment 279–80; and investigative work 193; Levels (National Curriculum assessments) 38, 49, 171; and out-of-classroom learning 252–3; pathways through the National Curriculum 37, 58; and schemes of work 138–9; science in the National Curriculum 36–41; and sex education 238; and technology-supported approaches 207 *see also* Key Stages; *specific subjects e.g.* Physics
National Healthy Schools Status (NHSS) 245
National Strategy for Teaching Science 2002 142, 169, 170–1, 272
natural selection 81–2
'negotiated' teaching styles 163
nervous system 81
Nespar, J. 273
neutrality, of teacher in discussion management 227
Newlands, 90
Newton, P. 227
non-formal learning 252
normal science vs scientific crisis 68–9
Northern Ireland: awarding bodies (examination boards) 53; Irish Baccalaureates 63; and the National Curriculum 35; sex education 239
Nott, M. 71, 197, 198
Nuffield courses 192–3
numeracy 40, 50

objectives, assessment 279
objectives, learning: assessment of 8; being explicit about 171; evidencing 135–6; and planning 132–3, 151; and use of different teaching strategies 166–7
observations (as assessment) 277
observation skills 193–4
observing others' lessons 20–1

Printed in Great Britain
by Amazon

27576618R00190